SAUDI ARABIA

SAUDI ARABIA

Government, Society and the Gulf Crisis

Mordechai Abir

London and New York

First published 1993
by Routledge
11 New Fetter Lane, London EC4P 4EE

Simultaneously published in the USA and Canada
by Routledge
29 West 35th Street, New York, NY 10001

© 1993 Mordechai Abir

Typeset in Baskerville by
Witwell Limited, Southport
Printed and bound in Great Britain by
Mackays of Chatham PLC, Chatham, Kent

British Library Cataloguing-in-Publication Data

*A catalogue record for this book is available from the
British Library*

ISBN 0-415-09325-2

Library of Congress Cataloging in Publication Data

has been applied for.

To my daughter, RONIT,
who had to share, unevenly, her mother with me
and to my wife, Rutha, for all her suffering
throughout the years of working with me

CONTENTS

CONTENTS

viii

TABLES

PREFACE AND
ACKNOWLEDGEMENTS

The first two parts of this book consist of an abbreviated and updated version of my book *Saudi Arabia in the Oil Era. Regime and Elites; Conflict and Collaboration* (listed in the bibliography). For the totally new part (nearly half) of the book I relied heavily on Arabic, Hebrew and European languages press and periodicals, American and Israeli monitoring services, recent Saudi Arabian Kingdom official publications and other sources.

Since *Saudi Arabia in the Oil Era* was published (1988) many more books have been written on the kingdom. Yet, to my knowledge, none deals with the impact of the crises of the 1980s and early 1990s on the society and government of Saudi Arabia. Nor am I aware of any work that treats the rise of 'neo-fundamentalism' in the kingdom since the late 1970s.

I faced the difficulty common to all Israeli socio-political historians dealing with Arab countries, that of being unable to conduct field work in the countries which they researched. The situation was exacerbated by my inability to exchange ideas and opinions with Saudi counterparts, although I tried to do so on several occasions.

I take this opportunity to thank the many Saudis whose books, articles and PhD and MA theses relating to Saudi Arabia I have used, and who unbeknownst to them helped me to understand better their country, society and government. Special thanks are due to Dr Ghazi al-Gosaybi the prominent Saudi scholar, poet and former cabinet minister, whose articles and books I have found enlightening. His 1991 book *Hatah la takun fitna*!!, in addition to other sources, greatly contributed to my understanding of the phenomenon of modern 'neo-fundamentalism' in Saudi Arabia.

I am grateful to Dr Joseph Kostiner and Dr Jacob Goldberg of the Dayan Centre of Tel-Aviv University, who allowed me to use yet unpublished drafts of the Kuwaiti and Saudi chapters which they prepared respectively for the 1990 Dayan Centre's *Middle East Contemporary Survey* (*MECS*). Dr Kostiner has also put at my disposal notes for his forthcoming 1991 *MECS* Kuwait chapter and some Arabic publications relating to Saudi Arabia. I am also grateful to my assistant Raz Zimt, for his help in researching material for the new part of the book.

To my dear friend of many years Dr Samuel Halperin I am indebted for obtaining for me recent Saudi statistical and other official publications which helped me update this book in Washington DC and Jerusalem. I also exploited Dr Halperin's short visit to Jerusalem to edit the English of Part III of my book. My brother-in-law, Dr Azriel Karny, to whom I always turn when in need, helped with several difficult Arabic (Saudi) texts relating to religious polemics. I am also grateful to my colleague, Professor Hava Lazarus-Yaffe, at the Hebrew University of Jerusalem, for comments on part of chapter 10 of this book relating to Saudi 'neo-fundamentalism'. She is, of course, not responsible for what I have written in that sub-chapter.

Last, but not least, this book, like all my previous works, could not have been produced without the partnership, meticulous work and infinite patience of my wife Rutha.

I have followed, whenever possible, the established system of transliteration of Arabic words and names. In the case of names and words which have become common in European languages, the common European transliteration has been used. Because of technical difficulties, diacritical signs have been kept to a minimum and simplified.

Mordechai Abir
Jerusalem and Washington DC

ABBREVIATIONS

ACC	Arab Co-operation Council
AFP	Agence France Presse
ANLF	Arab National Liberation Front
AP	Associated Press
Aramco	Arabian American Oil Company
EIU	*The Economist Intelligence Unit*
FBIS	Foreign Broadcasting Information Service
FT	*Financial Times*
GCC	Gulf Co-operation Council
ICO	Islamic Conference Organisation
IHT	*International Herald Tribune*
IJMES	*International Journal of Middle East Studies*
IPI	Israel Petrolem Institute's newsletter
IRO	Organisation of the Islamic Revolution for the Liberation of the Arabian Peninsula
JP	*Jerusalem Post*
JQ	*The Jerusalem Quarterly*
KFU	King Faysal University
KSU	King Saud University
KUNA	Kuwait News Agency
m.b.d.	million barrels daily
MECS	*Middle East Contemporary Survey*
MEED	*Middle East Economic Digest*
MEES	*Middle East Economic Survey*
MEI	*Middle East International*
MEJ	*The Middle East Journal*
NLF	National Liberation Front
NRF	National Reform Front
NYT	*New York Times*
PDF	Popular Democratic Front
PDFP	Popular Democratic Front for the Liberation of Palestine

PDP	Popular Democratic Party
PDRY	People's Democratic Republic of Yemen
Petromin	Saudi Petroleum and Minerals Organisation
PFLOAG	Popular Front for the Liberation of Oman and the Arabian Gulf
PFLP	Popular Front for the Liberation of Palestine
PLO	Palestine Liberation Organisation
P&M	College of Petroleum and Minerals
UAR	United Arab Republic
UK	United Kingdom
UPAP	Union of the Peoples of the Arabian Peninsula
UPM	The University of Petroleum and Minerals
SABIC	Saudi Arabian Basic Industries Corporation
SAMA	Saudi Arabian Monetary Agency
SR	Saudi riyal
WSJ	*Wall Street Journal*
WP	*Washington Post*

INTRODUCTION

Saudi Arabia has a territory of about 865,000 square miles and a citizen population of about six million. With the exception of Asir in the south and a score of oases, it is made up of a largely arid plateau of varied desert landscapes.

The kingdom of Saudi Arabia consists of five major regions. The core of the kingdom is Najd, the Central Region, the historical seat of the Wahhabi movement (*muwahhidun*) and the House of Saud. Al-Hasa, renamed the Eastern Province (*Al-Sharqiyya*), the Hijaz or the Western Region (the most populated), Asir or the Southern Region (the second most populated) and the Northern Region (part of the Syrian desert), were conquered between 1913 and 1934 by the founder of modern Saudi Arabia, King Abd al-Aziz Al Saud (better known as Ibn Saud).

Administratively, the kingdom's five regions are sub-divided into fourteen major provinces – *imarates* (the number has varied over time). The governor of each province is an amir (plural *umara'*) who is a prince of the royal house, or a member of one of the aristocratic families related to it. Until the development of the modern central government in the 1950s and 1960s, the amir ruled the province in the king's name and was the head of its administration. The traditional government hierarchy included local notables (*a'yan*) and tribal shaykhs, also known as *umara'*.

With minor exceptions all the kingdom's citizens are Muslim Arabs who speak Arabic; most are of tribal origin and the Arab culture is common to all. Yet, the Saudi society cannot be considered fully homogeneous. Although about 90 per cent of Saudis are Sunni Muslims, a large proportion of the population of Al-Hasa is Shi'ite Twelvers (*ithna 'ashariyya*). Small communities of Twelvers and Isma'ilis (seventh imam) are to be found in Asir and the Hijaz and Zaydis (fifth imam) in Asir. Although most of the population of Hijaz and Asir is now Wahhabi and adheres to the Hanbali school of theology and religious jurisprudence (*madhab*), followers of the Shafi'i, Hanafi and Maliki schools are still to be found in the above provinces as well as in Al-Hasa. Culturally, historically and climatically, agricultural Asir is an offshoot of Yemen.

Al-Hasa (the Eastern Province), with its large Shi'ite community and mixed coastal population, is also very different and more oriented to the population of the Gulf principalities and Iran. Historically, the Hijazi townspeople, considered by Najdis to be of mixed blood (an outcome of the settlement of non-Arab pilgrims and merchants and concubinage), are proud of their unique heritage, having given Islam to the world and being the guardians of Islam's holy cities. They are closely connected with the Muslim world through the hajj and trade; they are more sophisticated, cosmopolitan and religiously moderate than other Saudis, the Najdis in particular.

Cultural variations exist between the nomads (*badu*) and the settled (*hadr*) but more so between the 'aristocratic', conservative and religiously puritan Najdis who consider themselves 'racially pure', and the population of the other regions. By the middle of the twentieth century, more than half the population of Saudi Arabia were still nomads, and perhaps 35 per cent settled and semi-settled. Barely 10 per cent lived in the major towns. The tribe and clan were still the most important socio-political substructures in Arabia. The tribal *umara'* were considered *primus inter pares*; their position and the extent of their authority depended on their individual merit and leadership capability. The number of bedouin had begun to decline in the first half of the century, a process sharply accelerated after the 1950s by massive urbanisation sparked by increasing oil wealth and modernisation. By the late 1980s less than 5 per cent of the population was considered nomadic, while about 25 per cent were settled or semi-settled cultivators. The major urban centres grew dramatically and claimed over 50 per cent of the total population. Towns of under 100,000 people account for about 12–14 per cent.[1]

With urbanisation, traditional institutions began to decline, as oil wealth and modernisation increasingly bridged the differences between the population of the kingdom's provinces. Notwithstanding these processes, national integration and the stability of the regime in Saudi Arabia are largely the result of the kingdom's oil revenues and the delicate balance of power within the House of Saud, between the rulers and the religious leaders, the ulama (singular *'alim*), and between traditional elites and the expanding new middle class, led by the intelligentsia.

Part I

RULING CLASS AND ELITES IN SAUDI ARABIA

1

THE CONSOLIDATION OF THE RULING CLASS

The Saudi population, at the beginning of the twentieth century, could be considered, with some exceptions, a classless society. There was no upper class to speak of in Arabia at the time. Only a small proportion of the merchants and the ulama in the towns of Hijaz and Najd could be described as 'middle class'. The great majority of the Arabians – townspeople as well as the rural nomads and agriculturalists – lived at or near subsistence level. The unification of the Saudi kingdom by Abd al-Aziz ibn Saud, in the first decades of the century, consolidated the power and authority of a new Saudi ruling class – the aristocracy. The development of the kingdom's oil industry since 1938 and the modernisation of Saudi Arabia after World War II, produced, moreover – in addition to existing regional and other differences – new classes and a relatively rigid social structure. The latter depends not so much on power, wealth and education as on affiliation to the ruling family and on regional (Najd), tribal (noble) and urban or rural origin.

The reconquest of Dari'yya (Riyadh) in January 1902 is considered in Saudi annals as the beginning of the modern Saudi kingdom. The small army of Abd al-Aziz ibn Saud was composed at the time of a few score relatives, in-laws and some bedouin. Abdallah ibn Jiluwi was said to have twice saved the life of his 'cousin' Abd al-Aziz (henceforth also Ibn Saud). Subsequently, the Jiluwis, a cadet branch of Al Saud,[1] gained a key position in the kingdom's ruling class. Such a development is typical of considerations which influenced the formation of that class in Saudi Arabia. Indeed, members of other important families who helped Ibn Saud in the consolidation of his kingdom were incorporated into the Saudi aristocracy. At their side, the ulama led by Al al-Shaykh (the descendants of Muhammad b. Abd al-Wahhab, the founder of the Wahhabiyya), and important tribal and regional *umara'* (singular amir) who joined Ibn Saud's camp at this stage can be considered part of the Saudi ruling class.

Ibn Saud continued to expand his power base by numerous matrimonial arrangements with traditional regional rulers and important tribal shaykhs (*umara'*).[2] Most significant, however, was his affiliation with the powerful Sudayris of northern Arabia, who had already intermarried with the Sauds in the past.

Contrary to the Wahhabi–Saudi jihad of previous centuries, Ibn Saud's military campaigns were not aimed at spreading the Wahhabiyya but rather at re-establishing the authority of the House of Saud. The historical alliance between the Najdi ulama and Ibn Saud had not been automatically reinstated. The ulama viewed Ibn Saud's government with reservation, if not with suspicion, and did not regard him as sufficiently pious. He toyed with technological innovations which they considered heretical innovation (*bid'ah*). He did not conduct jihads against the polytheists (*mushrikun*) in the region, and he was known to associate with the British infidel authorities in the Persian Gulf.

The cementing of the relationship between Al Saud and Al al-Shaykh through matrimonial arrangements, and the preferential treatment accorded to the religious hierarchy, undoubtedly contributed to the improvement of relations between the king and the majority of the urban Najdi ulama. Moreover, in order to establish a loyal military force to carry out his plans and overcome the natural opposition of bedouin tribes to law and order, about 1912 Ibn Saud revived the *Ikhwan* movement. Ulama volunteers (*muttawwa'in*[3]), some of tribal origin, were sent to teach the bedouin the principles of the Wahhabiyya, and land and funds were apportioned for their settlement. By 1930 this movement led to the settlement of approximately 150,000 bedouin in over 200 military-agricultural villages (*hujar*).[4]

After 1913 the Ikhwan were principally responsible for Ibn Saud's conquests including Jabal Shammar, the Hijaz and Asir, and became the mainstay of his regime. As a result, the importance of the tribal *umara'* and the *muttawwa'in*, and the Najdi ulama in general, rapidly increased.

As he became more dependent on them, the leading tribal *umara'*, some of whom had previously been Ibn Saud's bitter enemies, and the more fanatic ulama, exploited their new leverage to coerce their ruler to accept their extreme interpretation of the Wahhabiyya and their right to intervene in the running of the kingdom. Yet Ibn Saud chose to overlook the Ikhwan's excesses in order to avoid an open breach with them.

After the First World War Ibn Saud accelerated his efforts to establish a united centralised kingdom in the Arabian Peninsula. For this purpose he planned to introduce aspects of modern administration and Western technology not contrary to the principles of Islam. Moreover, aware of the political realities in the region, he co-ordinated his activities, as much as possible, with the British authorities.

Such policies were anathema to the Ikhwan and to most of the Najdi ulama. The fact that the ruler had also begun to consolidate his dynastic rule and had taken to himself, instead of the traditional title of Amir

4

Najd, the title of 'Sultan of Najd and its Dependencies' (1921) and 'King of the Hijaz' (1926) added fuel to the fire. Indeed, both tribal shaykhs and ulama connected to the Ikhwan were convinced that if they were not to stop Ibn Saud, or at least limit his authority, they would be incapable of doing so in the future.

The Ikhwan rebellion (1927–30)[5] was not only a challenge to Ibn Saud's policy but also a desperate attempt on the part of the leading Ikhwan amirs and some fanatic ulama to preserve their power and the traditional socio-political frameworks from which they derived it. It was especially dangerous because its leaders, supported by a few prominent ulama, took on the mantle of defenders of puritanic Wahhabism and underscored the community's inherent right to replace a leader who betrayed its principles or who was incapable of carrying out his duties.

Ibn Saud's final victory over the Ikhwan in 1929/30, with the establishing of a national army and a centralised administration, deprived the tribal shaykhs and the ulama of the power to intervene, on their own initiative, in the conduct of state affairs. It led to a sharp decline in the power of the latter and eroded the ulama's political influence.

There are about 50 senior tribal amirs and a few hundred shaykhs (*umara'*) of secondary tribes and sub-tribes in Saudi Arabia.[6] The power and authority of these amirs has been gradually declining since 1930 as the power and authority of the Saudi kingdom and its government were consolidated and its administration and army expanded. Most important, Ibn Saud's revenues dramatically increased following the conquest of the Hijaz and commercial exploitation of oil in Saudi Arabia (1946). Thus the Saudi ruler was now able to purchase armaments and transport and to 'buy' the loyalty of the tribesmen. Thereafter the amirs' potential to resist him was completely nullified and they became part of the Saudi regime's power base. They are considered a component of the ruling class, although inferior to the others.

After 1930, Ibn Saud still upheld whenever possible the golden rule of *shura* (consultation) and *ijma'* (consensus) concerning most non-political major decisions. Nevertheless, he was now able to disregard the ulama's objections to his limited modernising measures, essential for the consolidation and development of his kingdom. Otherwise he devoutly espoused Wahhabi principles, his kingdom's *raison d'être*, and confined the process of modernisation to the most essential.

Notwithstanding the consolidation of his power, Ibn Saud continued to show respect for and pamper the ulama, whose support was still essential for the legitimisation of his regime. Yet, consultations with their rank and file during the king's daily council (*majlis*)[7] and with the senior ulama in a far more important weekly *majlis*, could no longer be viewed as a recognition of their supreme authority and right to participate in decision-making. Indeed, in matters of importance, although he consulted them, he made his final decision according to what he considered right and, whenever necessary, disregarded their opinion.

The ulama, who were coerced into accepting the new *status quo*, realised that, none the less, Wahhabi hegemony and their special position in the kingdom were still guaranteed, but their actual power and influence were to be dependent on the ruler's good will. Even as junior partners of the Sauds, they enjoyed high prestige, privileges and influence. As the kingdom's government and administration developed they were given, in addition to control of religious institutions, key positions in it, including justice and the educational system.

Paradoxically, the role and authority of the ulama further declined after the rise of King Faysal, whom they helped bring to the throne in 1964. Related through his mother to Al al-Shaykh, and known for his piety, Faysal, nevertheless, deliberately eroded the ulama's power and independence. Frequently he ignored their opposition to aspects of his accelerated modernisation. Lastly, he curbed the authority and activities of the Committees for Encouraging Virtue and Preventing Vice (*Hay'at al-Amr bi'l-Ma'ruf wa'l-Nahy 'an al-Munkar*) (henceforth the Morality Committees and the Morality Police).

The above notwithstanding, both the Sauds and the ulama, each for their own reasons, have a vested interest in the preservation of their historical alliance. On the one hand, it contributes to the regime's legitimisation, to stability and to national integration. On the other hand, it helps preserve the Wahhabi character of, and the role of the ulama in, the kingdom.

Regardless of the decline in their power and influence, the ulama thus remain an important component of the Saudi ruling class. In the scale of importance of the traditional elites they come immediately after the royal house and its collateral and associated families, but above the *umara'*. Indeed, in contrast to the *umara'* they are organised, have a hierarchy, leadership, state-supported institutions and common interests which bind them as a cohesive group. The activities of the Al-Shaykhs, moreover, are no longer restricted to religion. Many are now to be found in key positions in the administration, educational system, security services, armed forces and in the private sector of the Saudi economy.[8]

It is generally accepted that the House of Saud, the ulama and the *umara'* – the most important components of the regime's power base – are in fact the Saudi ruling class. The size of this class is difficult to determine. The 'recognised' branches of Al Saud, and their associated important families, are generally estimated to be about 10,000 strong. The ulama, their associates and all the members of the religious hierarchy in Saudi Arabia probably number tens of thousands. Indeed Al al-Shaykh has intermarried with all the other branches of the ruling class, by itself believed to consist of about 7,000 people. As for the *umara'* and

6

their extended families, their number is probably equal to that of the religious establishment. Thus, the size of the Saudi ruling class, in the wider sense, is quite substantial.

Some scholars classify the Saudi kingdom as an autocracy. Others call it a 'desert democracy'.[9] The more appropriate description of the Saudi regime after the death of Ibn Saud is probably an oligarchy whose pillars are the Saudi royal house, the ulama and the *umara'*. The conduct of its government still follows Ibn Saud's golden rule of consultation (*shura*) and consensus (*ijma'*) within the ruling class.

The monarch has a power of veto over all the decisions of the executive system (government and administration). Indeed, notwithstanding the principles of *shura* and *ijma'* the king can also veto, at least in theory, decisions of his informal royal Consultative Council (*majlis al-shura*),[10] the representative organ of the Saudi oligarchy. Yet in certain circumstances, the oligarchy, through its unofficial leadership – *ahl al-hal wa'l-'aqd* (lit. 'those who loosen and bind') – may overrule the king, limit his authority and, in extreme cases, even depose him, as was the case with King Saud (1964). Thus, if the policies of the king were to threaten the kingdom's stability and the regime's power, a similar coalition to that which deposed Saud could re-emerge.

Unlike the traditional Islamic concept of the *ahl al-hal wa'l-'aqd*, this informal institution is not dominated in Saudi Arabia by the ulama. Most sources agree that membership in the Saudi *ahl al-hal wa'l-'aqd* is limited to about a hundred and fifty members of Al Saud and its associated families – and some outstanding ulama and several extremely important *umara'*.[11] The criteria for membership in this authoritative body are origin, seniority, prestige and leadership qualities (scholarship and piety for the ulama), according to bedouin tradition.

Leading ulama have usually participated with the other components of *ahl al-hal wa'l-'aqd* in consultations preceding or following dramatic developments impacting the Saudi government. These included Saud's coerced abdication, the Mecca rebellion in 1979, the outbreak of the Iran-Iraq war in 1980 and Iraq's invasion of Kuwait and the invitation extended to the US to protect the kingdom in 1990. In several such instances *fatwas* (religious–legal opinion) were also issued by the ulama leadership. Yet, the ulama's participation in the above and in the informal royal Consultative Council, the kingdom's decision- and policy-making organ, is largely *ad hoc* and conditional on the need for religious sanction for specific decisions.[12]

The *umara'* – tribal shaykhs and members of regional dynasties – provide the third leg of the tripod of the Sauds' traditional power base. Yet, just a handful of the most important *umara'* are considered *ahl al-hal wa'l-'aqd*. Indeed, only a few exceptionally important amirs have been invited in times of crisis or in relation to major policy debates, to participate in consultations of the informal royal *majlis al-shura*.[13]

Despite their role in the provincial government, the importance of the *umara'*, as mentioned above, has declined steadily, a process accelerated by the reorganisation and strengthening of the central government by King Faysal. Simultaneously, the strengthening of central government and the extension of its administration and welfare services to the provinces eroded, until the early 1980s, the authority of the provincial governors (*umara' al-manatiq*) and government. Moreover, the decline in authority of the *umara'* gathered momentum after the 1960s, also, as a result of the rapid urbanisation of the bedouins and agricultural population. Indeed, the average Saudi found himself increasingly turning to the central government's representatives for services and help rather than to his amir. However, the *umara'*, still the link between the rural population and the Sauds, regained some of their influence in the 1980s when Fahd began to strengthen the authority of the provincial government.[14]

Obviously, the most important component of the Saudi ruling class and of *ahl al-hal wa'l-'aqd* is the royal family. It dominates the kingdom's decision-making apparatus through the king, his informal royal Consultative Council and *ahl al-hal wa'l-'aqd*.

The term 'royal house' in modern Saudi Arabia is exclusively used to describe the descendants of Abd al-Rahman ibn Turki ibn Faysal Al Saud, foremost among them the offspring of his son Abd al-Aziz, as well as a few cadet branches of the family. This definition received legal sanction in 1932 when only they and some branches of the Sauds allied to them were to be considered royalty and to receive a stipend. Indeed, regulations instituted by the Saudi civil service during Faysal's reign demand that all the direct descendants of King Abd al-Aziz should be referred to as 'His Royal Highness'. Those of his brothers and some of his uncles should be referred to as 'His Highness', and members of other recognised branches of the Sauds as 'His Excellency', a title they share with cabinet ministers, non-royal district amirs and other senior officials.[15]

All in all it is estimated that about 7,000 members of Al Saud are considered today part of the royal family of which nearly 1,000 are direct descendants of Ibn Saud. When Crown Prince Faysal reorganised the kingdom's financial and administrative systems in 1958 he also removed from the royal list members of remote branches of the family. In 1962 Saudi Arabia again faced a major financial crisis. Hence Faysal requested in 1963 his uncle and finance minister, Musa'id ibn Abd al-Rahman, to re-examine the royal list. Subsequently Prince Musa'id limited the recognised membership of the royal family to the offspring of Abd al-Aziz and his brothers and Saud al-Kabir, Abd al-Rahman's nephew, the

Jiluwis, and the less important Thunayans, Abd al-Aziz's kinsmen and companions since the beginning of his career.

The royal family (as defined above), the Sudayris (the powerful bedouin dynasty from northern Najd intermarried with all the branches of the Sauds) and the Al-Shaykhs are thus composed of the upper echelon of the kingdom's ruling class. This group is estimated at over 20,000 people. Together with their other non-royal partners in the kingdom's traditional elites (ulama, *umara'*), they probably number about 100,000 people.

The crucial criterion for membership in the ruling class, we believe, should be the ability to participate in policy formulation and decision-making. In short, to be represented in ahl al-hal wa'l-'aqd. Wealth, education and key positions in the administration, the military or the economy, proposed by some scholars as additional yardsticks for inclusion in the Saudi ruling class, prove incorrect when examined against the above criterion. Although consulted occasionally, Saudis of such background were never considered *ahl al-hal wa'l-'aqd* nor members of the king's informal *majlis al-shura*.

Following in the footsteps of their father the great Abd al-Aziz, the Saudi monarchs carefully adhere to the golden principle of *shura* and *ijma'*. Until today, however, they have applied this principle exclusively to the royal family and its traditional partners in the ruling class. Yet, the monarch's 'absolutism' is tempered by the fact that he consults with the informal *majlis al-shura* on every important issue and whenever policy decisions are required. In the case of a major crisis, moreover, a larger forum of *ahl al-hal wa'l-'aqd* is convened. The centralisation of the government, and the rapid modernisation of the kingdom, nevertheless, eroded the power of the *umara'* and ulama and, to a lesser degree, that of the related families: the Sudayris, the Jiluwis, Al al-Shaykh and the Thunayans. Thus the senior members of the recognised royal family dominate the ruling class and its informal consultative bodies.

'THE BOOK AND THE SWORD' – THE ULAMA AND THE SAUDS

The term 'ulama' is used in this book in its wider sense to include all recognised religious scholars: the judges (*qadis*) of the different ranks, religious lawyers and all the other *'alims* engaged in the judicial system; the various ranks of religious teachers (*mudarris*); imams and the other office holders of consequence in the mosques. It is estimated that the Saudi ulama numbered in the mid-1980s 'at least 10,000', but it could well be that their number is far larger, now that the three Islamic universities[16] produce several thousand graduates annually. Yet, not all the above are recognised 'ulama', nor are they of equal importance.

At the head of the religious pyramid is the Council of the Assembly of

Senior Ulama (*Majlis Hay'at Kibar al-Ulama*), said to be composed of twenty-five members. Leading members of several other institutions are either included in the above or are equally, or almost as important. Such institutions are: the Higher Council of Qadis (*Al-Majlis al-'Ali li'l-Qada*); the Institute for Scientific Study, the Issue of Religio-Legal Opinions and the Supervision of Religious Affairs (*Dar al-Ifta' wa'l Ishraf 'ala'l-Shu'un al-Diniyya*) and the Committee for the Commendation of Virtue and the Prevention of Evil (*Hay'at al-Amr bi'l-Ma'ruf wa'l-Nahy 'an al-Munkar*), whose Morality Police serve as the executive arm of the ulama.

Saudi Arabia is often described as a theocracy; its puritanical Islamic laws and regulations are maintained more strictly than ever since the 1950s. This, however, does not reflect the power of the ulama and their influence. Moreover, one must make a distinction between the ulama in general, who although numerous and organised, exercise little power and the handful of senior ulama, the apex of the religious establishment, who control the kingdom's religious institutions.

The ulama leadership, appointed by the ruler and numbering probably about 30 or 40 '*alims*,[17] have direct access to the king and all the senior princes. They are greatly respected, and are consulted on matters of importance in addition to those related to religious affairs. Thus, under certain circumstances, they may influence the rulers' decisions. Yet, in general, their role is limited to legitimising a decision previously reached by the informal royal *majlis al-shura* or *ahl al-hal wa'l-'aqd* and thus providing the required consensus (*ijma'*).

Particularly after King Faysal was enthroned, the regime progressively decentralised the ulama's power. Although Faysal placed the old and newly created religious institutions and the ministries of justice and education under the control of leading '*alims*, such ulama became *de facto* part of the establishment, accountable to him. Indeed, the most important fields of ulama activity, justice, education and hajj, became formal ministries whose heads are members of the cabinet chaired by the king.

The ulama's involvement in the Saudi political process after Ibn Saud's death (1953) remained marginal.[18] They played only a peripheral role in the dramatic developments in Saudi Arabia in the 1950s and 1960s. Their involvement in various crises was necessitated by the regime's need to legitimise succession, and/or other extraordinary political actions that required the issuing of a *fatwa* by the senior ulama. Such was the case when Faysal was appointed prime minister (1958 and 1962) and king (1964),[19] before the storming of the Ka'ba in 1979, and when 'infidel' forces were invited to protect the kingdom in 1990.

Most ulama since the 1950s have tended to accept, to some degree, the limited modernisation efforts and their subordinate position in the Saud–ulama traditional alliance, since they nevertheless do enjoy a special

10

status and practically control everyday life in Saudi Arabia. This somewhat revised form of alliance between the ulama and the Sauds was finalised by Faysal (1958–75). Yet, it seems that the ulama in the late 1980s and early 1990s were no longer satisfied with this situation.[20]

Although he noticeably accelerated modernisation, even Faysal, whenever possible, attempted to gain the ulama's consent for his reforms. Endeavouring to modernise and decentralise the religious hierarchy and to incorporate it in the Saudi establishment, Faysal created several very important religious institutions, some of which replaced the broad authority of the Grand Mufti who died in 1969. Those institutions, funded by the government, are today the centres of the ulama's authority in the kingdom and enjoy substantial prestige and influence.

Frequently when the Wahhabi conservatives opposed his evolutionary reforms, Faysal did not hesitate to confront them. For instance, when he pioneered girls' education in 1960 (when Saud's prime minister), Faysal suppressed with an iron hand the riots incited by the ulama in different parts of the kingdom. In 1965, the king's conservative nephew, Khalid ibn Musa'id, was killed following a violent demonstration against the opening of a television station in Riyadh.

As long as he was able to achieve his essential objectives, Faysal compromised with the ulama. Once television was introduced, for example, Faysal agreed that its broadcasts would be restricted largely to religious programmes and news.[21] After establishing The Female Education Authority and expanding the kingdom's higher education, the monarch entrusted their development and supervision to senior ulama. Saudi students, moreover, study many religious courses and are constantly reminded that the rulers are the protectors of the Wahhabi state. This process of indoctrination was accelerated and the 'Islamisation' of modern education was expanded after the 1979 Mecca rebellion. Thus, the Saudi education system produces largely conformist graduates, although this process may be undergoing a change since 1980.[22]

Most ulama of the 1960s and 1970s, rather than fight Faysal's accelerated modernisation, tried to curb the impact of Westernisation on the Saudi–Wahhabi kingdom's special character and culture. The lower and middle ranks of the religious hierarchy, gradually being filled with a new generation of ulama, who enjoyed prestige and affluence, were, with some important exceptions, willing to follow their mentors and tolerate, if not support, the regime's policy. It could be said, that by the 1970s most of the ulama had progressively been co-opted into the system. Even if some extremist senior *'alims* expressed their views in the religious universities and publications, such critics of modernisation were secure, affluent, old-school fundamentalists. While lashing at the kingdom's Westernisation and the erosion of the 'Saudi way of life' by foreigners and Western-trained technocrats, censuring other Muslim rulers for corrupting Islam, they absolved the Sauds of such guilt.[23] Such hypocrisy was totally rejected by the handful of semi-educated militant neo-Ikhwan who rebelled in Mecca in 1979. Moreover, in the 1980s, many university-educated *'alims* and, in recent years, some popular young religious zealots began to voice criticism of the Sauds, their regime and its policy.[24]

The development of secular nationalism and pan-Arabism in the Arab world brought to Saudi Arabia, between the 1940s and 1960s, Muslim Brothers (mainly Egyptian) and other fundamentalist (*salafi*) refugees, who opposed their governments' official ideologies and reforms. All were given sanctuary and generous stipends by the Saudi authorities, on the understanding that they would refrain from criticising their hosts. Faysal, who was fighting Nasser's pan-Arabism, established with their help in 1962 The World Islamic League (*Rabitat al-'Alam al-Islami* later renamed the Islamic Conference Organisation – ICO). Funded by the Saudis, it has become an important tool of Riyadh's foreign policy.

By the 1970s the Muslim world was experiencing an upsurge of Islamic militant (neo)fundamentalism. That and the presence in the kingdom of a large Western community with its abhorred lifestyle – an anathema to the 'believers' – was bound to affect the conservative Saudis, who feared that Western cultural influences would subvert their Wahhabi–Saudi 'way of life'. Hence, some Najdi *'alims* even began openly to criticise the regime's modernisation policy.[25]

Aware of the rise of militant fundamentalism in the Muslim world, Crown Prince Fahd strove in the late 1970s to improve his relations with the ulama, curbing any flagrant aspect of Westernisation. Wahhabi laws and a puritan code of behaviour were more strictly enforced by the Morality Police, now endowed with additional authority. Nevertheless, Fahd refused to slow down the kingdom's modernisation programmes and rarely consulted the ulama even on internal problems, unless they were related to religion.

While militant, socially oriented, fundamentalist ideologies were by the 1970s rapidly spreading and, to some extent, replacing pan-Arabism in the Arab world, this was far less the case in Saudi Arabia (the Shi'ites of the Eastern Province excepted). Here, on the one hand, the standard of living of the largely unsophisticated, conservative population was rapidly rising and the regime gradually succeeded in solving the pro-blems which caused hardship to the newly urbanised population. On the other hand, the co-operation between the Sauds and the establishment ulama, including the tame ultra-conservatives, produced a 'pragmatic fundamentalism'. The latter accepted modern technology and state organisation, closed its eyes to other aspects of modernisation, yet strongly rejected Western culture, its material values, consumerism and permissiveness. It also provided a legitimate outlet for Wahhabi xeno-phobia and the anti-Western sentiments of many Saudis.[26]

The Mecca rebellion of 1979,[27] rather than exposing the regime's vulnerability, underlined its strength and the dependence of the establishment Wahhabi ulama on their traditional alliance with the Al Sauds. The critical attitude of the Ikhwan toward the establishment, which neo-salafi jihad groups in the Muslim world propagated, is nevertheless consistent with the Wahhabi world view. Some senior Najdi ulama, it is claimed, sympathised with, and may have even encouraged, neo-Ikhwan groups and their criticism of the regime.[28] However, thirty senior ulama, including several arch-conservatives, produced a fatwa on 24 November 1979 permitting the storming of the Ka'ba and condemned the rebels. The Saudi regime, they claimed, 'had done nothing to warrant the rebellion'. The same ulama produced in 1990 a fatwa justifying the invitation of 'infidel' forces to protect Saudi Arabia.[29]

The Mecca affair and the success of the Islamic revolution in Iran had put the Saudi regime, and especially Crown Prince Fahd, on the defensive. Saudi 'institutionalised puritanism' was now facing the challenge of the new militant fundamentalism. The Saud rulers, therefore, decided to strengthen the historic alliance between 'church and state' which guaranteed the ulama's legitimisation of the Sauds. Despite the continuous erosion of the ulama's influence in the kingdom's power equation, their role was still indispensable notwithstanding criticism by fundamentalist circles of the Sauds' lifestyle and behaviour.

The alliance between the regime and the ulama has been even more carefully cultivated in the 1980s because of Tehran's revolutionary anti-Saudi propaganda and the Iran–Iraq war. King Fadh now consulted with senior ulama, on a variety of internal matters, every week and with lesser 'alims during his regular majlis.[30] Fahd, moreover, reversed the hesitant liberalisation of the mid-1970s and education has become more 'Islamic'. But although he bowed to their wishes on matters connected to religious and moral conduct and the curtailment of 'Westernisation', the monarch did not permit the ulama to interfere with the running of the kingdom, its development or its foreign policy.

The increased respect which the ulama enjoyed in the 1980s and the fact that King Fahd frequently underscored his devotion to Wahhabi principles notwithstanding, it seems that 'The ulama have exercised very little or no influence over major policies concerning foreign affairs, internal security, economic development, oil production and pricing, wealth distribution and regional allocation, or political participation' (the latter, however, has begun to change in the 1990s).[31]

The pace of modernisation initiated by Faysal from the late 1960s, sustained in the 1970s by increasing oil wealth, led to important changes in Saudi society and, to a lesser extent, in its cultural values. All social changes run against elements which cannot, or will not, adapt. That partly explains the 1979 'neo-Ikhwan' reaction, which protested against the corruption of the fundamentalist jihadist Wahhabi state by modernisation and gradual Westernisation. But in the age of jet airplanes and a complex security apparatus, such elements cannot hope to overthrow a regime, unless they enjoy widespread support. By the late 1970s, however, the Saudis were no longer an impoverished, backward people ready to embrace extremist puritan ideologies, but rather a society composed largely of a relatively affluent and educated urban middle class. Such a change, coupled with rapid modernisation, has made militant Wahhabi fundamentalism (neo-Ikhwan) unattractive to the Saudi masses, although being essentially conservative they continued to support the existing diluted version of Wahhabism.

The Wahhabiyya was always an antithesis of sophisticated religious philosophy. What was left in the 1980s of its original fundamentalist-jihadist message, besides old-fashioned unitarianism, was largely its traditional puritan moral code of public behaviour, feigned asceticism and xenophobia, merged with tribal customs and heritage, popularly referred to as the 'Saudi way of life'; it was sanctified by the Sauds and the ulama and transformed into a national ethos. This unique combination, coupled with oil wealth, provides the regime with a working formula for countering militant fundamentalism on the one hand and radical nationalism on the other. As long as the Sauds continued to nourish the above ethos and respected the special position of the ulama in the Saudi–Wahhabi kingdom, they were assured of the continuity of their historic alliance with the ulama. That and economic prosperity (now renewed) ensures the Sauds of the support of most of the conservative majority of their subjects. Yet by the 1990s, a new generation of *'alims*, largely graduates of Islamic universities, was no longer satisfied with the kingdom's pseudo-fundamentalism and their role in its power equation.[32]

2

MODERN EDUCATION AND THE RISE OF NEW ELITES*

MODERN EDUCATION AND THE ULAMA

Traditionally the ulama, in addition to their religious and judicial duties, were the teachers of the devout, and of the sons of the ruling elites. The puritanical Wahhabi ulama, however, limited themselves to the study of the *shari'a* and its recognised interpretations and totally ignored all other subjects. On the other hand the Hijaz, the most populated province, with its holy cities was of old a centre of Islamic scholarship in the broader sense, and at the beginning of the twentieth century it benefited from the development of modern education in the Ottoman Empire.

In 1926, Ibn Saud created in the newly conquered Hijaz a directorate of education, which opened the first secondary school, and introduced modern subjects into the curriculum of public schools. This innovation naturally aroused substantial opposition among the Wahhabi ulama. But the king, who considered such a development essential for his kingdom, practically ignored their protests. Ibn Saud, however, prudently tried to avoid a confrontation with the ulama. Indeed, as his meagre revenues suffered in the 1930s from the world economic recession, the development of modern education in Saudi Arabia was slow and illiteracy in the kingdom remained until the 1950s as high as 95 per cent.[1]

Commercial exploitation of oil in Saudi Arabia, after 1946, facilitated renewed efforts to advance Saudi education. Many Egyptian and other Arabic-speaking teachers were hired by Ibn Saud and suitable Saudis were sent to study in Egypt. This was the beginning of the progressive Egyptianisation of Saudi education.

In 1949 the Arabian–American Oil Company (Aramco) launched a five-year plan for the development of the skills of its employees. Selected Saudi employees were sent to the American University in Beirut and later on to the United States. Aramco also provided modern education for its employees' children and other children in the Eastern Province.[2]

Generally speaking, Aramco's contribution to the development of modern Saudi education, especially in the Eastern Province, was very important.

A ministry of education was created in 1953 by King Saud (r. 1953-64). Indeed, the number of schools and students in all levels of education tripled or quadrupled during Saud's reign. Furthermore, King Saud established in 1957 Riyadh University, the first secular university in the kingdom, and in 1958 adopted a three-cycle sequence of education.

Although he ignored the ulama's opposition to modernisation, Faysal followed his father's policy and tried to win their support for his reforms through concessions and compromises. For example, after pioneering girls' education in 1960 in the face of violent opposition, King Faysal placed the new general directorate of girls' education under the Grand Mufti. Subsequently, ulama-controlled female education became completely segregated.

In return for the ulama's acquiescence in his reforms, Faysal in effect granted them supervision of the modern education system and the appointment of a leading 'alim Shaykh Hassan Al al-Shaykh as minister of education. Thus, this ministry became a stronghold of conservative bureaucrats. In 1970 Faysal established the general directorate of religious institutions and colleges through which the government funded the religious system of education. When the government was reorganised by Prince Fahd in 1975 and a ministry of higher education created, Shaykh Hassan was appointed its head and a conservative technocrat replaced him as minister of education.

Paradoxically, the ulama, who at first opposed modern education, under Faysal practically controlled it. The curriculum of Saudi schools came to be focused on Islamic and Arabic studies, to the point where mandatory Islamic courses constitute about a third of the curriculum in Saudi schools. Indeed all students are constantly reminded of the organic relationship between the Saudi state and the Wahhabiyya.[3] Consequently, the younger Saudis, their minds conditioned by the educational system, become largely conservative in their outlook.

Faysal, believing that the modernisation of Saudi Arabia was conditional on the emergence of a large educated elite, was determined to provide a minimum level of education for every Saudi. Simultaneously he accelerated the development of secondary and higher education and the vocational system. The latter, however, failed to attract sufficient students (Al-Hasa excepted), owing to the stigma attached to manual work in Saudi society and the more attractive opportunities open to young Saudis.[4]

In the 1970s and early 1980s the mammoth expansion of the Saudi educational system was facilitated by the enormous rise in state revenues from the sale of oil. Because of the economic recession in the 1980s vocational education gained popularity, but many graduates of the system became in essence contractors, setting up with government loans, workshops or little factories employing foreign workers.[5]

The rapid development of modern education necessitated more than ever the employment of foreign teachers and administrators. Over the years more and more trained Saudis were employed in school administration and as teachers. Thus, elementary education is now completely Saudi-ised, but a good part of the intermediary and secondary levels still remains partly dependent on foreigners.

Possibly more serious is the poor quality of the Saudi educational system itself. Two major reasons for this are the low standard of foreign teachers and the Egyptian model followed by the Saudis: this is based on rote-learning, recitation and 'cramming'. Moreover, Saudi teachers who replace foreigners in elementary and secondary schools are generally no better than their predecessors. Educated Saudis generally avoided the teaching profession which was not considered sufficiently prestigious or rewarding. Yet in recent years, prompted by unemployment, many more better qualified graduates are joining the teaching profession.[6]

Following Faysal's death in 1975, King Fahd, who held the reins of power even while Khalid reigned (1975–82), stepped up the country's rapid industrialisation, which necessitated accelerated manpower training. The education system was expanded to an unprecedented rate; by 1989, the total number of students in Saudi schools had risen to about 2,650,000 (40 per cent of the population) of whom 1,160,000 were girls, compared with a total of 33,000 in 1953. A further growth of the system is projected by the kingdom's fifth development plan (1990–5).[7]

The enormous expansion of modern education and the substantial decline in illiteracy in Saudi Arabia are impressive achievements. Yet, Saudi statistics often conceal the low standard of the educational system and the social composition of its students. The quality of schools and students varies according to the geographical and social environment. Rural and urban lower-middle-class students, largely bedouin, with traditional backgrounds, are often unprepared for the systematic approach and foreign philosophy of modern education.[8] Beyond the first years, many rural and newly urbanised students are incapable of, or not interested in, continuing their studies, which have no economic value for them.

An exceptional case is that of the Shi'ites of the Eastern Province, who until the 1980s were officially discriminated against by the Wahhabi kingdom. Their best chance to acquire education above the elementary level then was through the Aramco schools, or on Aramco scholarships in foreign universities.[9] Others were the sons of the new Shi'ite *petite bourgeoisie*, which began to emerge in the late 1960s. The Saudi regime became, however, more sensitised to the Shi'ites' needs in the 1980s.

The standard of education in the urban centres catering to the Saudis of middle-class background is on the whole also relatively low. Memorising is still the backbone of the system, while the standard of English and science teaching is uneven and often very poor.[10] Saudi statistics take no account of the middle and upper classes' disproportionate benefits from subsidised education. Middle- and upper-class children, especially from the Hijaz and children of the Najdi *hadr*, are better prepared for modern education and have access to better schools. These groups also dominated secondary education and enrolment in Saudi or foreign universities in the 1980s.

However, the government is not unaware that the first two development plans (1970–80) favoured the urban population, especially the middle and upper classes. One of the aims of the third and fourth development plans (1980–90) was to improve and expand the education system. Nevertheless, the numerous successful 'lower-class'[11] entrepreneurs have not been constrained by minimal education. Together with their brethren who are school and university graduates, they have become in the last two decades part of the Saudi middle class.

THE DEVELOPMENT OF HIGHER EDUCATION

Determined not to remain completely dependent on foreign higher education, Ibn Saud established in Mecca a college of *shari'a* in 1949 and a teacher training college in 1952, with an extension in Ta'if.

The Grand Mufti, competing with the government system, also established in Riyadh a *shari'a* college in 1953 and an Arabic language college in 1954. This development helped prolong somewhat the conservatives' hegemony in education and in the Saudi administration.[12]

The establishment of Riyadh University in 1957 ushered in the second period in the development of Saudi higher education (1957–75). Older colleges were consolidated into, or merged with, full-scale universities, while new ones were opened elsewhere in the kingdom, to facilitate Saudi Arabia's modernisation and economic development. It was also the regime's hope, apparently, to offset the tensions arising from rapid social change by enabling talented Saudis to acquire university education and to benefit from their country's prosperity.

As a result, numerous Egyptian, Western and other professors and administrators were hired. Only in recent years did Saudi professors replace a good part of the foreign faculty who dominated the kingdom's universities. As in other fields, the path of modern educational development was facilitated by concessions to the ulama. In this case the state funded Islamic universities and schools, made religious courses mandatory in the curriculum of the 'secular' universities and handed to the religious leadership the supervision of women's colleges.[13]

Riyadh University (in 1980 King Saud University – KSU), the largest in

Saudi Arabia, is the stronghold of the Najdi 'aristocracy' and is somewhat more conservative than other 'secular' universities.[14]

The Islamic University of al-Madina was established in 1961 following consultations between foreign fundamentalists, Wahhabi ulama and the Saudi authorities. Designed to replace Al-Azhar (following the latter's reorganisation by Nasser in 1961) as an international Islamic university, its staff and students are largely foreign Muslims, while most of its Saudi ones are of bedouin origin, and other Saudis, with fundamentalist tendencies.

The University of Petroleum and Minerals (UPM), now King Fahd University, in Dhahran (Eastern Province) is by Western standards the best and most prestigious university in the kingdom. Established by Aramco in 1963 as a college (P&M), it became a university in 1975. The UPM is an American enclave in Saudi higher education: its teaching language is English, its faculty is largely foreign. Half of the students and some of its faculty are said to be Shi'ites.

The ulama-controlled Riyadh colleges became in 1974 the Imam Muhammad Ibn Saud Islamic University. A stronghold of Najdi–Wahhabi fundamentalism, this university, in addition to producing jurists and teachers, co-ordinates all Saudi religious schools and studies. It supervises the National Guard schools and the upgrading programme of the Morality Police.

King Abd al-Aziz Ibn Saud University at Jedda was founded in 1967/8 by local philanthropists as a Western-oriented business institution. In 1971, it became a state university ('secular') and its orientation became more Arabic–Islamic. In 1977 it opened a new campus in Madina and one in Abha (Asir) and is the second largest Saudi university.

King Faysal University (KFU), the fourth and latest 'secular' university, was established in 1974/5 with campuses in Hufuf and Damman (Eastern Province). After 1980, the university established a full range of faculties. A good part of its faculty is Western, and courses in the sciences and medicine are still taught in English (1987), a serious problem for the average Saudi student. Because of the regime's efforts to mitigate the traditional discrimination against the Shi'ite minority, the university has enrolled in the 1980s a growing number of Shi'ite students.

Umm al-Qura University (Mecca) was formed in 1980, its nucleus the colleges founded in 1949 and 1953. Umm al-Qura is apparently intended largely to serve the conservative population of the Hijaz, but one quarter of its students are foreigners. Like other Islamic universities, its aim is to supply the judges, imams and teachers required throughout the country; in the government its graduates occupy posts in the ministries concerned with education, justice and the 'preservation of virtue'.

By 1975 there were nearly 20,000 students in Saudi universities, and more than 5,000 Saudis studying abroad. While some of the latter, mainly

the offspring of wealthy Hijazi and some Najdi merchants and aristocrats, studied at their own expense, the others, mostly of urban middle-
class background, were given government stipends throughout their
graduate and postgraduate studies. Upon their return to Saudi Arabia,
these graduates of foreign universities were often appointed to important
positions in Faysal's and Fahd's administrations and governments.
Graduates of 'secular' domestic universities (mostly of *hadr* or urbanised
middle-class background), were appointed to lesser but still prestigious
positions when they chose not to go into the private sector. Subsequently,
bureaucrats of middle- and upper-class background, largely Hijazis and
to a lesser degree Najdis, came to dominate the Saudi administration
(with the exception of the ulama-controlled ministries and the legal
system), at the expense of traditional bureaucrats and graduates of
religious institutions.

The third period in the development of higher education in Saudi
Arabia (1975–85) coincides with the rise to power of Fahd and the second
and third development plans. This was a period of almost uncontrolled
growth in Saudi higher education. Unfortunately it saw the decline of
quality and standards. As the demand for educated Saudi manpower
increased following the accelerated modernisation, the enormous budgets
for the 'development of human resources' were comparatively increased.
Thousands of foreigners, again mainly Egyptians, were hired to teach in
the universities, many of inferior quality. The Saudis who opted for an
academic career were also, in many cases, poorly qualified.

Already in 1974, enrolment requirements in the 'secular' universities
(the UPM excepted) were noticeably lowered 'by order of the government'
and thereafter frequently overlooked altogether.[15] In addition to free
education, housing, stipends and other privileges, students were assured
(until 1986) of government employment on graduation. Such concessions
were obviously motivated by the regime's need to defuse socio-economic
tensions. The majority of students normally opted for the less demanding
humanities and social sciences, where the teaching and text-books were
in Arabic; only a minority chose engineering, sciences, business and
medicine, which were badly needed in the kingdom's developing economy but where the teaching language was often English, professors
foreigners and admission requirements more difficult.[16]

Although the number of university graduates rose quickly in the 1970s
and early 1980s, it could not satisfy the demand. Nevertheless, women
graduates were discouraged from seeking work and only a small percentage of female graduates were employed in the Saudi economy in the
1980s. As a result of King Fahd's political difficulties after he was
enthroned (1982), the separation of sexes in institutes of higher education
and the limited employment opportunities for women became even more
pronounced than before.[17]

In 1985, Saudi Arabia's seven universities and fourteen women's colleges had a total student population of about 80,000. The number of Saudi students abroad, nevertheless, continued to rise, and about 18,000 were believed to be attending American universities. However, the severe recession in the kingdom in recent years gradually caused that number to decline. Simultaneously, the number of students in Saudi universities has risen by 1989 to about 100,000, with 20,000 graduates annually.[18]

By the early 1980s large sections of the administration had become over-inflated with university-trained bureaucrats, exacerbating the prevailing inefficiency;[19] but as senior and even middle-range positions were hard to come by, university graduates, including seasoned bureaucrats, progressively opted for provincial offices of the ministries. Indeed, after 1985, owing to the economic recession, which was caused by the crisis in the oil market, government offices and agencies were instructed (1986) not to hire additional personnel. Thus unemployment among school and university graduates was on the increase.[20]

Graduates who returned to Saudi Arabia in the 1960s and early 1970s with PhD and Master's degrees were appointed to key positions in the government's bureaucracy and education system. The wave of foreign-trained graduates returning home after the mid-1970s dominated most of the middle level of the civil service and government agencies, and increasingly joined the staff of the 'secular' universities. Besides their influence on the central government and its policy, their manners, ideas and way of life have been copied by many others. Thus, even the transformation of the universities from the Egyptian to the American system in 1975 seemed to the conservatives another aspect of the growing 'Americanisation' of Saudi Arabia.

Frustrated by what they perceived as the Westernisation of the Wahhabi kingdom through uncontrolled modernisation, many conservatives accused the government and its US-educated technocrats of helping supplant Wahhabi puritanism and 'the Saudi way of life' with Western culture and 'the American way of life'. Even before the 1979 Mecca rebellion Prince Fahd had come under growing pressure from the more extreme ulama and Saudi middle-class nationalists to reduce Western influence in the kingdom. Indeed, after the Mecca incident even Crown Prince Fahd found it prudent to restate his declared opposition to the Westernisation of Saudi Arabia. By the early 1980s, even some American-trained Saudis began to question Western values and the aims of modern Saudi education which they helped develop.[21] The growing number of graduates of Saudi universities, who knew very little English and had little contact with the West, were largely conservative and increasingly anti-American. The ulama were given greater control of the education system and their influence seemed again to be on the increase.[22]

CONCLUSIONS

As in other fields, Riyadh tried to bridge over centuries of stagnation by allocating larger and larger budgets for education. Certainly, for a nation whose illiteracy rate was 95 per cent in mid-century, the development of Saudi education is phenomenal. Yet its quality leaves much to be desired and the low level of the Saudi education system and of its graduates is an accepted norm related, to a great extent, to the kingdom's political realities. Moreover, it seems an absurd situation that Saudi Arabia, experiencing an acute shortage of manpower and needing to employ millions of foreigners, keeps at an enormous cost to its treasury about 35 per cent of its population in school (some for indefinite periods) and excludes women graduates from the job market. Indeed, for a nation of this size, the number of its students in domestic and foreign universities seems excessive.

Saudi Arabia's oil revenue has declined from about 108 billion dollars in 1981 to about 18 billion dollars in 1986 (16.5–17.5 billion in 1987–8). Consequently Riyadh has been trimming its expenditures on one hand and drawing on its financial reserves on the other. For political reasons, the allocations to education, welfare services and subsidies, which benefit all Saudis, have been reduced only marginally. By the late 1980s, however, Saudi Arabia was unable to maintain its previous level of expenditure and continue to drain its financial reserves. Thus, the education and manpower development budget, over 10 per cent of the kingdom's budget, could not be sustained at the previous level.[23] Yet the war against Iraq and the sharp rise in oil revenue in 1990 may again change the situation.

Until 1986 the Saudi regime employed all the university and school graduates who chose to join its inefficient administration. By the mid-1980s, unless they had a UPM degree or the necessary professional or vocational speciality, graduates had to be satisfied with whatever job they could get in the provinces. Indeed, students have begun progressively to adapt their studies to their country's needs and some, in addition to Al-Hasa and peripheral areas, are finally joining the science and engineering faculties and the vocational stream. The question, nevertheless, remains (even in 1992) whether Saudi Arabia can afford its extensive, wasteful and inadequate educational system. Further economies by the government and the slowly reviving private sector make it extremely difficult to provide suitable employment for over 100,000 school and 20,000 university graduates annually.[24] But this is a political and social rather than just an economic issue, and one of which the Sauds are well aware.

The relatively small but growing proportion of 'lower-class' students with secondary education in the last decade often chose the Islamic universities with their traditional character and curriculum, easy admission requirements and higher stipends. 'Lower-class' graduates, from both Islamic and 'secular' universities, rarely reached high positions in the administration. This undoubtedly contributed to the interest of some in fundamentalist (neo-Ikhwan) ideologies and to the growing tension between graduates of Saudi religious universities and of the 'secular' ones – and between both these groups and their Western-trained colleagues, who have captured most of the key positions in the central government and its agencies.[25]

As the number of university graduates continued to grow in the 1980s, the three-sided competition for jobs, exacerbated by growing unemployment among the educated, peaking in 1986–9, has been extended to the lesser positions in the middle level even in the provincial administration. Indeed, unemployment among the new elites has become a serious socio-political problem that could undermine the kingdom's stability, accompanied as it is by conflicting ideologies and socio-religious tension. The rise in oil revenue since 1989 may help the Saudi regime partly to overcome the problem if properly handled.

The rise of the Saudi middle class has been greatly enhanced by the growth of Saudi oil revenue. The acceleration of the kingdom's modernisation on the one hand and the dramatic rise in the number of educated Saudis on the other have given new dimensions to this phenomenon. Faysal's policy in the 1960s and early 1970s, which enabled the new elites to participate in his government and share in the country's wealth, encouraged them to co-operate with his regime and, largely, to join its power base. Thus, notwithstanding two abortive attempts at coups in 1969 and unrest in 1977 and the early 1980s, social fermentation among the new middle class was avoided. Yet, despite the decisive role played by the new elites in their country's modernisation and the dramatic expansion of their ranks, the Saudi oligarchy is only now, in 1992, hesitantly relinquishing its monopoly of the kingdom's decision- and policy-making.[26]

Part II

MODERNISATION AND STRUGGLE FOR POLITICAL REFORM

3

THE REIGN OF SAUD (1953–64): STRUGGLE FOR POWER AND NATIONALISM

It is often assumed that the nationalist upheavals which had shaken the Middle East from the late 1940s to the early 1970s left Saudi Arabia's society relatively unaffected. Indeed, after the suppression of the Ikhwan uprising in 1929/30 the patriarchal Saudi regime seemed to rule the kingdom unchallenged at least until 1979. The uprising in Mecca in that year, moreover, was the outcome of a Wahhabi fundamentalist reaction to rapid modernisation and had nothing to do with the rather secular socio-politically motivated opposition to the monarchical regime. Yet, the changes which Saudi society has experienced in recent decades, the emergence of a new elite and of social ideologies, and the growing frustration of the Shi'ite minority, have produced in the kingdom a militant nationalist opposition to the Sauds' authoritarian government. Despite its relatively limited following, this militant opposition has affected the kingdom's policy and in certain instances threatened the regime's stability. Even more important, however, was the rise in the kingdom of new powerful middle-class elites whose struggle for political participation became a major issue in Saudi Arabia in the 1970s and 1980s.

The development of a militant nationalist (Shi'ites included) and middle-class opposition to the Saudi regime, the reason for its failure to gain power despite the dramatic expansion in the ranks of the new middle-class elites and the latter's partial incorporation into the ruling class's power base, will be discussed in the following chapters.

SOCIO-POLITICAL CHANGE IN THE POST-WORLD WAR II YEARS (TO 1958)

Authoritarianism and the growth of Arab nationalism

Policy decisions in Arabia were usually adopted through deliberations with the tribal elders or regional notables rather than unilaterally by the Shaykh (amir). Abd al-Aziz Ibn Saud, a strong leader, once his power was

27

consolidated often dispensed with this procedure. In the 1920s, as his power grew the ruler increasingly made major policy decisions himself or consulted his unofficial *majlis al-shura* (Consultative Council) made up of his most senior kinsmen and devoted friends.

A milestone in this process was the collapse of the Ikhwan rebellion in 1929/30 and the dramatic rise of Ibn Saud's revenues after the conquest of the Hijaz (1924) and following commercial exploitation of oil in the late 1940s. Ample funds not only enabled the ruler to begin building the kingdom's armed forces and dispensing with the military services of tribal and regional amirs but also, whenever possible, to buy off rather than fight the opposition – the Sauds' golden rule to this day.

The monarch still met tribesmen, merchants and ulama in his daily *majlis*. Such audiences served largely as a forum for petitions and complaints. On rare occasions the king convened large gatherings of tribal shaykhs, notables and ulama. This was to obtain through *ijma'* (consensus) their formal sanction for a major policy decision which would have been reached previously after consulting senior members of *ahl al-hal wa'l-'aqd*. Considering Ibn Saud's strong personality, his reluctance to delegate authority and tendency to identify the kingdom with himself (*l'état c'est moi*), his government after 1930 could be considered paternalistic and authoritarian rather than, as described by some authors, a 'desert democracy'.

The Ikhwan rebellion, the last serious challenge to Ibn Saud's increasingly centralist government and relations with the British, was crushed by 1930. Nevertheless, Saudi Arabia remained relatively insular until the end of World War II. Yet the traditional links which the Hijaz maintained with the Muslim world served Ibn Saud as a channel for communication with the Arab countries. Indeed when appointed Viceroy of the Hijaz (1926) Prince Faysal was also put in charge of relations with the outside world.

Though they largely embraced the Wahhabiyya after 1926, most urban Hijazis, compared with their Najdi compatriots, remained tolerant and open-minded. Modern education, the press and broadcasting developed in the Hijaz faster than elsewhere in Saudi Arabia. In fact most of the reforms introduced under Ibn Saud were first tried out in the Hijaz, Saudi Arabia's most developed and populous province. Furthermore, up to the 1970s, the growth of the foreign Arab community in the province outpaced that in the other regions in the kingdom.

A nascent educated elite had already emerged in the kingdom by the 1940s. The ranks of the new middle-class intelligentsia gradually expanded in proportion to the growing number of Saudis studying in universities abroad. At this stage the majority of such students came from urban Hijazi families. Sons of merchant families, some Najdis and others from the Eastern Province who had won Aramco scholarships also studied in foreign countries. Yet until the 1970s Hijazis remained the majority of those studying in foreign universities. On returning home they formed the backbone of the new middle class and the upper echelons of the modern administration.

After World War II, the Hijaz was quick to respond to the rise of nationalism and anti-colonialism in the Middle East. These were reinforced by the strongly anti-Western foreign Arab community living in the province. Accelerated modernisation and the 1948 war brought to the Hijaz many more Egyptians and Palestinians to join relatives who had already obtained employment there. The size of the foreign Arab communities was constantly growing through increased opportunities in the Saudi oil industry and the administrative and educational networks. These communities were important in fostering nationalist agitation in Saudi Arabia as a whole. In the early 1950s, events in the Middle East and the growing foreign presence helped disseminate these sentiments which were reinforced by the press, particularly in the Hijaz, and by radio broadcasts from neighbouring countries. Aware of developments in the Arab world the nascent Hijazi urban middle class served as the vanguard of Arab nationalism in Saudi Arabia.

Rivalry in the royal house (1953-8)

Despite his uncontested succession to the throne in November 1953 King Saud (r. 1953-64) could not hope for the kind of authoritarian regime which his father had enjoyed. He had to contend with personal shortcomings and serious health problems; also, his smooth succession was conditional on two factors: first sharing his power with Faysal his heir apparent, who was to become prime minister, and second, sometimes consulting the informal *majlis al-shura* made up of the senior members of the royal family. Saud faced a variety of complex problems both within and outside the kingdom. The Middle East was in constant turmoil because of Nasser's militant nationalist leadership, while in Saudi Arabia oil wealth and modernisation were beginning to change the face of Saudi society.

Lacking the strength of character, finesse and *savoir faire* of his brother and rival Faysal, Saud was unable to consolidate a power base within the royal family. A conservative, he turned for support to the ulama and the tribal amirs but also tried to win favour with the emerging middle class. Unhappy at the loss of their power and the erosion of the traditional way of life, the old elite demanded an end to modernisation. Conversely, the new middle class, and some young princes, wished for constitutional reforms, faster development and limits on the power of the conservatives. Although he speeded up the modernisation of the government and expanded the educational system, Saud gave in on the whole to the demands of the traditionalists.

Saud established the Council of Ministers at the beginning of 1954 (decreed by Ibn Saud in October 1953) and later appointed Faysal to be its head. Yet he did not delegate authority to this body but rather tried to rule the country with the help of unscrupulous advisers, in the same patriarchal style as his father. His management of the modern apparatus, however, frequently revealed his incompetence. There was no distinction between the king's privy purse and the kingdom's treasury. The larger the revenue from oil, the more Saud managed to squander, and the kingdom's financial situation rapidly deteriorated.

Matters were aggravated by the 1956 Suez war. Though Saudi oil installations were spared because of Saud's support of Nasser, the closure of the canal proved a setback to the kingdom's oil industry. By 1957 the kingdom was on the verge of bankruptcy and dissatisfaction with Saud's incompetence reached a peak.

The cohesiveness of the kingdom, which Ibn Saud had achieved through political marriages, proved to be its undoing after his death. His numerous sons contended for power and wealth. By the beginning of 1958, after Saud dramatically reversed his foreign policy and clashed with Nasser, it was clear that the country was heading for political and financial crisis. By this time, the royal family was split up into three camps. The first was made up of the king, the few princes who still supported him, Saud's numerous sons and most of the tribal amirs who rejected the modernisation which eroded their power. The second consisted of most of the senior princes who supported Faysal's demands for financial reforms and evolutionary modernisation which would consolidate the power of the monarchy in the face of rising radical nationalism in the Middle East. The third consisted of a group of younger liberal princes, led by Talal who, until 1955, was minister of communications. Prince Talal, who frequently visited Nasser between 1955 and 1958, wished to turn Saudi Arabia into a constitutional monarchy and favoured more rapid modernisation of the kingdom.

When Saud's complicity in a plot against Nasser became public in March 1958, Faysal immediately resigned from his position as prime minister. Pro-Nasser and pan-Arab sentiments in the Middle East, including Saudi Arabia, reached an unprecedented peak following the establishment of Nasser's United Arab Republic in February 1958. The royal family, naturally, became exceedingly worried lest Saud's bungling should cause the overthrow of the regime. Subsequently, after consulting the senior ulama and some tribal amirs, the majority of the senior members of the House of Saud decided to divest Saud of most of his responsibilities and to request Faysal to assume the position of prime minister with full authority. Facing a *fait accompli* Saud agreed to these demands and Faysal began his first term as *de facto* ruler of Saudi Arabia.

King Saud, Arab nationalism and the West

The Middle East began to change rapidly in the last years of the reign of King Ibn Saud and especially after the 1948 war in Palestine. A new generation of Arab nationalists became increasingly impatient with the 'neo-colonial' presence in the region and with the traditional regimes and politics of their countries. The unrest in the Arab countries reached a climax with the 1952 officers' revolution in Egypt. The Middle East holds a major part of the proven oil reserves in the world, and this made the region a zone of contention between the superpowers. Together with its revenues from oil, the Arab nationalists considered Saudi strategic importance crucial for the achievement of their aspirations. As its expanding oil industry and fast modernisation were beginning to have an impact on its society, Saudi Arabia could no longer remain insular.

Ibn Saud's attempts, between 1949 and 1951, to persuade Washington to sign a defence agreement with Saudi Arabia failed despite Aramco's support. However, they led to the expansion of Washington's military and financial aid to the kingdom and to the extension until 1956 of an agreement under which the US leased the Dhahran air base. A training mission commanded by a USAF brigadier joined the military advisory group which had helped to organise the Saudi armed forces since 1946. Thus, military personnel further bolstered the American presence in the Eastern Province, which was constantly growing at this time because of the intensification of Aramco's activities in the region.

England, as was to be expected, was the main target of the Egyptian-led Arab nationalist propaganda. Following the 1952 revolution in Egypt and the undermining of Premier Musadeq's government in Iran by the CIA after the nationalisation of the Anglo-Persian Oil Company, sympathy for the United States in the Arab world also declined. The US, moreover, now the leader of the West, lent support to Israel and had initiated regional anti-Soviet defence pacts incompatible with Arab nationalist aspirations.

Even before he came to power, the traditionally-minded Saud, heavily reliant on his father's Syrian and Palestinian political advisers, was believed to be unfriendly to the West. Immediately after his succession King Saud declared that he was not favourably inclined to the proposed American Middle East defence pact. He was apprehensive of the closer relations America was forging with Hashemite Iraq, and critical of US support for Israel. Early in 1954 Saud informed Washington that he wished to dispense with its Point Four aid and he instructed the Point Four Mission to leave the kingdom.[1]

31

A strange alliance emerged in 1954 between Saud and President Nasser. Each needed the other's help in fighting the Western-sponsored regional defence pacts. Saudi oil and financial resources temporarily made Saud an ideal partner for Nasser, who was leading the struggle against British and French colonialism in the Arab world. For his part, Saud hoped to capitalise on Nasser's popularity and prestige as a leader of Arab nationalism.

Aramco's relations with Saud were less amicable than they were during the reign of his father because of his political bias and his insatiable need for funds. Aware of the company's vital help in various fields, and with events in Iran unfolding before his eyes, Saud was careful not to antagonise Aramco. The monarch, however, faced a difficult dilemma just before he came to power in November 1953 when confronted by growing unrest in the oil fields of the Eastern Province.

THE GROWTH OF OPPOSITION AND THE ISSUE OF POLITICAL REFORM (1953-8)

The Aramco 1953 strike and the rise of nationalist opposition

Until the 1940s, the Eastern Province (*Al-Mantiqa al-Sharqiyya* or Al-Hasa), was generally considered backward, as well as being unpleasant in climate. Its population was largely made up of nomadic Sunni tribesmen, Shi'ite agriculturalists (mainly in the Al-Hasa and Qatif oases) and a mixed coastal population which engaged in trade, fishing and pearl diving. The discovery of oil in Al-Hasa in the 1930s, and its commercial exploitation from 1946 onwards, completely changed the character of the province.

Many American and other Western oil men came to live in 'Aramco towns' with their families. They maintained their own lifestyle as far as possible. In addition, Aramco employed thousands of Italians, Indians, Pakistanis, Palestinians and Lebanese clerks and technicians. The expatriate Arab employees introduced to the province social, cultural and political values common in the Middle East but not compatible with those existing in the archaic Wahhabi kingdom. Thousands of bedouins, who despised manual work because of social mores, also settled temporarily on the peripheries of the 'oil towns' and provided the company with unskilled transient labour. Local Shi'ites, about one-third and possibly one-half of the province's Saudi population, formed the backbone of Aramco's permanent unskilled and semi-skilled workforce. Traditionally discriminated against by the authorities, their only chance for a better life was with Aramco, whose recruitment policy was 'colour blind'.[2]

The growth of Aramco's operations triggered off fundamental changes in the Eastern Province. Its coastal 'oil towns' rapidly developed and economic activity in the region intensified. The business of the oil company, the requirements of its foreign employees and the wages earned by its Saudi workers caused the cost of living to rise sharply, and the local population, including Aramco's Saudi workers, experienced hardship. The proud Wahhabi bedouin found it difficult to adjust to a Western work regime. To their eyes they were being patronised and discriminated against in their own country by 'infidels' whom they had been taught to despise, and they resented this.[3]

Undoubtedly the Shi'ite community in Al-Hasa as a whole greatly benefited from Aramco's activity and its liberal employment policy and training programmes. Some qualified Shi'ite employees were even sent abroad by the company for further training and were later appointed to medium-level clerical and technical positions in the company (but not managerial ones). As members of an oppressed minority with a tendency to extremism, many Shi'ites were attracted by radical anti-Western Arab nationalism, which held promise of social and political equality. The deep frustration of the Shi'ites of the Eastern Province with the Saudi–Wahhabi regime which oppressed them could find expression in the anti-Western manifestations of unrest in Aramco.

In the early 1950s after Ibn Saud's health rapidly deteriorated the kingdom was governed *de facto* by a council of regents. It was widely believed that when the old king died a struggle for power would break out in the country. Such an atmosphere of uncertainty, combined with the nationalist fervour which swept the region after the Egyptian revolution, increased the unrest in Al-Hasa and in the Hijaz.

Aramco began to experience labour difficulties in the first months of 1953. At the end of June a workers' committee, largely made up of Saudis trained abroad, handed the management a petition, demanding higher salaries, improved work conditions and facilities and the right to organise the workers. A copy was also handed to the government.[4]

As the situation in the oil industry, which provided the government with its main source of revenue, continued to deteriorate, Amir Saud, the heir apparent, was asked to handle the crisis. He appointed a royal commission to look at the workers' grievances. The arrest of the twelve members of the Workers Committee, who became popular heroes over-night, for their abusive treatment of the royal commissioners, sparked off a general strike by the Saudi workforce.

The strike ended only after the king ordered the workers to return to work and the strikers' leaders were released from jail. On 9 November, King Abd al-Aziz died and Saud succeeded him. The new king, striving to consolidate his authority, immediately issued a royal decree granting Aramco workers a 20 per cent pay rise and many other concessions.[5]

The 1953 Aramco strike is often described as a spontaneous protest by

Saudi workers, who were forbidden by law from organising to contest unsatisfactory pay and amenities. The value of Aramco's salaries was eroded by the high cost of living in the Aramco towns and by inflation. The Saudi workforce was incensed by the luxurious housing and other facilities enjoyed by the American employees.[6] However, another element – the strong xenophobic and anti-Western sentiments of the domestic Aramco workforce – is frequently ignored. These were fomented by native and expatriate Arab (largely Palestinian) nationalist employees.

The scale of discontent and nationalist ferment in Saudi Arabia in the early 1950s is usually underestimated. Five centres of opposition to the Sauds' patriarchal regime emerged inside the kingdom during this period. The first was among the urban middle-class Hijazis, the second among the Shi'ites and the Aramco workforce. The third was among tribal and *hadr* elements in northern Najd and in the Eastern Province, who had resisted the rise of the House of Saud in the first decades of the century. The fourth emerged in Asir, where some tribes were still not reconciled to the Saudi domination. The fifth was in the armed forces, generally among officers who had gone abroad for training[7] or came into contact with their Egyptian and other Arab colleagues.

The sophisticated Hijazis were not only closely attuned to nationalist activity in the Arab world but, after 1924/5, found themselves governed by the Najdis, whom they considered uncouth. The Najdis, who looked down upon the Hijazis as being of mixed blood and religiously lax, imposed the restrictions of the Wahhabiyya upon them. To add insult to injury, King Saud, shortly after his succession, abolished the special status of the Hijaz, granted by his father and nourished by Faysal, which gave its population a degree of self-government.[8] He also ordered all government offices to be moved to Riyadh.

Although separatist tendencies were common in the province, it was inconceivable that the Hijazis would really wish to cut themselves off from Saudi oil revenue once the benefits became apparent.[9] The Hijazi intelligentsia, however, hoped that either a reform of the Najdi-dominated archaic regime, or its overthrow, would enable them to assume a more fitting role in the government of their country and *inter alia* abolish, or at least reduce, the ability of the Wahhabi ulama to constrain its development.

The Shi'ites and some of the Sunni tribes of the Eastern Province who fought Ibn Saud and participated in the Ikhwan movement ('Ujman), had no reason to like the regime. The Shi'ites, subject to religious persecution and ill treatment, and their Sunni neighbours, believed that their oil was enriching their oppressors while its benefits were denied to them.

The 1953 strike was an important milestone in the re-emergence of militant opposition to the Al Saud government. Anti-monarchical overtones became apparent in the later stages of the strike and the workers, despite the many concessions they had won, remained discontented and critical of the regime. In the following years, the Aramco workforce and the Eastern Province as a whole became the focus of nationalist and radical leftist activism.[10] Saudis, along with foreign Arab workers, most notably Palestinians, agitated against the Americans and the regime. They formed clandestine organisations demanding reforms, the right to unionise, the phasing-out of the US air base in Dhahran and increasingly the ending of discrimination against the Shi'ites.

The Hijazi urban middle class had access to the whole of the Arab world, its press and radio broadcasts. Their opposition to the Sauds in this period reflected the Egyptian-led mainstream of Arab nationalism. Several small clandestine nationalist groups, made up of only a small number of active members belonging largely to the educated well-to-do urban middle class, demanded a constitutional–parliamentary regime and a faster pace of modernisation.

Far more militant was the National Reform Front (NRF) which emerged at the end of 1953 or early in 1954. Founded by the leaders of the 1953 Aramco strike and of the small Najdi intelligentsia, it also claimed members in the Hijaz and the armed forces. The socialist and secular orientation of this organisation, influenced by contacts with the Palestinian Arab Nationalists (*Qawmiyyin al-'Arab*), called for social and political reforms and the abolition of the Committees of Public Morality. As the NRF intensified its activities among the Aramco workforce and the military in 1954 and 1955, its more outspoken leaders were often imprisoned and some were forced to flee the country.

The NRF, renamed the National Liberation Front (NLF) in 1957/8, continued its activities as a socialist pro-Nasserite movement both in Saudi Arabia and abroad until the 1970s. Its leftist leanings, militancy and roots in the oil industry, in the armed forces and among some Najdi tribal elements, made the NLF exceptionally dangerous to the regime and a primary target for its security services.

The Saudi NLF moved further left from the Nasserite mainstream of Arab nationalism in the 1960s and was ideologically related to the Marxist South Yemeni NLF and Palestinian Liberation Fronts (especially the PDFP). Repeatedly splitting away from and regrouping with its mainstream Arab Nationalists and its left wing, the Popular Democratic Front (PDF), in the 1970s the NLF became the nucleus of the small Saudi communist and Ba'th parties (both Syrian- and Iraqi-oriented).

A member of the Workers Committee of the 1953 strike, Nassir Sa'id, a Najdi, the best-known Saudi opposition leader until the 1970s, was a founding member of the NRF. He was the chief instigator of the 1956 disturbances in Al-Hasa, and, following an attempt to form an Arabian

Trade Union Association, escaped to Syria (1956). In 1958 he founded the *Ittihad Shu'ub al-Jazira al-'Arabiyya* later renamed *Ittihad Abna' al-Jazira al-'Arabiyya* (Union of the Sons of the Arabian Peninsula) active against the Saudi regime in the 1960s and 1970s. Support for this organisation among Saudis seems to have been limited to the Aramco workforce and Jabal Shammar and it was especially popular among the Yemenis and other foreign Arabs residing in the kingdom.

The Popular Democratic Front and the Organisation of the National Revolution, offshoots of the Arab Nationalists (*Qawmiyyin al-'Arab*), also appeared in the 1960s. Their support in Saudi Arabia was minuscule and largely among foreign workers.

A Saudi branch of the Ba'th movement was founded in 1958, shortly after the emergence of the UAR. At first it looked to the Syrian Ba'th for guidance, and the little support it found in Saudi Arabia came mainly from townspeople in the Hijaz and Asir. After the early 1960s, with the rise in power of the Iraqi Ba'th, the small Saudi Ba'th movement became largely Iraqi-oriented and its activities spread to the Eastern Province and Hijaz. It also won some support among Saudi students abroad.[11]

In other Arab countries, discontented young nationalist army officers represented the more serious opposition to their regimes. In the 1950s the Saudi armed forces were still in an embryonic form. They lacked prestige and were easily counterbalanced by the tribal National Guard loyal to the Sauds. It seems that although suspected and discriminated against, educated Hijazi commoners reached key positions in its command.

A movement called the Free Officers had already emerged in the armed forces by 1954. In the spring of 1955, members of this group were arrested and their leaders executed because of an alleged plot against the regime. The Free Officers and members of the Arab Nationalists in the armed forces also participated in anti-monarchical activities until 1959. But such activities were of little consequence and only made Faysal more determined, in 1958, to freeze plans for the development of Saudi Arabia's army and air force. Following the Egyptian intervention in Yemen, some officers of the Saudi air force deserted to Egypt with their planes. But the most serious, albeit amateurish, attempt by the military to overthrow the regime was to come, ironically, in 1969 after the *rapprochement* between Nasser and Saudi Arabia.

King Saud was not unaware of the discontent in the kingdom. Thus, paradoxically, while he courted pan-Arabism, he took steps to suppress the nationalist and radical opposition to his regime. A royal decree was published at the beginning of 1954 prohibiting strikes and demonstrations, and control on the media was tightened. The security services began to hunt down 'communists' and radical nationalists. Foreign Arabs, particularly Palestinians, were also accused of agitation or of membership in pan-Arab movements.

The efforts of the regime to suppress the middle-class and socialist-nationalist opposition were not very effective because of rivalry in the royal family between 1955 and 1961 and because the security services were inadequate. The bleeding of the country's economy by the royal family and Saud's pro-Western and anti-Nasserite policy infuriated the nationalists. Indeed agitation among the military, the intelligentsia and Aramco's workforce was to continue, and even intensify, in the years to come.

The 1956 strike and the collapse of the Egyptian–Saudi axis

Ironically, the intensification of anti-monarchical activities among the new elites and the Aramco workforce coincided with the climax of the Egyptian–Saudi co-operation. The Baghdad Pact was launched in February 1955. Only the joint efforts of Egypt and Saudi Arabia prevented Jordan from joining as well. Yet Saud's anti-Hashemite and anti-Western activities could not offset the fact that his corrupt and reactionary regime was unacceptable to the new elites and other Saudi nationalists.

From 1955 anti-Western and anti-American agitation, aimed, as well, against the regime, escalated in the Hijaz and the Eastern Province. When King Saud visited Dhahran in May of 1956 he was confronted by a hostile demonstration 'organised by nationalists and communists' demanding the phasing-out of the American base there and the nationalisation of Aramco.

At the beginning of June, Aramco was paralysed by a general strike. There was little doubt that in addition to legitimate grievances the strike was politically motivated and directed against the regime and the West. This time the strike was quickly and harshly suppressed on Saud's orders and a number of demonstrators and strike leaders were killed or executed and others were imprisoned. Furthermore, a new royal decree strictly forbade strikes and demonstrations of any kind.[12]

It should not be overlooked that modern education and the economic development of the Eastern Province had begun to make the Shi'ite population of the region more conscious of their disadvantages. Since 1953 Aramco had gradually divested itself of different operations which it had carried out in the past by passing them on to local contractors. Because of this and the higher skill of its workforce and the termination of labour-intensive infrastructure projects, the company gradually reduced its workforce. At the same time, it was trying to increase the proportion of local employees and the number of Saudis in its administration and management.[13] Yet, coming as it did during a period of financial crisis in the kingdom, this reduction in manpower was especially painful for the Shi'ite population of the Eastern Province. To some extent Aramco became in the next decade a focal point of radical anti-government and anti-American activity in Saudi Arabia.[14]

President Nasser arrived in Dhahran in September for the meeting with King Saud and President Kuwatly. His nationalisation of the Suez Canal two months earlier and the humiliation of the West had aroused Arab pride and turned Nasser into the idol of the Arab masses. He was met in Al-Hasa by huge crowds, who manifested their admiration for him with great emotion. Saud was not only ignored but, according to one source,[15] 'stones were thrown at the royal entourage and slogans denouncing the House of Saud were displayed by some of the demonstrators'. Shortly afterwards, when Nasser arrived in Riyadh, the whole population turned out to accord him a hero's welcome.

Disturbances in the Eastern Province in 1956 during Nasser's visit there were an extension of the Arab nationalist struggle, led by the Egyptian President, against Western colonialism in the Middle East. The Aramco concession and the Dhahran air base were viewed as a symbol of the 'neocolonialist' presence in the region and constituted a challenge to Saudi pride and Arab independence. Together with the authorities' harsh suppression of the Al-Hasa demonstrations and strike, they exacerbated the resentment of the population of the Eastern Province and Saudi nationalists towards their regime.

Nasser's visit to Saudi Arabia, it seems, was also a turning point in the relationship between Saud and the Egyptian leader. Apprehensive of the universal empathy in the kingdom for Nasser and his policy, Saud became determined to resist Nasser's growing power in the Arab world. When the Suez war broke out the king prudently severed Saudi Arabia's relations with Britain and France and slapped an oil embargo on them. He also helped Nasser to coerce King Hussayn to withdraw the military facilities England enjoyed in Jordan; but despite the universal rejection of the Eisenhower Doctrine (January 1957) by Arab nationalists, Saud visited the US at the end of January and undertook to support the Doctrine. In exchange for an agreement to extend the lease of the Dhahran air base for five more years Saud obtained from Washington an undertaking of economic and military assistance.

Relations between Saud and Nasser rapidly deteriorated in 1957. King Saud attempted to stop the unification of Syria and Egypt which led to the establishment of the UAR in February 1958. In March it came out that the Saudi monarch had financed a plot to assassinate President Nasser. As this happened when Arab euphoria at the establishment of the UAR was at its peak, the Egyptian and Syrian media exploited the affair for an all-out attack on the Saudi regime, and called upon the kingdom's population to rise against its corrupt rulers.

Faysal, who supported Saud's opposition to the Western defence pacts, disagreed with his anti-Western extremism and his support for the subversion of Nasser in the Arab world. Always an advocate of a cautious and passive policy, Faysal was naturally unhappy with Saud's total change of attitude at the end of 1956. It was obvious to him that overt opposition to the Egyptian leader was bound to cause Nasser and the nationalist camp to focus their efforts on undermining the Saudi regime. Although careful not to challenge his brother openly, Faysal took advantage of his mistakes practically to rule Saudi Arabia in his name.

POWER STRUGGLE IN THE ROYAL FAMILY AND THE NEW ELITES (1958-64)

Faysal's first cabinet (1958-60)

As soon as he assumed power Faysal adopted a policy of appeasement towards Nasser and quickly declared his support for his positive neutralism. He froze all the king's agreements with the US to assure Nasser of Saudi opposition to America's Middle Eastern policy. However, relations between the traditionalist kingdom and its revolutionary neighbours remained at best correct.

By 1960, while Nasser preached socialism and militant pan-Arabism, Faysal began to experiment with a pan-Islamic policy meant to block the spread of radical ideologies. Earlier, the kingdom had become a haven for Syrian and Egyptian Muslim fundamentalists, who were now permitted to use the media to criticise Egypt's secularisation and 'socialisation' of Islam.[16]

The period of Faysal's government in the late 1950s is marked by the success of his financial reforms, the reorganisation and modernisation of the cabinet and administration, and the rapid expansion of the educational system. Many technocrats from foreign universities were given key positions in the administration.[17] Yet, ironically, Faysal's achievements caused him to lose many of his supporters. His austerity policy estranged the Hijazi merchant class. The substantially reduced allocations to the numerous princes and to the tribal *umara'* antagonised both. The Liberal Princes led by Prince Talal were disillusioned with Faysal's conservative measures designed to preserve the system rather than reform it. They considered the strong and capable crown prince a more serious obstacle to change and to their own aspirations than Saud had been. As for the nationalists, when they realised that Faysal's limited reforms were meant to perpetuate the Sauds' authoritarian regime, they were determined to transform Saudi Arabia into a constitutional monarchy, or get rid of the House of Saud altogether.

Once it became apparent that Faysal had no intention of instituting a constitutional monarchy, and as the crown prince and the king wished to win their sympathy, the nationalists skilfully manoeuvred between the

39

two and in practice enjoyed the advantage of overt political activity. At the time the Saudi security services were extremely ineffective and the regime, attempting to appease Arab nationalism, did not wish to undermine its own efforts by persecuting the local progressives.

Between 1958 and 1960 opposition organisations frequently distributed pamphlets demanding a reform in the kingdom's political system and its policies. The Saudi press, dominated by Egyptians and the Hijazi intelligentsia, openly defied the censorship and frequently published articles promoting the cause of Arab nationalism and indirectly attacking the regime. The establishment of the UAR caused many more Saudi officers and NCOs to join the Free Officers movement and other Saudi clandestine organisations. Yet the result of Faysal's policy was that the armed forces remained weak and incapable of seriously threatening the regime.

By the beginning of 1960, Faysal's popularity was at a low ebb. A strange alliance emerged at the end of 1959 between Saud and his conservative supporters, the Liberal Princes and the intelligentsia. In an effort to win the good will of the new elite, Faysal employed many in his administration, speeded up the process of modernisation, allocated greater funds to modern education and abolished the censorship laws. Yet, when the Liberal Princes and the nationalist intelligentsia submitted a proposal to him in June for a constitutional monarchy and an elected body with legislative powers, Faysal, backed by most of the senior princes, rejected it out of hand.[18]

The rise and fall of Saud's 'progressive' government (1960–2)

By the last months of 1960 Saud felt sufficiently strong to oust Faysal. Subsequently, on 21 December, the king announced the formation of a new government which he would lead.

Saud's new 'progressive' government was probably the nearest that the nationalists and constitutionalists ever got to gaining power in Saudi Arabia. The new cabinet did not include any of the senior princes of the royal house. In addition to Saud's son, the cabinet consisted of three Liberal Princes led by Talal, who was appointed minister of finance and national economy as well as deputy president of the Supreme Planning Council. Six out of eleven ministries in the cabinet were held by commoners, five of whom, mostly with university degrees, were moderate nationalists. Abdallah ibn Hamud Tariki (a Najdi and a co-founder of OPEC) was the exception: his appointment as the head of the newly created Ministry of Petroleum and Mineral Resources represented the militant element among the nationalists.

The June 1960 programme for constitutional reforms which the Liberal Princes and the intelligentsia submitted to Faysal was strongly condemned by the ulama on the ground that it contravened the *shari'a*. Even Saud dissociated himself from the document, declaring that the Qur'an was Saudi Arabia's constitution and the only source for its social principles. Notwithstanding, immediately following the formation of the new cabinet Radio Mecca announced in its name the promulgation of 'basic laws' and the establishment of a legislative council: two-thirds of the members were to be elected and one-third appointed. The announcement was refuted by the king two days later in a radio broadcast and press interviews.

Evidently the conservative king was opposed all along to his allies' constitutional reforms. Nevertheless, the Liberal Princes and the nationalist commoners in the government, inspired by Nasser's revolutionary nationalism, believed that the days of the Saudi monarchy were numbered. Indeed, as finance minister and deputy president of the Supreme Planning Council, Talal frequently attempted to usurp the power of the Council of Ministers in order to achieve his aims, but he thereby alienated the king and the more moderate ministers.[19]

Not unaware of the progressives' attempt to manipulate the weak king, the senior princes and the other conservatives in the Saudi ruling class exerted pressure on Saud to limit the influence of leftist nationalists in his court and government. The king dismissed his progressive advisers at the end of February 1961. In the next few months he began to strengthen the moderates in the government, ignoring the outraged protests of the Liberal Princes.

A harsh State Security Law was promulgated by the king in March 1961, paradoxically, while a 'liberal' government was ruling the country. It prescribed the death penalty or twenty-five years' imprisonment for any aggressive act against the royal family or the state (including treason, attempts to change the regime, or to spread disaffection among the armed forces). It also forbade the profession of any ideology other than Islam, or the formation of political parties. This was necessitated by the rising tide of leftist-oriented clandestine activities aimed against the regime, which followed on the shelving of the constitutional reforms and the dismissal of Saud's progressive advisers.[20]

The American presence in Dhahran became a source of increasing embarrassment to King Saud, who was accused of providing the imperialists with a base in Saudi Arabia. The Eastern Province, a centre of radical nationalism, did not benefit, moreover, from government-sponsored development and suffered from growing unemployment. Thus, during a visit to the region in the first months of 1961, Saud was met by hostile demonstrations. That, and pressure from Arab nationalists at home and abroad, caused the king, in mid-March, to announce his decision to terminate the Dhahran agreement on its expiry in April 1962.[21] None the less, nationalist ferment all over the kingdom was

41

aggravated in the spring of 1961 by economic problems and rising unemployment among the newly urbanised unskilled rural population.

All the different ideologies prevalent at this time in the Arab world – Communism, Socialism, Ba'thism and Nasserism – were represented in Saudi Arabia, although their actual following was limited in number. Yet all were united in their demands for constitutional reforms, for attuning Saudi foreign policy to pan-Arabism and for faster development. Some even plotted to assassinate members of the royal family and to hasten the kingdom towards a popular revolution. Indeed, unrest in the armed forces following the outbreak of war in Yemen in 1962 demonstrated the wisdom of Faysal's decision to freeze its development.

Tension between Nasser and King Saud resurfaced in 1961 because of the difficulties the former was encountering in Syria. Wahhabi ulama and Muslim Brothers, who found refuge in the kingdom, attacked the secularisation of the UAR and its relations with the Soviet atheists. The Saudi regime, exploiting pan-Islam to counter pan-Arabism, authorised non-Saudi fundamentalists to establish an Islamic University in Al-Madina to compete with the 'socialised' Al-Azhar. The Saudi government, claiming that the principle of Islamic solidarity supersedes foreign ideologies, also founded in 1962 the World Islamic League (*Rabitat al-'Alam al-Islami*) which later set up a permanent secretariat in Mecca.[22]

Inter-Arab relations on the whole became increasingly polarised in this period because of Nasser's militant pan-Arabism and the rivalry between the Egyptian and the Iraqi revolutionary regimes. Ironically, when Iraq attempted to annex Kuwait at the end of June 1961 shortly after its independence, Riyadh found itself in the same camp as Cairo. Yet, when the UAR collapsed in September, the Egyptian media again viciously attacked the Saudi regime.

Isolated in the royal family, and again facing a political and economic crisis, the ailing Saud sought reconciliation with Faysal, though he did not wish to relinquish the government to him. The shrewd crown prince agreed to co-operate on condition that Saud dismiss Talal and the other Liberal Princes from the cabinet. Although he accepted this condition, Saud, when he left the kingdom for medical treatment in November, entrusted the premiership to Faysal on condition that the latter would not make any changes in the cabinet. Thus, from mid-November 1961 to the beginning of March 1962, Faysal presided over a cabinet made up largely of nationalists and Saud's supporters.

The usually cautious Faysal, abandoning his traditional appeasement policy concerning Egypt, dismissed many of the Egyptian advisers employed by the Saudi administration. Because of allegations of Egyptian espionage, each government withdrew its ambassador from the other's capital. Faysal was no longer willing, as well, to tolerate a hostile Saudi press. Egyptian and local nationalist journalists were dismissed and a ministry of information was established in 1962 in order, *inter alia*, to monitor the press and help fight against the Egyptian propaganda. A press law was promulgated in November 1963, but strict state control over newspapers was re-established even earlier (and exists to this day). In 1962 Faysal obtained the consent of the ulama for the expansion of radio broadcasting to counter the vitriolic attacks from Egypt's *Sawt al'Arab* (the Voice of the Arabs). Notwithstanding the ulama's strong objection, the government authorised shortly afterwards the construction of TV stations in Jedda and Riyadh.[23]

When Saud returned to Saudi Arabia in March 1962 he was coerced by a coalition of senior princes to surrender his responsibilities as prime minister to Faysal. Abdallah Tariki and several of Saud's commoner ministers were replaced by more moderate Hijazi notables and technocrats (Zaki Yamani replaced the Najdi Tariki as minister of petroleum). Most important, Shaykh Hassan bin Abdallah Al al-Shaykh was appointed minister of education, thus ensuring the support of the ulama for Faysal, despite the modernisation of the kingdom and the rapid development of 'secular' education, and Musa'id ibn Abd al-Rahman, Faysal's uncle, became minister of finance. The latter ministry was essential to the success of Faysal's modernisation policy and his intention to channel much of the kingdom's oil revenues to the population through government and welfare services. Musa'id's prestige, moreover, enabled Faysal to reduce substantially the royal list and the stipends allocated to each prince who remained on it.

Muzzling the press and purging the cabinet of radicals and the Liberal Princes served as a warning to the Saudi nationalists that a new era in their relations with the Sauds' regime had begun. Indeed, Abdallah Tariki slipped out of Saudi Arabia and settled in Beirut. He was later followed by Talal and some of his brothers. Yet the attraction of pan-Arabism was still considerable, and most of the moderate Hijazi nationalists in the cabinet did not hesitate to challenge Faysal's policy when it clashed with Nasserism.

While negotiations between Egypt and Syrian and Iraqi Ba'thists about a new unit plan were going on, Faysal's Islamic entente and the *de facto* renewal of the leasing of the Dhahran base to America were viciously attacked. The overthrow of the monarchy in Yemen at the end of September 1962, and the Egyptian involvement there soon after, began a new era in active opposition to the Sauds' regime. Radical nationalist organisations now turned increasingly to sabotage and acts of terrorism; but the Hijazi middle-class nationalists became less supportive of Nasser after his intervention in Yemen.

The war in Yemen precipitated a new crisis in the Saudi government. The royal house could no longer afford to be led by the irresolute and incapable Saud. Thus, with the blessing of the ulama, the monarch was

43

coerced into handing over the office of prime minister with unlimited authority to Faysal. On 31 October, the crown prince formed a new government in which all the major power groups, excluding Saud's supporters, were represented. In addition to Faysal and Prince Musa'id, who continued to hold foreign affairs and finance portfolios respectively, Prince Fahd (king in 1982),[24] Faysal's staunchest ally and the leading reformer, became minister of the interior, his full brother Sultan replaced Saud's son Muhammad as minister of defence and their older half-brother Khalid became deputy prime minister. The *'alim* Shaykh Hassan was appointed minister of education and another *'alim* became minister of pilgrimage and *awqaf*. Six Hijazis, most of whom were technocrats known for their moderation in internal and external affairs, were appointed to the remaining ministries.[25]

When Faysal assumed the premiership at the end of October 1962 the future of the Saudi regime looked quite grim. Nasser considered Yemen a jumping board to the control of the enormous oil wealth of the Arabian Peninsula, and he committed a large army and substantial resources to the war in Yemen. The Egyptian expeditionary force, supporting the republicans in Yemen, succeeded in defeating the royalists, and Egyptian planes bombed the border towns of Asir which served as staging bases to the royalists' tribal army.

The Saudi armed forces at the time were small and poorly equipped and many of its officers sympathised with Nasser's aspirations. Saudi air force planes, despatched with supplies for the loyalists, were flown by their crews to Egypt, and several rebellions erupted in remote garrisons. Furthermore, the National Guard was incapable of waging a modern war and most of its commanders (tribal amirs) were loyal to King Saud.

In September Prince Talal with his brothers Abdul Muhsin, Fawwaz and Badr, and his cousin Sa'd ibn Fahd, founded in Cairo the Free Princes Movement. Later on, together with the Saudi Nasserite and leftist organisations, they formed the Arab National Liberation Front (ANLF). In its name, Egyptian, Syrian and Yemeni radio stations called upon the Saudis to overthrow their 'corrupt' and 'reactionary' regime.

When he was in the United States in September and October of 1962, Faysal realised that his policy had estranged America and that the kingdom could not count on the Kennedy administration for support in relation to Yemen. Nevertheless, contrary to his traditional policy of appeasement and caution, Faysal was now determined not to allow Nasser to have his way, and so he actively supported the Yemen royalists.

Faysal was not unaware of the rapid social change taking place in the country and of the growing strength of the new Saudi middle class. By 1962, for instance, the number of students profiting from the modern educational system had risen to more than 113,000, compared with 33,000 in 1953. Students in local institutes of higher learning numbered several thousand while those studying abroad, with government or Aramco sponsorship, were conservatively estimated at about 1,200. Many more, the offspring of well-to-do families, were attending foreign universities at their own expense.[26] Indeed, by the early 1960s the ranks of the educated middle class, especially in the Hijaz, had expanded to such an extent that they could support nineteen newspapers and periodicals compared with the four of the early 1950s.

In such circumstances it was of the utmost importance for the regime to gain the support of the moderate nationalists, who were mainly from the Hijazi middle classes and, to a lesser extent, of Najdi *hadr* origin. These nationalists mainly aspired to a constitutional monarchy, and the modernisation of the kingdom but were not fired by the idea of Nasser's new socialist radicalism, nor by the Palestinian-inspired militant socialism widespread in Al-Hasa.

Aware of the inherent weakness of the traditional conservative Wahhabi kingdom in a rapidly changing Middle East, Faysal, encouraged by Prince Fahd, was determined to modernise Saudi Arabia with the help of the new elites. Yet even though he was given a lot of latitude by *ahl al-hal wa'l-'aqd* to deal with the grave crisis threatening the regime, Faysal knew that there was a limit to the concessions that he could offer. He was aware that the majority of the ruling class would not agree to sharing decision-making with the new elites, a step which would begin the erosion of their power and privileges, nor did he himself truly wish for such a change. His experience with the Hijazi middle-class elite led Faysal to believe that it would co-operate with him. All they needed were the right incentives: the chance to share in running the country's development and the hope of eventually participating in decision-making.

Diluted reform and the Yemen war

On 6 November, the day that relations with Egypt were cut off after the bombing of Saudi towns near the Yemen border and a week after he became prime minister, Faysal announced his ten-point programme; he promised a wide range of social and political reforms, rapid modernisation and economic development. The proposals were the closest to constitutional monarchy ever promised officially and in detail by the regime. The following were the most important:

1 To promulgate a fundamental law, based on the Koran and the Sunna, that would allow for a National Consultative Assembly (*majlis al-shura*).

2 To regulate the provincial government and provide for provincial councils.

3 To guarantee freedom of expression (within the context of Islamic laws).

4 To preserve the independence of the judiciary and to create a Ministry of Justice.

5 As 'one of the government's most important functions is to raise the national social level', to establish welfare services that would take care of the needy and the unemployed.

6 To provide free education and medical services.

7 'As the financial and economic development of the kingdom are of primary concern to the government' to enact laws to promote the above.[27]

The promised fundamental law incorporating a National Consultative Assembly (*majlis al-shura*) and the reorganisation of the provincial government with their councils have not yet materialised, although reiterated by Saudi monarchs during the last thirty years following every crisis. Rather, shortly after undertaking to guarantee freedom of expression, Faysal launched a campaign to suppress the nationalist-oriented Saudi press. However, all the other points, some substantially modified, were carried through immediately or in the next few years. Within a decade, they led to a rapid modernisation of the Saudi kingdom, an impressive rise in the standard of living and the involvement of its new elites in running the affairs of its government.

Free modern education and medical treatment, social security laws, welfare services and efforts to deal with unemployment were forthwith tackled by Faysal's governments. Together with modernisation and economic developments they were made easier by the growing revenue from oil.

Past experience had taught Faysal that the ulama will resist any attempt to undermine their control of institutions, such as education and justice, traditionally within their jurisdiction. Yet, he also knew that determination to carry out the reforms seemingly resulting from *shura* and *ijma'* (consultation and consensus) would convince them that they should accept a compromise, especially if control of the modernised institutions was to be left in the hands of an *'alim*. Nevertheless, the promised independence of the judiciary and the creation of a Ministry of Justice met with strong opposition from the ulama and other conservatives from the ruling class.

As early as June 1963 Faysal attempted to reorganise his government and establish new ministries of justice and municipal affairs. But the bitter opposition of the ulama, his uncle Musa'id's refusal to accept the justice ministry and the hostility of the *umara'* to the proposed reorganisation of the rural government, caused Faysal to postpone this plan (only in 1970, following the death of the kingdom's powerful Grand

46

Mufti, did Faysal establish the ministry of justice). By the end of 1963, no longer worried about the Yemen war, Faysal published an edict for the formation of provincial government and councils but did nothing about it. Yet, in later years, he systematically strengthened the authority of his central government at the expense of the power of the *umara'*.

Faysal again avoided a confrontation with the ulama in relation to his promise to establish a judiciary council by creating the Institute for the Issue of Religio-Legal Opinions and the Supervision of Religious Affairs (*Dar al-Ifta' wa'l Ishraf 'ala'l-Shu'un al-Diniyya*) and the Higher Council of *Qadis* (*Al Majlis al-'Ali li'l-Qada*). Both were directed by, and composed of, senior jurists.[28] Another touchy problem was Faysal's undertaking to reform and restrict the authority of the ulama-controlled Committees of Public Morality. Their power, which Saud had re-established, and the zeal of their Morality Police was strongly resented by the new elites and the middle classes. Faysal, believing this extremist body to be a dangerous anachronism, restored the *status quo* which had existed until 1953.

Faysal's strategy proved most successful. The old elites accepted his policy because it enhanced both stability and the regime's ability to overcome the grave threat facing it. The ulama, as expected, were ready to compromise as long as the Wahhabi character of the kingdom was preserved and their role in it outwardly respected. The larger part of the middle-class intelligentsia, apprehensive of Nasser's increasing radicalism, welcomed the ten-point programme. Their main aim in any case was to achieve faster development in the country and constitutional reform granting them participation in decision-making, both of which Faysal appeared to promise.[29]

Although it became evident later that the king had no intention of carrying out the promised constitutional reforms, the majority of the new elites, tempted by power, prestige and wealth, or induced by the cruel suppression of the militants, opted to continue co-operating with the regime. Many even misled themselves into believing that Faysal's evolutionary reforms, the modernisation of the kingdom and their increasing influence in the government and administration, would eventually lead to their participation in policy-making. Some, however, felt that they had been misled by the ruler and in addition to the leftist opposition that had rejected Faysal's evolutionary reform programme from the start, began to plot the overthrow of the regime.

Welfare benefits, government services and subsidies increased in the following years, in proportion to the country's rising oil revenue. This ensured the support of the rural population, the newly urbanised and the middle class for the Al Saud regime. Most important was the fact that Faysal had publicly declared that the welfare of the population was the government's first concern and that the country's wealth was to be used to improve the population's standard of living.[30]

In his relations with the nationalist new elites Faysal adopted the carrot-and-stick principle. He differentiated between the moderate middle-class nationalists, mainly Hijazis who had been carried away by the early success of Nasser's anti-colonial struggle and the idea of pan-Arabism, and the hard-line militant leftists in the province and elsewhere in the kingdom. Some of the latter came from Najd and Al-Hasa families traditionally unfriendly towards the Sauds. For this minority, the cadres of the different offshoots of the NLF, the Nasserites, socialists, Ba'thists and the communists, he had no compassion. They were mercilessly hunted and tortured and imprisoned when caught.[31]

The ANLF disintegrated in September 1963. Talal and the other princes, despairing of gaining support in Saudi Arabia and objecting to the use of their names in the vitriolic Egyptian propaganda offensive against Al Saud, begged Faysal's forgiveness. Their return to Saudi Arabia in 1964 signalled the demise of their quixotic movement and of open liberalism in the royal family (until recent years).

The war in the Yemen, and the escalation in the activities of the clandestine opposition organisations, caused Faysal to expand and modernise the security services with the help of American experts. A directorate of internal security was established by the Ministry of the Interior in 1964 (*Al-Mabahith al-'Amma*) as well as the Security Force College (in Riyadh). The National Guard, enjoying the favour of the royal house, was to be expanded and, with British help, upgraded in quality. In 1963 it was put under the command of Prince Abdallah (now crown prince), the leader of the conservatives among the senior princes supporting Faysal, and its command structure was purged of King Saud's appointees.

By the latter part of 1963 it was already clear that the Egyptians were not going to win an easy victory in Yemen, and by the end of the year Syria succeeded in focusing Arab attention on the river Jordan project undertaken by Israel. This caused a temporary détente in inter-Arab relations and led to the Cairo summit of January 1964.

Once enthroned in October 1964, and no longer apprehensive about the future of the Sauds' regime, Faysal gradually rescinded his promise to institute constitutional reforms. In an interview which followed his succession to the throne in 1964, he declared that 'Saudi Arabia has no need for a constitution because it has the Qur'an, which is the oldest and most efficient constitution in the world.' Later he added that 'the only true criterion of a regime, monarchical or republican alike, is the degree of reciprocity between ruler and ruled and the extent to which it symbolises prosperity, progress and healthy initiative'.[32]

By the second half of 1964, although Nasser realised that his Yemeni adventure had failed, he renewed his attacks on the Saudi regime. Saudi radical opposition movements enjoyed the support of Cairo, San'a and the Ba'th regimes of Damascus and Baghdad and were encouraged to escalate their operations in the kingdom. In addition to occasional bombing incidents and the distribution of anti-government pamphlets throughout the provinces, leftist organisations attempted to foment unrest in Al-Hasa and its oil industry. The Aramco College of Petroleum and Minerals, with its partly Shi'ite student body became, shortly after its establishment, an additional focus of nationalist agitation.[33]

Faysal's hard-line policy towards the radical opposition was demonstrated immediately by the widespread arrests in the Southern Region (Asir) and the Eastern Province among the local intelligentsia and the Yemeni and Shi'ite workers. New anti-strike laws, announced in 1964, prescribed harsher punishment for incitement to strike and widespread arrests of opposition activists accused of communism were carried out in the Eastern Province. Yet tension in Al-Hasa continued and demonstrations, rioting and even bombing incidents were reported in the following years.[34]

CONCLUSIONS (1953-64)

The reign of Saud (1953-64) which coincided with the rise and continued success of Nasser's pan-Arabism, could be considered the golden era of Saudi nationalism. The weakness of the ruler and his ambivalent policies, and the struggle for power within the royal family, presented the Saudi nationalist opposition with the opportunity to expand its activities practically unchecked. The potential threat to the power monopoly of the Saudi oligarchy by the largely bourgeois pan-Arab nationalists of the Hijaz, their socialist and even Marxist-oriented counterparts of northern Najd, Asir and Al-Hasa (including Shi'ites in the latter), and by frustrated pro-Nasserite officers (many of whom were Hijazis), was not underestimated by the rulers. Both Saud and Faysal, struggling for power, tried to win their favour, especially after 1958 when a wave of euphoria swept the Arab world following the establishment of the UAR.

In December 1960 when he ousted Faysal and established his 'progressive government', Saud valued the support of the nationalist intelligentsia to such an extent that they were strongly represented in his cabinet and among his advisers. When he again became prime minister in 1962, Faysal considered winning the sympathy of the nationalist public sufficiently important to merit his ten-point programme. The very fact that Faysal ruthlessly persecuted the nationalists who were either dissatisfied with his partial reforms or unwilling to join his camp, was a tribute to their estimated power. Indeed, the potential threat of the militant pan-Arabists to the conservative Saudi monarchy was seriously exacerbated in the last months of 1962 by the establishment of a

49

republican regime in Yemen and the presence of Egyptian expeditionary forces there.

The failure of the Saudi nationalists to oust the relatively weak and divided regime was the result of several factors. The Saudi armed forces were still in an embryonic state and were balanced by the tribal National Guard. Most Saudis in the 1950s and early 1960s were still country people, backward and conservative. Their allegiance was to their tribes and traditional institutions, including the paternalistic Saud monarchy, rather than to the 'Saudi nation'. The nationalists, moreover, were identified with the urban (*hadr*) middle class whom the bedouins traditionally disliked. The socialists, even Najdis, were considered atheists or identified with the despised Shi'ites and their struggle for equality. On its part the regime increasingly channelled oil revenues to improve the standard of living of the population. Thus, notwithstanding the climax of pan-Arabism in the region, nationalism in Saudi Arabia failed to win popular support other than from the intelligentsia, Aramco's Shi'ite and expatriate Arab workforce and from the non-aristocratic officers in the inconsequential armed forces. Finally, at the end of 1962, faced with a serious threat, the royal family and the ruling class overcame its differences and closed ranks behind Faysal.

The Egyptian intervention in Yemen provided Saudi nationalists with what seemed their best chance ever to win a share in policy-making. Faysal's decision to abandon his appeasement policy signalled the end of the radical nationalists' overt political activity and their attempts to share in power and decision-making from within the establishment. It also led to the growing radicalisation and militancy of the small Saudi left and widened the rift between the latter and the largely Hijazi middle-class nationalists, many of whom were becoming disillusioned with Nasser's radical pan-Arabism which now threatened their country. Attracted by new opportunities opened for them by Faysal, the majority opted, thereafter, to co-operate with the traditional elites and provided the numerous technocrats which Faysal's plans for speedy modernisation and his evolutionary reforms needed. Finally, it brought to the throne Faysal, a capable, strong leader with political *savoir faire*, who mercilessly suppressed the militant Saudi opposition.

50

4

THE REIGN OF FAYSAL
(1964–75): NEW ELITES, OIL
AND RAPID DEVELOPMENT

MODERNISATION AND NEW ELITES, FROM
CONFRONTATION TO CO-OPERATION (1964–70)

After he was enthroned in November 1964, Faysal continued to strength-
en the central government and expand its responsibilities at the expense
of the traditional socio-political institutions. With the exception of
foreign relations, security and religious-oriented ministries, all cabinet
positions were placed in the hands of commoners. Other ministries
relating to social and economic development and modernisation, created
in later years, naturally required the expertise of Western-educated
technocrats. Subsequently many more educated Saudis were incorporated
into the administration, gradually replacing the officials with traditional
backgrounds or establishing new government departments and services.

The ever-increasing need for an educated and skilled Saudi workforce
necessitated the expansion of the kingdom's educational system and the
establishment of additional 'secular' and Islamic universities. Together
with the increased enrolment of Saudis in foreign universities, the growth
of higher education swelled the ranks of the Saudi new elites. However,
the rapid urbanisation of the unskilled rural population, resulting from
accelerated modernisation, presented Faysal's government with serious
problems of unemployment, inadequate housing and welfare services
and rising cost of living in the cities of the Hijaz, the Eastern Province
and Riyadh. Paradoxically, modernisation necessitated the employment
of large numbers of skilled and unskilled foreigners, most of them
expatriate Arabs, to do the jobs that Saudis could not, or were unwilling
to do.

On the whole the bourgeois new elites were satisfied with Faysal's rate
of modernisation and they reconciled themselves to the fact that some of
his promised reforms seemed to take longer to materialise. Indeed, even
Saudis who professed leftist ideologies during their studies abroad were
enticed into joining Faysal's service on their return home: the promise of
high office, prestige and wealth soon facilitated their becoming part of

51

the fold.[1] Yet, radical elements of the new elites and some graduates of foreign universities, as well as some Sunni and Shi'ite worker activists in the Eastern Province, remained sceptical about Faysal's reforms and were determined to bring down the Al Saud regime.

While rapidly expanding the responsibilities entrusted to the new elites in his government and the number of agencies involved in the modernisation project, Faysal also increased the central role of the royal family in policy decisions by consulting regularly with the informal *majlis al-shura*.

By 1964 President Nasser was searching for a face-saving formula to extract himself from the Yemeni quagmire. The Arab–Israeli conflict provided a temporary solution. But Nasser's attention was again diverted to Arabia in the second half of 1964. The deteriorating situation in Yemen in the following year coerced Nasser to sign in August 1965, in Jedda, a humiliating agreement designed to enable him to terminate the costly Yemen adventure. Shortly afterwards, however, the British announced their intention of evacuating their forces from Aden by the beginning of 1968 (and from the Gulf by 1970), and Nasser's ambitions to control the Gulf oil were rekindled.

At the end of 1966 the Constituent Assembly of the World Islamic League in Jedda denounced the inter-Muslim war in Yemen and the persecution of the Muslim Brotherhood in Egypt. Faysal forged closer relations with the United States, bringing about the American–British military aid package in 1965, and renewed American guarantees for Saudi Arabia's territorial integrity in June 1966 as well as the military assistance agreement in September.[2] All this caused Nasser to pursue the war in Yemen with renewed vigour. The bombing of Saudi border towns and villages was resumed and anti-regime operations by Saudi and expatriate Arab clandestine organisations were escalated.

Unrest in the Eastern Province again erupted in 1965 and in 1966. This led to the detention of scores of nationalists and labour activists. At the end of 1966 rumoured coup attempts followed bombs which exploded near sensitive targets in different provinces of the kingdom and in Riyadh.

The Arab Nationalist movement (*Qawmiyyin al-'Arab*), which by the mid-1960s could be considered Marxist, encouraged its Saudi offshoots to escalate their operations in co-operation with Palestinian and Yemeni groups in the kingdom and in nearby countries. Not surprisingly various Saudi groups identified with the *Qawmiyyin* became the primary target of the kingdom's security services. Yet, most of the bombings were carried out by Yemeni and Palestinian infiltrators and residents in Saudi Arabia. Scores of Yemenis and Palestinians and hundreds of Shi'ites were arrested at the end of 1966 on suspicion of being members of the Ba'th and other illegal organisations, and a large number of foreign Arabs were deported from the kingdom.[3]

During the Alexandria Arab summit of September 1964, Faysal realised that the era of inter-Arab détente was over. Faced with the expanding camp of hostile radical Arab regimes, and escalated Egyptian operations in Yemen in the first half of 1965, he was resolved to develop the Saudi armed forces. Despite strong opposition in the royal house, the Saudi defence budget was increased from about 104 million dollars in 1964/5 to 335 million in 1966/7. By 1967 the Saudi armed forces numbered about 35,000 men compared with about 18,000 a few years earlier.[4]

Considering the kingdom's enormous territory and its sparse population, Faysal (or his American advisers) rightly gave priority to the development of the Saudi air force and air defence system. The inadequacy of the latter was underscored by the renewed Egyptian air strikes on Asir's towns and villages. Faysal requested and received, in 1965, the assistance of the US Department of Defense in the form of an American–British military aid package worth several hundred million dollars. In addition to American-made Hercules transport planes and Hawk missiles, the Saudis purchased English-made Lightning fighters and SAM missiles. While some British and Pakistani mercenaries began to fly Saudi planes, ex-RAF pilots trained Saudi air and ground crews, many of whom were the better educated and more sophisticated Hijazis.[5]

Faysal's determination to build up the power of the armed forces was strengthened by the British decision to evacuate their forces from Aden and the Persian Gulf. The departure of the Egyptian forces from Yemen at the end of 1967, in Faysal's view, worsened the situation in the Arabian Peninsula. An NLF government replaced the British in Aden (South Yemen) in December 1967. Marxist elements, benefiting from Soviet aid, attempted to take power in San'a and another *Qawmiyyin* offshoot, the Popular Front for the Liberation of Oman and the Arabian Gulf (PFLOAG), began to operate in Dhofar and Oman in 1968. So Saudi efforts to develop their armed forces were further accelerated after 1967. Indeed the Saudi defence budget jumped to 2,331 million dollars in 1970/1.[6]

The Six-Day War brought to a climax the anti-Western sentiments among Saudi and expatriate Arabs. Anti-American demonstrations took place in the Hijaz and in Riyadh. More serious incidents, with anti-regime overtones, erupted in the Eastern Province, culminating in large-scale demonstrations organised by the UPAP in Qatif, Damman, Al-Khobar and Ras-Tanura. In Dhahran mobs, led by students of Aramco's P&M and by leftist nationalists, attacked the company's installations, the American air base and the US consulate. Only the intervention of the National Guard prevented serious damage and bloodshed. Oil production was paralysed for a week by a strike of the Saudi workforce, despite the strict laws prohibiting strikes, and the Tapline was sabotaged in several places. Faysal prudently decided to stop the sale of oil to the West, a measure which had previously been demanded by radical Arab leaders and rejected. But, following the Khartoum summit in December, the direct sale of oil to the West was resumed.

ARAB NATIONALISM, AND OPPOSITION IN THE SAUDI KINGDOM

Radicalisation in the Arab world and the suppression of Saudi militants

By 1968, the Nasser regime was no longer considered radical in the Arab camp. Egypt's relations with Saudi Arabia greatly improved, although they remained cool until Nasser's death in 1970. The Ba'th governments in Damascus and Baghdad now led the radical camp and actively supported revolutionary pan-Arabism. Damascus became the focal point for the activities of the Saudi leftist dissidents, while Baghdad hosted Saudi Ba'thists and other dissidents (including some Shi'ites) and facilitated their broadcasts to Saudi Arabia and the publication of their journal *Sawt al-Tali'a*.[7] Apart from this, the radical Saudi opposition seemed relatively inactive.

The Iraqi Ba'th had a special axe to grind. It still laid claim to Kuwait, but more important, as Britain was preparing to evacuate its forces from the Persian Gulf, Baghdad became increasingly frustrated with the American–British plans that Iran, and to a lesser degree Saudi Arabia, should replace the UK as guardians of the region's stability. Baghdad therefore tried hard to undermine the British-sponsored arrangements and the pro-Western conservative regimes of the Gulf, which were led by Saudi Arabia.

Although Saudi Arabia's income from oil was constantly growing, 1968/9 proved to be a period of increasing economic difficulties. Saudi revenues in 1969 were about one billion dollars. But, in addition to the aid promised to the 'confrontation countries' and the Palestine Liberation Organisation (PLO), defence expenditures grew substantially. The kingdom's involvement in the affairs of North Yemen and its subversion of the Aden regime also proved costly. Finally, Faysal's modernisation plans demanded ever-increasing funds. The Saudi government was thus forced to seek loans from Aramco and from commercial banks.

The Central Planning Organisation, a most important tool for the kingdom's modernisation, was formed by Faysal in 1968. Another of his protégés, Hisham Nazir (petroleum minister since November 1986), a moderate American-educated technocrat from a prominent Hijazi family, was appointed its head.[8] With American help, Nazir hastily prepared in 1969 an eight billion dollar five-year development plan (1970/5).

Aware of the hardships facing the masses of newly urbanised Saudis Faysal, with the help of other technocrats, took steps to deal with the country's economic stagnation. Following a decade of growing unemployment and tension at Aramco in spite of the many benefits the company's workforce enjoyed, Faysal issued in 1969 new Labour and Workers Regulations which were far more beneficial to the workers than the previous laws. Loathed by the regime and their fellow citizens and still discriminated against, the Al-Hasa Shi'ites would not have shared at all in their country's growing prosperity, had it not been for Aramco's liberal employment policy and services. Paradoxically, it was this community that produced the most radical anti-American elements in the kingdom.[9]

The 1969 abortive coup attempts and their aftermath

By the late 1960s Faysal's handling of the kingdom's affairs had produced stability and substantially reduced the tension in the kingdom. Increasing oil wealth, and Faysal's development policies, helped speed a change in Saudi society. Urbanisation was greatly accelerated. The major towns in the Hijaz and the Eastern Province, and the capital, Riyadh, now held a greater proportion of the Saudi people, whereas the rural population, especially the bedouin, rapidly fell in number. By 1970 the kingdom boasted 7,000 students in its institutes of higher education and about half a million youngsters attending the modern schools – about 15 per cent of the kingdom's total population.[10] Saudi Arabia's prestige in the Arab and Muslim world was rising quickly. The Rabat (Morocco) Summit of the World Islamic League in September 1969 was attended by 25 Arab and non-Arab Muslim heads of state, with several radical ones among the participants; it adopted a decision to establish a permanent secretariat for the organisation in Jedda.[11]

The year 1969 was one of growing tension and upheaval in the whole of the Arab world. In addition to several abortive coups, the traditional regimes of Libya, Sudan and Somalia were overthrown by the military. After the decline of pan-Arabism, the Nasserists were in search of a new ideology and leadership. The nationalist camp gradually radicalised its position and differences between it and the Arab conservatives were polarised. In the Gulf, the British had begun to evacuate their forces. This increased tension in the region as well as the activities of Marxist and Ba'thist-oriented organisations. Thus many believed that even the archaic conservative Saudi regime could become the target of a *coup d'état*.

Reacting to Saudi Arabia's undeclared war against it, the Marxist NLF government of South Yemen (later People's Democratic Republic of Yemen – PDRY) retaliated by launching incursions into the Rub' al-Khali in the first half of 1969, while its Arab Nationalist allies in the kingdom and nearby countries escalated their clandestine operations against the Saudi regime. The Popular Front for the Liberation of Palestine (PFLP – established by George Habash), for instance, blew up the Saudi Tapline in the Golan Heights in May.[12] The Saudi security services arrested in early June many Aramco oil workers, especially Palestinians, suspected of membership in the 'Arab Nationalists'. Investigation uncovered a *Qawmiyyin* plot to overthrow the regime. This in turn led to the arrest of a large number of Saudis in the Eastern Province, in Riyadh and in the Hijaz. Among those arrested were army officers and government officials, suspected of membership in the NLF.[13]

Simultaneously (mainly in September) the security services rounded up several hundred officers, technocrats and other Saudis involved in another plot. About a hundred were air force personnel, more than a score were senior officers – a few were even generals. Among the civilians, largely Hijazis, were senior technocrats, including the head of the Institute of Public Administration and several of the directors of the Saudi Petroleum and Minerals Organisation (Petromin) and other members of the new elites.

A second wave of arrests took place at the end of the year and in 1970. It was estimated that the total number of those arrested was about 2,000, among them students who were recalled from the US and the Shi'ite dean of the P&M in Dhahran, whose two radical brothers-in-law had previously been detained for involvement in the 1966 bomb outrages.

A few hundred Shi'ites were also rounded up by the authorities at the end of 1970 on suspicion of membership in the Ba'th, but more likely in relation to the almost yearly politically or religiously motivated disturbances (*'ashura*) in the Eastern Province. These were partly, but clearly, an outcome of the Shi'ites' frustration resulting from humiliation by the authorities and the lagging development of Al-Hasa province.

As the Saudi government never disclosed the nature of the 1969–70 events, nor commented on the confused information published about them abroad, the story of the abortive coups remains unclear. It seems that the authorities dealt with four different and largely unrelated opposition groups in 1969 and 1970, and that several thousands were detained for interrogation, of whom about two thousand were jailed. It also appears that the 'plots' were blown out of proportion and led to disagreement between Faysal and the more liberal Fahd.

Among the first to be arrested, in April and May 1969, were Hadrami (PDRY) residents of the kingdom and Asir tribesmen suspected of sympathising with the Aden and San'a regimes. More serious was the wave of arrests on 5 and 6 June, when a large number of Saudis and non-

Saudis suspected of membership in different NLF offshoots were detained. It was alleged that, encouraged by the PDRY (South Yemen) and probably by the Ba'th regimes, they planned to overthrow the Saud government. Although the Eastern Province was the NLF's power base, its offshoots flourished among the Najdi and Hijazi new elites as well.

The regime at first believed that the largely military conspiracy constituted the more serious threat to its existence. About a quarter of the air force officers, including several generals commanding air force bases and academies in the Hijaz and in the Eastern Province, and others holding, or who had once held, key positions in the general staff and the army technical services, as well as many technocrats, were involved. It was alleged that the Committee for the Liberation of Saudi Arabia, as they called themselves, plotted to assassinate the king and the senior princes and to declare Saudi Arabia a republic.

Many of the culprits were of Hijazi origin. To add to the confusion, Yusuf Tawwil, a prosperous Hijazi merchant, and an acquaintance of Prince Fahd, was believed to be central to this plot. Yet, he and his family were known to sympathise with the idea of Hijazi separatism. Others involved in this plot were Najdis or Sunnis from the Eastern Province.

The high ranks of a large number of the officers involved in the conspiracy rather indicated that the organisers may have been members of the pan-Arab 'Free Officers' or 'Free Saudis' movements in the 1950s and early 1960s. Probably in their late forties, successful and well-to-do in 1969, it is unlikely that they would have been attracted by Marxist–Leninist ideologies. There were even indications that relations between members of this group and the Egyptian secret services went back to the early 1960s. By 1969, however, such connections were no longer relevant to the alleged amateurish coup plan.

By the end of 1970, when the naive nature of the 'Hijazi air force plot' was more fully comprehended, most of the two to three hundred officers and civilians involved in it were moved to officers' quarters in military barracks or were held in an old palace on Prince Fahd's orders. Some were pardoned by Faysal in 1972 and most of the others were freed immediately after his assassination in 1975. All were able to share, thereafter, in the booming Saudi economy. None the less, large-scale arrests of members of the radical opposition continued in 1971 and early in 1972.

The treatment of the members of the different parts of the radical NLF, especially those actually involved in the plot against the Sauds' regime, was far harsher than that of the 'air force conspirators'. However, even the hard-core leftists arrested in 1969–72 were pardoned by King Khalid and Crown Prince Fahd in the years following Faysal's assassination[14] and the Saudi state helped in their physical and financial rehabilitation. Indeed, by the mid-1970s the Saudi regime no longer felt threatened by the handful of home-bred radicals nor by its Marxist and Ba'thist neighbours. By then the oil boom had turned Saudi Arabia into a world economic power and a leader in the Arab camp.

Holden and Johns[15] term the 1969 abortive coups 'half baked', 'flamboyant' and lacking in determination and a clear plan. Yet, the dissidents, though coming from peripheral groups, had a strong power base in the armed forces. Moreover, successful revolutions in the Middle East were of similar character and their triumph was largely facilitated by the weakness of the traditional regimes which they overthrew and the alienation of their peoples. This was not the case in Saudi Arabia.

By 1969 the kingdom's security forces had been reorganised, expanded and trained by American experts and they enjoyed practically unlimited budgets. The tribal-based National Guard, on whose loyalty the Sauds could count since the 1930s, had been strengthened in the 1950s and 1960s. The Saudi regime, moreover, did not depend on one person or one small family but on a widely-based ruling oligarchy, and its head, King Faysal, was a capable and strong monarch.

As a result of the 1969–70 abortive coups, the relatively small active opposition to the Sauds' regime was reduced to insignificance. The widespread arrests, repressive measures and rumours about the fate of those imprisoned, demoralised the radical new elites and other dissident groups. Their activities within the kingdom were negligible and they no longer constituted a serious factor in the Saudi power equation. In the following years, as the kingdom became immensely rich and politically powerful, the Saudi opposition was further hindered by the seemingly endless funds at the disposal of the regime.

Dr Shaker, a Saudi intellectual clearly sympathetic towards the radical new elites, conducted in 1970 an informal survey of Saudi public opinion concerning the abortive coups.[16] Her conclusions (corresponding with the writer's belief) are that the great majority of the kingdom's population, the intelligentsia and Shi'ites excepted, utterly condemned the conspirators. Part of the new elites 'with vested interest in the regime', and the older generation of the well-to-do urban middle class, were also unreservedly critical of the dissidents and glad that members of their families were not involved with them.

Shaker's survey also shows that the great majority of the technocrats disapproved of the conspiracy because they were either worried about their personal achievements or apprehensive lest the abortive coups prove detrimental to the country's development 'because the conservatives in the ruling class will have the upper hand in the government'. Though many were dissatisfied with different aspects of the traditional regime, they praised the progress achieved by Faysal's government, and were of the opinion that an attempt to change the system by force would be counter-productive (true to this day). Only a very small minority of the educated (some educated abroad) young middle-class Saudis whom she met supported the abortive coups fully. A smaller percentage said that they were willing to participate in one, if it were the only way to bring about a meaningful change in Saudi Arabia.

Faysal's decision in 1958, but especially at the end of 1962, to allocate most of Saudi Arabia's increasing oil revenue to the kingdom's modernisation and to improve the population's standard of living, was fully vindicated by the events of 1969-70. So was his carrot-and-stick policy for dealing with the new elites. Nearly all ordinary citizens were supportive of the Sauds' government (*hukuma*) in 1970 and most of the new elites, enticed by prestige, power and wealth and Faysal's modernisation and development programmes, identified with the regime, if not joined its power base (true for the 1970s and 1980s as well). Others in the new elites were frightened into accepting co-operation with Faysal's government as the second-best option in Saudi Arabia.

The 1969 failed coups polarised the differences between the majority of the new elites, largely Hijazis, of urban middle-class origin and the radical minority. The latter consisted of Najdi elements inimical to the Sauds and a mixture of leftist–nationalist Sunnis and Shi'ites from Al-Hasa, to a lesser degree from Asir and a handful of Hijazis. The majority of the middle-class elites co-operated with the Sauds, although many were privately critical of their paternalistic archaic government, and their refusal to allow them to participate in decision-making. The radicals, mainly active abroad after 1970, with a growing Shi'ite membership, joined the small leftist opposition groups supported by the Ba'th regimes, the PDRY and communist parties universally. The débâcle of the PLO in Jordan during 'Black September' (1970), however, reduced the possibility of help for the beleaguered Saudi offshoots of the *Qawmiyyin* from their Palestinian associates.

A natural outcome of the events of 1969-70 was the stepping-up of the security measures in the kingdom. The ulama, a foreign visitor cynically observed, were co-operative with the authorities in matters of security: they sanctioned an edict in 1970 which required a photograph in the passports of Yemeni and other Arab women wishing to enter the kingdom.[17] Even more important was the decision of the Saudi rulers to replace expatriate Arabs working in the kingdom with non-Arab Muslim Asians or non-Muslims whenever possible. The preference was to use short-term Asian contract labour. These Asian workers were not allowed to settle in the country or bring their families with them.[18]

The period from 1970 to 1975 saw a dramatic rise in Saudi Arabia's economic power and leadership in the Arab world. It coincided with the first five-year development plan which Faysal had launched and which at first looked unrealistic because it involved eight billion dollars. This plan outgrew its original framework and budget, sparking off enormous changes in Saudi Arabia throughout the 1970s and accelerated the social revolution that the Saudi population was undergoing. Yet, inasmuch as the local opposition to the Sauds was practically paralysed, it was also a period of growing apprehension of foreign intervention.

The 1969 abortive coups aroused opposition to further modernisation, and particularly to the development of the armed forces, among the conservatives in the ruling class, led by Prince Abdallah, the National Guard commander. Such a policy, they argued, was bound eventually to enable 'Young Turks' in the armed forces to overthrow the Sauds. Purges slowed the development of the air force and army and the National Guard was given additional funds for expansion and modernisation. Yet, King Faysal, supported by Prince Sultan, the minister of defence, and Fahd, the minister of the interior (responsible for internal security), reached the conclusion that the 'air force conspiracy' was not serious enough to justify a total halt to the modernisation and expansion of the armed forces. That, just when the British were about to withdraw from the Gulf and Saudi Arabia was being threatened by radical forces in the region. The National Guard, moreover, vindicated at the time the claim that it remained an ineffective and anachronistic militia.

In November 1969 PDRY's regular units conquered the Saudi southern outpost of Wadi'a. Only an air strike by Saudi planes flown by Pakistani pilots forced the South Yemenis to retreat after army and National Guard units failed to dislodge them from the area. Threatened by the Ba'thist regimes in the north, Riyadh feared the unification plans of the two Yemens (a reality in 1990) initiated by the Marxist regime in Aden. Furthermore, by 1971 a Soviet flotilla appeared in the Arabian Sea shortly after the British evacuated their forces from the Gulf.

All the above and the Iranian high-handedness in the region culminating with the forceful conquest of islands near Hormuz and claims to Bahrayn, caused the Saudis to seek military aid in Europe and, when time was opportune, to turn again to the US for help (Peace-Hawk project, 1973). The kingdom's territorial size and manpower problem on the one hand and the availability of funds on the other, again made the air force the natural choice for priority. In the 1970s, thousands of educated youngsters, either of middle-class origin or Aramco-trained, were commissioned as officers and NCOs in the armed forces. Yet, they were counterbalanced by hundreds of aristocratic offspring who were encouraged to join the armed services, especially the air force, and thousands of foreign mercenaries, among them Pakistani, American, English and French pilots, technicians, instructors and advisers, who were hired by the Ministry of Defence.[19]

REGIME AND NEW ELITES - THE SHELVING OF POLITICAL REFORMS (1970-5)

Faysal, the technocrats and the central government

Having imprisoned most of the active opposition to the regime, King Faysal repeated his promise to establish a National Consultative Assembly at the beginning of 1970. Despite the opposition of the conservative members of the ruling class, Faysal, supported by a majority of his informal *majlis al-shura*, continued the kingdom's course towards rapid modernisation, and increased the role of its central government at the expense of the traditional institutions (including the provincial amirs). The monarch expanded the authority and responsibilities of the cabinet, regularly attended its meetings and encouraged discussion in it. He consulted his ministers daily before taking decisions, exploiting their expertise to devise a strategy for modernisation.

Despite the involvement of some senior technocrats in the abortive coups, Faysal continued to appoint Hijazi, and when available Najdi, graduates of foreign universities, to key positions in the government and its new agencies. Out of four new ministers appointed to his cabinet in July 1971, for instance, two were Hijazi graduates of Western universities – Hisham Nazir, the head of the Central Planning Board (now minister of petroleum) and Abd al-Aziz al-Qurayshi, the head of the Saudi Arabian Monetary Agency (SAMA). The other two (one Hijazi) were administrators from traditional backgrounds. In 1972 Muhammad Aba'l-Khayl was the first foreign-educated commoner Najdi to be appointed minister (without portfolio and finance minister in 1975) since Tariki. On the whole, graduates of the modern education system rapidly replaced the traditional bureaucrats in all ministries other than the religious-oriented ones.

However, Faysal continued the paternalistic Saudi style of government. As he increased the proportion of technocrats in his cabinet and strengthened the authority of the modern central government, he only grudgingly delegated authority to his commoner ministers. Even then, he supervised them closely and frequently intervened in the running of their ministries.[20] The repeated promise to establish a National Consultative Assembly was again ignored; and despite the growth of their numbers and their crucial role in governing and modernising the kingdom, the new elites were prevented from taking part in the decision-making process.

By the early 1970s Faysal no longer tolerated questions about a constitution. He even insisted on the use of the term 'social development' rather than 'social change' and in his meeting with Dr Shaker in 1970 he told her: 'revolutionary change is out of context with our traditional heritage and Islamic culture'.[21] The king, who was strongly opposed to the democratisation of the system, believed that the kingdom needed to modernise its patriarchal system which ensured the welfare of its population according to Islamic principles, rather than adopt the 'corrupt material Western democracy' or 'atheist communism'.

New elites and the modernisation of the bureaucracy

From the mid-1960s, increasing oil wealth facilitated the rapid modernisation of the kingdom and the consolidation of the Faysal regime. It provided endless opportunities of advancement for the educated Saudis who joined the government service and of prosperity for the ones who opted for the private sector. As demand for trained Saudis in the 1960s and 1970s became almost insatiable, Faysal abandoned any attempt to improve the quality of the educational system, and allocated vast funds for its expansion. By the mid-1970s a million Saudis, about 20 per cent of the kingdom's citizen population, were studying in the different levels of the educational system, about 25,000 students were registered in the kingdom's universities, and more than 5,000 were studying abroad. This, and rapid urbanisation, totally changed the character of Saudi society, while the millions of foreign workers introduced cultural influences incompatible with the character of the Saudi–Wahhabi kingdom.

The ranks of the new elites were now further expanded by many graduates of Saudi and foreign institutes of higher education. The majority (Hijazis) chose to join the administration and rapidly changed its character by replacing or superseding the traditional civil servants (Najdis). Government appointments to high positions unrelated to security or religious affairs were determined, more and more, by education and ability, rather than by social status. The new government ministries, departments, agencies and institutions created to facilitate the country's development were, in most cases, run by bureaucrats with doctorates and master's degrees from Western universities, many with little or no practical experience, and often trained in other fields altogether. The majority owed their appointment to academic achievements, the recommendation of 'first wave' senior technocrats, nepotism or Faysal's relations with leading Hijazi merchant families. Although by the mid-1970s it was becoming apparent that academic excellence did not by itself provide administrative capability, only in the late 1970s, as inefficiency in the government service became more apparent, did practical experience became a major criterion.[22]

As early as 1962, Faysal's government included several Western-trained Hijazi technocrats besides traditionally-trained commoners. Yet, the heyday of the Western-educated Hijazi new elites' 'aristocracy' was the decade from the late 1960s to the late 1970s when many Hijazi graduates of Western, particularly American, universities, were appointed to senior positions in the kingdom's administration. This was not only due to

Faysal's sympathy for the usually moderate and open-minded Hijazi middle-class intelligentsia (whom he befriended when Viceroy of the Hijaz), nor was it just an outcome of nepotism, but mostly because the more sophisticated Hijazis were quicker than the conservative and xenophobic Najdis to take advantage of modern education and were not inhibited from enrolling in Western universities. The Hijazi merchant community, and the middle class in general, could also afford to educate their offspring abroad, whenever necessary, without government subsidies.

Nepotism, moreover, is a common and acceptable norm in Saudi society. Once established in a government ministry or agency, the technocrat was expected to hire applicants for jobs who were his kinsmen or who belonged to his tribe and region. Even the lowliest position in any unit in the administration went to clients of the technocrat's family or that of other important officials in this administrative unit. Thus, the proportion of traditionally-educated Najdis in the civil service declined in the 1970s while that of modern-educated Hijazis and, to a far lesser degree, Najdis grew.[23]

Some Najdis of *hadr* origin were also appointed by Faysal to senior positions in the government. A few merchant and Najdi notables' families, who had assisted Ibn Saud when the kingdom was formed, were far-sighted enough to help their sons to obtain modern education in the 1950s and to enrol in foreign universities.[24] Many more Najdis graduated from the Saudi modern educational system in the early 1970s and joined or replaced their traditionally-educated Najdi kinsmen who had joined the civil service under Abd al-Aziz and Saud. Najdis increasingly enrolled in local religious and secular universities or went abroad for further studies. By the 1960s, especially in the 1970s, tension and competition began to emerge between the Hijazi and traditional Najdi civil servants and by the mid-1970s between the former and the Najdi new-elite bureaucrats and between both and graduates of the Islamic universities.[25]

In the years following Faysal's assassination it became increasingly clear that Najdis again enjoyed preferential treatment by the regime owing to the dislike and suspicion in which the Hijazis were held by many senior princes.[26] As the Saudi university system developed in the 1970s a clear distinction also emerged between the Western-educated senior technocrats, who, in most cases, joined the government service in the 1950s, 1960s and 1970s and the numerous new-elite bureaucrats, the product of the Saudi educational system or of foreign universities (BAs), who joined it in the late 1970s and 1980s. The first, if they had proved capable, caught Faysal's, and later Fahd's, attention, and were appointed as heads of new and existing ministries, departments or agencies. This new 'commoner aristocracy' enjoyed enormous power, prestige and wealth by the early 1970s. Although it did not participate in decision-making proper, it could greatly influence it through membership in the cabinet, control of ministries and budgets and the fact that the king and his Consultative Council sought its advice. As the government was expanded by the creation of specialised ministries, departments and agencies, the foreign-trained technocrats at their head had a better chance of influencing policy decisions relating to their particular field of expertise. For their part, the senior and middle-level technocrats have a vested interest in the continuity of the Sauds' regime and closely identify with it. An aristocratic PhD student[27] visiting Saudi Arabia about 1980 wrote the following:

> The [senior] technocrats seem to be content with the system; as one minister [Al-Gosaybi] observed, 'the Royal Family command of the structure is not weakened because they have responded to the need for technocrats. They got them into the government to keep the system going; the [senior] technocrats are grateful for the stability this system provides'.

However, in the final analysis, policy decisions were arrived at only in the royal *majlis al-shura* or by *ahl al-hal wa'l-'aqd*, to the exclusion of the senior technocrats.

The rise of the foreign-educated technocratic 'aristocracy' was resented by the traditional non-royal elites whom they largely replaced and led to competition if not hostility between the two. In addition to reform and modernisation which affected the 'Saudi way of life', their rise caused a noticeable erosion of the status and authority of the non-royal members of the ruling class. The decline of the ulama's power under Faysal has already been discussed above. Even more noticeable was the eroding authority of the tribal and regional amirs. Many of their responsibilities had been taken over by the central government, their subsidies were substantially slashed, and Faysal received them scarcely once a week in the 1970s, compared with his almost daily meetings with them at the beginning of his reign.[28]

In the 1970s and early 1980s the number of rank and file new-elite bureaucrats grew constantly. Opportunities for personal advancement, for achieving great wealth and for participation in the country's development enticed the majority to join the service of the regime. This did not mean that the 'new men' were not critical of the paternalistic and 'corrupt' character of the Sauds' government and its refusal to allow them, and the middle class as a whole, to participate in the power system. Faysal's constitutional reforms were totally ignored and the frequently promised National Consultative Assembly did not take shape.[29] But inasmuch as such criticism existed, it did not mean that the successful new elites were ready actively to challenge the ruling class as they had in the 1950s and 1960s. Only a minority sympathised with the clandestine radical organisations and a handful of those, some students in foreign universities and graduates returning from them, and members of the nascent Shi'ite intelligentsia, actually joined them.

Elsewhere in this book[30] it has been pointed out that the expansion of the educational system largely benefited the traditional urban middle class until the 1970s, primarily the Hijazis, and, since the 1970s, Najdis of *hadr* origin. The city-dwellers, more than the rural population and the newly urbanised, also enjoyed the fruit of rapid modernisation and development in other fields. By the mid-1970s the middle class of *hadr* origin largely monopolised the technocratic 'aristocracy', the new elites' bureaucracy and new middle class as a whole. The evidence indicates that the traditional tension between 'noble' Najdis and 'sophisticated' Hijazis still prevails, and the historic aversion of the rural population for the *hadr* and vice versa has now also been extended to the relationship between newly urbanised groups and the central government administration, controlled by the new middle-class elite of urban origin.[31] Social change in Saudi Arabia has thus far proceeded with limited national integration.

ARAB NATIONALISM AND SAUDI 'OIL POWER' (1970-5)

Wholesale arrests and harsh persecution virtually eliminated the whole spectrum of clandestine movements in the kingdom in 1969-70 and minimised their activities within Saudi Arabia to this day. Some radical members of the new elites who were still free in 1970 told Dr Shaker with bravado 'let them [the royal family] do as they please . . . repression will breed more hatred and frustration, which in turn will bring the existence of the monarchy to doom'.[32] Yet, the cruel suppression of the opposition brought stability and encouraged the majority of discontented intelligentsia to accept the Sauds' regime and the role which Faysal allocated to them. Faysal's biographer Vincent Sheean[33] claimed in the early 1970s that 'The question of an alternative to Faisal's rule is, indeed, seldom considered . . . except in the youngest and most advanced circles of students returned from foreign countries . . .' This is largely true of the Saudi new elites to this day.

Inconsequential and rarely active in the kingdom, in the 1970s, the militant opposition to the Sauds' regime consisted of three groups. The first, the old NLF, now Marxist, was 'officially' renamed in Baghdad in 1975 the Saudi Communist Party. The second was Nassir Sai'd's UPAP, still ideologically Nasserite and pan-Arabist, with some supporters in the armed forces, in the northern parts of Najd (Shammar) and in the Aramco workforce. The last was the Popular Democratic Party (PDP) created by the amalgamation of the remnants of the Saudi Ba'th (both Iraqi- and Syrian-oriented) and a leftist Nasserite faction of the NLF. The militant opposition remained inactive until the late 1970s. This was partly due to

65

the prosperity enjoyed by nearly all the Saudis and partly because of Faysal's iron-fist policy until 1975 and Fahd's carrot-and-stick policy thereafter.[34] But the most important reason was the relative cohesion within the royal family under Faysal and immediately after his succession.

By 1970 the oil market had undergone a dramatic change. The United States had become a net oil importer, and demand for oil in the industrial West was increasing at an average rate of about 10 per cent per annum and exceeded supply. Not only was OPEC now able to flex its muscles but the balance of power in it had been changed, with Ghadhafi's Libya joining the militant camp of the organisation. Thus, the price of oil in the early 1970s began to rise dramatically compared with the 1960s, as did Saudi Arabia's revenue from it (655 million dollars in 1959, 1,214 million in 1970, 4,340 million in 1973 and 22,574 million in 1974).[35]

Pressure had been building on Saudi Arabia since the 1950s both from its sister Arab countries and from different circles in the kingdom to use its oil as political leverage against the West and the United States in particular because of the Arab–Israeli conflict. Faysal resisted this until 1970 on political and economic grounds; but then, as the situation in the oil market changed, he decided that confrontation with the United States over this issue was unavoidable and that the kingdom was in a position to undertake it. In 1972, therefore, Zaki Yamani informed Washington that Saudi Arabia was no longer willing or able to separate oil supply from Arab political interests and that unless the US were to take a more balanced (i.e. pro-Arab) stance in relation to the Arab–Israeli conflict, the kingdom might be forced to use oil as a weapon against the West.

Although there are conflicting reports about Riyadh's role in the preparation for the Yom Kippur war of 1973 it is evident that the use of the 'oil weapon' during and after the October war, and the embargo on oil exports to the United States and Holland, earned Faysal, at least temporarily, the respect and affection of most Arabs. As the kingdom's revenues from oil grew dramatically, Saudi Arabia came to be the financier of the Arab and Muslim world, thus 'buying' her peace even with the more radical Arab countries (riyal politik). Egypt, now under President Sadat, became an ally and even Syria, following a coup that brought Hafiz al-Assad to power in 1971 after he had overcome the leftist elements in the Syrian Ba'th, improved its relations with the 'reactionary' Saudis. Only Baghdad, with its dogmatic Ba'thist regime and interests in the Gulf, and the PDRY because of its NLF Marxist ideology, continued after 1973 the militant campaign against the Saudi regime, and gave shelter and support to the small leftist Saudi groups. With the ruling class united around Faysal, the regime seemed to be stable and secure, notwithstanding the rapid change which Saudi society was undergoing.

After a period of tension with Washington, Faysal and Fahd felt confident enough in 1974 to improve their relations with the United States once again. These were considered essential to the security of the kingdom in view of the Soviet presence in Aden and the fact that the Gulf had become a focus of power politics. Following earlier arrangements, Prince Fahd visited Washington in June with a retinue of key cabinet ministers and high-ranking officers. The result was a far-reaching understanding on economic, technical and military co-operation. Riyadh expressed its readiness to help maintain a regular supply of oil to the market and to curb the rise in oil prices. For its part, America undertook to help in finding a solution to the Arab–Israeli conflict acceptable to the Arabs, and help the Saudis build up their defence capabilities through the construction of suitable military infrastructure (which the US used in 1990), the sale of sophisticated weaponry and the training of Saudi personnel. Close relations with the United States, co-operation concerning oil supply and pricing, and Saudi involvement in negotiations relating to the settlement of the Arab–Israeli conflict, became important strands in Fahd's government after the death of Faysal.

King Faysal was assassinated by a deranged nephew in March 1975. The succession arrangements established by him after 1964 facilitated a smooth transfer of power. With the blessing of the ulama, Khalid was pronounced king and Fahd crown prince and acting prime minister. Abdallah, commander of the National Guard and a conservative with strong ties with the tribal leaders, known for his dislike of the West and for his relations with anti-American Arab nationalist leaders, became second in the line of succession and second deputy prime minister.

CONCLUSIONS (1964-75)

Faysal had been confronted with Nasser's pan-Arabism which established a foothold in Yemen and initiated a rising tide of militant nationalism in the kingdom when he again became acting prime minister in 1962. Faysal believed the challenge to be so grave that at first he attempted to win the moderate new middle class by his 'ten-point programme', which included promises of constitutional reforms and participation in decision-making through a national *majlis al-shura*. At the same time, abandoning his traditional caution, he challenged Nasser's intervention in Yemen by supporting the loyalists, while suppressing with an iron hand the active opposition to his regime at home. While the militant nationalists were mercilessly persecuted, the moderate middle-class elite was practically 'bribed' by Faysal to participate in the government of the kingdom and its accelerated modernisation.

Faysal's reforms and the expansion of modern education in Saudi Arabia, made possible by increased revenue from oil, led to substantial growth in the new middle class and educated elite. Yet, although Faysal increasingly incorporated university graduates in his government and its agencies, enabling them to gain prestige and to share in the country's wealth, he conveniently forgot the constitutional reforms and participation in decision-making which he had promised them. The ideological foundations of his (and his heirs') paternalistic regime rested on the premise that the Qur'an was the constitution of a Muslim state and that institutions of Western democracies were incompatible with the principles of Islamic society (in which the people are represented by *ahl al-hal wa'l-'aqd* and the rulers are obliged to safeguard the citizens' interests).

Faysal prudently channelled the major part of the kingdom's increasing wealth to modernisation and development and to improving the standard of living of the various classes of Saudis through a network of subsidies, welfare services and opportunities for advancement. Thus, the danger of social upheaval resulting from accelerated modernisation and rapid urbanisation was largely avoided. Notwithstanding the increasing power of a central government dominated by the new, largely *hadr*, elites, the Sauds' paternalistic regime continued to enjoy the loyalty of the newly urbanised masses and rural population, whose allegiance to their traditional institutions began to erode.

Following the abortive coups of 1969 Faysal mercilessly crushed the vestiges of opposition to his regime. Indeed, after his demise, when the struggle for power within the royal family re-emerged, the great majority of the intelligentsia neither opted for militant nationalism, nor attempted to challenge Al Saud's authority, as they had in the 1950s and 1960s. Even their half-hearted efforts to gain a share in the decision-making process through the often promised National Consultative Assembly were easily frustrated by the ruling class. With the exception of insignificant radical–nationalist leftist and Shi'ite opposition organisations, largely based abroad, the disunited new elites on the whole preferred personal achievement, prestige and wealth to a confrontation with the regime and reconciled themselves to the existing situation.

5

POWER STRUGGLE, MODERNISATION AND REACTION (1975–80)

OIL WEALTH, MODERNISATION, POLITICAL PARTICIPATION AND ROYAL HOUSE RIVALRY

King Khalid, a conservative with little experience in administrative or political affairs, was in a very poor state of health when he came to power. From the outset, whether by design or necessity, he delegated much of his authority to Crown Prince Fahd, the acting prime minister, but the final power rested in the hands of the king. Like Faysal thirteen years earlier, Fahd used the Council of Ministers to fortify his own position in relation to Khalid. But the appointment of Prince Abdallah as next in line of succession and second deputy prime minister limited somewhat the ability of Fahd and the modernist camp to act unilaterally and ensured the family's consensus in all major matters.

For six months after Fahd's accession to authority Faysal's appointed government continued to function almost unchanged. The only significant exceptions were the following: the appointment of Faysal's son, Saud al-Faysal, a representative of the third-generation royal family, as foreign minister – Prince Na'if, Fahd's full brother, replaced him as minister of the interior, and another of the 'Sudayri Seven', Ahmad, was appointed his deputy.[1]

In order to win the general support of the new middle-class elites whom he consistently befriended, Fahd, with Khalid's blessing, announced (1975) the regime's intention to establish a National Consultative Council (*majlis al-shura*). This was to be composed of appointed 'young' tribal leaders, technocrats, professionals and businessmen of the new middle class, as well as the ulama. Yet, once the regime had consolidated its position and felt secure, the promise was again conveniently forgotten.[2]

As minister of the interior responsible for security under Faysal, Fahd was considered far more lenient than the king in dealing with the opposition. Now that he was practically in power, Fahd pardoned all those still imprisoned as a result of the 1969 abortive coups and ordered the authorities to help rehabilitate them. Censorship of the media was also relaxed and 'positive constructive criticism' of the administration, but not the Saudi regime, was permitted.[3] At the same time Na'if, the new minister of the interior, reorganised and expanded the Internal Security Services, the feared *Al-Mabahith al-'Amma* (lit. 'the General Investigations'; popularly known as *mabahith*).[4] Na'if also cultivated intelligence co-operation between Saudi Arabia and the nearby Gulf principalities, to counter subversive organisations supported by the PDRY and Iraq. As an extension of such activities Na'if initiated in 1976 negotiations that eventually led to the establishment (1981) of the Gulf Co-operation Council (GCC) which excluded Iraq and Iran.[5]

Fahd was always considered the leading modernist in Faysal's camp. His enthusiasm was restrained, however, by the king, who was determined to preserve the balance of power between modernists and conservatives. Once in power, relying heavily on the technocratic upper-crust, the crown prince began to accelerate Saudi Arabia's development. The kingdom's second five-year development plan (1975–80) estimated at 142 billion dollars (final cost over 180 billion) was, to a great extent, Fahd's responsibility. In addition to the enormous defence allocations (over 20 per cent of the total), the plan concentrated on building the kingdom's infrastructure, diversifying its economy and expanding its welfare and other services which benefited the citizenry. This necessitated a substantial increase in the workforce, at a time when Saudi manpower was already in short supply. It also necessitated that the central government administration and its specialised agencies be expanded. The employment demands of the late 1970s required, in addition to a large number of foreigners, many more educated Saudis in the government services and in managerial positions in the private sector.

In October, the cabinet was thoroughly reshuffled, showing more than ever the modernising trend of Crown Prince Fahd's regime. It now had twenty-six members, eight of whom were princes and the rest commoners, sixteen with university degrees. Yet to counter the Sudayris' power in the cabinet, two younger sons of Abd al-Aziz were appointed ministers and Faysal's younger son Turki was appointed shortly afterwards director of the General (external) Intelligence Services (*Al-Istikhbarat al-'Amma*).

Unlike Faysal, Fahd delegated real authority to his commoner ministers and encouraged them to take initiatives. Once a policy was decided upon by the royal *majlis al-shura*, it was the minister's responsibility to carry it out and thus, within their respective areas of responsibility, the non-aristocratic ministers enjoyed a measure of decision-making. According to an American observer who had spent the 1970s and early 1980s in the kingdom, 'When Khalid and Fahd promoted the ambitious plans of the 1970s, they set in motion forces which necessitated the diffusion of power and the delegation of increasing responsibilities to the Council of Ministers.'[6]

Another distinguishing feature of Fahd's cabinet of October 1975 was the assimilation to it of Western-educated Najdi technocrats (the first after Tariki left the cabinet) such as Sulayman Sulaym, minister of commerce, Ghazi al-Gosaybi, minister of industry and electricity, and later Muhammad Aba'l-Khayl as minister of finance. This marked the beginning of the erosion of the Hijazi predominance and the re-establishment of the Najdi hegemony in the Saudi government service and armed forces.[7] The preference for their Najdi *hadr* 'constituency' was mainly an outcome of a royal family consensus, supported by King Khalid, despite Fahd's ambivalency on this matter.

The above trend was also strongly resented by the Hijazi middle class because of its economic ramifications. In the first place it undermined the advantage that the Hijazi businessmen and entrepreneurs had in obtaining fat commissions from foreign companies or winning government contracts for themselves and their foreign partners. Furthermore, it also affected employment opportunities for Hijazi school leavers and university graduates, as the Najdi minister and senior technocrats looked after their own.

Faysal's appointment as prime minister in 1958 and his return to power in 1962–4 were facilitated to a great extent by a group of senior princes led by the 'Sudayri Seven' and Faysal's uncles. Among these princes, Fahd enthusiastically supported Faysal's reform plans even before he joined the Saudi government in 1954. A coalition, formed between the above group and other senior princes related to the Jiluwi branch of the royal family led to the enthronement of Faysal in 1964. The more loosely connected Jiluwi group was led by Prince (later king) Khalid and his elder brother, Muhammad, Abd al-Aziz's sons by a Jiluwi wife. Prince Abdallah, another member of the group, was related to the Jiluwis through his mother and had married a Jiluwi. Another important member was the Jiluwi governor of the Eastern Province. This conservative group offset the modernising zeal of the Sudayris. In contrast the Princeton graduate Prince Saud al-Faysal, and Faysal's two other sons by his Jiluwi wife, were modernists. Nevertheless, Saud al-Faysal and his brothers were considered by many to be likely allies of the Jiluwi faction in the royal family.

The strains between the Sudayri and the Jiluwi camps among the senior members of the royal family were exacerbated at the end of 1975, when the Sudayris pressed on with their demand that Prince Abdallah, now second in line of succession and second deputy prime minister, relinquish the command of the National Guard. Yet, the conservatives encouraged Abdallah to resist this demand because, at a time when the Saudi armed forces, under Sultan, were rapidly being upgraded and

Prince Na'if as minister of the interior controlled the strengthened security services, the National Guard was their only power base. The conservatives and other members of the aristocracy also protested against the kingdom's pro-American policy revived by Faysal with Fahd's help, and now vigorously pursued.

Paradoxically, an important faction of the new elites supported the conservatives rather than Fahd's modernist camp, as had been the case with Saud and Faysal in the late 1950s. Although Fahd was always considered their patron, some of the graduates of the foreign and the 'secular' domestic universities were dissatisfied with his lukewarm position on political reform. Others were critical of his unbridled, extravagant modernisation. Practically all of the expanding, domestically-trained, modernist and conservative intelligentsia criticised Fahd's pro-American and oil policies.

Fahd's pro-American policy, and 'archaic' Saudi regime, became the target of a propaganda campaign directed by Iraq, Libya and the PDRY on one side and their subversive affiliate organisations in the Gulf on the other. But in essence, anti-Western sentiments were widely shared as well by the conservatives and by most new elites in Saudi Arabia. The regime, moreover, faced increasing financial, as well as social, difficulties resulting from the rapid pace of change due to the second five-year development plan (1975–80) and the decline of oil revenues.

The kingdom's oil revenues declined in 1976/7 because of a decreasing demand for oil while supply increased. Income no longer sufficed to finance the enormous expenditure relating to developments and defence. American 'gold-plated' military projects concentrated on multi-billion defence-related construction and, to a lesser degree, on the acquisition of very costly sophisticated weapons. Building the country's communications infrastructure proved exceedingly costly, as did the enormous petrochemical complexes of Jubayl and Yanbu, meant to diversify the Saudi economy. All this necessitated the additional employment by 1977 of more than two million, mostly non-Arab, foreigners, including about 100,000 Westerners. They all constituted a heavy burden on Saudi finances. Riyadh, moreover, was also expanding the costly subsidies and network of welfare and other services which benefited the population.[8]

The first and second five-year development plans (1970–80) greatly accelerated changes in Saudi society that had been under way since the 1940s. The expenditure of tens of billions of dollars on development, which in the 1970s largely benefited the urban population, further expedited the movement of the rural population into the towns. Thus, by the end of the 1970s, the proportion of urban to rural population was completely reversed. Indeed, by 1980 the percentage of true bedouin, who had constituted the larger part of the population until the middle of the century, declined to less than 10 per cent. City-dwellers and inhabitants of small towns made up about two-thirds of the population.[9] Ironically, while Saudi Arabia was employing millions of foreign manual workers and technicians of different kinds, unemployment among newly urbanised Saudis, resulting from social mores and lack of skills, was a grave problem. At the same time, as the economy overheated, the cost of living and inflation in the kingdom were skyrocketing, and the government was unable to provide sufficient housing and social services for the ever-growing urban 'proletariat'. For a time, the frustration of the 'lower class' was intensified by the increasing polarisation between rich and poor and by tales of corruption and scandals relating to the Sauds. Such infringements on Wahhabi puritanism, moreover, incensed the fundamentalists and especially the less sophisticated Najdi.

Yet, by the late 1970s, the Saudi government, with practically unlimited funds at its disposal, succeeded in overcoming most of the economic and some of the social problems which it faced. The kingdom's citizens now enjoyed housing and a wide range of other subsidies, free education and extensive welfare services. Guaranteed employment and advancement in government service, coupled with financial support to businessmen and entrepreneurs, enabled most Saudis to share in their country's wealth and facilitated the rapid rise of 'lower-class' Saudis, mainly of rural origin, to membership in the flourishing middle class. The threat to the traditional sympathy for the Saud regime of the rural and part of the urban population was thus averted.

Widespread corruption in the Saudi government was nourished by the numerous multi-billion defence, infrastructure and other development contracts. The kingdom's spending spree and commission system at every level of economic activity enriched many Saudis, particularly senior members of the Saudi ruling class and their 'constituencies' as well as Saudis related to the technocratic upper-crust. That, and the fortunes which members of the royal family had amassed through parasitical involvement (fictitious partnerships) in the country's trade and other economic activities since Faysal's period, enraged the Saudi intelligentsia and the business community. Only a few commoner cabinet ministers and other senior technocrats refused commissions and bribes offered by foreign contractors and freely accepted by their associates and members of the royal family. The patronage and commission systems were in fact major means by which the regime channelled wealth to the ruling class and the new elites and through them to all levels of the middle class. Indeed, in 1977 Crown Prince Fahd enacted the 'Tender Law' by which, *inter alia,* no Saudi was allowed to represent more than ten foreign companies so as to enable many more technocrats, businessmen and princes to benefit from the sponsor and commission system.[10]

The ulama were also becoming increasingly frustrated with the impact of modernisation and the presence in the kingdom of many foreigners, especially Western experts, whose cultural influences threatened the Wahhabi–Saudi 'way of life'. Some even began openly to criticise the Saudi ruling class for betraying the principles of (Wahhabi) Islam.

Rivalry in the royal family again broke out into the open and endangered the Sauds' external common front in February 1977 when the ailing Khalid was rushed to London for urgent treatment. Rumours that the king's health was rapidly failing exacerbated the rivalry in the royal family and undermined the consensus essential for upholding the regime's stability. The Sudayris again demanded that Prince Abdallah, whose position was considered weak because he did not have any full brothers, surrender control of the National Guard. It was widely believed, moreover, that Fahd and his brothers wished to replace Abdallah as second deputy prime minister, and second in line of succession, with Sultan and thus consolidate the Sudayris' hold on the government.

The Sudayris' alleged attempt to monopolise all power in the royal family enraged many of the senior members of Al Saud but mostly the conservative ones. Frustrated as well by the erosion of the kingdom's traditional character through modernisation and Western influences, they rejected the new balance of power which the Sudayris wished to impose upon the ruling class and encouraged Abdallah to resist the Sudayris' demands. The conservatives, moreover, attributed the socio-economic difficulties faced by the kingdom to Fahd's government and alleged that its pro-Western oil and foreign policy served Western interests rather than those of Saudi Arabia and its Arab sisters.[11]

The conservatives attempted to form a coalition with elements of the new elites dissatisfied with Fahd and with the younger generation of princes, led by Faysal's university-educated sons. But despite blood affiliation, the younger princes chose not to identify with any faction of their elder kinsmen and avoided as well the pitfall of allying themselves with the nationalist new elite with whom they shared some common interests.[12]

The complacent bourgeois new elites of the late 1970s avoided a confrontation with the regime and did not seriously press the ruling class for constitutional reforms. By contrast with the 1950s and 1960s they operated, by and large, within the framework of the establishment and shunned the militant clandestine organisations. The officers of the modernised armed forces, who enjoyed high salaries and many privileges, were closely watched by the security services. More often than not, the ones appointed to key sensitive positions were the offspring of the aristocracy and of loyal bedouin amirs. The Saudi officer corps, it seemed, no longer bred frustrated 'Young Turks'.[13]

Responding to demands of the new middle class for political reform, Crown Prince Fahd in April 1977 expressed an understanding of the need for a National Consultative Council and for similar provincial institutions, stressing that the matter was under review.[14]

Clearly Fahd was trying to win the support of the middle class at a time of crisis. The 1977 'Tender Law', for instance, was also meant to further spread the kingdom's oil wealth among the new elites. Indeed, in the mid-1970s Fahd could be a benevolent ruler with regard to imprisoned opposition members and an ultra-modernist when it came to economic, technological and administrative development. Yet, when it came to political modernisation, although more liberal than Faysal, Fahd was unwilling to antagonise the ruling family by granting the intelligentsia participation in decision-making. Such a step, his peers believed, was bound eventually to undermine the foundation of the Sauds' regime.

At the end of April King Khalid returned to Saudi Arabia and began immediately an extensive tour of the various provinces. On their part, fearing that the stability of the regime would be threatened by the inter-factional rivalry, the Sudayris temporarily accepted the existing arrangements by which Abdallah was to succeed Fahd as king. Nevertheless, they continued their efforts to reduce the power of the National Guard.

In May 1977 Fahd flew to Washington to discuss two major issues with President Carter: the supply of oil to the West and its price, and American policy relating to the settlement of the Arab–Israeli conflict. Although Fahd prudently co-ordinated the Saudi stance with President Sadat and President Assad, the crown prince's American-oriented policy again caused discord within the ruling class and antagonised a sizeable part of the nationalist (anti-American) new elites.

Earlier, opposing OPEC's decision to raise the price of oil by 15 per cent (December 1976), the Saudi government increased its oil production and coerced the organisation into accepting its proposed 5 per cent rise in oil prices. The radical, mainly Palestinian-controlled, press in Beirut and the Gulf, accused the Saudi regime of being an instrument of Western imperialism and of US policy. Reports of unrest among Aramco workers were followed in May 1977 by two fires in the huge Abqaiq oil field, which caused serious damage.

A quixotic attempt at a coup against the regime involving thirteen Hijazi pilots of a squadron of the Saudi air force based in Tabuk and a number of civilians was also uncovered in mid-1977. Their 'plan' was to bombard and rocket government buildings and royal palaces in Jedda and Riyadh, and then proclaim the establishment of an Arabian Republic. Although the participants were, it seems, Ba'thists connected to Iraq, the plot was masterminded and financed by Libya. Ironically, the head of Libya's military intelligence involved in this affair was 'turned' by the Saudi security services (or the CIA) and Riyadh was aware of this naive plot from its inception. All those involved, with the exception of three pilots who escaped to Iraq, were arrested and, for a time, all air force planes were forbidden to carry munitions and were restricted to enough fuel for only thirty minutes' flying time. Coincidentally, the salaries of all civil servants were doubled, as were those of soldiers and NCOs. Officers of different ranks also received salary rises, land grants and other benefits.[15]

A serious setback to Crown Prince Fahd's policy was President Sadat's visit to Jerusalem in November 1977. The kingdom's policy in OPEC and its stance concerning the American peace efforts, in addition to antagonising the Arab militants, caused growing dissatisfaction among the Saudi new elites and the conservatives. The latter were also increasingly critical of the unbridled modernisation pursued by Fahd which, they claimed, undermined the kingdom's religious and cultural foundation. Thus, discontent with Fahd's government noticeably intensified. The crown prince prudently dissociated himself from Sadat's peace initiative and reduced the profile of Saudi relations with Washington. France and England, but especially the first, subsequently benefited from military contracts meant to diversify the kingdom's sources of weapons.

Tension in the ruling class continued in 1978. Discontent with Fahd's pro-Western policy and government in general among the conservatives and new elites also became increasingly evident. The latter now openly aired demands for political participation. Subsequently, Fahd promised to review proposals for a Consultative Assembly. Yet a text of a draft proposal for municipal elections later published in the Saudi press awakened little enthusiasm among educated Saudis.[16]

The limited amount of anti-regime activity of the small leftist clandestine organisations in Saudi Arabia in the 1970s took place mainly in the Eastern Province and to a lesser degree in Asir. In the former, the Shi'ite community increasingly protested at the discrimination practised against it by the government. The development and prosperity enjoyed by the kingdom's Sunni population, the Southern Region excepted, resulting from the sale of 'their' oil, frustrated the Shi'ites of Al-Hasa and enhanced the growth of local radical and separatist organisations.

In the last months of 1978 it was alleged that tribal elements inimical to the Sauds had staged an 'uprising' in the Eastern Province which coincided with labour problems in Dhahran. Tension was also reported in Asir, which suffered badly from poverty and neglect. Pamphlets of regional separatist movements such as the Organisation for the Liberation of Al-Hasa, Asir and the Hijaz were circulated, it was reported, in various parts of the kingdom. At the beginning of 1979 the radical Arab press even alleged that Saudi Arabia was 'on the verge of an explosion'.[17]

The renewed unrest in Saudi Arabia emanated partly from the socio-cultural ramifications of hasty modernisation and the growing tension within Al Saud related to the rise in the power of Arab radicals following the Camp David talks; but it was greatly enhanced by the collapse of the

Shah's regime in Iran in 1978, and the decline of American credibility in the region. The success of the Iranian revolution, although involving Shi'ite fundamentalism, fanned neo-Ikhwan sentiments among elements of the kingdom's Sunni population. It instilled, moreover, new pride among the Shi'ites and by 1979 the Organisation of the Islamic Revolution for the Liberation of the Arabian Peninsula (*Munazamat al-Thawra al-Islamiyya litahrir al-Jazira al-'Arabiyya*), popularly called *Al-Thawra al-Islamiyya* – the Islamic Revolution (henceforth IRO) – began to operate in the Eastern Province.[18]

The Saudi ruling class was seriously shaken by the collapse of the monarchy and the rise of the fundamentalist regime in Iran, prior to the Camp David agreement (March 1979). Fahd's pro-American policy was totally discredited and blamed for the grave situation which the kingdom faced. The crown prince prudently even left the country in the spring for a long 'vacation'. Feeling exposed to Arab radicalism during the short-lived *rapprochement* between Syria and Iraq (September 1978 to July 1979) on the one hand and the rising tide of Shi'ite militant fundamentalism on the other, the royal *majlis al-shura*, presided over by Prince Abdallah, known for his friendly relations with Syria and anti-Western sentiments, and Fahd's brother Sultan, hurriedly disengaged the kingdom from its special relations with the United States. In contrast to the moderate policy they had followed in the past, the Saudis, at the Baghdad summit in March 1979, supported the imposition of a boycott on Egypt, and strongly condemned the Camp David agreement and the US policy in the region. A humbled Zaki Yamani accepted a substantial raising of oil prices advocated by OPEC's 'hawks' and Saudi nationalists, causing the second 'oil crisis' in 1980 which later led, as he and Fahd expected, to the collapse of oil prices with grave consequences for Saudi Arabia.

The Saudi rulers, in disarray, aimlessly followed in the coming months the radicals in the Arab camp. With the conservatives attempting to undermine the Sudayris' position and the middle-class new elites more vigorously pressing for power and participation in policy-making, the situation in the kingdom in the spring of 1979 somewhat resembled that of the early 1960s. The more radical among the new elites hoped and even believed that the end of the Sauds' regime was rapidly approaching.[19]

By mid-1979, the crown prince was back in Saudi Arabia resuming his responsibilities. Although he temporarily dissociated himself from the United States and condemned its policy, specifically the Camp David agreement, his position remained precarious. Only the shock of the Mecca rebellion and the Shi'ite rioting in the Eastern Province at the end of 1979 and the beginning of 1980 re-established solidarity within the ruling class and, paradoxically, helped consolidate the regime's stability.

Saudi Arabia's influence and prestige in the Arab camp and the international arena continued to rise after the death of Faysal despite the struggle for power in the royal family. The kingdom with its enormous oil reserves and wealth was now considered by the international community a mini-superpower. While Saudi relations with Egypt and Syria had already improved under Faysal, Crown Prince Fahd, exploiting Iraq's resentment of the coerced 1975 (Algiers) border agreement with Iran, managed superficially to smooth the differences between Riyadh and Baghdad and to reduce temporarily the tension with the Marxist PDRY, partly the outcome of Riyadh's efforts to prevent the unification of the two Yemens.

Despite its power, partly gained at the expense of the traditional institutions, the intelligentsia-dominated central government did not enjoy the sympathy of the newly urbanised and rural population.[20] The latter, as well as all classes of Saudis, shared in the country's prosperity through Fahd's accelerated development and the expanding network of welfare services and subsidies. The ruling class, with its wide power base, estimated that the fragmented new elites, corrupted by prestige and wealth, despite their expanding ranks, did not constitute a sufficiently serious challenge to merit special consideration. Thus, meaningful constitutional reform was rejected as being un-Islamic and the promised national (Islamic) *majlis al-shura*, resurfacing with every crisis, was again ignored.

In so far as the backbone of the leftist opposition was broken in the late 1960s and early 1970s, the mainstream of the Saudi intelligentsia, enjoying prestige and economic prosperity, continued loyally to serve the ruling class. The tame, successful and deeply divided bourgeois new elites of the 1970s half-heartedly attempted in 1977–9 to exploit the rift in the royal family to advance political change in the kingdom and radicalise its oil and foreign policy. Yet, it carefully avoided a confrontation with the regime over demands for meaningful constitutional reforms. The relatively conservative majority of the new elites was either satisfied with the existing situation, or naively hoped that aware of their expanding ranks and role in the kingdom's government and economy, the ruling class would eventually agree to including them in some way in decision-making. In the meantime, the technocratic 'aristocracy' endeavoured to expand the measure of decision-making which it enjoyed in the central government and within the ministries by using its members' control of budgets and role in the cabinet. Their efforts, however, were usually blocked by the antagonism of the ulama and of the royal family. They were eventually more successful in pressing for a rise in oil prices following a reduction in the kingdom's production.

Even though the rival camps in the aristocracy occasionally courted the new middle class, its support was considered secondary to that of the ulama, the source of the Saud's legitimacy. The eruption of the conflict in the royal family and the rising wave of fundamentalism in Iran and in the Muslim world as a whole rather prompted Fahd to improve the Sudayris' image as guardians of the kingdom's Wahhabi character and to reverse Faysal's relatively liberal policy. Thereafter, the regime again increased the authority of the ulama and their Morality Police, who supervised the piety of the citizens and curtailed the 'privileges' of Westerners residing in the kingdom.[21]

THE MECCA REBELLION AND THE SHI'ITE RIOTS (1979)

Saudi Arabia's rapid modernisation since the late 1960s, and the socio-cultural changes which it induced, rekindled the fundamentalist senti-ments which had been dormant after the suppression of the 1927–30 Ikhwan rebellion. The ulama, who strongly objected to innovations introduced by Ibn Saud and his heirs, reconciled themselves, in most cases, to the rulers' decisions. During Faysal's reign, the ulama increas-ingly became part of the state establishment. Indeed, although some ulama bitterly criticised other Muslim rulers for introducing modernisa-tion and foreign influences which were contrary to the principles of Islam, they were careful not to point an accusing finger at the Sauds' regime.

Even before the 1979 uprising, the Sauds and most new elites, not to mention the ulama, became growingly concerned about the impact on their society of rapid modernisation, accompanied by Westernisation. Traditional anti-Western sentiments were enhanced in this period by the sense of power (oil) and the presence in Saudi Arabia of many foreigners. Hence, in the late 1970s, members of the ruling class and even some Western-trained officials began to pay lip-service to the need to protect the 'Saudi way of life' from the corrupt Western culture with its materialistic values and permissiveness, in order to advance national solidarity.

To a simple but proud people whose oil has recently purchased their rapid modernisation and made them into a world (economic) power, the 'Saudi way of life' has come to represent their uniqueness and has become their national ethos. The 'Saudi way of life' is, in fact, a synthesis of customs of the pre-oil, impoverished Arabian society, symbols of the tribal–nomadic people (the camel, the tent, the dress) and aspects of Wahhabi asceticism and beliefs, many of these features being alien to the traditional urban elements, especially to the Hijazis who dominate the Saudi bureaucracy.[22]

The accelerated development and change, which Saudi society was experiencing under Fahd, exacerbated the discontent of the Najdi-led fundamentalists. The conservative ulama frequently felt threatened as well by the Western-educated technocrats and bureaucrats, who were often critical, however discreetly, of the ulama. The students and faculty of Riyadh's Islamic University including Abd al-Aziz bin Baz (rector of Al-Madina Islamic University and the president of the Administration of Scientific Study, [Religious] Legal Opinions, Islamic Propagation and Guidance) claimed in 1978 that programmes screened by the state television were anti-Islamic and subversive of Wahhabi society. In the same year the furious ulama criticised the television for presenting the opinions of 'modernists' on the status of Saudi women, another sore point with the ulama, and described them as anti-Islamic. After Ghazi al-Gosaybi, the minister of industry and electricity, considered the doyen of the Saudi intelligentsia, was quoted as having said in an interview that the kingdom's modernisation had 'bridged over three thousand years of sub-human existence', Bin Baz, whose ultra-conservatism often embarrassed the rulers, condemned Al-Gosaybi in an article published in a Kuwaiti periodical for insulting Islam.[23]

The accelerated urbanisation which began during Faysal's reign brought to the towns many illiterate or semi-literate, yet deeply religious bedouin, including offspring of Ikhwan who participated in the 1927–29 rebellion. Some newly urbanised young Saudis attended the Al-Madina University with its largely foreign student body, very low admission requirements and Islamic character and curriculum. This university, run by foreign fundamentalists and some ultra-conservative Wahhabi ulama who often condemned the evils of modernisation and the Western culture, became the focus of Saudi 'neo-fundamentalism'. A Najdi *'alim* discussing the Mecca incident in 1980 said the following: 'An atmosphere favourable to Islamic heresy sprang up at Medina because of the presence of large numbers of foreign students . . .'[24]

As the frustration of the conservatives rapidly grew after the mid-1970s, the wave of 'neo-fundamentalism' began to spread from Al-Madina to the Imam Muhammad ibn Saud Islamic University (Riyadh) and to the theology faculty in Mecca and the one at Riyadh's 'secular' KSU. Many of the *'alims* and the students (a sizeable percentage of whom were foreigners) of the above were openly critical of many of the innovations and Western influences introduced by the government.[25] Yet, the most outspoken critics of the regime, it seems, were offspring of the Ikhwan and dropouts from the modern education system, mainly of bedouin origin, overwhelmed by the revolutionary changes which their society was undergoing. Disillusioned with the establishment fundamentalists whom they considered hypocrites corrupted by the regime, some turned to a synthesis of militant 'neo-Ikhwan' and Muslim millenarianism.

A son of an Ikhwan warrior who fought Ibn Saud, Juhayman ibn Sayf al-'Utaybi, an ex-National Guard NCO, attended lectures by the Najdi ultra-conservative *'alim* Abd al-Aziz bin Baz at Al-Madina University. In

1974 the disillusioned Juhayman left al-Madina for his native Qasim (Najd) followed by a handful of bedouin and foreign students. In the coming years he preached his version of 'neo-Ikhwan' ideology in the towns and oases of the Najd where his kinsmen, many of them Ikhwan descendants, had settled. During this period additional university dropouts joined his group and he managed to link up with militant neo-fundamentalist organisations in nearby Arab and Muslim countries.

By 1978 Juhayman and his followers moved to Riyadh, where they began to preach in several mosques against the evils of modernisation, insinuating that the regime was responsible for the corruption of Islam by foreign influences. The Saudi secret services always kept an eye on the activities of extremist religious fanatics. Thus, in the summer of 1978 Juhayman and about 100 of his followers were arrested and interrogated by the *mabahith*; but they were released from jail after Bin Baz and other ultra-conservative ulama interceded on their behalf, declaring them harmless crackpots.

With the help of local *salafis*, Juhayman printed in Kuwait four pamphlets in which he emulated the Ikhwan's philosophy, attire and criticism of the 'corruption of Islam' by the rulers through modernisation. 'For Juhaiman . . . ulema and state had combined in a truly unholy alliance.' In a pamphlet that appeared in 1978 Juhayman wrote that the 'Nejd ulema had been bought . . . Where is it that the ulema and sheikhs find their money, except through corruption?'; 'how the religious authorities could be so prosperous without active financial support from the Royal Family?'.[26]

About this time Juhayman convinced Muhammad ibn Abdallah al-Qahtani, a bedouin theology student in Riyadh, that he was the expected Mahdi. Indeed, in the pamphlets which he published and distributed at the end of 1978 and in 1979, Juhayman refers to the coming of a Mahdi from the tribe of Quraysh who would redeem the Muslim world. Here he is indirectly accusing the Sauds of being usurpers not of Quraysh origin.

On the night of 19 November, at the end of the Muslim fourteenth century, Juhayman and about 400–500 of his followers, including womenfolk and children, entered the grounds of the Mecca mosque with quantities of weapons and food. On the following morning, they seized the Ka'ba *haram*, denounced the corrupt government of the Sauds and especially the ulama who supported them, and declared Muhammad ibn Abdallah al-Qahtani the expected Mahdi.

It took the regime two weeks to crush the rebellion and regain control of the Ka'ba. The rulers awaited at first a *fatwa* of the ulama permitting the seizure of the Mecca mosque by force; but the Sauds were also indecisive and apprehensive of the reaction of the population and of tribal elements in the armed forces to the events. On their part, the rebels bravely fought off the superior forces which surrounded them, expecting that all the believers who rejected the corruption of Islam by the Sauds would rally to the flag of the 'expected Mahdi'.

When granted, after debates lasting several days, the *fatwa* proclaimed by the ulama did not denounce the rebels for heresy but rather for using weapons in the holy Ka'ba and rising against a legitimate regime. Among the 30 ulama who signed the *fatwa* were, ironically, leading Najdi ultra-fundamentalists known for their opposition to modernisation including Abd al-Aziz bin Baz.

In the meantime the shocked population of the kingdom was largely angry at the rebels for defiling the holiest shrine of Islam. It became clear that by choosing the Ka'ba as the site of their uprising the Ikhwan rebellion had misfired.[27]

Despite the enormous forces brought by the regime to Mecca, it took a great effort to overcome the rebels. Only on 3 December did the exhausted remnants of the Ikhwan, including Juhayman, surrender to the authorities. Their execution in the different towns of the kingdom several months later was generally considered appropriate and did not seem to arouse any sympathy.

While the legitimacy of the Saudi regime was being challenged in Mecca the authority of Al Saud was threatened from another quarter by the unrelated eruption on 28 November of serious violence in the Eastern Province. The Shi'ites in Al-Hasa had increasingly been protesting since the 1950s against their oppression and discrimination by the regime. The success of the Iranian revolution gave them new pride and encouraged them to press their demands for equality. In addition, Tehran repeatedly called upon them to rise against their corrupt rulers. The above, and the Shi'ites' proportion among Aramco's workers, and Al-Hasa's population, made the unrest in Al-Sharqiyya seem extremely dangerous for the regime.

In the early 1980s it was estimated that the Shi'ites in Saudi Arabia numbered about 500,000, or 10 per cent of the population. Nearly all Saudi Shi'ites (Twelvers) live in the Eastern Province, and are concentrated in the oases of Al-Hasa and Qatif.[28] This community is closely related to its co-religionists in Bahrayn and Kuwait and relations between it and most of its Sunni neighbours are relatively good.

After the rise of the Wahhabiyya in the eighteenth century the Al-Hasa Shi'ites, considered by the *muwahhidun* worse than infidels, were constantly persecuted. When Ibn Saud reconquered the region from the Turks in 1913 its Shi'ites unsuccessfully sought the protection of the British in Bahrayn. They renewed this attempt in 1927 when, under the pressure of the Ikhwan, the Wahhabi ulama instructed Ibn Saud to increase their oppression. Even though the treatment of the Shi'ites improved after the collapse of the Ikhwan rebellion, they were despised by the Sunnis, and were considered at the bottom of the Saudi social

stratification. They were officially discriminated against by the authorities in many matters including employment, and prohibited from
having their own mosques and judicial system. Above all they were
prevented from holding public religious ceremonies, especially the
annual 'ashura processions commemorating the assassination of
Hussayn ibn'Ali.

The development of the Saudi oil industry has had a most beneficial
impact on the oppressed, largely agricultural, Shi'ite community of the
Eastern Province. Many Shi'ites from the rural areas of the large Al-Hasa
oasis, seeking employment and a better life, moved to the peripheries of
the coastal 'oil towns': Dammam, Al-Khobar, Ras Tanura and Dhahran.
Originally small, poverty-striken, villages, such towns prospered and
rapidly grew in size.

Aramco's 'colour blind' employment policy was not an outcome of
moral principles but of necessity. The Shi'ites constitute about 40 per
cent (possibly one-half) of Al-Sharqiyya's population and their work
ethics are quite different from those of most Sunni Saudis who, because of
social mores, consider manual labour demeaning. For the Shi'ites,
employment in Aramco, in most cases, was the only way to earn a decent
living and to advance in life. Thus, by 1978, Shi'ites were estimated to
make up more than half of Aramco's workforce and while institutes of
vocational training elsewhere in the kingdom failed to attract students,
the ones in the Eastern Province had more candidates than they could
handle. In the 1950s, moreover, Aramco encouraged its more enterprising
employees to provide the company with supplies and services on a
contractual basis. Thus, it was instrumental in the rise of a relatively
sophisticated Shi'ite middle class and intelligentsia alongside a socially
conscious working class.

Aramco not only provided employment but also education, which was
partly the reason for Al-Hasa's having the lowest illiteracy rate in the
kingdom. Many young Shi'ites trained by the company or in schools
established by it found their way to domestic and foreign technical
institutions and universities. Indeed, by 1980 half of the students of Saudi
Arabia's most prestigious university, the UPM, and the majority of those
of King Faysal University were Shi'ites. A high percentage of the students
sent to study abroad by Aramco, and some by the Saudi government, were
also Shi'ites, not to mention the ones who were supported by their
middle-class families.[29]

Notwithstanding the above, the Shi'ites remained a minority, discriminated against, if not persecuted. The Najdi establishment continued to
distrust and abhor the Shi'ites and considered them, despite their
achievements, backward if not mentally retarded. The testimony of
Shi'ites, whose doctrines are viewed as heretical, was not admissible in
Saudi courts of law, and units of the bedouin National Guard were

stationed in the province's main towns. A foreign correspondent observed in 1980 that 'Cultural discrimination is perhaps the most bitter for them. Shi'ite literature is banned and Shi'ite history is not allowed to be taught in the local schools and university.' The teaching profession was closed to Shi'ites, who are virtually excluded from all but the lowest ranks of the civil service and inhibited from serving in the army and the security forces. A young Shi'ite told the above reporter: 'There are Sunnis, below them are Christians and below them are Jews; we are below the Jews.'[30]

Not surprisingly, the educated Shi'ites and 'working class' have become involved with trade unionism and radical nationalist clandestine movements since the 1950s. The emergence of a new Shi'ite middle class and intelligentsia provided the community with the means to protest against their treatment and discrimination. Thus, as early as 1960, a Shi'ite delegation petitioned King Saud about a defamatory article published by a semi-official periodical and demanded an end to discrimination against them. Tension among the Shi'ites grew in the 1960s simultaneously with the rise of pan-Arabism in Saudi Arabia. Shi'ite workers and intellectuals joined offshoots of the *Qawmiyyin al-'Arab*, the UPAP and the Ba'th and were involved in different anti-government activities.[31]

Although the older generation and part of the new Shi'ite middle class were reconciled to the gradual improvement in their position, the younger and better-educated Shi'ites became progressively more militant, anti-Najdi and anti-American. Their frustration was enhanced by the fact that revenue from 'their oil' financed the accelerated development of Saudi Arabia, yet only marginally benefited their province.

When Khalid–Fahd came to power in 1975 and 'liberalised' Faysal's policy, the Shi'ites benefited, to some extent, as well. More funds were allocated for the building of communications and industrial infrastructure in Al-Sharqiyya and to expand the province's education system, including the new King Faysal University in Hufuf and Dammam. A few Shi'ites were advanced in the administration and one was appointed in 1976 the head of the Jubayl industrial complex. Many Shi'ites benefited indirectly as well from Aramco's and the government's development projects, and joined the Saudi middle class, but not its upper levels, which were composed solely of successful Sunni businessmen, industrialists and contractors. Yet in the eyes of the Najdi establishment, the Shi'ites remained a despised and abhorred minority. Despite the measure of liberalisation in regard to Shi'ite religious practices, their *'ashura* processions were still strictly prohibited, nor were they allowed to have their own religious courts. Shi'ite graduates of the education system and universities met with difficulties in finding suitable positions in the government and were rejected by the armed and security forces.

The growing unrest in the Saudi kingdom and the revolution in Iran were bound to have an impact on Al-Hasa's and the Gulf Emirates' Shi'ite communities. The 1978 violence in Al-Sharqiyya was followed at the beginning of 1979 by labour unrest in the oil fields and the oil towns. Aramco had indeed been expecting trouble in the region following the victory of the Islamic revolution in Iran and the propaganda broadcasts from Tehran aimed at the Shi'ite population in Arabia. Bahrayn, with its Shi'ite majority, a short distance from the Saudi oil towns, experienced in September 1979 very serious riots which led to massive repression of Shi'ite and other radical elements. By November the *mujtahids* of Qatif and the nearby Shi'ite villages announced their determination to hold the *'ashura* processions in defiance of the government's prohibition.[32] Several days before the event news of the rebellion in Mecca galvanised the Al-Hasa Shi'ites. When the police attempted to disperse the large crowds who participated in the *'ashura* procession in Qatif on 28 November, the Shi'ites went on a rampage. The trouble spread to Sayhat and other Shi'ite settlements in the region and oil installations near Ras Tanura and Dhahran were sabotaged.

The rioting lasted for three days. Demonstrators carried pictures of Ayatollah Khomayni and placards denouncing the House of Saud and the American imperialists. They chanted anti-American slogans, and demanded that Saudi Arabia stop supplying the United States with oil and that it support the Iranian Islamic revolution. Others demanded the establishment of an Islamic republic in Al-Hasa. The reinforced units of the National Guard, who had no love for the Shi'ites, opened fire on the demonstrators on several occasions. A total of seventeen people were killed, many were wounded and hundreds arrested.

Apprehensive of the impact of the ferment among the Shi'ites and the Iranian revolution on the security of its oil industry, the Saudi government immediately despatched Prince Ahmad, the deputy minister of the interior (a Sudayri) to the province. Ahmad prudently admitted that the regime had neglected the Eastern Province and discriminated against its Shi'ites, and announced the beginning of a new era. He promised massive investments in Al-Hasa's development and economic infrastructure, education system and other services. Yet, simultaneously, he warned the Shi'ites that if they were to undermine law and order they would be severely punished.

In spite of the above, tension among the younger Shi'ites continued to rise. A declaration by Prince Na'if, the minister of the interior, that the Shi'ite rioting was inconsequential added fuel to the fire, as did the anti-Saudi propaganda from Tehran. More politicised and resentful of the Najdi establishment, the young Shi'ites were more receptive to the Iranian incitement. Indeed, the IRO claimed (in 1981) that it had deliberately prepared the continuation of the *'ashura* demonstrations in order to bring about the release from prison of all those arrested following the November riots. Violent demonstrations again erupted in Qatif and Al-Hasa following the Friday prayers on the first of February, the anniversary of the return of Ayatollah Khomayni to Iran. Anti-Saudi and anti-American slogans were chanted and students from the UPM university set buses and private cars on fire, but Saudi banks were the main target of the demonstrators this time. Four people were killed, and many arrested, during this spate of rioting which also lasted several days.[33]

The Shi'ite rioting caused the regime to realise that it could not continue blatantly to discriminate against the Shi'ites. Previously prepared, but shelved, plans for the development of Al-Sharqiyya were now quickly implemented. A modern vocational training centre opened in Dammam. It was designed to produce technicians for the huge Jubayl industrial complex which offered attractive job opportunities for the local population. New commercial centres were built and Shi'ite businessmen were helped to expand their enterprises. Some traditional administrators in Al-Hasa were replaced by university-trained technocrats and additional faculties were opened in the KFU.[34]

In spite of these measures and the change in the authorities' attitude, discrimination against the Shi'ite population was not eradicated. Rather the appointment of two Shi'ite officials to high, yet secondary, positions in the administration, and the relatively modest success of several Shi'ite businessmen (in many cases related to Aramco) underscored the fact that on the whole Shi'ites were still excluded from the medium and upper levels of the Saudi administration and economy and totally from the security and armed forces. At the UPM Shi'ites composed about half the student body, yet they could not be elected as officers of the students' union. Shi'ite requests that they be allowed to settle personal judicial matters such as inheritance according to their customs were rejected out of hand. Even though the authorities legalised low-profile 'ashura processions, the Shi'ite leaders were warned against exaggerated expressions of grief, typical of such processions, which anger Wahhabi puritanists.[35]

In September 1980, following the eruption of the Iran–Iraq war, the Saudi government substantially bolstered its armed forces in the Eastern Province. Security in the oil installations, relatively lax in the past, was markedly tightened. A new Ministry of the Interior security force was established solely to protect essential installations, largely in the oil province. The Shi'ite community in Al-Hasa, constantly incited by the revolutionary regime in Iran, and especially discontented elements among the intelligentsia, fundamentalists and workers, were closely watched, if not harassed, by the authorities. Moreover, although the GCC was formally launched in 1981, security co-operation between Saudi Arabia and its Gulf allies was promoted by Prince Na'if (even earlier).

Simultaneously, the development of the Eastern Province supervised by Prince Ahmad was accelerated. Between 1980 and 1982, roads were paved, schools built, sewage systems constructed and a hospital opened. When King Khalid visited the province in November 1980 he announced that 1 billion dollars were being allocated for 'public service projects' in Al-Hasa. All those incarcerated during the November 1979 and February 1980 riots were pardoned and a general amnesty enabled political refugees to return to their homes. The legalised *'ashura* processions which took place shortly afterwards went off without incident, with the security forces keeping out of sight.[36]

The regime's carrot-and-stick policy in Al-Hasa proved quite successful. The efforts to develop the region and grant its Shi'ite population the nearest thing to equality in a Wahhabi state were appreciated by most of the community. This, in addition to the quantitative and qualitative upgrading of the security forces, prevented an outbreak of serious anti-government activity in Al-Sharqiyya in the following years, despite Iran's vicious anti-Saudi propaganda and support of subversion in the Gulf, and the impact of the Iran–Iraq war.

Yet, the unrest among the young Shi'ites and other radical elements in the Eastern Province persisted under the surface. Anti-regime, separatist, radical socialist or fundamentalist sentiments were now fanned by Iranian militant propaganda. An Iranian plot to destabilise the regimes of Bahrayn and Saudi Arabia was uncovered at the end of 1981. Among the many who were arrested in Bahrayn were Saudi Shi'ites who had undergone training in Iran.

The IRO, which began to operate in 1979, joined in the 1980s existing small groups of Shi'ite workers and intelligentsia-supported Marxist, Ba'thist and pro-Iranian organisations in their limited anti-regime activities at home and abroad. In the ensuing years it was responsible for subversive activities in Al-Hasa's towns and villages. Although suppressed by the Saudi security services with an iron fist, it remained active and had followers among the students and other Shi'ite elements.[37]

The limited activity of the Saudi militant opposition in the early 1980s focused largely on Al-Hasa. There, in addition to the IRO, Shi'ites are an important component of the relatively inconsequential Saudi leftist clandestine movements. Undoubtedly, the rapidly growing Shi'ite intelligentsia and working class (the nearest thing to a proletariat in Saudi Arabia) would be among the first to join an anti-Saud nationalist–radical revolution if it were to erupt. Yet, a Shi'ite uprising in Al-Hasa is, ironically, likely to consolidate Sunni support for the regime because of the latter's nearly universal dislike of Shi'ites, fear of fundamentalist Iran and concern about Al-Sharqiyya's oil revenue. The frustrated and dissatisfied Shi'ite minority represents, nevertheless, a threat, even if not a major one, to the regime because it constitutes such a high proportion of

Al-Hasa's population and of Aramco's workforce. The Iran–Iraq war and Tehran's subversive propaganda (until 1989) underscored this danger. Thus, besides stepping up security measures since 1980, Riyadh has accelerated Al-Sharqiyya's development and strengthened and improved its administration. Progressively, the regime was able to pacify, if not win the good will of, the majority of the Shi'ites.

In retrospect the failure of the Mecca rebellion and the little support that the 'Ikhwan' won rather demonstrated that, in contradiction to other Arab and Muslim countries, 'neo-fundamentalism' in Saudi Arabia, in this period, appealed only to peripheral elements. Most Saudis, especially the religious and conservative 'lower classes', are quite happy with the synthesis of 'puritanism', modernism and material prosperity, provided by Al Saud and legitimised by the ongoing alliance between the latter and the ulama. Tribal loyalties, which began to erode at the time of the Ikhwan rebellion, moreover, proved of little consequence fifty years later during the Mecca incident. Indeed, despite rumours to the contrary, nearly all the bedouin and the newly urbanised masses and the National Guard remained absolutely loyal to the Sauds. Such support was conditional on the continued prosperity of the population and their satisfaction with the regime's performance. Yet in spite of the economic recession which the kingdom experienced in the 1980s, the population, on the whole, continued to support the Sauds.[38]

The damage caused by the Mecca affair to the prestige of the Saudi regime was considerable. The Sauds, who took to themselves the role of 'protectors of the holy places' when they conquered the Hijaz, were widely criticised for their inability to prevent the Mecca rebellion and their mishandling of its suppression. Juhayman's condemnation of the royal family's corruption, the scandalous behaviour of many of its members and their association with infidels did not go unheeded either. Prince Fawwaz, the governor of Mecca, accused by Juhayman of indulging in alcoholic beverages, was removed from office, some senior officers in charge of the kingdom's internal security were retired, and restrictions concerning the possession of spirits and the behaviour of foreign residents were more strictly enforced. Aware of the grass-roots apprehension concerning the kingdom's rapid development, King Khalid and Crown Prince Fahd expanded, moreover, the ulama's authority in relation to the supervision of the kingdom's Wahhabi character, demonstrating whenever possible their own piety and devoutedness. As long as the ulama did not interfere with the kingdom's modernisation and politics Fahd, disregarding the reaction of his Western-educated technocrats, was willing to grant the ulama's demands concerning a stricter observation of the Wahhabi edicts and feigned asceticism. Thus Summer Scott Huyette, who lived in the kingdom in the 1970s and early

1980s and wrote her PhD thesis on Saudi Arabia's 'political adaptation', observed:

> They [the graduates of the three religious universities] remain the mainstay of the legitimacy of the Al Saud and they do not hesitate to make their presence felt, enjoining the king to adhere to the tenets of ibn 'Abd al-Wahhab, but their impact is felt more in the social than in the political realm.[39]

Fahd's new policy of course outraged the intelligentsia, particularly its Hijazi members and most of the Western-educated technocrats.

6

THE ZENITH OF THE NEW ELITES' POWER: A FALSE DAWN (1979-83)

THE MIDDLE-CLASS ELITES' STRUGGLE FOR POLITICAL PARTICIPATION

By 1980 the Saudi school population was about one and a half million strong. Nearly 11,000 Saudis graduated that year from local and foreign institutions of higher learning; the majority of them joined the prestigious civil service. In addition to sixteen cabinet ministers, 2,000 senior technocrats held a PhD or an MA degree. Many other university and high school graduates joined the private sector of the economy and became members of the professions, businessmen, industrialists and contractors or were employed in the private sector in managerial positions.[1]

In the early 1980s it seemed that the new middle class, led by the technocratic 'aristocracy', had reached the zenith of its power. Although the ruling class did not grant them political participation, the 'new men' were largely absorbed into the system and formed a non-royal elite which exerted enormous power and competed for authority with the traditional non-royal elite. The technocratic upper-crust shared indirectly in policy-making, by controlling the huge government budgets, by participating in the cabinet discussions or by acting as advisers to the informal royal *majlis al-shura*, not to mention their active role in their respective ministries.[2]

The technocratic elite seemed to enjoy wealth and prestige in addition to enormous power and some, such as Zaki Yamani, were considered all-powerful in the West. They had gradually replaced the non-royal traditional elites as a source of influence since the mid-1960s as the central government had eroded the traditional socio-political institutions. Their role in the internal power struggle was often exaggerated. Their impact on the kingdom's foreign and oil policies, which manifested itself in the 1979–80 crisis, was believed by some to be also a reflection of the technocrats' growing power. By the early 1980s many foreign observers believed that in view of their expanding ranks it was only a matter of time before the new elites would gain full political participation, or even replace altogether the Sauds' regime.

In reality, the technocrats, notwithstanding the honours and authority they enjoyed, remained senior executives and advisers to the king and the royal *majlis al-shura*, their power being totally dependent on those who appointed them. The *ahl al-hal wa'l-'aqd* jealously guarded the ruling class's monopoly of decision-making and retained the key positions in the cabinet essential for safeguarding its supreme authority. Although occasionally disagreeing with their mentors, aware of the limitations of their power, members of the technocratic upper-crust, especially the new Najdi executives, reconciled themselves to the situation.[3]

The rise of fundamentalism in Tehran and the 1979 neo-Ikhwan rebellion did not strengthen the intelligentsia's position but rather forced it further into the arms of the regime. With the example of Iran fresh in their minds, the new elites now feared a fundamentalist backlash aimed against modernisation and the secular, especially Western-educated, middle class. Despite the constant expansion of their ranks, the importance of the Hijazi-led secular bureaucrats suffered a grave blow when Crown Prince Fahd decided to abort his relatively liberal policy and seek, whenever possible, the ulama's blessing for his modernisation programme. Although he still needed their co-operation to govern and develop the kingdom and to resist the conservative opposition within the ruling class, when it came to a choice between the new elites and the ulama Fahd, considering the circumstances, opted for the latter.

Moreover, the new elites' growing criticism of the royal family's corrupt practices and extravaganza, while many of the bureaurocrats benefited far more from the commission system and kickbacks, hardened the ruling class's opposition to 'democratising' the regime. It also accelerated the trend to prefer 'local' Najdi technocrats and civil servants to the politically sophisticated and conscious, and religiously 'liberal', Hijazi bourgeois elite.[4]

Even before the Mecca rebellion was over, the rulers revived the committee charged with exploring ways and means to involve the new middle class in the political process. On 10 January 1980, Crown Prince Fahd announced the government's intention to promulgate a basic law (based on the *shari'a*), to establish a national *majlis al-shura* 'that would share with the cabinet the responsibilities of government' and to re-organise the provincial government. An eight-member committee made up of ulama and conservative ministers headed by Prince Na'if was appointed on 18 March to study and propose a Basic Law of Government (*Nizam Asasi li'l-Hukm*), a framework for a National Consultative Assembly and a Provincial Government Act (*Nizam li'l-Muqata'at*), meant to modernise the latter.

The new *majlis al-shura* of 50-70 members, it was claimed, was to represent the different powers in the kingdom: the royal family and the ruling class as a whole, the ulama, the technocrats and other educated elements. Yet, the members of this 'National Assembly' were to be appointed and not elected. Their role in the government was limited to participation in the legislative process but they lacked authority to veto the king's decisions. The new *Nizam li'l-Muqata'at* was to re-define the kingdom's provinces (and towns), their status and the authority of the provincial amir and his subordinated governors in all matters relating to their administrative unit not in the purlieu of the central government. On the day following King Khalid's previous edict, the monarch also appointed new amirs for the provinces of Mecca, Al-Qasim, Tabuk and Ha'il, all of whom were younger and capable sons of Abd al-Aziz. This was the beginning of a trend to strengthen the provincial government and expand the authority of its amirs, to some degree at the expense of the central government, reversing Faysal's policy.[5]

It was evident from the start that, even if carried out, this reform would not turn Saudi Arabia into a 'constitutional democracy' and indeed members of the *majlis al-shura* were to be largely appointed from among the old and new elites. This, Crown Prince Fahd stressed, was in line with the Islamic mode of government (*ahl al-hal wa'l-'aqd*), 'as the Qur'an was the country's constitution'.[6]

In the spring of 1980, when questioned about the progress made by their 'constitutional' committee, Princes Na'if and Salman responded that it was still meeting regularly but underscored the fact that the committee was not preparing a constitution because 'the Qur'an is Saudi Arabia's constitution'. In a press interview in March 1982, Fahd claimed that the recommendations concerning the promised *majlis al-shura* would be implemented in a matter of months, although the committee's report was still not ready.[7]

Quite obviously, once the storm was over, the Saudi ruling class had no intention of enabling the new elites to share in decision-making. This policy was vindicated by the difficulties experienced by the Kuwaiti and Bahrayni rulers, who had experimented with parliaments, which included nationalistic and fundamentalist members.

Yet Fahd, who sympathised with the middle-class elites, felt compelled at least to reassure them that he still intended to grant them some participation in decision-making, especially since he needed their co-operation. By reiterating previous promises of limited political reforms, the crown prince, in addition to responding to their demands for participation in decision-making, wished to appease the new elites, especially the Hijazi middle class. This was also necessary because the ulama had won concessions which led to a more vigorous enforcement of Wahhabi laws and customs in the Hijaz and the Eastern Province.

The Saudi bourgeoisie – strength or weakness?

As mentioned before, it appeared that the Saudi new elites were steadily becoming a power that could no longer be ignored, because of its sheer size. By the early 1980s the technocrats and bureaucrats, professionals and the middle and upper ranks of the business community components of the middle-class elites probably numbered hundreds of thousands. Yet, the new elites of the early 1980s were even less monolithic than in the 1950s and the 1960s. Rather, the differences that had emerged in the past, besides the Najdi–Hijazi cleavage, were now exacerbated. The intelligentsia was not necessarily socially liberal and supportive of reform. Most remained deeply committed to Islam and the Saudi way of life and critical of Western lifestyle. While a large number became very wealthy, the majority were well off or modestly so.

Western-educated technocrats, who dominated the key positions in the government and its agencies, and professionals were largely the ones most anxious to modernise the kingdom and generally impatient with its traditional institutions including the quality of the domestic universities and their 'product'; but graduates of Saudi 'secular' universities, jealous of the former, though they supported modernisation and reform in principle, were more traditionally oriented and introvert and therefore more concerned about the impact of modernisation on their society and culture. Graduates of religious universities and institutions, many of rural origin, were, as expected, the most conservative in their outlook and critical of many aspects of modernisation and government. They resented, moreover, the preference given by the regime in the employment and advancement of their secular (*hadr*) counterparts and accused the foreign-educated intelligentsia of introducing into the kingdom Western influences which 'corrupted the principles of the Wahhabi state'. A foreign professor who had spent several years in Saudi universities described the above cleavage in the following way: 'English and Arabic are forces which have powerful symbolic valence in Saudi Arabia; they stand for modern/traditional; secular/sacred; alien/comfortable.'[8]

The new elites were also polarised by social status determined by position, income, level of education and connections with the ruling class. The number of 'technocrats' (bureaucrats) employed in the government administration and its agencies in 1980 was 173,290. Only a tiny fraction (0.77%) received the highest grades' monthly salaries (SR6,491–11,460) on the civil service pay scale and belonged to the technocratic upper-crust, largely composed of graduates of Western universities. About 21% receiving upper medium- and medium-grade salaries (SR3,076–6,490) were mostly Saudi university-educated technocrats. Over 78% of the civil servants received the lower grade of the monthly pay scale (SR1,610–3,075) and were probably largely traditional civil servants, graduates of religious institutions and of the different levels of the modern educational system. The standard of living of the last group could be considered relatively low when compared with the other two groups of bureaucrats, or with their counterparts who opted for the less prestigious and more lucrative private sector. They thus belonged to the lower rungs of the middle class. Clearly the interests and sympathies of such varied components of the 'new elites' were very divergent, adding to its weakness. Salary scale aside, all the above, particularly senior technocrats, usually amassed wealth through their connections with the country's development and very frequently were involved in business enterprises in addition to their government jobs.[9]

It would be wrong to think of the middle-class elites as being synonymous with the technocrats and bureaucrats. Many graduates of domestic and foreign universities, especially the ones whose studies were financed by their families, became professionals, businessmen or entrepreneurs. Some of the most successful Saudi businessmen–entrepreneurs, however, did not acquire a university degree or even a secondary or an intermediary school certificate. The numerous members of the lower middle class who ran petty business enterprises such as small trucking and taxi ventures, gasoline stations and shops, or who became paid sponsors (*kafil*) of foreign workers, often of bedouin origin, obtained only minimal education, if any. Obviously, in addition to the gap in wealth and standard of living between the latter and the middle-class elites, their interests and sympathies were also different and often opposed to those of the members of the intelligentisa and the upper-crust technocrats and wealthy businessmen–entrepreneurs.

The 'lower-class' Saudis between *dawla* and *hukuma*

The Saudi 'lower classes', with the exception of an insignificant element, faithfully supported the regime, its policy and the conservative–Wahhabi character of the Saudi kingdom. Their allegiance to the government of the Sauds (*hukuma*) goes back to the pre-kingdom (1932) era and has been maintained through the network of traditional socio-political institutions. Even after the establishment of the modern Saudi kingdom in 1932, townspeople, nomads and agriculturalists were still governed through their respective hierarchy of village, town, district and provincial amir, tribal shaykh (amirs) and *'umda*. The leadership of the rural population was integrated in the regime's power base through numerous matrimonial arrangements and managed to some extent to preserve their influence in the rural areas and provincial government system. The Saudi patriarchal system, moreover, provided for the needs of the largely nomadic rural society through the *majalis* system, welfare services, stipends, subsidies and employment in the National Guard, the armed forces and the internal security forces.

The accelerated development of the kingdom since the 1960s and through the first and second five-year development plans (1970-80), mainly benefited the townspeople, though they sparked off rapid changes in the rural society. By creating attractive employment opportunities in the cities, moreover, they accelerated the urbanisation of the bedouin and settled rural population. This, and the development of a centralised government administration, caused an erosion of the traditional socio-political institutions of the tribal society. Yet, the newly urbanised, on the whole, maintained their contacts with their tribes, villages and amirs. The third five-year plan (1980-5) already gave the highest priority to the rural population with the aim of equating their standard of living to that of the townspeople and curbing the process of urbanisation. Indeed, the development of the rural areas was one of the major goals of the fourth development plan (1985-90), but owing to the economic recession by the mid-1980s circumstances somewhat changed.[10]

Oil wealth and its dispensation to all levels of Saudis through welfare services, subsidies and the like, and by the senior princes directly to their constituencies, helped maintain the links between the regime and the people. Al Saud continues to exercise its patriarchal rule based on patronage, marital ties with the important tribes and families and personal relationship between the rulers and the ruled. Such contacts with the tribal population, both rural and newly urbanised, are maintained through the hierarchy of amirs and other traditional institutions. Most important are the *majalis* held by the king, all the senior princes and their offspring, the leaders of the aristocratic families and the provincial and district amirs. The royal family up to the monarch is thus, at least in theory, accessible to the lowliest citizen. He can petition for, and receive, financial and other help, or may bring before the ruler any grievance he has. Individuals and groups, moreover, also use the *majalis* to lobby for 'worthy' public and regional causes.[11]

Despite the erosion of tribal or regional loyalties and the penetration of the central government through urbanisation, the tribal fraternity still eased the settlement of the individual *badu* or villager in the towns by providing financial support and/or the necessary connections in the new and foreign environments. Thus, although the authority of the traditional socio-political institutions of the rural population was often replaced by the bureaucrats of the central government (*dawla*) who now provide services and subsidies to the newly urbansied masses, the latter's allegiance is still largely reserved for the Sauds' regime (*hukuma*) and its representatives. The deeply religious new townspeople, moreover, may have occasionally heard the imam of their mosque criticising foreign

95

Muslim rulers, the *dawla* and the technocrats but, nearly always, only praise of the Sauds' *hukuma*.

The distinction made by the Saudi 'lower class' between *hukuma* and *dawla*, both of which literally mean 'government', is quite significant. To the simple Saudi, *dawla* is a synonym of the modern central government and its agencies, largely controlled by Western-educated bureaucrats of urban origin. The expansion of the central government's services, and rapid urbanisation, brought the Saudi 'lower and lower middle classes', both largely of bedouin origin, into daily contact with the *dawla* and made them dependent on services and subsidies provided by it. Nevertheless, the new townspeople usually dislike the bureaucrats, whom they consider inferior and crafty and who despise them. In contrast, the Sauds' paternalistic *hukuma*, which retains personal contact with them, they believe, respects them, understands their problems and, as befits a government, provides their requirements whenever the need arises.[12]

Some authors espousing radical ideologies lament the fact that the Saudi 'lower class' is not really a lower class *per se* because the poorer Saudis have already elevated themselves to the middle class, or are in the process of doing so, and hence are not proper 'revolutionary material'.[13] The rapid expansion of modern education among the rural and recently urbanised Saudis, and the rise in their standard of living, may gradually bridge the differences between the Saudi 'lower class' and the new elite. But at present the new elites, mainly of urban middle-class origin, can expect little sympathy or support from the lower-middle-class Saudis in the former's bid to penetrate or overthrow the Saudi regime.

After the Mecca rebellion Crown Prince Fahd was determined to reinforce, reorganise and modernise the provincial administration. Young, educated and dynamic princes gradually replaced ineffective traditional provincial governors. The new amirs, using their royal connections and exploiting the priority given to rural areas and the less developed provinces in the third (1980–5) development plan, expedited the modernisation of their provinces or districts. Thus, for instance, Khalid al-Faysal, appointed in the 1970s governor of Asir, began to improve the situation in the backward and neglected Southern Region. No less impressive were the achievements of Prince Muqrin b. Abd al-Aziz, a former air force major, appointed (1980) as governor of the Shammar (Ha'il) province. Besides infrastructure and other development projects which he brought to the region, Muqrin took advantage of the generous subsidies to agriculture and the fossil water reservoirs in the region and brought prosperity to the population (of Muhammad al-Fahd and Al-Hasa, see below).

Obviously the ability to overcome the red tape of the bureaucracy and access to the king, the senior princes and ministers, were essential to the success of the new *umara'*; yet education, dedication to modernisation and special relations between the rulers and the ruled, which did not pertain in the case of the modern bureaucrats, were important as well.

The previously neglected largely nomadic northern, the largely agricultural southern and the Shi'ite-dominated eastern provinces were granted substantial budgets in the third development plan, and are undergoing accelerated development. In recent years their *umara'* of all ranks were given additional responsibilities and authority and they were put in charge of the co-ordination of all projects initiated by the different ministries in their governorates. King Fahd believes, it seems, that this will not only compensate the loyal rural population for past neglect and curb migration to the big towns but that the modernised patriarchal provincial government may also offset the influence of his conservative rivals, led by Abdallah, and of the new elites, who dominate the central government.[14]

7

THE REIGN OF KING FAHD: ECONOMIC CRISIS AND OPPOSITION (1982-7)

King Khalid died in June 1982 and Fahd was declared king. Abdallah became crown prince and first deputy prime minister, and Sultan second in line of succession and second deputy prime minister. Although the prearranged succession went through smoothly, the struggle for power within the royal family soon re-emerged. Abdallah refused to surrender the command of the National Guard, thus violating the understanding that the crown prince and deputy prime minister should not hold a cabinet portfolio. On his part, Abdallah strongly resented the fact the unlike Fahd, who ruled the kingdom in Khalid's name, he was given a title without real authority. Furthermore, he also believed, as did many others, that the Sudayris were planning to get rid of him and appoint Sultan as Fahd's successor.

Abdallah opposed Fahd's inter-Arab and pro-American policy which found expression in his Eight-Point Programme for the settlement of the Arab–Israeli conflict (August 1981) and co-operation with the US during and after the Israeli invasion of Lebanon (1982/3). He disagreed with the kingdom's (and OPEC's) oil policy and its involvement with the GCC, and advocated a more balanced policy with regard to the Iran–Iraq war.[1] Known for his integrity, Abdallah was critical of the moral corruption and extravaganza in the royal family and the administration and of Saudi Arabia's inflated budgets.

Most conservatives, including many princes, urban *a'yan* and tribal *umara'*, supported Abdallah. The group of Western-educated, third-generation princes, led by Saud al-Faysal, sided more openly with the anti-Sudayri camp this time, at least in matters relating to foreign affairs and oil policy. They, as the majority of the intelligentsia, would also have preferred that the kingdom follow a more neutralist line in world and inter-Arab affairs. They were also displeased with the excesses and lifestyle of members of the royal house, led by the 'Fahd clan', in a period of rising economic and social difficulties. They were also suspicious of the Sudayris' intentions regarding the succession to the throne, believing that the time had come for the younger generation of Sauds to take over.

Table 7.1 Saudi Arabia's oil revenues 1981-92

Year	Billion $
1981	108
1982	70
1983	37
1984	35
1985	22
1986	16-18 (est.)
1987	17.8
1988	16.6
1989	23 (est.)
1990	43
1992	over 40 (est.)

Source: FT, 22 July 1985, 21 April 1986, supplement, 30 April 1986, 2 January 1987; Knauerhase, 'Future', p. 75; *IHT,* 3 June 1986, 3-4 January 1987; *NYT,* 8 February 1987; *IHT,* 20 December 1989, according to SAMA; Budget for 1989; *FT,* 2 January 1991, estimate of the Gulf International Bank; *FT,* 30 January 1992, supplement Saudi Arabia, p. II.

OPEC's substantial price hikes in 1980 caused demand for its oil, and oil prices, to decline in the coming years. This was due to the introduction of conservation measures and alternative sources of energy by the industrial countries and rising production of non-OPEC oil. In order to maintain OPEC's shaky unity and its leadership in it, Saudi Arabia gradually became the organisation's 'swing producer' (reducing its production as demand for oil declined on the understanding that it would increase it when demand rose). Saudi production thus fell from about ten million barrels daily in 1981 to about two million by September 1985. Hence, the kingdom's revenue from oil, its main source of income, rapidly declined from 1982 onwards (see Table 7.1), owing to the fall in production as well as decreasing oil prices. The intense power struggle in the royal family since 1982/3 was thus accompanied by growing criticism of Fahd's 'catastrophic' oil policy, responsible for the kingdom's economic crisis, on the one hand and his 'inept' foreign policy on the other (America's pro-Israeli policy, decline of the Saudi role and prestige in the Arab world and Iran's inimical attitude to the Saudi kingdom).

The Saudi government's budget was largely dependent on its oil revenue because the regime was unable, and unwilling, owing to religious and political factors, to tax the population. Although Riyadh continued to draw upon its enormous financial reserves (estimated in 1981/2 at over 150 billion dollars), it was obliged, nevertheless, progressively to reduce its annual budget by 1985/6 to just over one-half of its size in 1982/3 (see Table 7.2) and to 37.5 billion in 1988. Subsequently the kingdom's economic activity, largely dependent on government spending, totally stagnated. The private sector faced, therefore, increasing

Table 7.2 Saudi Arabia's budgets 1981/2 - 1992

Year	Billion $
1981–2	82.7
1982–3	91
1983–4	75
1984–5	75
1985–6	56.3
1987	45.3
1988	37.50
1989	37.60
1990	38.13
1991	No budget
1992	48.3

Source: Business America, 13 July 1981; Field, *FT*, 22 April 1985, supplement; Reuter from Riyadh, 5 January 1987; *Saudi Budget Estimates*, The Royal Embassy of Saudi Arabia, Commercial Office (Washington, DC, 6 August 1991); *FT*, 30 January 1992, supplement Saudi Arabia, p. II.

hardships as business contracted and thousands of companies, some among the largest in the kingdom, faced cash-flow difficulties, and even went bankrupt. As their income declined the Saudi population naturally reduced its spending. This affected not only importers but also the nascent domestic industry. The petrochemical and other oil- and energy-intensive industries, in which the Saudi government invested through Saudi Arabian Basic Industries Corporation (SABIC) tens of billions of dollars, also proved far less profitable than expected. Thus, its contribution to the diversification of the kingdom's sources of revenue is still small compared with the enormous investment in it.[2]

For a country of about eight million people of whom only about six million are citizens, the Saudi budget in 1985/6, in the vicinity of 56 billion, was still extravagant. Yet, for political reasons the Sudayris were unwilling significantly to reduce the enormous budgets of the ministries of defence and interior or halt the development of the poorer Northern and Southern Regions and the problematic Eastern Province, neglected until 1980. Nor were they willing to cut meaningfully the enormous subsidies and extensive welfare services which the population enjoyed. Indeed, when the government attempted to scale down the unrealistic subsidies for agriculture (largely benefiting companies established by the wealthy) and gasoline, the matter caused such an outcry that the regime quickly shelved the plans.[3] That nearly a million foreign workers and experts, including tens of thousands of Westerners, left Saudi Arabia between 1982 and 1987 may have pleased the ulama and the nationalists, but it further aggravated the country's economic stagnation. Economic activity declined, tens of thousands of villas and numerous office

100

buildings in the kingdom's main towns stood empty; rents which provided many Saudis with a handsome income were halved, and in some cases reduced to about a third compared with 1982.[4]

What at first was believed to be a temporary crisis developed into a prolonged economic recession. Paradoxically, while Saudi Arabia still employed nearly two and a half million foreigners, the phenomenon of unemployment among Saudi citizens re-emerged, owing to social mores and lack of skills. School leavers, moreover, met with increasing difficulties in finding employment, while salaries were noticeably reduced. The vocational school system, however, which other than in the Eastern Province failed to attract students, benefited from the new situation because of the country's continued need for technicians and mechanics. Yet, most of the 'lower-class' students, who enrolled in, and graduated from, vocational institutions, rather than replacing foreign mechanics and technicians, became workshop and garage owners, exploiting the generous government grants and hiring foreign foremen and workers.[5]

University graduates, who were previously snapped up by the civil service or the private sector, met with growing difficulties in finding employment; this was particularly true of those with degrees in Islamic studies, humanities and social sciences. In the early 1980s most graduates of the domestic universities still insisted on employment in the metropolitan towns, although they had to settle for progressively less important positions. By the mid-1980s such graduates were considered lucky to get an appointment in the rural areas, previously socially unacceptable. A higher percentage of students, although still less than a third, turned, therefore, to the more demanding and less prestigious (in Saudi Arabia) engineering and science faculties, the graduates of which could still find attractive employment opportunites. But as the recession became more severe in 1986, unemployment among university graduates became a common phenomenon and was openly discussed in the Saudi press. The universities tightened their admission requirements and reduced the students' stipends. They also failed many more students in their final exams, allegedly on government instructions, to reduce the pressure on it to provide suitable employment. Yet occasionally the regime intervened on behalf of students owing to political consider-ations.[6]

By 1984 the Association of Chambers of Commerce and Industry (below), lobbied the king, albeit unsuccessfully, to disregard OPEC and increase the kingdom's oil production and, subsequently, government spending. They managed, nevertheless, to persuade the government to promulgate a law requiring foreign contractors operating in Saudi Arabia to purchase in the kingdom supplies, services and Saudi products to the value of at least 30 per cent of their contract. Later on the 'offset' requirements were expanded to include the setting up of joint ventures with Saudi entrepreneurs in the field of high technology. Indeed the fourth development plan (1985–90) was based on the assumption that the private sector would take over from the government the burden of diversifying the kingdom's economy.[7]

Apprehensive of the future of their country's economy, many Saudi businessmen preferred to invest their wealth, valued at between 100 and 200 billion dollars, in the economies of the major Western industrial countries. During the second conference of the Association of Chambers of Commerce and Industry in March 1985 King Fahd, hinting at the flight of capital from the kingdom, invited Saudi businessmen to take advantage of the infrastructure provided by their government and the absence of taxation in Saudi Arabia to invest in their country's economy. The Saudi capitalists, however, used to government support and subsidies, considered the ruler's request a warning signal and many transferred additional funds to foreign countries.[8]

By the last quarter of 1985 the kingdom's economic situation rapidly deteriorated and its oil production bottomed at about two million barrels daily. King Fahd now gave in to the pressure of many senior princes, and of the business community, and decided to abandon the kingdom's role as 'swing producer'. At the beginning of 1986 he accepted Zaki Yamani's strategy to step up Saudi production substantially and cause the oil price to decline to under 20 dollars a barrel, possibly as low as 15 dollars. This, it was hoped, would discipline OPEC members and coerce non-OPEC oil countries into agreeing to limit their production, enabling OPEC (and Saudi Arabia) to regain its 'fair share of the market'. However, this strategy backfired and led to a total collapse of oil prices.

In 1986 the Saudi oil industry was generating a fraction of the revenue that it had produced in the early 1980s. Still insisting on providing the citizens with all the services and most of the subsidies that they enjoyed in the past, the government was drawing upon the country's financial reserves at an unprecedented rate.[9] Unwilling to reveal its predicament, the Saudi regime postponed the publication in March of its annual budget for 1986/7. Even earlier, it became common for all ministries to delay, as long as possible, payment to contractors and suppliers, a policy that aggravated the difficulties of local and foreign companies in Saudi Arabia and led to many bankruptcies.

The situation so deteriorated that rumours began to circulate that government employees would have to forgo part of their pay. Thus in a speech to the nation on 10 March, King Fahd assured the population that ample funds were available for salaries and for all the planned expenditures of the government.[10] The budget, however, was not published until the end of the year, after the king, in desperation, abandoned the 'fair

102

share of the market' strategy, and sacked Yamani, and after OPEC agreed to limit its production and adopt an 18-dollars-a-barrel reference price.

Even then the kingdom's budget was based on the assumption that a deficit of about 13 billion dollars (in reality about 17 billion) would be drawn from reserves. Speaking for the government, Prince Sultan justified the size of the budget (over 30 per cent of which went to defence), which drew criticism from the technocrats, by the need to maintain the level of services and the standard of living to which the Saudi population was accustomed.[11] Obviously, at a time when the regime's prestige was at a low ebb, it was essential to keep the Saudi masses content, so as to maintain their support for the Sauds.

FAHD'S POLICIES AND INTERNAL CHALLENGES

The consolidation of the Sudayris' hegemony

Aggravated by budgetary cuts the friction between the two major camps in the royal house reached a climax in the first months of 1983. By March it was widely rumoured that Crown Prince Abdallah and the National Guard were involved in an abortive coup against King Fahd. The polarisation in the ruling class, as portrayed by the foreign media, seemed so acute that Abdallah broke the usual silence of the Sauds about royal family politics and prudently granted an interview to a Kuwaiti newspaper,[12] in which he categorically denied the rumoured coup and his involvement in any plot against the king. Yet he admitted the serious differences in the royal house regarding the kingdom's internal (modernisation) and external policies (relations with the West, Iran, the Arabs and oil) and, indirectly, accused Fahd of indecisive leadership. This interview was partly an outcome of endeavours by the *ahl al-hal wa'l-'aqd* to reunite the ruling class at a time of growing challenges to the regime.

Faced with a financial crisis, subversion by a victorious fundamentalist Iran and rising discontent among the new middle class, the *ahl al-hal wa'l-'aqd* accelerated in 1983 and early 1984 their efforts to re-establish the royal family's wavering external consensus (*ijma'*). The outcome was the consolidation of the 'collective leadership' and the increased influence of the royal Consultative Council on decision-making. By 1984, moreover, the Sudayris no longer seemed to challenge Crown Prince Abdallah's position as heir apparent and commander of the relatively weak National Guard and agreed to let the latter develop alongside the armed forces. On his part, Abdallah refrained thereafter from publicly challenging King Fahd's policies and appeared to accept the latter's role as active prime minister.[13]

A most significant feature of Fahd's policies in the 1980s was the large-

103

scale appointment of young members of the royal family and offspring of other components of the ruling class to important positions in the civil service, the *imarates* (provincial administration) and the armed and security forces. The recognised branches of Al Saud, the Al-Shaykh, Jiluwis, Thunayans and Al Sudayri, by themselves probably number over 20,000 males. Thus, candidates for such appointments abounded. In his previously mentioned PhD thesis (1982), Mashaal Abdullah Turki Al Saud suggested the involvement of the numerous young Sauds in the administration. Eager to assume an active role in the kingdom's government these young men, he claimed, are ideologically dedicated to the kingdom's Saudi–Wahhabi character and have a vested interest in the regime's survival, unlike the secular, nationalistic middle-class technocrats.[14]

Shortly after the reconciliation in the ruling house, Mishari, one of King Saud's numerous sons, was appointed commander of the National Guard in the crucial Eastern Province. This, and other appointments of King Saud's sons in the following years, requiring the authorisation of the royal *majlis al-shura* and the king, were probably an outcome of efforts to reconcile the different branches of the royal family. They were also in line with Fahd's policy to involve Ibn Saud's younger sons and the disgruntled third-generation Sauds in the kingdom's administration and the provincial government.[15]

When Fahd was minister of the interior (1963–75) he gradually began to implant members of the 'Sudayri Seven' clan, their clients and their 'tribal' relatives in the provincial government. Prince Salman (born 1936), probably the most capable and popular of his full brothers, was appointed amir of the key Riyadh province (*imara*) as early as 1962. The authority of such *umara'* was partly to offset the influence enjoyed by Princes Khalid and Abdallah among the rural population and ulama. The gradual 'Sudayri-isation' of the provincial government was further accelerated when Na'if took over from Crown Prince Fahd in 1975 the Ministry of the Interior, directly responsible for provincial government and governors (*umara' al-manatiq*). In this he was occasionally assisted by commoner ministers loyal to him who controlled the budgets of the royal ministries allied with Abdallah (Prince Majid resigned from the government in 1979). In 1977 Fahd exploited the reorganisation of the provinces, expanded substantially the Riyadh province governed by Salman and implanted Sudayri supporters in other provinces. As crown prince, Fahd was also able to help appoint and advance his kinsmen and his allies to key positions in the government and its administration. Thus, by the early 1980s, we find Sudayris and their allies as governors, deputy governors and senior administrators, of many of the kingdom's fourteen provinces and by 1985 of the Eastern Region as well.[16]

The same strategy was used by Fahd's full brothers Na'if and Sultan with regard to their ministries and sensitive positions in the security and armed forces. Nearly all of Prince Sultan's sons served as senior air force officers (Salman's son, an air force major, took part in a US space flight). Many sons of his Sudayri brothers and their royal and non-royal traditional elites allies (including the descendants of their uncles and many Al-Shaykhs) also hold key positions in the armed forces, the Ministry of Defence and other ministries. Indeed, the fourth command of the Saudi armed forces, the air defence command, organised in 1986, was entrusted to Sultan's son Prince Khalid, who was promoted to major general (commander of the Arab forces in the 1990/1 Gulf war). Sudayris and their allies hold as well all the important departments of the Ministry of the Interior and command its various security forces, including the feared *mabahith*.[17]

The strengthening of the provincial government by Fahd, reversing Faysal's policy, eroded somewhat the authority of the central government, controlled by the new elites, and was also consistent with the regime's policy of balancing centres of power. Yet the main thrust of this policy was aimed, it seems, at countering the influence of Prince Abdallah and, until 1982, of King Khalid and his brother Muhammad (Jiluwi camp) among the tribes and other rural elements. In addition to the *Mujahidun* Department dealing with offspring of Ibn Saud's early bedouin followers, the Ministry of the Interior is also responsible for the provincial governments and their budgets and for co-ordinating the activities of their *umara'*. Especially since 1980 (the third development plan) the ministry has been increasingly involved, together with the provincial governors, in the accelerated development of the rural areas and the improvement of the standard of living of their population. The ministry's special security forces recruited their personnel largely from among rural or ex-tribal population. These forces were rapidly expanded in the 1980s and are approaching in manpower the strength of the National Guard. The 'security training city', established in 1982, gave Na'if a role in the defence and security fields equal to those of Abdallah and Sultan.[18]

Control of the Ministry of the Interior thus enabled the Sudayris to consolidate and expand their influence among the rural and the newly urbanised lower middle class. Not surprisingly, with the resources of the Ministry of Defence, not to mention the monarchy, also at their disposal, the Sudayris have lured to their camp in recent years many bedouin *umara'*, regional *a'yan* and their followers, previously supporters of Crown Prince Abdallah.

The Sudayris, it seems, expanded their control to the media as well. Prince Turki ibn Sultan is the director of the department of press in the Ministry of Information, whose minister, General Ali al-Sha'ir, is Fahd's son-in-law, and many editors of Saudi newspapers are Sudayris. Indeed,

Fahd frequently utilises the Saudi television and radio to inform his subjects of their country's progress and problems. He often visits universities and academies and answers students' queries and this fact, and what he says, is always prominently reported by the media.[19]

The consolidation of the Sudayris' power base at the expense of the Jiluwi camp, despite the seeming 'collective leadership' and the claimed erosion in the king's prestige in the mid-1980s, was evident in other areas as well. Prince Ahmad (deputy minister of the interior), and later his nephew Muhammad al-Fahd, took over after 1981 some of the duties of Abd al-Muhsin al-Jiluwi, the reactionary and ineffective governor of the crucial Eastern Province. Nevertheless, by giving a free hand to the Wahhabi ulama and their Morality Police, Abd al-Muhsin enhanced the tension with the Shi'ites in this crucial province where many Americans and other Westerners employed by Aramco and the Ministry of Defence lived. After an earlier attempt to get rid of Abd al-Muhsin failed, Muhammad al-Fahd and his cousin Fahd al-Salman (Prince Salman's son), officially replaced the governor and his deputy respectively at the beginning of 1985 and brought to an end the government of the Jiluwi 'dynasty' in Al-Sharqiyya. Another son of King Fahd, Saud, was appointed in 1985 deputy to Turki al-Faysal, the head of external intelligence (*Istikhbarat al-'Amma*), King Faysal's son. Bandar Ibn Sultan (married to Turki al-Faysal's sister), the Western-educated ex-pilot son of the minister of defence, was appointed in 1983 ambassador to the United States. Thus, King Fahd provided himself with a direct link to Washington, bypassing the foreign office, controlled by Saud al-Faysal.[20]

It is evident that the Sudayris enjoyed the support of a number of the 'younger' sons of King Abd al-Aziz and other members of the royal family, who themselves, or their offspring, were appointed to different positions in the government and the '*imarates* system' or granted special concessions which enriched them. Even more important was the alliance between the 'Fahd clan' and the descendants of some of the king's paternal and maternal uncles and leading representatives of Al al-Shaykh. Hence, if a new confrontation were to break out in the royal house in regard to the monarch's authority or the problem of succession, the Sudayris could count on substantial support in the ruling class as well. Indeed the Iran–Iraq war has further strengthened the Sudayris' position in the Saudi ruling class.

Yet, on the other hand, there was intensive opposition in the royal house, both among senior and frustrated 'third-generation' princes, to the Sudayris' dynastical tendencies and endeavours to monopolise power. Moreover, as was the case with Faysal between 1958 and 1960, the support for Fahd among the different components of the aristocracy and the middle class (it is alleged even among the Sudayris) was conditional on his success as a ruler, which has been somewhat tarnished as a result of events in the region and the economic crisis in Saudi Arabia until 1990. Between 1985 and 1989, owing to the decline of the oil revenue which had fuelled the kingdom's prosperity and contributed to its stability, government budgets have been halved and economic activity has stagnated. Saudi Arabia's prestige has also undergone an erosion due to its inability to continue subsidising Arab and Third World countries and Riyadh's inability to influence America's pro-Israeli policy. The proliferation of royal officials in the provincial government and of royal technocrats in the central government also antagonises the middle-class elites with whom they compete.

Tension within the royal family, though still covert, was rising; but it was tempered by apprehension about the rise of Wahhabi fundamentalism, dissatisfaction among the masses and middle class and the fear of Iran's power. The recession experienced by the kingdom was partly attributed, by elements in the aristocracy and the middle class, to Fahd's inaptitude as a ruler, and to the 'failure' of his foreign policy.[21] Similar accusations led to the dethroning of King Saud in 1964, yet Fahd is by far a better statesman and ruler than Saud and commands a broad support which he has managed to consolidate in recent years.

The regime and national integration

A 1982 doctoral thesis of Abdallah Ali al-Ibrahim demonstrates how the modernisation of Saudi Arabia until the 1980s favoured the central province (Najd) and the more developed Western Province (Hijaz). Development has, however, largely bypassed the desert bedouin-inhabited Northern Region (Ha'il, Qurayat, Tabuk and Al-Jawf provinces) and, to a lesser extent, the Eastern Province.[22] The northern and the southern provinces still had in the early 1980s 'a high rate of illiteracy, inadequate access to social services and physical infrastructure'. Subsequently their population migrated to Hijaz and Najd, where attractive employment opportunities and government services abounded. Minimal development and a very high rate of migration were particularly noticeable in relation to the densely populated Southern Region (over 25 per cent of the Saudi population). An offshoot of Yemen, it supplied cheap labour to Saudi rural and urban areas. In the sparsely populated north, the settlement of bedouin nomads has gathered momentum with government help since the late 1960s. Yet, in both regions jealousy of the prosperity of Najd and Hijaz caused frustration and alienation. In Asir, for instance, support grew for Nasserism in the 1960s and for radical nationalism and separatist tendencies in the 1970s and 1980s.[23]

The appointment of young, dynamic governors such as Princes Khalid al-Faysal (Asir – to further strengthen the Sudayris' alliance with Al-Faysal), Muqrin bin Abd al-Aziz (Ha'il) and Fahd bin Khalid al-Sudayri (who replaced his father, the 'Sudayri Seven' maternal uncle, as governor of Najran), coincided with the third five-year development plan (1980–5) which gave the highest priority to the development of the peripheral rural areas. The generous development allocations and subsidies for agriculture completely changed the above regions by the mid-1980s and halted migration from them. Schools, infirmaries, hospitals, roads and airfields were constructed, running water, electricity and telephones were introduced, land was distributed and the standard of living of the population was noticeably improved. Attempting to promote national integration and win the favour of the rural population, King Fahd insisted that despite the drastic cuts in the government's budget in the mid-1980s and thereafter development allocations for the Northern, Southern and Eastern regions should remain a priority.[24]

Comparatively speaking, the Eastern Province experienced some development in the 1960s and 1970s due to the oil industry and Aramco's operations, yet its Shi'ite population was the most discriminated against in the kingdom. After the 1979–80 riots and the rise of Iranian subversive activities in the Gulf, Prince Muhammad was instructed by Crown Prince Fahd personally to supervise the speeded-up development of the Eastern Province and to improve the treatment of its Shi'ite community. More-over, Fahd and King Khalid (after 1982 King Fahd) regularly visited Al-Sharqiyya's major towns, meeting with their sectarian leadership and business communities and with the students and faculty of its two universities.

The instability in the kingdom following Fahd's succession and the rise of subversion in the Eastern Province in 1982–3 caused the regime to accelerate its effort to develop the region, improve the standard of living and abolish the inferior status of the Shi'ite community. Following a visit by King Fahd to Al-Sharqiyya in the summer of 1983, it was decided to give priority to developing parts of the Eastern Province with high Shi'ite concentrations, especially the towns of Qatif and Hufuf which did not benefit from the oil boom. Simultaneously, in the face of the intensified activities of leftist-supported workers and intellectuals and pro-Iranian Shi'ite organisations, the government accelerated the construction of a National Guard town near Dammam and a 'military town' near Hufuf and reinforced the security forces in the province.[25]

The pace of development activity in the Eastern Province in the years 1980 to 1985 was the most intense in the kingdom, surpassing that of Najd and Hijaz. Airfields, ports, hospitals, schools, roads and other facilities were feverishly constructed all over Al-Sharqiyya. The Jubayl super-modern oil-related industrial centre became operational and was followed by three industrial sites around the town of Dammam.[26]

The appointment of his son and nephew as governor and deputy governor may have been prompted by royal family politics. Yet Fahd probably intended Muhammad, his able (and controversial) son, to accelerate as well Al-Hasa's development and reduce sectarian tensions in the province during a difficult period to his regime, when it was vulnerable to the effects of Iran's victories and the economic recession. Prince Muhammad and his deputy introduced a new style of relations with the Shi'ites and endeavoured to convince them that they were now to enjoy full citizen rights. The governor and his deputy visited members of the community and made Shi'ite leaders welcome in their *majalis*. A special effort was made to win over the Shi'ite new elites and students, who tended to be the most radical.[27]

Prince Muhammad's enlightened policy met with difficulties, however. Predictably, the economic recession gravely affected the Eastern Province. Aramco and its daughter companies, the largest single employer in Al-Sharqiyya, were forced to adopt severe austerity measures and substantially reduce the workforce. Furthermore, the attempt of Prince Ahmad, and later of his nephew Muhammad, to elevate the Shi'ites to an equal position to that of the Sunnis met with strong opposition by local conservatives. Traditionally strongly anti-Shi'ite, the Wahhabi *'alims'* revulsion for this sect was now rekindled by the Gulf war, Iran's fundamentalist anti-Saudi propaganda and terrorist activities of extremist Shi'ite elements. In sermons and lectures in mosques, public institutions and even the official media, the local ulama lashed out at the Shi'ites' religious practices and beliefs, characterising the latter as infidels 'more dangerous than the Zionists and the Communists'.[28] Whenever they could they harassed the Shi'ites, using the Morality Policy *muttawwa'in*. By the mid-1980s, however, having regained their self-respect and confidence, the Shi'ite leadership and middle class fought back and signed petitions to the king demanding his personal intervention and the punishment of those responsible for the semi-official campaign against them.

The regime and the ulama (1982-6)

The ulama's support for and legitimisation of the regime seemed even more important in a period of rising fundamentalism in the Muslim world. Even before his succession to the throne Fahd became convinced of the wisdom of accepting some of the ulama's demands concerning the enforcement of Wahhabi religious practices, as long as the ulama did not attempt to interfere with the kingdom's development and conduct of government. In reality, however, the pace of modernisation was slowed down in the early 1980s, and in some areas there was a marked regression from the relative liberalism introduced in the 1970s.

After his succession in June 1982, Fahd, not known for his piety in his younger days, attempted further to improve his relations with the ulama.

He now met, as did his predecessors, with the religious establishment in a weekly *majlis* and frequently consulted them on various matters. Inasmuch as he encouraged them to 'codify' laws 'in accordance with the needs of modern life' (within the context of the *shari'a*) he also prudently supported their efforts to protect the kingdom's Wahhabi character and 'Saudi way of life'. This meant, *inter alia*, that the largely uncouth Morality Police were permitted to intensify the enforcement of Islamic-Wahhabi laws in the kingdom's towns. Even Westerners in the Aramco enclaves in Al-Hasa were now exposed to their interference and not immune to *shari'a* punishment. King Fahd's policies also resulted in the expansion of religious studies within the 'secular' education system, stricter separation of sexes in the universities and reduced employment opportunities for women.[29]

As he advanced in age and gradually assumed the full responsibility of government, Fahd, it seems, had begun to appreciate the importance to the regime's stability of the conservative orientation of the Saudi populace and its acceptance of the principles of 'Islamic government' propagated by the ulama. Confronted by rising criticism of his regime by the intelligentsia and fundamentalists and increasingly also by the middle class, King Fahd decided to encourage the reorganisation and modernisation of the archaic Directorate for Islamic Propagation in order to improve the 'indoctrination' of the masses. Obviously the monarch hoped that better trained and educated *muttawwa'in* would also be more palatable to the new elites. His policy resembled, to a degree, that of Faysal, who brought the ulama into the fold of the establishment, yet Fahd lacked Faysal's pious reputation and authority and therefore could not force the ulama to accept his wishes.

Fahd's earlier readiness to safeguard the kingdom's 'Wahhabi character' and his declared opposition to 'Westernisation', helped win the ulama's co-operation. Although the younger, better-educated *'alims* were increasingly dissatisfied with the monarch's policy, nearly all the ulama were willing, even keen, to modernise the religious propagation apparatus and help carry out Fahd's indoctrination policy.

At the apex of the religious hierarchy, Shaykh Abd al-Aziz Al al-Shaykh, the head of the Committee for Encouraging Virtue and Preventing Vice, the most reactionary body in the kingdom, was thus co-opted by the king to modernise and upgrade the Morality Police. Returning to the original concept of the *muttawwa'in*, he undertook to train them for Islamic propagation and expand their activities in the different provinces in co-operation with the Ministry of the Interior. Simultaneously, Abd al-Aziz bin Baz, the reactionary president of the Administration of Scientific Study, [Religious] Legal Opinions, Islamic Propagation and Guidance, also helped the king's efforts to indoctrinate the rural population.[30]

By the mid-1980s King Fahd not only appeared as the protector of the special character of the 'Saudi–Wahhabi theocracy' but, making up for past reputation, he made an effort to project the image of an ideal Islamic ruler. Indeed, in October 1986 he officially adopted the title 'servant of the holy places' (*khadim al-haramayn*) instead of 'His Majesty'. Inasmuch as Fahd needed religious legitimacy at a time when his credibility was somewhat eroded, the establishment ulama also had a vested interest in the stability of the regime. This was an outcome of Iran's conquest of Iraq's Faw Peninsula in 1986 (below) which increased the threat to the Wahhabi kingdom and of the establishment ulama's determination to preserve Saudi Arabia's special character in the face of criticism by the middle-class elite on the one hand and a group of 'neo-fundamentalist' *'alims* on the other.[31]

While members of the royal family continued to indulge in excesses (after 1985), the economic recession was progressively eroding the standard of living of most other Saudis. The newly urbanised masses were particularly affected by the recession and had also become more aware of the Sauds' extravagances. The dissatisfaction of the rural and urban 'lower classes' was expressed through letters to the editor, often published in the Saudi press. A non-Saudi Muslim scholar, who visited Hijaz during this period, remarked that 'The sermons at Friday prayers in Mecca and Madina are filled with parables of Omar, the second Caliph, who was known for simple living and humility.'[32]

RULERS AND OPPOSITION IN THE 1980s

The succession of Fahd to the throne, and the struggle for power in the ruling class, signalled a resurgence of the activities of militant fundamentalists and leftist–nationalist circles in the kingdom, but especially in Al-Hasa. To make things worse, Saudi Arabia became the target of subversion and propaganda campaigns initiated by Iran and, to a lesser degree, by Syria, the PDRY (until 1984) and Libya. Radio broadcasts from, and agents of, these countries agitated against the royal family and the Sudayris in particular, emphasising the reactionary 'anti-Islamic' character of their regime and the squandering by the Sauds of the country's oil wealth.[33]

The opposition Saudi and leftist Arab press claimed in 1983-4 that many students, intellectuals, workers and members of the armed forces in Najran, Hijaz and particularly in the Eastern Province, had been incarcerated for participating in an 'abortive coup'. The organisations involved in the 'plots' against the regime, it seems, were the Union of Democratic Youth, the Socialist Workers Party and the Shi'ite-dominated IRO.[34]

By the 1980s, most of the original radical opposition organisations such as that of Nassir Sa'id (abducted by the Saudi intelligence services from Beirut in 1980) People's Democratic Party (formerly UPAP), the Free Saudis, and the offshoots of the Arab Nationalists (*Qawmiyyin al-'Arab*), had been replaced by, or had developed into, a number of small, extreme leftist-oriented or Marxist ones. These included the Saudi Communist Party, the Socialist Workers Party of the Arabian Peninsula (related to the Palestinian PFLP), the Union of Democratic Youth (related to the Palestinian PDFP) and a Syrian-related Ba'thist party. Each had, it seems, several hundred supporters among students, intellectuals and workers, largely in the Eastern Province but also in Hijaz and Asir (the Saudi diaspora's publications were the main source for information about their existence). By far the most important, however, judging by its publications and the number of its jailed members, was the Shi'ite IRO. The latter's ideology combined Iranian-inspired fundamentalism and radical socialism and was probably supported by Tehran.[35]

While accelerating efforts to improve the standard of living in Asir, the northern border regions and the Eastern Province and endeavouring to mollify Al-Hasa's Shi'ite community, the regime intensified its suppression of the militant opposition groups. This was facilitated by the modernisation of the Saudi security services with American help and through closer co-operation with the GCC countries.

Already in 1981 the Saudi government had installed in Riyadh, with French help, a central computer with a data bank and terminals in all airports, sea ports, major towns and the provinces. The US trained 400 Saudis to operate the interior ministry's National Information Centre (*Markaz al-Ma'lumat al-Watani*). With the help of this centre, the Passport Department, and the newly introduced identity cards, the ministry was now able to supervise both the millions of foreign residents in the kingdom and the Saudi citizens. The government, moreover, required the *'umda* of each neighbourhood, as it did the amirs of rural areas, to serve also as representatives of the security services.

Thousands of suspected members and sympathisers of the opposition groups, mainly in the Eastern Province, were questioned and hundreds incarcerated between 1982 and 1984.

A new wave of arrests of suspected members of the IRO and different leftist organisations, residing largely in the Eastern Province, began at the end of 1984. By 1986 the number of Saudi political prisoners was about 900. This is confirmed by a detailed list of political prisoners from the Eastern Province (but not Hijaz and Asir) arrested between 1982 and 1986, published jointly by Shi'ite and leftist-oriented Saudi opposition circles in London and New York.[36]

Many non-Saudi Arabs (mainly Palestinians) were deported from the kingdom in this period and replaced, it is claimed, by Pakistani and other non-Arab Muslims. This followed evidence of increasing co-operation between the Marxist factions of the PLO, their Saudi counterparts and Shi'ite fundamentalist organisations in Lebanon and the Gulf. Such co-operation led in 1984-5 to hijacking attempts on Saudi airlines, attacks on Saudi diplomats and embassies abroad, and attempts to smuggle weapons and explosives into the kingdom from neighbouring countries. Among those arrested were, it is alleged, students, intellectuals, members of the armed forces, workers and Aramco employees. The fact that 'Committees for the Defence of Political Prisoners in the Arabian Peninsula', which mushroomed in Britain, the USA and in some Middle Eastern countries, were jointly sponsored by the Shi'ite IRO and Arab nationalist-leftist organisations, vindicated claims that such co-operation existed throughout the 1980s.[37]

The small leftist opposition organisations in Saudi Arabia were based largely in the Eastern Province. Other than their publications abroad, their main activity in the kingdom was the distribution of leaflets. Occasionally they also sabotaged oil installations and police and government vehicles, planted bombs, and attacked the security forces. Their activities caused the authorities to adopt severe security measures in airports, government offices, military installations and even in hotels. At the end of 1984 the interior ministry established, moreover, a special force to protect such targets. In addition, in 1986 Aramco strengthened the security measures aimed at protecting American and European residential enclaves.[38]

Despite the above, it is evident that the regime's 'carrot-and-stick' policy proved quite successful. The majority of the Saudi Shi'ites were, by and large, satisfied with the government's new policy, although they would have wished for further improvement in their status, and sympathy for Iran's Islamic revolution has declined.[39] The size of the anti-regime organisations operating in the kingdom in the middle and latter part of the 1980s was far smaller than the size of the militant opposition to the regime of the 1950s and 1960s. Their operations were relatively inconsequential and to judge by what is said in the publications of the Committees for the Protection of the Rights of Political Prisoners in the Arabian Peninsula, the authorities were able to arrest most of their activists.

Fear of Tehran's propaganda and its military success, the vulnerability of the Saudi oil industry, and the size of the Shi'ite community in Al-Hasa, were probably responsible for the more liberal policy introduced by the Saudi authorities in the Eastern Province. The continued success of this new policy, which led to the province's rapid development and growth of its Shi'ite middle class, was, nevertheless, affected by the prolonged crisis in the oil industry and the decline of the kingom's oil revenues until 1989.

Middle-class elites in the mid-1980s – from co-operation to confrontation?

Far more serious than the militant opposition was the growing discontent with the regime on the part of middle-class new elites, whose size and potential power increased annually. Their dissatisfaction, especially in the Hijaz, emanated partly from their being excluded from political power, while the ulama were pampered and granted additional authority. Businessmen and entrepreneurs resented as well the numerous princes who competed with them or often forced themselves upon them as partners. Yet, as long as the kingdom prospered and everyone got a share of its wealth, they reconciled themselves to the situation. But as recession began to set in, both merchant-entrepreneurs and technocrats became increasingly outraged with the 'corrupt and extravagant Sauds' who were wasting the kingdom's patrimony and increasingly monopolising, as well, business opportunities and key positions in the central and provincial administration. The Hijazi new elites, moreover, were angered by the preference given by the Sauds to the Najdi technocrats.

Always the staunchest supporter of modernisation in the ruling-class inner circle and sympathetic to the middle-class new elites, King Fahd believed that their exclusion from participation in the kingdom's political system was the major source of their frustration. When he had tried to advance their cause in the past, however, he met with strong opposition from the senior princes and the ulama. The former opposed such a move because they believed that a change in the kingdom's political system would eventually erode the Sauds' power. The latter rejected any change in the *status quo*, because they feared that if the new elites were to gain access to decision-making, they would gradually change the character of the Saudi-Wahhabi state. Bound by the golden rule of consultation and consensus and lacking Faysal's power and prestige, Fahd gave in to the conservatives' pressure. He hoped, nevertheless, that in the long run the Sauds and the ulama would accept his proposed 'Islamic' national *majlis al-shura* and grant the new elites minimal participation in decision-making. As was the case in 1979/80, Fahd endeavoured in the meantime to keep the middle class within the regime's power base by reiterating his support for the elusive National Consultative Assembly.

Fahd was cognisant of the revolution which the Saudi society had undergone as a result of the kingdom's modernisation and the rapid development of its educational system. Though far from constituting a cohesive class,[10] the new elites, largely Hijazi and Najdi and to a lesser degree from the Eastern Province, numbered several hundred thousands. Indeed, in addition to bureaucrats (about 200,000) and professionals, the Association of Chambers of Commerce and Industry representing middle- and upper-level merchants and entrepreneurs already had in

1984 a membership of about 100,000 in eighteen branches in the kingdom's main cities.[41]

The growth of the Saudi Association of Chambers of Commerce and Industry is a case in point. The association is a legacy of the pre-Saudi Hijaz. Its nucleus was the Jedda chamber whose members after 1925 served in the new administration and proved most helpful to Ibn Saud and useful to his regent Faysal in dealing with foreign representatives and the kingdom's trade. When Faysal became king in 1964 members of the Hijazi Chamber of Commerce assisted him in developing the economy and modernising the kingdom. The organisation truly blossomed, however, in the 1970s, when it benefited from Saudi Arabia's rapid development and its enormous oil wealth.

The Council of the Saudi Chambers of Commerce and Industry, representing the upper layers of businessmen, industrialists and con-tractors, is located in Riyadh. It plays an essential role in consolidating middle-class support for the royal family and susbsequently is believed to enjoy a lot of influence over the regime. It is the only major organisation in the kingdom to elect its officers (two-thirds of its governing board are elected and a third are appointed by the minister of commerce), has its own publications and is permitted complete freedom within the scope of its interests.[42]

Still opposed to any form of professional organisations, the Saudi government in the second part of the 1980s gave its blessing to profes-sional congresses of university professors, engineers, doctors, pharma-cists, chemists and others, whose numbers in the kingdom had grown dramatically since the 1970s. In the first congress of engineers, which took place in Jedda, some participants proposed that the congress request government permission to form a professional organisation. Although the proposal was not adopted, it was another milestone in the process of consolidating the new elites' power in Saudi Arabia. Similar demands resurfaced in the wake of the Gulf war.[43]

Even before he was enthroned Fahd again attempted to win the Sauds' and the ulama's backing for a watered-down formula that would enable the middle-class elites to participate in decision-making. Using Ibn Saud's tactic of confronting the orthodoxy with Qur'anic precedents (or the lack of them), Fahd instructed Prince Na'if, in charge of the committee for 'political reforms', to extract from the Qur'an all the verses (about two hundred) relating to the principle of *shura*. These were to serve as a guideline for the proposed 'Islamic' National Consultative Council. Within a month of coming to power, King Fahd vowed that

the principles of the basic system of government and the con-sultative council . . . will, God willing, be in the forefront of the issues of concern to me . . . This will be accompanied or preceded by moves to bring to completion the necessary measures to put into force the provinces' law.[44]

Always the most liberal among the senior Sauds, Fahd was keen on winning the support of the expanding middle class. But once again, in the face of the royal family's and the ulama's opposition, and in view of the stronger role which the royal Consultative Council had exercised since 1983, the matter was shelved. None the less Iranian victories over Iraq, the growing unrest in the kingdom and the deteriorating state of the economy were probably partly responsible for the submission by Prince Na'if of his committee's recommendations in mid-1984. Those included a 'Basic Law of Government' (Qur'anic constitution) and the modernisation of the provincial administration. Each province was thus to have a partly elected assembly, some of whose members were to be members of the proposed, largely appointed, National Consultative Assembly.

On 12 September 1984, a tender was issued for the construction of the *majlis al-shura* building. Shortly afterwards King Fahd declared that the planned National Consultative Assembly 'whose members will be appointed, will begin to operate in the first months of 1985'. The role of the new 'parliament', Fahd continued, would be to 'express opinion and supervise the execution of government policy' and thus 'ensure the participation of the people in government'.[45]

In April 1985 the king again reassured his people that he intended soon to establish the promised National Consultative Assembly, 'composed of members drawn from the proposed partly elected provincial councils'. Although the king meant what he said, the delay in the implementation, of his promises, his supporters argued, was again the result of the strong opposition of the conservative members of Al Saud and the religious establishment.[46] Leading intellectuals, on the other hand, called this explanation a farce, claiming that the ruler could easily overcome the ulama's opposition had he truly wished to do so. Not only did such claims ignore the Saudi realities, especially at this stage of the Iran–Iraq war, but after the militant nationalist–fundamentalist Kuwaiti parliament was dissolved in mid-1986, the likelihood that the Sauds would agree to grant political participation to the middle-class elites further diminished.[47]

The tension between the middle class and the regime, and even between the latter and the technocratic upper-crust, reached a new climax immediately after Fahd's succession. Having willingly or unwillingly disregarded promises concerning political participation while increasingly appointing royal technocrats to high positions, the economic-financial nexus which held the middle class within the regime's power base was also beginning to crumble. As the kingdom's oil revenue declined from 108 billion dollars in 1981 to under 17 billion in 1986, the

Saudi budget was reduced to an estimated 45 billion in 1986, about half of its 1982/3 size. The balance was made up from income from other sources and from the kingdom's financial reserves. Considered by the new elites their national patrimony, particularly in view of the limited success of the costly Saudi industrialisation programme in the 1970s and early 1980s, the kingdom's liquid assets shrank from over 150 billion in 1982 to under 40 billion at the end of 1986.[48]

While the business community and entrepreneurs were displeased with the government for serving as OPEC's 'swing producer' and reducing government spending, the middle-class elites were critical of the regime's inflated 'political budgeting'. The size of the Saudi budget, many claimed, had no economic justification and was a by-product of the avidity of members of the royal family and the need of the rulers to 'buy' the people's goodwill and political influence in the Arab countries and the world.

As the kingdom's financial situation deteriorated, members of the technocratic upper-crust, largely Hijazis, often disagreed with the royal Consultative Council and the aristocratic cabinet members over policy matters. Some non-royal ministers even dared to challenge policy decisions related to finance made by their royal mentors. They, the middle-class as a whole and younger, university-educated 'non-conformist' ulama, increasingly criticised the excesses and corruption of members of the royal family and the system of commissions (sponsorship) and coerced partnerships, which enriched the ruling class (and the technocratic elites) but inflated the kingdom's budget and the cost of its development. Such excesses continued at the same time that ministries, other than defence and interior, were instructed to trim their expenditures and not to hire school graduates, when salaries were cut and bankruptcies became common.[49] To add insult to injury, some senior Sauds argued that the technocrats' policy and inefficiency were responsible, at least partly, for the difficulties which the kingdom faced.

The dependency of the technocratic upper-crust and the middle-class elites on the whims of the Saud rulers became now even more apparent, when cabinet ministers and leading technocrats, previously considered 'the pillars of the government', the majority of whom were Hijazis, resigned, were dismissed or were practically exiled. In most cases they were replaced by 'loyal' Najdi and other technocrats or by civil servants who were the Sudayris' old retainers.[50]

The first commoner to resign from the government *in protest* (unheard of in the past) was Abd al-Aziz al-Qurayshi, a member of a prominent Hijazi merchant family and the head of SAMA (with the rank of cabinet minister). Al-Qurayshi's resignation was caused by his strong objection to the proposed inflated budget for 1983/4, which would further drain the Saudi financial reserves. He was soon followed by Muhammad Abdu

Yamani, the Asiri information minister, who was dismissed because of the displeasure of the ulama and the Sauds with the way that he handled the domestic media and the coverage of the international press (Abdu Yamani was a signatory in 1991 of the liberal intelligentsia's 'open letter' to King Fahd requesting reform).[51]

The most significant cabinet change was the dismissal in 1984 of the 'leftist'-oriented minister of health (previously of industry and electricity), Dr Ghazi al-Gosaybi, universally regarded as the *doyen* of the Saudi intelligentsia. Al-Gosaybi, from a prominent Al-Hasa Sunni merchant family of Najdi origin, believed in the ability of the Sauds and the new elites to co-exist, yet was critical of the extravagance of the ruling class. Always supportive of Fahd's modernisation policy, he also praised him for truly delegating authority to his commoner ministers and his handling of the government, compared with Faysal's era. When he clashed with Prince Sultan over his misappropriation of the enormous defence budget, he naively hoped for the monarch's support. As such support did not materialise, Gosaybi dared to express his feelings in a poem which he managed to publish in a Saudi daily. For this act he was dismissed and was appointed ambassador to Bahrayn. (From there he counter-attacked in the late 1980s and early 1990s the rising tide of militant 'neo-fundamentalism' in the kingdom.)[52]

The most publicised dismissal of a senior Saudi technocrat was that of Zaki Yamani, the petroleum minister, followed by the discharge of his Hijazi friend and associate, Abdul Hadi Tahri, as head of Petromin (with the rank of a minister). Yamani's dismissal in October 1986 proved, if proof was needed, how insecure is the position of the technocratic uppercrust and the middle-class elites, when they incur the displeasure of the Sauds.

Yamani was hand-picked by King Faysal, as were many of the Hijazi commoner technocrats who served in the Saudi cabinets in the last three decades. This in itself did not endear him to the Sudayris and the ulama. Yet, his loyalty, expertise and international prestige made him invaluable to Fahd. His position was seriously eroded, however, when in 1984, during a serious crisis in the oil market, he strongly objected to Prince Sultan's 'oil for Boeings'[53] and similar barter deals. Yamani believed that such transations, meant to channel commissions to Sultan, his protégés and to other princes, would erode the kingdom's credibility in the oil market and its financial stability. When in 1986 his strategy for regaining Saudi Arabia's and OPEC's 'fair share of the market' backfired and oil prices collapsed to about nine dollars a barrel, Yamani was summarily dismissed by Fahd, although the king had supported his plan from its inception.

The Hijazis have seen their influence dwindle, as the new Najdi intelligentsia and royal technocrats have filled many of the prominent positions in the government and its bureaucracy. This seemed even more threatening because of the continuing pre-eminence of the conservative Najdi ulama, whose influence on the government, in addition to the traditional political censorship, increasingly stifled intellectual debate on religious, social and political matters. The Hijazi technocrats, merchants and entrepreneurs viewed Yamani's dismissal as another symptom of the erosion of their position and the 'Najdi-isation' of the government and economy, which followed King Faysal's assassination.[54]

The seat of the modern government had already been removed from Hijaz to Riyadh during the reign of Saud. It was followed in the 1970s by the migration of the headquarters of most foreign enterprises and several domestic ones from Jedda to Riyadh. The pattern repeated itself with most major banks in the early 1980s. By the mid-1980s, after the Foreign Office moved into its new headquarters in the capital, it was the turn of the foreign embassies, the forerunners of which were established in Jedda in the period preceding the Saudi conquest of the Hijaz, to move to Riyadh.[55] The departure of the embassies was received by the sophisticated and traditionally extrovert Hijazis as the supreme insult, particularly because the traditionally introvert and xenophobic Najdis had discouraged Westerners until the 1960s from even visiting Riyadh. Some Hijazis bitterly remarked that, if the Najdis could have, they would have removed the holy towns from the Hijaz to their province as well.

It is unlikely that the Hijazi middle class still entertains separatist tendencies (although some tiny groups do), which mean cutting themselves off from the kingdom's oil wealth. Yet, by virtue of their relative liberalism, and the fact that they constitute a majority of the new elites, they have become the vanguard of the growing middle-class criticism of the Sauds' regime. Such sentiments were nourished, for some time, by the growing success of the Najdi entrepreneurs and merchants. Indeed, as the recession in the kingdom spiralled, the exasperation of the Hijazi-led new elites with 'the traditional royal system of acquiring and distributing wealth', with the Sauds' government of the kingdom as a feudal fiefdom, and with their handling of the economic crisis markedly increased.[56]

The military as a component of the new elites

The modernisation and expansion of the Saudi armed forces since the 1960s made the House of Saud even less dependent on the traditional power brokers. It also reduced, by the 1970s, the importance of the lightly armed, undisciplined and inefficient National Guard, the conservatives' source of power. Younger members of the ruling elites increasingly joined the armed forces, especially the air force, and many were appointed to key positions in the latter.

Yet, despite the enormous investment in the 1970s and 1980s, largely in infrastructure for the Saudi armed forces (which enriched many Sauds), and to a lesser degree in the air force, the Saudi military remained weak and inefficient. They were also dependent on a polyglot host of foreign advisers, technicians and mercenaries. Their weakness and inefficiency was made apparant even in border clashes with the Yemens.

The multi-billion, systematic, qualitative and quantitative upgrading of the armed forces planned with American help, particularly since the mid-1970s,[57] necessitated the recruitment of many thousands of better-educated officers, and skilled NCOs, which the oligarchy was incapable of providing. The chronic shortage of suitable Najdis and related tribesmen to handle the progressively more sophisticated weapon systems, and apprehension at turning its armed forces into a 'foreign legion', forced the regime to enlist educated Hijazis and technically skilled Al-Hasa Sunnis. By setting up extensive security services and appointing many royal officers to key positions, and employing numerous foreign advisers and security experts (Americans and Europeans) and foreign mercenaries, the regime hoped to reduce the possibility of a military coup.[58] Plans to introduce universal (male) compulsory military service, reiterated by Prince Sultan possibly owing to the pressure of the middle class, were repeatedly postponed because the regime preferred to keep the armed forces small, loyal and manageable, through selective recruitment. The army, unlike the trusted National Guard, moreover, is largely kept in military towns in the peripheries of the kingdom.

The likelihood of an emergence of 'free officers' in the Saudi armed forces in the 1980s was minimal in view of the system of checks and balances instituted by the rulers, the elaborate security services and the substantial benefits enjoyed by officers and ranks.[59] Nevertheless, the gradually increased numbers of middle-class officers add another dimension to the tension between the new elites and the ruling class. The war with Iraq (1990/1) demonstrated, moreover, the ineffectiveness of the Saudi military, despite the enormous sums invested in it. This has shaken all classes of Saudis and the pressure for universal compulsory service is now coming even from the ranks of the ulama.

As revenue from oil and other sources fell short of the government's expenditures, and the kingdom's financial reserves continued to erode in the second half of the 1980s, the exasperation of the middle-class elites with the Sauds was rising. The newly cemented alliance of the regime with the ulama, for which the king opted in the face of the Iranian threat and the economic crisis, further exacerbated the new middle-class elites' dissatisfaction, as did the 'Saudi-isation' of the central and provincial government at a time of growing unemployment among the new intelligentsia. Apprehensive of the ramifications of change in the kingdom's power structure, the *ahl al-hal wa'l-'aqd*, moreover, were even less

120

likely, in the existing circumstances, to grant the middle class participation in decision-making which, they feared, could lead to the erosion of the Sauds' hegemony. Yet, as long as the war between Iran and Iraq continued, as did Shi'ite subversion in the kingdom, the Saudi new elites and the population as a whole closed their ranks behind Fahd's government, together with the whole of the royal family.

Part III

CRISES IN THE GULF

8

SAUDI ARABIA AND THE IRAN-IRAQ WAR

BACKGROUND

Existing in the shadow of Iran and Iraq – the two Persian Gulf giants – Saudi Arabia, with a population of about six million, attempted to walk the tightrope between the two after the British forces evacuated the region in 1971. Despite its power, emanating from oil wealth, Riyadh constantly felt insecure. It maintained close relations with Washington, invested heavily in defence and, from 1976 on, strove to establish an Arab Gulf co-operation alliance with Kuwait, Bahrayn, Qatar, the UAE and Oman, excluding Iraq. Its endeavours to create a conservative regional pact, however, met with opposition from Gulf states and members of the Saudi oligarchy and were criticised by Arab nationalists, as contradictory to the spirit of pan-Arabism.

In the late 1960s and 1970s, Saudi Arabia resented the Shah's high-handed policy in the Gulf which, while aimed at curbing Moscow's influence and its local allies' subversive activities in the Gulf, furthered Iran's national, and the Shah's personal, ambitions in the region. Riyadh was even more apprehensive about Iraq's pan-Arab socialist–Ba'thist aspirations.[1] From 1979 onward, however, Khomayni's Shi'ite fundamentalist regime, determined to export its revolutionary message to its Arab neighbours – all with large Shi'ite minorities – posed the greater threat. Indeed, the Saudi–Wahhabi state, with a large Shi'ite community in its oil-rich Eastern Province, felt particularly vulnerable.

Notwithstanding efforts to diversify its economy, Saudi Arabia remains largely dependent on revenue from oil and oil-related exports. The Eastern Province's oppressed Shi'ite population, largely barred from government employment and only minimally sharing in their country's wealth and privileges (until the mid-1980s), was especially receptive to Iranian propaganda. The latter, from 1979, questioned the very legitimacy of the Saudi regime and its right to protect Islam's holy shrines.

As discussed above,[2] Saudi Arabia experienced social, religious and political unrest in the late 1970s. Furthermore, in the struggle for power which erupted in the royal family after 1975, both conservatives and the 'younger', 'nationalist' princes, objected to the Sudayris' pro-American policy and stance in OPEC, which they claimed served Western, rather than Saudi and Arab, interests.

Fahd's unpopular pro-American policy was discredited by the Camp David agreement and the fall of the Shah of Iran. The first caused the collapse of the conservative moderate camp in the Arab League and the expulsion from it of Egypt. The second led to the rise of Khomayni's fundamentalist regime and seriously eroded American prestige and credibility in the region. Determined to export its revolution, Tehran, moreover, directed subversive propaganda and activities against Riyadh and the Gulf's other Arab regimes with sizeable Shi'ite citizenry.

The Iran-Iraq war which erupted in September 1980 could not have happened at a more opportune moment for Riyadh. Saudi Arabia was in a state of disarray. Despite vast investments in defence since the late 1960s, the Saudi armed forces were weak and incapable of protecting the kingdom against Iranian or Iraqi aggression. Saudi relations with the US were still shaky. Notwithstanding the change in the administration in Washington, Riyadh was doubtful if it could count on American assistance.[3] As the Iraqi army rolled into Iran, lured into a destructive eight-year war by Saddam Hussayn's belief that Tehran's Islamic revolutionary regime was about to collapse, Riyadh was free to put its house in order just before it faced the economic crisis of 1983-9.

Shortly after the war broke out Saudi Arabia, notwithstanding past differences, declared its unreserved support for its 'sister' Iraq. Fahd, it is believed, was informed in advance by Saddam Hussayn of his intention to invade Iran and at least approved, if not encouraged, the Iraqi plan. By this time Tehran's vicious anti-Saudi propaganda and subversive activities were beginning to have an impact on the kingdom's and the Gulf principalities' Shi'ites. An Iranian plot in 1981 to overthrow Bahrayn's ruler, involving Shi'ites from Al-Hasa trained by Tehran, caused serious concern in Riyadh regarding its regime's security.

The Iran-Iraq war diverted the attention of the two Gulf giants from Saudi Arabia and was, therefore, welcomed by Riyadh. It enabled Fahd to consolidate his power in the royal family and to deal with the kingdom's most pressing problems. The war, moreover, eroded the power of the radical Arab camp and caused Baghdad to woo the conservative Arab countries and, eventually, to improve its relations with Washington.

The war also provided the Saudi regime with a golden opportunity to improve its image in the kingdom and in the Arab world, badly tarnished in the late 1970s. Fahd attempted to foster an Arab consensus on the Iran-Iraq war by bridging the differences between Iraq and Syria and by rebuilding the power of the moderate Arab camp with Egypt returned to the Arab fold.

Cognisant of the strong anti-American sentiments in the Arab world and in the kingdom, Fahd, especially after the events of 1978/9, was careful to avoid any impression that he was promoting America's interests. Immediately after the outbreak of the Iran–Iraq war, he applied to President Carter for help but indicated his apprehension lest such aid be interpreted by Arab nationalists as an invitation to establish a US military presence in the kingdom or in the Gulf. The five AWACS which Washington despatched to Saudi Arabia, based at Dhahran, were admirably suited for the situation. They indicated, on the one hand, Washington's new determination to support its allies and, from a military point of view, were highly visible and useful. On the other hand, they necessitated only a limited American presence in the kingdom and did not awaken the wrath of the fundamentalists as did the massive American–Western presence in the kingdom a decade later. Soon afterwards, Riyadh acquired five AWACS of its own to replace the ones carrying the American emblem. None the less, this was a meaningful departure from the Saudi traditional vocal rejection of any American presence in the Gulf, based on apprehension about the reaction of Arab nationalists and its own conservatives and new elites.

In August 1981, Fahd announced an eight-point plan to resolve the Arab–Israeli conflict, which was soon abandoned when it met with Syrian and PLO opposition, in favour of a watered-down resolution adopted at the 1982 Fez summit. Yet, after his succession in June 1982, when victorious Iranian forces penetrated Iraq, and Tehran increasingly lashed out at the Arab countries which supported Baghdad, Fahd declared on several occasions that the Iran–Iraq conflict overshadowed the Arab–Israeli one because it more seriously threatened the Arab world. While basically wishing to focus Arab attention on the Gulf war, Fahd's policy aimed, as well, at winning American sympathy and the US Congress's approval of Saudi military requirements.

Earlier, in February 1981, the Iran–Iraq war enabled the Sudayris to establish the GCC, comprising Saudi Arabia, Kuwait, Bahrayn, Qatar, the UAE and Oman. Although it was officially an economic and cultural co-operation organisation, Riyadh strove to turn the GCC into a regional defence organisation which would co-ordinate the internal security activities of its members.[4] Ironically, Kuwait was the most reserved about the GCC and joined its mutual defence agreement only at the end of 1986. It also continued to object vociferously to any form of US presence in the Gulf.

The conservative faction of the Saudi oligarchy, led by Prince Abdallah (crown prince in 1982) who had befriended Syria, challenged the Sudayris' policies. This faction approved at first of the Islamic zeal of the new Iranian regime and admired its anti-Western and anti-Israeli stance. But as Tehran escalated its verbal attacks on the Sauds and the Wahhabi establishment, the conservatives turned their backs on Tehran and opted for a neutral policy in the Gulf war.

The younger and better-educated third-generation Saudi princes, led by Saud al-Faysal, always advocated that their country strengthen its ties with the 'nationalist' Arab camp and improve its relations with Moscow – at the expense of its relations with Washington. Sympathetic at first to Iran's revolution and its anti-American, anti-Israeli policy, they opposed its fundamentalist character. They also advocated that Riyadh remain neutral in the Gulf war and opposed its involvement with the conservative GCC. This camp was critical, as well, of the Sudayris' oil policy which, it claimed, served Western interests by glutting the market and commended Iran's demand that OPEC reduce production to raise oil prices.

IRAN–IRAQ WAR AND SAUDI POLICY – STAGE ONE (1981–6)

Three interrelated objectives dominated Fahd's considerations in formulating his Gulf policy: the need to protect the kingdom; the wish to maintain the regime's stability and to uphold the Sudayri hegemony in Riyadh; and, lastly, the kingdom's dedication to Islamic and Arab solidarity. Matters were somewhat complicated by disagreement within Al Saud over Fahd's policy, and, within the GCC and other Arab countries, over the question of solidarity with (Arab) Iraq fighting (Persian) Iran.

Major constraints, some inherent and some the result of new economic and political dynamics, were also taken into account by Fahd. Foremost was Saudi Arabia's sparse population and the weakness of its armed forces in relation to its vast area. The kingdom's vulnerability was further increased by the fact that its economy (and that of all the GCC countries), and ultimately its stability, were largely dependent on its oil revenues. Indeed, all Saudi oil was located in the Eastern Province (until 1989, when the discovery of new oil fields south of Riyadh was disclosed) with its large Shi'ite population just across the Persian Gulf from Iran. Moreover, from the first days of the war the Iranian navy dominated the Gulf and the Straits of Hormuz, the only outlet for the region's oil and shipping in general.[5]

The Saudi stance regarding the Gulf war seemed consistent. Riyadh unreservedly supported Iraq from the outbreak of the war in September 1980 and throughout its eight years. In 1981, when the tide began to turn against Baghdad, Riyadh and Kuwait began to subsidise Iraq's war effort and to help it logistically to resist Iran (and thus to protect themselves).

At the same time they repeatedly attempted to appease Tehran and supported or initiated various efforts to terminate the war through Islamic or Third World mediation or United Nations intervention.

In reality, Riyadh's policy was pragmatic, influenced by the fortunes of the war and their effect on Saudi interests. An outcome of the Saudi regime's golden rule of *shura* and *ijma'* (consultation and consensus), it reflected as well the different opinions within the Saudi ruling class. In the final analysis, Riyadh's policy was determined by Fahd and his informal *majlis al-shura*, dominated by his Sudayri brothers.

A staunch advocate of Arab (moderate) solidarity since the 1970s and fearing Iran's extreme fundamentalism, Fahd could not but support Iraq, especially when the tide turned against it at the end of 1981. The Saudi people, sensitive to any external threat to Arab territory, largely sympathised with Iraq and disagreed with demands for a more neutral stance in the Gulf war, as advocated by Arab radicals and elements within the Saudi ruling class and intelligentsia. Although Muslims, the Iranians were 'abhorred' Shi'ites and aroused memories of historic confrontations between Arabs and Persians, Sunnis and Shi'ites. Iranian Shi'ite fundamentalism, based on Imam Khomayni's principle of 'Governance of the Jurist' (*vilayat faqih*), was anathema both to the Wahhabi ulama and to the Saudi new elites. The Iranians, moreover, antagonised the Saudi population by political demonstrations during the hajj season (starting in 1981) in Islam's holiest towns. Such events caused the great majority of Saudis rather to coalesce behind their rulers and the ulama and to support Fahd's Gulf policy.

Iraq had been a most troublesome neighbour to Arabia's conservative regimes before 1980 and twice (1960, 1973) had attempted to annex Kuwait, whose territory, it asserted, was historically hers. Nor did Baghdad renounce its militant Ba'th ideology, its claim to be the vanguard of socialist pan-Arabism in the Gulf or its alliance with 'atheist' Moscow. Thus, although Riyadh constantly advocated ending the Gulf war through negotiations, it was not totally displeased (until the beginning of 1986) with the stalemate in the battle front which exhausted both combatants. Furthermore, as Baghdad became more dependent on its conservative neighbours' aid it courted Riyadh, improved its relations with the US and, ironically, considering its crusade to expel Egypt from the Arab camp in 1978/9, it gradually came to support Saudi endeavours to bring Egypt back into the Arab fold.

When things began to go badly for Baghdad at the end of 1981, the war with Iran was portrayed by Iraq as a new 'Persian invasion of the Arab world' and it clamoured for help from its Arab sister states. Riyadh and its GCC allies also became increasingly worried about Tehran's subversive activities among their Shi'ite subjects. Hence, Saudi Arabia solicited the good offices of the ICO (Islamic Conference Organisation), the non-aligned countries and the UN to end the war. At the same time, together with Kuwait, Saudi Arabia expanded financial and logistic assistance to Iraq (total cost about 40 billion dollars). Kuwait was exceptionally valuable to Iraq because Tehran had blockaded Iraq's only outlet to the sea and brought its oil exports to a virtual stand-still, not to mention its supply of war material. Its neighbours' financial help was crucial because Baghdad was incapable of conducting a protracted war without it, as it was unable to export its oil. To add insult to injury, 'sisterly' Ba'thist Syria under Hafiz al-Assad not only supported Iran but also stopped the flow of Iraq's oil to its Mediterranean terminals through the pipeline crossing its territory.

With a stalemate emerging in the Gulf war between 1982 and 1983, after Iran had reconquered all the territory it had lost to Iraq, the Saudis intermittently encouraged new mediation attempts to end the war, but to no avail because Iran's demands included the removal of President Saddam Hussayn from office. This period, moreover, witnessed rising tension in the Saudi royal family following Fahd's succession. Subsequently, in addition to endeavours to appease Tehran and luke-warm attempts to improve relations with it (and with Moscow[6]), Riyadh also increased its efforts to bridge the differences among the Arabs concerning the Iran–Iraq war and Egypt's rehabilitation. Although it was obliged, together with Kuwait, to increase aid to Baghdad, Riyadh was not displeased with the no-win situation in the war.[7]

The third phase of the war, beginning in 1984, was signalled by increased Iranian efforts to penetrate Iraq's heartland and to cause its Shi'ite (Arab) majority population to rise against Saddam Hussayn's Sunni minority regime. It was also highlighted by Iraq's launching, in March 1984, of tanker warfare aimed at undermining Iran's ability to sustain its war effort. This development soon began to have an impact on Saudi Arabia and Kuwait, whose shipping became the target of Tehran's retaliatory attacks (May and July 1984 and February 1985) because of the two countries' growing aid to Iraq. Repeated Iranian violation of Kuwaiti and Saudi territorial water and air space culminated in June 1984 when Saudi F–15s shot down two Iranian F–4s which approached the kingdom's Eastern Province.[8] The low-profile treatment of such incidents was typical of the kingdom's timid policy. It was related, as well, to the GCC's efforts, spearheaded by the UAE and Oman, to improve relations with Iran. Yet, simultaneously, Riyadh wished to indicate clearly to Tehran the 'red line' which, if transgressed, would cause Saudi Arabia to hit back. Obviously, in such an event the Saudis hoped for US military intervention, but Washington's Gulf policy was still ambivalent.[9]

With its large Palestinian community and its parliament dominated by a nationalist–fundamentalist group, and hosting a large and the only

Soviet embassy in the GCC, Kuwait frequently and vociferously condemned US Middle Eastern policy and American 'plots' in the Gulf.[10] Riyadh, also, overtly rejected any superpower's presence in the Persian Gulf but covertly implored American statesmen and diplomats to maintain a strong presence 'over the horizon', meaning in the Arabian Sea and at their Diego Garcia base, in case of an emergency. Despite increasing financial difficulties, the Saudis continued as well the construction of a huge military infrastructure, far beyond the requirements of their inconsequential armed forces. In addition, Prince Bandar ibn Sultan (the minister of defence's son) was appointed ambassador to Washington to liaise directly between the Sudayris and the US government, thus bypassing Saud al-Faysal, the minister of foreign affairs.[11]

Notwithstanding Iranian attempts to assassinate Kuwait's amir and to smuggle weapons into Saudi Arabia in 1985, Riyadh, in addition to encouraging mediation attempts, stepped up its efforts to appease Tehran. This policy was welcome to the advocates within the Saudi ruling class of a more neutral stance in the Gulf war. In so far as the kingdom's Gulf policy was entrusted to Prince Na'if, the 'creator' of the GCC, and to King Fahd, who co-ordinated with Saddam Hussayn, the person in charge of relations with Iran was Saud al-Faysal. Thus, in May 1985 the latter visited Tehran reciprocating visits to Riyadh by Iranian ministers and officials.[12] Indeed, the regent, Prince Abdallah, was also recruited to help improve relations with Iran, utilising his special connections with Syria, Iran's foremost friend in the Arab camp.

To win Tehran's goodwill and Washington's favour, Riyadh, through Prince Bandar, paradoxically became involved in 1985/6 in Washington's attempt to improve relations with Tehran and to free the American hostages through a limited supply of arms to Iran, which led to its involvement (still not fully known) in the Iran–Contra fiasco. Saudi Arabia not only facilitated the flying of American weapons to Iran but itself sold the latter badly-needed refined oil products.[13] On its part, Tehran replaced its pilgrimage director who had enraged the Saudis, and in 1986 intervened with the Lebanese Hizbollah to free a Saudi diplomat abducted in Beirut.[14] Yet, all the Saudi efforts to end the Iran–Iraq war were doomed because Tehran insisted that Iraq be pronounced the aggressor in the war and that Saddam Hussayn be removed from power in Baghdad.

The relative stalemate in the Iran–Iraq war came to an end in February 1986 with the conquest by Iran of the Faw Peninsula, the larger part of Iraq's Persian Gulf coast, and by renewed Iranian efforts to take Basra. Iranian soldiers were now virtually positioned on Kuwait's border, a short distance from Saudi Arabia's Eastern Province and its oil fields. Tehran, thereafter, often threatened Riyadh and Kuwait that it would attack them unless they ceased their massive financial and logistic assistance to Iraq. The Iranians now occasionally violated Kuwaiti territory and escalated their attacks on both countries' tankers. Iranian-backed subversive Shi'ite groups also intensified their terrorist activities in Kuwait and in Saudi Arabia's Eastern Province.[15]

Baghdad's inability to stop Tehran and counter the religious zeal of the 'human waves' tactic of the Iranian Revolutionary Guard and Basji volunteers terrified Riyadh (and Kuwait). A Saudi nightmare was that an Iranian victory would produce a fundamentalist Shi'ite regime in Baghdad. Alternatively, that Iran would conquer Kuwait and invade Saudi Arabia's Eastern Province, or sabotage its oil fields with the help of local Shi'ites. All along, Tehran had the ability seriously to damage the Saudi oil industry or to stop the passage of tankers and ships going to and from its ports. Such a radical step, it was widely believed, would cause a strong American reaction. Yet, in view of Washington's poor track record, Riyadh was uncertain if it was truly willing to act against Iran. Even if the US were to intervene, Riyadh feared that such intervention would come too late to prevent the eruption of unrest in the kingdom and the destruction of its oil industry. All this also prompted Riyadh's appeasement policy towards Tehran and led to the relatively frequent meetings between Saudi and Iranian personalities in 1985/6.

The conquest of Iraq's Faw Peninsula by Iran in 1986 was, undoubtedly, a turning point in Riyadh's policy concerning the Iran-Iraq war. It now became imperative for Saudi Arabia and Kuwait to terminate the war as soon as possible, by all means, before it could spill over into their territories. As Tehran refused to agree to an unconditional cease-fire, Riyadh and Kuwait were determined to strengthen their and Iraq's ability to resist Tehran's power and to gain universal Arab support for their position.[16] Egypt's rehabilitation and inclusion in the GCC's defence plans now became more desirable than ever before. Furthermore, although Washington began to suffer the results of the disclosure of its dealings with Tehran (the 'Irangate' fiasco), King Fahd again turned to the United States for low-profile help. His request received immediate attention.

Shocked into action by Washington's near success in improving its relations with Tehran, still considered the most important strategic asset in the region, Moscow, despite the opening of a new era in US–USSR relations, increased its efforts to win Iran's (and the GCC countries') friendship. Thus, the Soviet deputy foreign minister, Gregory Kornyenko, visited Tehran in August. Shortly afterwards, Iran's deputy foreign minister, Muhammad Jawad Larijani, arrived in Moscow to discuss political and economic agreements between the two countries.[17]

Notwithstanding Iran's endeavours to undermine Kuwait's stability and attacks on Kuwaiti and Saudi shipping, Riyadh continued, in line with its timid traditional policy, to avoid confrontation with Tehran and to keep its criticism low-key. At the same time, it stepped up its efforts to purchase sophisticated weapons in the West and, in 1986, secretly acquired from China CSS2 ballistic missiles with a range of about 1,650 miles. Unwillingly at first, Riyadh facilitated Iraq's air strikes against Iranian oil terminals near and beyond Hormuz.[18] Even earlier Saudi Arabia hesitantly began to improve its relations with the Soviet Union, a step welcomed by some younger princes and the nationalist-oriented element in the intelligentsia. Following the establishment of diplomatic relations between Moscow and the UAE and Oman (1985), Soviet officials began to visit Riyadh and other GCC capitals.

An additional factor which made the conclusion of the Gulf war a priority for Riyadh was the severe recession experienced by the kingdom as a result of the sharp decline of oil sales and prices, which affected the Saudi expenditure budget (slashed from over 90 billion dollars in 1982 to 37.5 in 1987, while revenue from oil declined from 108 billion dollars to 17.8 billion dollars in the same period).[19] Thus, as previously mentioned, many Saudi businessmen and entrepreneurs faced growing cash-flow difficulties or went bankrupt. Inasmuch as Riyadh endeavoured to protect the 'lower-income' Saudis from hardship, it reduced, by various means, some subsidies on consumer goods and increased indirect taxation. By mid-1987, Riyadh took steps to curb the growth in the number of students in domestic and foreign universities and its expenditure on them. Many graduates were unable, moreover, to find work, following the government's decision in 1987 to freeze the hiring of new employees.[20]

Concerned about restless, unemployed intelligentsia and a dissatisfied middle class, King Fahd hoped that, if the war was ended, Saudi Arabia could discontinue its multi-billion aid to Baghdad and be better able to restrain both OPEC and non-OPEC producers. In the meantime, Iran's conquest of the Faw Peninsula generated fear in all classes of Saudis. While the oligarchy closed its ranks behind King Fahd, the population tightened its belts and generally adjusted to the new situation and, hoping for better days, supported the regime.

Riyadh's relations with Tehran in OPEC were, at best, strained. While Iran wished to maximise oil revenues by reducing production and raising prices, Saudi Arabia firmly believed that reasonable oil prices and co-operation between producers and consumers in the industrial countries were essential for long-range market stability and its own security. Riyadh also wished, until the end of 1986, to penalise non-OPEC producers who increased their output and glutted the market at OPEC's expense. King Fahd's policy, which, after 1986, dramatically reduced the price of oil, was considered by Iran and Arab nationalists a betrayal of the producers' interests in order to benefit the Western economy. The Saudi oil policy, in conjunction with Iraq's air offensive, may have aimed, as well, at reducing Iran's revenues from oil drastically and thus coercing it to agree to peace terms acceptable to Iraq.[21]

The 'fair share of the market' policy, which caused oil prices to collapse to about nine dollars a barrel in the last months of 1986, threatened Saudi Arabia's economic stability and standard of living. This caused growing discontent in the Saudi aristocracy and middle class. Fahd's competence as a ruler was questioned by many. Some even opined that he, as had been the case with Saud, should be replaced by a more capable member of the family or that the Saudi government system should be reformed. The monarch, on his part, fired Yamani and agreed to a pricing and quota formula for OPEC, acceptable to Tehran and the other members which, by the beginning of 1987, somewhat stabilised oil prices at about 12–13 dollars a barrel.[22] By this time, Riyadh's ability and willingness to subsidise Baghdad's war effort had markedly diminished.[23]

Following the Irangate fiasco, Tehran became more receptive to Moscow's wooing. Senior Soviet and Iranian officials visited each other's capitals and it was rumoured that in addition to discussing economic and political agreements, Moscow was willing to sell Tehran sophisticated arms. That, together with the continued Iranian insistence on peace conditions unacceptable to Iraq, and Iran's increasing belligerence in the Gulf, caused King Fahd to explore again the possibility of American help.

Following Faw's conquest and frequent Iranian threats against Kuwait and Riyadh in 1986, the Saud and Al-Sabah rulers began seriously to consider Iraq's previously rejected strategy to de-escalate the Gulf conflict by internationalising it through superpower involvement. Traditionally suspicious of Moscow, Riyadh was reluctant to adopt a strategy that could advance Soviet interests in the area. Hence, while Saudi Arabia again vocally condemned the great powers' involvement in the Gulf, Prince Bandar was discussing with Washington options to counter the Iranian threats and Soviet aspirations in the region.

The second part of 1986 witnessed intensified Iranian attempts to conquer Basra, Iraq's second largest city. Tehran announced its intention to launch a new 'final' offensive against Iraq at the end of the year. On its part Baghdad escalated its strategic bombing of Iran proper and its oil installations in the Gulf. These developments, and the Saudi–Kuwaiti support for them, led Tehran to intensify its retaliatory attacks on their shipping and its anti-Saudi propaganda. As the morale of the Iraqi army and population was generally believed to be at a low ebb, Riyadh feared that if Iran were to launch its much-heralded offensive, Iraqi resistance might collapse. To counter Tehran's propaganda attacks against the Saudi regime and his own piety, King Fahd, *inter alia*, adopted the title of 'Servant of the two Holy Shrines', instead of 'His Majesty', and further strengthened the authority of the ulama's Morality Police.

The rumoured agreement on the sale of Soviet sophisticated arms to Iran caused apprehension in Saudi Arabia. So did Tehran's increasing intimidation of Kuwait and Iranian-sponsored sabotage incidents in the kingdom in the second part of 1986. Subsequently, Kuwait's ruler, Shaykh Jabir al-Sabah, giving in to lengthy Saudi pressure, dissolved in mid-1986 Kuwait's parliament, which had been dominated by nationalist-fundamentalists (it was previously dissolved in 1975 and re-established in 1980), and later signed the GCC's mutual defence pact. Most important, in consultation with Riyadh and in defiance of Iran, Kuwait decided at year's end to seek the superpowers' help.

A GCC summit meeting held in Ta'if (Saudi Arabia) at the beginning of 1987 approved Kuwait's chartering of three Soviet tankers which Moscow undertook to protect, and its intention to negotiate a similar agreement with Washington. However, when informed that the US did not have any tankers, Kuwait agreed to register its own tanker fleet in the US and reflag it to enable America to protect it in the Gulf. This was a total reversal of Kuwait's and Riyadh's oft-repeated rejection, meant to please Arab nationalists, of any superpower presence in the Gulf. It was also a serious challenge to Tehran's hegemony in the Persian Gulf and, indirectly, a rebuff to Moscow's aspirations in the region.

By sanctioning Kuwait's plan, the Saudi-led GCC *de facto* adopted Iraq's strategy to internationalise the Gulf conflict. King Fahd who was aware of, if not deeply involved in, the formulation of Kuwait's plan from its inception, had secretly desired a meaningful American presence in the region all along. The Kuwaiti scheme now enabled the Saudi and Kuwaiti rulers to seek American protection and presence in the Gulf with relative impunity and with minimal Soviet involvement. Riyadh, nevertheless, cynically continued, in 1987, to declare its displeasure at Kuwait's decision to invite the US navy to the Gulf.[24]

While Kuwait's proposal was being debated by the GCC in December 1986 and January 1987, Hisham Nazir, the new Saudi petroleum minister, visited Moscow, ostensibly to win Soviet support for the latest OPEC agreement aimed at stabilising oil prices, which was obviously welcomed by the Soviets. Nazir's visit was meant as well to signal Riyadh's willingness to improve relations with Moscow, gauge Moscow's reaction to the Kuwaiti plan and learn details about Soviet-Iranian negotiations.

Although both Riyadh and Moscow wished to end the Iran-Iraq war, their motivations were diametrically opposed. Moscow, wishing to develop friendly relations with both Tehran and Baghdad, could gain nothing from the prolongation of the conflict. The Soviet Union preferred to refocus Arab attention on the Arab-Israeli conflict, where it could benefit from its pro-Arab stance. In contrast, Riyadh wished to draw Arab attention to the Gulf war and away from the Arab-Israeli conflict. Nor did Riyadh wish to see the USSR replacing the US in

Tehran or gaining a foothold in the Gulf. Rather Riyadh wished to free Baghdad from Moscow's 'stranglehold' and draw it into a moderate pro-Western axis along with Egypt and Jordan.

ENTER THE SUPERPOWERS – STAGE TWO (1986–8)

A new stage in the Iran–Iraq war began in March–April 1987 after Washington had officially agreed to protect the reflagged Kuwaiti tankers and despatched a powerful armada to the Arabian Sea. Prudently, Saudi Arabia and Kuwait refused to grant facilities to the American fleet, which reached the area by mid-1987. Besides bases leased from Britain in Oman, America was covertly granted some support facilities by both Saudi Arabia and Kuwait. In addition to the AWACS based in Dhahran, the US navy used large floating platforms, anchored off Kuwaiti and Saudi territorial water, as service depots for its warships.[25] Riyadh also approved Bahrayn's decision to enable the US to upgrade its small naval base there, near Ras Tanura on the Saudi mainland and not far from Kuwait.

Tehran, in the meantime, escalated its attacks on Kuwaiti and Saudi ships. In May, a Soviet freighter was shelled and a Soviet tanker hit a mine. Shortly after his return to Moscow from a tour of Oman, UAE, Kuwait and Iraq on 2 June, the Soviet deputy foreign minister Vladimir Petrovsky strongly criticised Tehran.[26] None the less, a few weeks later, Moscow pragmatically renewed its attempts to win Iran's friendship.

Riyadh now felt sufficiently secure to adopt a more bellicose stance in its relations with Iran, abandoning its traditional timid and hesitant foreign policy. It intensified its effort to win Arab consensus to coerce Iran to end its 'aggression' against its Arab neighbours. Exploiting Syria's economic crisis, it tried to entice Damascus away from Tehran, promising President Assad generous financial aid.[27] The escalation in the 'tanker war' and Washington's and Moscow's involvement in it, moreover, prompted the Security Council to produce on 20 July Resolution 598, which called upon Iran and Iraq to declare a cease-fire. The Council agreed, as well, to 'meet again as necessary to consider further steps to ensure compliance'.[28] Baghdad immediately acquiesced but Tehran delayed its answer, again demanding that Iraq first admit to being the aggressor and that Saddam Hussayn be removed from office.

As Iran did not comply with the Security Council's resolution, Washington proposed that the Council declare a mandatory arms embargo against it. The proposal was blocked by the Soviet (and Chinese) delegate, claiming that diplomatic means were not exhausted, thus showing the USSR's displeasure with the Saudi–American handling of the situation. Indeed, the Iranian deputy foreign minister Larijani signed in Moscow in July a general agreement for economic and political co-operation between Iran and the Soviet Union. The two sides also condemned the US naval presence in the Gulf and 'anonymous' Soviet officials expressed concern over Iraq's continued air attacks on Iran, despite the Security Council's call for a cease-fire.

The deterioration of relations between Riyadh and Tehran came to a climax on 30 July with the bloody suppression in Mecca of a violent demonstration by Iranian pilgrims. At the day's end, 408 people, largely Iranians, were dead and many more wounded. Putting the blame squarely on Tehran, Riyadh rejected claims that its security forces had indiscriminately opened fire on the rioters near Islam's holiest shrines. On their part, Iran's leaders claimed that a 'Saudi–American plot' was responsible for the massacre.[29] Indeed, some evidence indicates that the incident was not a spontaneous one.

Iranian demonstrations accompanied by rioting and sabotage attempts had occurred in Mecca in previous years.[30] Yet, they never caused the Saudis to react so violently. This time Riyadh not only brought beforehand to Mecca units of its special forces and National Guard but, it is claimed, a Jordanian anti-terrorist battalion was also positioned there.[31] 'Amateur' photographers, 'fortuitously' present at the site of the rioting, conveniently supplied the Saudis with video film of the event, released immediately to TV networks and shown all over the Muslim world. Thus, it seems that the incident may have been orchestrated by a more confident and assertive Riyadh, intent on stopping Iranian political and subversive activity in its territory and on winning Arab and Muslim support for its policy. Hereafter, Riyadh no longer attempted to appease Iran or hide its efforts to coerce the latter to end the Gulf war on terms acceptable to Iraq.[32]

When they were informed of what had happened in Mecca, angry Iranian crowds stormed the Saudi embassy and caused the death of a Saudi diplomat. A new wave of terrorist activities erupted in Saudi Arabia and Kuwait.[33] Simultaneously Tehran directed a vitriolic propaganda crusade against Riyadh, challenging the House of Saud's legitimacy and suitability to serve as the guardian of Islam's holy shrines. The Saudi regime, described by Ayatollah Khomayni as 'infidel', was also accused of serving American and Israeli interests in the region (an accusation repeated by Arab Sunni and Shi'ite radicals in 1990/1). This campaign was accompanied by threats to punish Saudi Arabia for its 'sins' and for its support, together with Kuwait, or Iraq.

At home, King Fahd endeavoured to project an even more pious image by granting additional authority to the ulama and reducing the profile of Western, especially American, presence in the kingdom. He also exerted himself to win the Shi'ite community's favour through accelerated development, by lifting discriminatory restrictions and by granting amnesty to political prisoners. Fahd's son, Muhammad, the Eastern

Province's governor, convincingly demonstrated the regime's determination to crush with an iron fist any plot against it. Thus, Saudi Shi'ites hardly reacted to the Mecca massacre.[34] On the other hand, the Hizbollah and its offshoots stepped up their terror campaign against Saudi targets world-wide.

The July 1987 Mecca riots, followed by violent Iranian threats against Saudi Arabia, served further to consolidate King Fahd's regime. The Saudi oligarchy and modern elites, who coalesced behind the king immediately after the conquest of the Faw Peninsula, now fully endorsed his assertive policy *vis-à-vis* Iran and his endeavours to win Arab and Western support to end the Gulf war.

As the economic recession deepened and oil revenue declined in 1987 to about 18 billion and government expenditure to less than 37 billion dollars, all classes of Saudis and the private sector of the economy experienced increasing hardship. Among other things, the administration reduced subsidies and allocations to higher education and further limited the hiring of university graduates by the administration and government agencies. Although the government even attempted to cut subsidies for foodstuffs and services, Fahd prudently continued to protect the standard of living of 'lower-income' Saudis. The monarch, furthermore, instructed administrators to improve services to citizens and to handle their requests more efficiently.[35] All the above notwithstanding, the great majority of the Saudi masses and intelligentsia, not to mention the ruling class, were supportive of the regime's policy as they felt threatened by the Persian Shi'ites' power, now practically next door. Nevertheless, criticism of the behaviour, avidity and 'corruption' of members of the artistocracy was quite common among the intelligentsia and younger, better-educated, 'non-conformist' ulama.[36]

Exploiting the widespread condemnation of Iran in the Muslim world, Riyadh wished to win Arab endorsement for its tough anti-Iranian stance. It again attempted to entice Damascus away from Tehran and to bridge Syria's differences with Iraq. It also endeavoured to persuade Damascus to attend an Arab summit which it wished to convene and which it hoped would decide to boycott Iran and bring Egypt back into the Arab fold. While Crown Prince Abdallah aptly 'lobbied' Syria, Algeria and the UAE, Prince Saud al-Faysal, failing to persuade the Arab League's foreign ministers' meeting in Tunis in August to adopt a strong anti-Iranian resolution, managed, nevertheless, to get the meeting to request the Security Council to take immediate steps against Iran for disregarding its resolution.[37]

Although the massive American presence in the Gulf altered the regional balance of power and limited Iran's options, it soon became apparent to Riyadh that its problems were not over. In July, Iran captured the Hajj Omran heights in Kurdistan. Shortly afterwards it launched an abortive offensive from Mehran in the direction of Baghdad. Tehran's defiance of Washington was demonstrated by its mining of maritime routes used by the US navy. A reflagged Kuwaiti supertanker in the first escorted convoy hit a mine on 26 July. US prestige was further damaged in mid-October when the Iranians fired Scud missiles at Kuwait harbour on two consecutive days, hitting an American tanker on the first and damaging a decoy target on the second. Yet, when asked about the matter while visiting Riyadh, Secretary of State Schultz advised Kuwait to complain about the matter to the Security Council as Tehran had attacked Kuwait's territory, not covered by its agreement with the US.[38]

The GCC, somewhat disillusioned with Washington's attitude, despatched a high-level delegation to Moscow in September, followed by Kuwait's foreign minister accompanied by senior officials. Both missions, particularly the Kuwaiti, requested Moscow to use its influence to stop Iran's attacks on Kuwait and to support a UN arms embargo against Tehran, which the Soviets had long opposed.

At the beginning of October, a flotilla of armed Iranian speedboats penetrated Saudi territorial water and was chased away by the Saudi air force and navy. Later in the month, a Saudi offshore oil field near Kuwait was sabotaged by a pro-Iranian Shi'ite underground group. When Iran escalated its attacks on Saudi and Kuwaiti tankers in retaliation for Iraqi strikes against its oil installations, Riyadh unsuccessfully requested the US, Britain and France to protect its tankers on a basis similar to the Kuwaiti arrangement with Washington. As the situation continued to deteriorate, the Saudis again pressured Washington and other members of the Security Council to declare an arms embargo against Iran. Such efforts were doomed to failure because the Soviets were displeased with the Saudi support for the Pax Americana in the Gulf. Riyadh again attempted, therefore, to activate its Arab and Muslim sisters.

The meeting of the Arab League's summit in Amman in November 1987 was an important achievement for Saudi diplomacy. Through Riyadh's efforts, the Gulf war now became the focus of Arab interest, rather than the Arab–Israeli conflict, something Riyadh had sought to bring about since the early stages of the Iran–Iraq war. Although Egypt was not readmitted to the League as Riyadh wished, each Arab country was now free to resume unilaterally its relations with Cairo. Thus, shortly after the summit, Saudi Arabia and the other Arab states, with the exception of Syria, Libya and Algeria, joined the ones which had already resumed their relations with Cairo, despite the fact that Egypt had not rescinded its peace accords with Israel. On the other hand, although the summit agreed to monitor Iranian 'aggression' closely, and to reconvene if Tehran were to threaten its Arab neighbours' security, Syria managed to block any decision to adopt concrete measures against Iran. Damascus undertook, nevertheless, to persuade Tehran to agree to a cease-fire.

Riyadh was aware of Moscow's displeasure with its exclusion from the 'policing' of the Gulf. Convinced that the Security Council could not act without its co-operation, and fearing that the Moscow–Tehran *rapprochement* would enable Tehran to obtain Soviet weapons, and particularly Scud missiles, the Saudis despatched a high-level delegation, led by Prince Saud al-Faysal, to Moscow in February 1988.

Not by chance, the other senior member of the delegation was Prince Bandar ibn Sultan, the Saudi ambassador to Washington, a known anti-communist, who was considered the Sudayris' special emissary. This visit, undoubtedly, indicated Riyadh's frustration with America's inability to bring the Security Council to implement Resolution 598. Yet, the Saudis also wanted reassurances that Moscow was still committed to maintaining stability in the Gulf and was not selling weapons, especially the longer range and more accurate Scud-B missiles, to Tehran. Fêted by Moscow, the delegation met with the top Soviet leadership. The Saudis were assured of Moscow's friendship for Saudi Arabia and the Arabs in general, and of its continued support for Resolution 598, but they were also told of Moscow's displeasure with the American naval presence in the Gulf and of the need to replace it with a UN force which Moscow would co-sponsor.[39]

Riyadh was not happy with America's 'embarrassing pressure to do the politically impossible and collude openly with Washington . . . and . . . successfully resisted political pressures to allow US forces basing rights on Saudi soil'.[40] Relations between the two countries deteriorated at the beginning of 1988 as a result of the US's 'special relation' with Israel during the Reagan administration and its refusal to sell Saudi Arabia additional F-15s and other sophisticated weapons. Riyadh was also angry about Washington's reaction to the disclosure that it had secretly obtained Chinese ballistic missiles. Subsequently, the US ambassador in Riyadh was practically declared *persona non grata* and was replaced in April to prevent further deterioration in US–Saudi relations. Yet, realising the US Congress's growing anger with its policy, Riyadh quickly endeavoured to repair its relations with America.[41]

The visit to Moscow of such a high-level Saudi delegation gave rise to rumours about the re-establishment of diplomatic relations between the Soviet Union and Saudi Arabia. Although untrue, the rumours greatly annoyed the Saudi ulama and were quickly denied by Riyadh. Nevertheless, this visit and the rapidly improving relations between Moscow and the GCC signalled the opening of a new era in Soviet–Saudi relations and were welcomed by the Saudi nationalist–neutralist camp. Above all, they indicated Riyadh's determination to end the Gulf war as soon as possible.

LAST STAGE - SAUDI ARABIA AND IRAN (1988-9)

February and March 1988 saw the renewal of the 'war of the cities', with Iraq and (to some degree) Iran terrorising each other's populations with Russian-made Scud-B missiles. This was followed by an Iranian offensive in Kurdistan, which turned out to be Tehran's last. Iranian forces, moreover, frequently violated Kuwaiti territorial water and, on one occasion, landed on its Bubyan Island. As Baghdad intensified its air strikes against Iranian oil targets, Tehran, in turn, escalated its attacks on Saudi and Kuwaiti tankers. This and the failure of Syria's mediation efforts and Tehran's scathing attacks on Riyadh over its new 'pilgrims' quota' policy which permitted only 45,000 Iranians to participate in the hajj (compared with 150,000 in 1987), produced a sharp Saudi reaction. The Saudi-sponsored ICO in its annual meeting in Amman strongly condemned Iran for its 'un-Islamic behaviour' and refusal to negotiate peace with Iraq.

Iran's continued 'brutal' pressure to rescind Riyadh's decision concerning the pilgrims' quota, its repeated attacks on Saudi tankers and the bombing of Saudi oil installations by Shi'ite saboteurs caused King Fahd on 26 April to break off relations with Tehran. The Saudi monarch declared on this occasion that any Iranian aggression against the kingdom would be met with force; Riyadh might even use its Chinese-made missiles.[42] This bellicose stance, so atypical for Riyadh, was undoubtedly promoted by the reassuring US presence in the Gulf and the belief that Tehran was nearly exhausted and its army about to collapse.

April 1988 saw the opening of the final stage in the Iran–Iraq war. In a surprise attack which met with minimal resistance, Iraq recaptured the Faw Peninsula. Thereafter, the initiative passed into Baghdad's hands. In addition, the Reagan administration was now ready to take its gloves off and teach Tehran a belated lesson for past humiliations. Thus, renewed Iranian mining of the Gulf's navigation routes, which caused damage to the USS *Roberts* on 14 April, led to the destruction by US forces of two oil platforms used by Iran's Revolutionary Guards. Following additional incidents, the US navy destroyed about half of the Iranian navy. Washington's new aggressiveness was also reflected by its decision to extend its protection to neutral ships in the Gulf if they were attacked in the vicinity of a US warship. (A US navy ship mistakenly shot down an Iranian passenger plane with heavy loss of life, believing that it was a war plane.) Tehran's ability to operate in the Gulf was thus practically nullified.

Repeated Iraqi victories in May, June and July, following the total collapse of Iran's military and logistical infrastructure, forced Ayatollah Khomayni to accept reality. Tehran informed the UN Secretary General on 18 July that it was ready to accept a cease-fire unconditionally.

Ironically, Riyadh was now compelled to persuade Saddam Hussayn to agree to halt the Iraqi offensive. The cautious and far-sighted Saudis, unlike Iraq, did not wish to further humiliate Iran and thus perpetuate the 'Persian–Arab war'. President Hussayn, however, agreed to the cease-fire only after Iran acquiesced in opening immediate peace negotiations with Iraq. A cease-fire was declared on 20 August.

Once the war was over, Iran quickly re-established diplomatic relations with Kuwait and endeavoured to improve its relations with the other GCC countries. In turn, King Fahd ordered the Saudi media in October 1988 to stop their attacks on Iran. Relations between Tehran and Riyadh slowly improved, despite the execution by Saudi Arabia of four Saudi Shi'ites responsible for sabotage activities.[43] This process was somewhat accelerated by the decline of oil prices, which both sides wished to halt, and because Riyadh and Kuwait again began to fear Iraq's ambitions in the region. Thus, for instance, an Iranian delegation was invited by Riyadh in March 1989 to attend an Islamic conference to debate Salman Rushdie's *Satanic Verses*. Yet, while Fahd preached tolerance, the Iranians wanted Rushdie's blood. Indeed, Iran's relations with Saudi Arabia again deteriorated over the matter of Riyadh's pilgrims' quota, over which Imam Khomayni would not compromise. Iran, in addition, continued to strengthen its ties with Moscow, hoping to counterbalance the Western presence and influence in the Gulf region and to acquire sophisticated weapons which the USSR was ready to sell both for political and economic reasons.

A major factor which influenced Iran's foreign policy after August 1988 and well after Khomayni's demise in June 1989, was the struggle for power between the dogmatic and the pragmatic radical Iranian leadership. The first, which controlled the *da'wa* office responsible for religious propaganda and clandestine activities abroad (traditionally so in Shi'ite empires), was led by Ali Akbar Mohtashemi, the powerful interior minister, by Ayatollah Montazeri, Imam Khomayni's ousted heir (responsible for the *da'wa* office), and by Khomayni's son Ahmad. This faction strongly opposed any normalisation of relations with the 'infidel' Gulf regimes and the West. The second faction, led by the wily Hashemi Rafsanjani, the powerful *majlis* speaker, and the armed forces' commander-in-chief, President Khamena'i (later elected heir to Khomayni), and foreign minister Vilayeti, was more realistic and pragmatic.

The hajj issue, and the beheading in Riyadh in September 1989 of sixteen largely Kuwaiti Shi'ites accused of a bombing incident in Mecca in July during the hajj period and masterminded by an Iranian diplomat in Kuwait, again increased the tension between Tehran and Riyadh. This, and other Iranian-inspired terrorist activities in the world[44] occurring after Khomayni's death were probably initiated by the radical and dogmatic Iranian leadership, which remained loyal to Khomayni's teachings and which sought to undermine the still shaky government of President Rafsanjani elected in August. Indeed, the Iranian radical and anti-Western opposition to Rafsanjani's regime enjoys majority support in the clergy-dominated Iranian *majlis* and until mid-1992 retained, some of its power both abroad and in Iran, where it continues to mastermind clandestine operations and political assassinations in the Middle East and Europe.[45] Yet, Rafsanjani's pragmatic government is itself engaged in spreading militant fundamentalism in the Arab world (Sudan, Algeria and Lebanon), supports the 'jihad' against Israel, and is developing, at great cost, nuclear and other unconventional capabilities as well as conventional military power.

Faced with the enormous task of rebuilding Iran's ruined economy, with severe unemployment and spiralling inflation and with an empty treasury, Rafsanjani wished to increase Tehran's revenue from oil. Abandoning Iran's unrealistic hawkish stance in OPEC, he supported moderately higher OPEC oil prices while safeguarding production quotas and co-operating with Riyadh's prudent production and pricing policy aimed at increasing demand for oil by stabilising prices. Iran also wished to restore its oil production capacity to the level attained before the anarchy following the Islamic revolution. That necessitated substantial foreign capital. Well aware that Tehran's involvement in international terrorism and its image in the world frightens off potential foreign investors, Rafsanjani has been endeavouring to improve Iran's image. In the final analysis, expanding Iran's oil industry for the benefit of the Iranian people, Rafsanjani believes, should help Tehran to resume its dominant position in the Gulf, and possibly in the Islamic world.

King Fahd's government emerged from the Iran–Iraq war more stable and confident and with its pro-American policy vindicated.[46] Fahd's policy even seemed to have produced a powerful, moderate Arab block incorporating, in addition to Saudi Arabia, Iraq, Egypt and Jordan. In 1989, moreover, with demand for oil beginning to rise and prices temporarily increasing, it appeared that the kingdom was beginning to emerge out of the acute recession which it had suffered since the mid-1980s.[47] Thus, Riyadh's leading position in the Arab world and in OPEC seemed assured.

Despite periods of tension with Tehran, Riyadh exerted itself to convince Baghdad after August 1988 that it should abandon its extreme demands upon Iran and sign a peace agreement with it. Still apprehensive about Tehran's regime, on the one hand, and again anxious about Saddam's 'pan-Arab' ambitions, on the other, Riyadh endeavoured to maintain amicable relations with Baghdad and to improve its relations with Tehran. Above all, Fahd continued to nurture Saudi Arabia's relations with Washington and the West generally and to acquire additional sophisticated weapons.

On 16 February 1989, Iraq established the Arab Co-operation Council (ACC) with Jordan, Cairo and Yemen. Observers believed, at first, that the ACC was part of a 'moderate pro-Western axis' emerging out of the Iran–Iraq war. But Riyadh was under no illusions about this so-called economic co-operation organisation.[48] Thus, after the US decided to withdraw most of its naval force from the region, as well as two of the four AWACS lent to Riyadh,[49] Saudi Arabia tacitly approved an increased American naval presence in the Gulf.

CONCLUSION

Even before Iraq invaded Iran, Riyadh was concerned with the impact of Tehran's propaganda and subversive activities on the Saudi people, and particularly on the region's Shi'ite population. After the war broke out, Riyadh also feared the consequences it might have on its oil industry, the kingdom's life-line. Once the tide turned against Iraq, King Fahd encouraged Muslim organisations and Third World countries to mediate between the two combatants. Following Riyadh's customary role of 'peace broker' in the Arab world, Fahd unsuccessfully sought to unite the polarised Arab camp in support of Baghdad. Yet, Riyadh considered the extended war as favouring its interests. While the Gulf giants were bleeding each other, King Fahd won wide support for his policy and consolidated the regime's position both at home and in the Arab camp.

Riyadh increased its efforts to end the Iran–Iraq war through mediation in 1984, after Iraq launched the 'tanker war' and Iran attempted to penetrate Iraq's heartlands. However, the Saudi-initiated mediation efforts were still half-hearted and doomed to failure because Iran insisted that Iraq be branded the aggressor and that Saddam Hussayn be removed from office. Riyadh was not altogether displeased with the stalemate in the battlefields.

Between 1984 and 1986 the Saudi regime also endeavoured to improve its relations with Tehran and to co-ordinate its activities with Washington, hoping, *inter alia*, to win its favour. King Fahd thus became involved in Washington's 'arms for hostages' negotiations (the Irangate fiasco) and, temporarily, Riyadh's relations with Tehran somewhat improved.

The Saudi attitude concerning the Iran–Iraq war dramatically changed following the conquest of the Faw Peninsula by Iran in February 1986. Riyadh and Kuwait now feared that the war could spill over into their territories or seriously affect their Shi'ite minorities. That, and Moscow's attempts to replace Washington's influence in Tehran, considered by both superpowers the region's most important strategic power asset, now made it imperative for Riyadh to end the war quickly. The fact that 'Persian' Shi'ite soldiers were now positioned near the Wahabbi kingdom's northern border caused the Saudi oligarchy, the ulama and new elites to coalesce behind King Fahd. The serious economic recession, the results of which caused hardships to Saudis of all classes, did not erode the support of the Sunni masses for the regime. On his part, King Fahd prudently protected, as far as he could, the standard of living of 'lower-income' Saudis by largely maintaining the kingdom's extensive welfare system and subsidies. In addition, Fahd pampered the ulama and expanded the activity of their Morality Police. The regime successfully used the 'carrot-and-stick' formula in treating its Shi'ite subjects and thus, throughout the Iran–Iraq war, the Saudi Shi'ites never truly threatened the country's security.

While increasing its financial and logistic assistance to Iraq, Riyadh strove to bring the Security Council to coerce Tehran to agree to a cease-fire. Simultaneously, it intensified its efforts to bring Egypt back into the Arab fold and to unite the Arab countries to resist the 'Persian' threat to Eastern Arabia. Lastly, Saudi Arabia and Kuwait now believed that the most likely way to de-escalate the Gulf conflict was to internationalise it.

Fahd covertly co-ordinated with the US Riyadh's political efforts in the Gulf and, it seems, co-operated with America's efforts to settle the Arab–Israeli conflict. The latter was not just to please Washington but more because he wished to focus Arab attention on the 'Persian threat' which undermined his regime's stability. Despite traditional apprehension of Arab nationalist reaction, Riyadh also facilitated the presence in the Gulf of an American 'armada', to the great consternation of Tehran and Moscow and radical Arab nationalists.

The US naval presence in the Gulf completely changed Riyadh's timid and ambivalent policy *vis-à-vis* Iran. This policy was replaced by a new assertive stance which, *inter alia*, was responsible for the harsh suppression of the Mecca riots in July 1987. The riots further united all Saudi Sunnis behind Fahd's regime and increased Saudi Arabia's self-confidence.

The Mecca riots helped turn most Arabs against Iran and focused their attention on the Gulf war. They helped stem any remaining criticism in the kingdom and the Arab world concerning the US presence in the Gulf and facilitated Egypt's reacceptance by the Arab camp. At home, they strengthened the oligarchy's and the people's support for King Fahd's policy.

Saudi diplomatic efforts to de-escalate the Iran–Iraq conflict may not have been very successful until 1987. None the less, they helped gradually to isolate Tehran and, in July 1987, produced Security Council Resolution 598. That, the tightening of the embargo on Iran, and the US naval presence in the Gulf, rather than Iraq's military performance, practically brought Iran to its knees in July 1988.

Washington's rapidly growing dependence on imported oil reinforced the traditional US policy of safeguarding the Saudi regime. On his part, in spite of occasional disagreement with America over arms sales and Washington's Middle East policy in relation to Israel, King Fahd was determined to continue to nurture Saudi relations with the US. These relations assumed additional importance in view of Riyadh's renewed concerns over Iran and Iraq's renewed ambitions in the region.

9

PRELUDE TO THE
IRAQ-KUWAIT CRISIS

SAUDI ECONOMY AND SOCIETY IN THE AFTERMATH OF THE IRAN-IRAQ WAR

At the beginning of 1988, after five years of economic recession, there was still no sign of improvement in the Saudi economy. This was reflected by the 1988 budget, announced at the end of December 1987. Expenditure remained at 37.6 billion dollars, while revenue from oil, projected at 18.4 billion, was by year's end only about 16.5 billion (the lowest since the mid-1970s). The projected budget deficit was about 10 billion dollars. As the kingdom's liquid assets had shrunk dramatically since 1982, Riyadh decided to launch another internal bond issue of about 8 billion dollars, rather than continue to draw on the remnant of its financial reserves.[1]

In his budget speech delivered on 30 December 1987, King Fahd told his nation that he would curb spending, 'although an unsuitable political situation in the Gulf region necessitates further military spending' (30-35 per cent of each year's budget). He also promised to protect the Saudi people from any hardship resulting from the economic crisis. Yet, it was clear that if oil prices remained depressed Saudi Arabia would not be able to finance its huge budget deficit.

Government expenditure on subsidies for agriculture and a variety of commodities and services, in 1987, amounted to 3 to 4 billion dollars. In addition, Riyadh was spending many billions on its extensive welfare services, the like of which were not to be found elsewhere. These subsidies and services were a pillar of the paternal relations between the regime and the Saudi people. But, as the kingdom's oil revenue was not likely to rise, and Riyadh was no longer willing to draw upon its reserves, it preferred to reduce its substantial subsidies for gasoline, electricity, basic food-stuffs, airplane tickets and some services. A similar attempt in 1985 'was scaled back . . . following a public outcry'.[2]

Sensing popular discontent, King Fahd, at the beginning of 1988, again rescinded his government's decision. A plan to tax the income of foreign employees, which caused many to threaten to leave the kingdom, was also cancelled.[3] Indeed, during a meeting with Saudi notables shortly afterwards, Fahd declared that his government would endeavour to alleviate the hardship suffered by the citizens and would improve the standard of the services provided to the population by both the central government's administration and that of the provinces. Moreover, the regime established three funds to subsidise agriculture, industry and real estate. The latter, for instance, granted Saudi citizens wishing to build houses on land granted by the government without charge interest-free loans, which were partly forgiven if repaid on time.[4]

Notwithstanding the government's efforts, the *per capita* income in Saudi Arabia, about 11,000 dollars in the early 1980s, declined to 7,000–8,000 dollars by 1989.[5] The private sector of the Saudi economy continued to suffer from the prolonged recession. Bankruptcies were common and many businessmen and entrepreneurs defaulted on payments of loans received from Saudi and foreign banks. As Western-type banks were not viewed sympathetically by *shari'a* courts because they charged interest, little could be done by them to retrieve unpaid debts. In turn, the banks, especially foreign ones, were reluctant to lend money to Saudis. Hence, SAMA established a three-man banking committee (the Negotiable Instruments Committee) to deal with non-payment of debts and thus bypass the *shari'a* courts. Theoretically, this body had the authority to take serious steps against defaulters. Yet, apprehensive of confronting the *shari'a* courts, especially when the debtor was related to the royal family or had friends in high positions, the new committee did little to solve the problem.[6]

Another element in the population which seriously suffered from the economic crisis, was the tens of thousands of high school and university graduates. Most could not find employment in the coveted government service, while the private sector, suffering from the economic recession, could not provide a viable alternative. Yet, a claim that unemployed students were responsible for a wave of crimes in the Eastern Province was either untrue or related to Shi'ite terrorist activities in that region.[7]

Addressing students at Umm al-Qura University (Mecca) in October 1988, King Fahd, in view of the increased unemployment among Saudi graduates, 70 per cent of whom held degrees in Islamic studies and liberal arts, called upon graduates to join the armed forces and security services. The monarch advised them, upon termination of their service, to opt for technical training. King Fahd told his audience that enrolment at military academies of all kinds had substantially increased. Hisham Nazir, the Saudi petroleum minister, also focusing on the problem of graduates' unemployment, encouraged graduate students to join one of the various branches of the oil industry. He also claimed that the policy of Saudi-isation was being accelerated in order to provide additional jobs for graduates.[8]

148

Generally speaking, it seems that by 1989, despite the difficulties they faced, Saudi graduates, with the exception of some from the Islamic universities, adjusted to the new situation and did not constitute a challenge to the regime's stability. They now sought employment wherever available and were ready to accept lower-paid jobs, even in remote provinces, as long as they did not entail manual work.

Indeed, the Saudi population as a whole adapted itself to the 'hardship' resulting from economic recession.[9] This adaptation was cushioned by the government's efforts to maintain its generous welfare system and most of the subsidies which preserved an acceptable standard of living for the Saudi population. The regime's policy was facilitated by further drawing on the kingdom's limited liquid reserves in addition to internal borrowing through bond issues and indirect borrowing from foreign banks.[10] That, and the Iranian threat emphasised by the Mecca carnage in 1987 and Shi'ite terrorist activities, which were viewed as a serious threat to the Sunni majority, were the main reasons for the kingdom's stability and the wide-based support for the Al Saud regime despite the recession. In so far as the power struggle within the royal family was largely contained after 1983, the Saudi oligarchy coalesced behind King Fahd, particularly following Iran's conquest of the Faw Peninsula in 1986 and the Mecca rioting in 1987.

Notwithstanding the armistice signed between Iran and Iraq in July 1988, Riyadh still felt insecure because Baghdad and Tehran had failed to reach a peace agreement. Not only did the Saudi regime become the target of a new wave of Shi'ite fundamentalist terrorism and propaganda, but it was becoming increasingly apprehensive concerning Iraq's renewed ambitions in the Arab camp and aggressive policy in OPEC. Moreover, during 1989 despite, or perhaps because of, signs of recuperation in the kingdom's economy, some discontent was becoming evident in the ranks of the intelligentsia concerning their non-participation in the kingdom's policy-making and the increased influence of the ulama.[11] On the other hand, the conservatives were dissatisfied with their country's relations with the United States and resentful of foreign cultural influence on the 'Saudi way of life', attributed partly to Western-trained technocrats. Both modernists and conservatives deplored the Sauds' involvement in business and the commissions system which enriched them, as well as their ostentatious lifestyle and excesses.[12] Above all, now that the Iranian threat had receded, Saudi businessmen and people as a whole were becoming increasingly displeased with the lengthy economic crisis and the government's handling of it.

Acutely aware of the correlation between the economy and the country's stability,[13] King Fahd frequently visited army units, academies and universities in the kingdom's different regions. In his speeches, he repeatedly underscored the tremendous development achieved by the kingdom, made possible by oil revenue. Indeed, in October 1988, the Saudi government announced a special development plan for the years 1989–93 with the following targets:

1 To continue to develop the kingdom's defence forces and 'to *strengthen loyalty of citizens*'.
2 '. . . to increase the state's revenues *providing this does not lead to undesirable social or economic effect . . .*'.
3 To improve the performance and efficiency of the government administration, 'which will lead *to reducing government expenditure without affecting the level of services . . . to citizens*'.
4 To increase the activity of the private sector in the national economy.
5 To achieve a balanced development among the various regions of the kingdom.
6 To encourage the private sector *to provide job opportunities for citizens.*
7 *To replace non-Saudi manpower with Saudi manpower.*[14]

Evidently, the regime believed that its stability in the 1990s depended on its ability to revive the country's prosperity and development, which would benefit all Saudis. That clearly depended on the state of the oil market and on oil prices.

OPEC AND THE OIL MARKET (1987–90)

Following the 1986/7 oil crisis, when prices sank to about 9 dollars a barrel, Saudi Arabia abandoned its crusade for a 'fair share of the market', largely aimed against non-OPEC producers. At the December 1986 OPEC summit, Riyadh was one of the main proponents of the decision to limit the organisation's total production to 15.5 m.b.d. (32.5 m.b.d. in 1980/1) and to set a reference price of 18 dollars a barrel. This decision caused prices to rise to 12–13 dollars a barrel by the beginning of 1987, and even higher when it became evident that OPEC's members had actually reduced their production to the prescribed limit.

Shortly afterwards Riyadh declared its determination not to serve any longer as OPEC's 'swing producer', and gradually raised its share of OPEC's production to nearly 25 per cent, equivalent to its share of the 'non-communist world's proven reserves'.[15] Subsequently Saudi oil production, which at one point in 1987 had shrunk to under 3 m.b.d. from 10 million in 1979, rose by mid-1988 to 4.35 m.b.d. Riyadh's insistence on achieving a 25 per cent market share of OPEC's total production, while other members of the organisation also exceeded their quotas, caused oil prices to remain under 15 dollars a barrel in the second half of 1987. Oil rose to about 16 dollars in the beginning of 1988 only to collapse again to about 12 dollars a barrel shortly afterwards owing to a glutted market.[16]

In view of the kingdom's grave financial situation the Saudi government implored its OPEC partners to observe their production quotas so that the price of oil would rise to as close to 18 dollars a barrel as possible. Such a price ceiling did not contradict the kingdom's long-range oil policy based on its enormous proven reserves,[17] which necessitated low oil prices to encourage higher consumption. By this time, moreover, non-OPEC producers, whose output had peaked, were eager to co-operate with OPEC to help raise oil prices.

However, Riyadh's efforts in the first half of 1988 to maintain OPEC's production discipline in order to raise oil prices did not succeed. This was largely due to Iraq's refusal to participate in OPEC's quota agreements as long as it was not granted a quota equal to that of Iran (2.3 m.b.d.). Iraq's production, which was marginal in the early stages of its war with Iran, rose by 1988 to nearly 3 m.b.d., compared to its 1.3. m.b.d. quota. This was facilitated by the construction of two pipelines from its northern (Kirkuk) fields to the Mediterranean via Turkey (capable of carrying about 1.9 m.b.d.) and another, from its southern (Rumayla) field to the Saudi Trans-Arabian pipeline, through which it was allowed by Riyadh to pump about 500,000 barrels daily. Baghdad was also trucking 200,000–300,000 barrels daily through Jordan to the port of Aqaba.[18]

Iraq's claim to a higher quota was based on its past production and possession of over 10 per cent of the world's proven reserves. Baghdad claimed, moreover, that new oil discoveries in central Iraq made it second only to Saudi Arabia as far as 'proven' reserves were concerned. Supported by Saudi Arabia and Kuwait, its demand was finally accepted by OPEC's extraordinary meeting in Spain in October 1988 when Baghdad was granted a 2.3 m.b.d. quota – equal to that of Iran.[19]

Once Iraq joined OPEC's quota arrangement in December 1988 and endorsed OPEC's new production ceiling of 17.5 m.b.d., oil prices rose sharply to about 17–18 dollars a barrel. Ironically, Baghdad now began to play the role of OPEC's policeman, attempting to persuade other members, especially its small Gulf neighbours, to restrain their production in order to achieve OPEC's reference price. Indeed, Issam Shalabi, Iraq's minister of petroleum, forecast at the end of 1988 a revival of OPEC's influence on oil prices and declared that his country 'would pursue a policy of maximizing revenue from oil'.[20] Yet, prices again fell to less than 15 dollars a barrel by the second quarter of 1989 because both Kuwait and the UAE were producing nearly twice their quota of under 1 m.b.d. at a time when demand for oil had seasonally declined.

Kuwait and the UAE argued that, as in the case of Iraq, they were entitled to a quota of at least 1.5 m.b.d., reflecting Kuwait's 10 per cent, and the UAE's claimed 5–10 per cent, share of the 'world's proven reserves', not to mention their respective existing production capacity. Their over-production, and that of other OPEC members, more than offset the continuous growth of demand for OPEC's oil, resulting from a revival in the world's economy and the fact that non-OPEC countries' production had peaked.

Dividing the incremental demand for its oil, OPEC, at the Vienna summit in June, increased Kuwait's quota to about 1.1 m.b.d. and the UAE's to about 1 m.b.d., about 10 per cent higher than in the past. Although both countries rejected this decision, Kuwait's powerful petroleum minister, 'Ali Al Khalifa al-Adabi, and his UAE counterpart, Mana al-Utayba, promised that their countries would 'somewhat' reduce their production, which was still nearly twice their quota.

The oil market remained unstable in the coming months, with prices fluctuating well under OPEC's 18-dollar ceiling. Nevertheless, in view of the constantly rising demand for OPEC's oil, and despite the opposition of its price hawks, the organisation decided in September to raise its production ceiling to 20.5 m.b.d., but did not deal with the thorny problem of individual quotas. Thus, by the beginning of October, OPEC's members were producing nearly 23 m.b.d. and, subsequently, in spite of seasonal and incremental rise in demand for OPEC's oil, prices remained between 16 and 17 dollars a barrel, a price considered insufficient by most members of the organisation in view of their financial difficulties.[21] Finally, after OPEC raised its production ceiling to about 22 m.b.d. in its November summit in Vienna, Kuwait was granted the 1.5. m.b.d. quota which it had requested, and the UAE 1.1 m.b.d. Iraq and Iran's quotas were raised to 2.9 m.b.d. and Saudi Arabia's to 5.1 m.b.d. OPEC's oil prices now temporarily rose to 18 dollars.[22]

It was evident that OPEC's price hawks, led by Algeria, who strove to drive oil prices up by reducing the organisation's total production were, Iran excluded, member countries with limited reserves, some no longer able to produce even their full quota. Yet, as demand for OPEC's oil continued to rise, Iraq and Saudi Arabia, each for its own reason, also began in 1989 to advocate increasing OPEC's 18-dollar reference price. This policy was strongly resisted by Kuwait (supported by the UAE), whose petroleum minister admitted at the beginning of 1990 that his country was intentionally exceeding its quota in order to prevent a rise of OPEC's reference price. Because of its vast proven reserves, he claimed, Kuwait's policy was long-range, aimed at encouraging a steady rise in the world's demand for oil (a policy endorsed by Saudi Arabia until the end of 1988).[23]

In February 1990, Saddam Hussayn personally contacted the rulers of Saudi Arabia, Kuwait and the UAE about the need to safeguard OPEC's production quotas and to raise its oil price. A meeting between the oil ministers of Iraq, Kuwait and Saudi Arabia, held in Kuwait at the beginning of March, failed to overcome the differences among them. On Fahd's instructions, Hisham Nazir immediately flew to Baghdad to discuss with Saddam Hussayn a formula which would be acceptable to OPEC's pricing committee scheduled to meet in Vienna on 16 March.[24] The Vienna meeting, too, failed to reach agreement. By April OPEC was producing over 24 m.b.d., while its production ceiling was about 22 million, and oil prices had plunged to 15 dollars a barrel. Another meeting of the Saudi, Kuwaiti and the UAE's oil ministers, convened by King Fahd in Jedda in mid-April, failed to persuade Kuwait and the UAE to curb their production, and oil prices declined to less than 15 dollars a barrel. An emergency OPEC meeting held in Geneva on 1 and 2 May did not produce concrete results despite Iraqi threats against 'quota-busters'.[25]

Desperately in need of funds, Baghdad was hoping to benefit from both OPEC's increasing market share and higher oil prices. Frustrated, in a speech delivered on 2 April 1990 Saddam Hussayn accused 'certain Gulf regimes' of being implicated in a 'Powers' (i.e. the US) conspiracy' to undermine Iraq's economy and 'stabbing it in the back'.[26] Iraq advocated the adoption by OPEC of a reference price of 25 dollars a barrel, which it claimed was 'economic' as far as the industrial countries were concerned.[27]

While disagreeing with Saddam Hussayn's 'conspiracy' theory and his denunciation of the US, King Fahd was exasperated, as well, by Kuwait's and the UAE's obstinacy, although they were following the policy he had previously advocated. This policy assumed that cheap oil would encourage increased consumption, undermine alternative energy sources and benefit producers with substantial oil reserves. Yet Riyadh was more attuned to Saddam Hussayn's aspirations and growing belligerence. Furthermore, having practically exhausted its financial reserves and suffering from chronic budget deficits, Saudi Arabia now opted for a short-term remedy to help maintain the regime's stability.

Saudi Arabia's expenditure budget between 1987 and 1990 remained steady at about 37.5 billion dollars, of which about 35 per cent was allocated to defence. Revenue from oil, which declined in 1988 to about 16.5 billion, rose to about 18.5 billion in 1989 and was projected to rise to over 22 billion in 1990.[28] As mentioned above, the kingdom's substantial budgetary deficit in 1988 was largely financed by drawing upon its previously accumulated liquid assets. In that year Riyadh also floated an 8-billion-dollar internal bond issue. Additional bond issues in 1989 and 1990 were also meant to finance budgetary deficits. Furthermore, Riyadh, for the first time, indirectly borrowed in 1989 about 600 million dollars from a consortium of Gulf banks for its development fund and seriously attempted to reduce government expenses.[29]

As demand for OPEC's oil was constantly rising in this period, Riyadh's oil policy was focused on maintaining its share of about 25 per cent of OPEC's total production. For this purpose, probably, Saudi

Arabia announced in 1989 that its 'proven' oil reserves now exceeded 250 billion barrels, about 80 per cent more than its previous estimate. Another target of the Saudi oil policy since 1989 was again to increase its production capacity to over 10 m.b.d. for which Riyadh budgeted 15 billion dollars (1989-94).[30]

Although the kingdom's economy slowly began to recuperate in 1989 and its GDP rose by 3.2 per cent, it was still only half of the peak of 147.5 billion dollars in 1981.[31] Determined to increase further its revenue from oil now that demand was steadily growing, Saudi Arabia in mid-1989 joined Iraq and Iran, as well as other OPEC members, who wished to increase the organisation's reference price by at least 10 per cent (Iraq demanded that the price should be raised to at least 25 dollars a barrel).[32] Indeed, already in May 1989, while endeavouring to persuade OPEC members to observe their quota, King Fahd declared that if they were to do so, there was no reason why oil should not reach 26 dollars a barrel by the beginning of 1990. Immediately afterwards, Hisham Nazir, his petroleum minister, explained that the king did not mean that OPEC should push prices up by curbing production but that prices would go up through 'a free play of market forces' and 'a rise in demand'.[33]

Riyadh's relations with Kuwait began to deteriorate shortly after the end of the Iran–Iraq war. Foremost among the reasons for this development was the fact that Kuwait continued to undermine oil prices by grossly exceeding its OPEC allocation. Before it was granted its requested quota of 1.5 m.b.d. in November 1989, Kuwait excused its excessive production by claiming that its quota was not in correct proportion to its reserves and production capacity. Yet, when it again over-produced at the beginning of 1990, Kuwait's petroleum minister, Shaykh 'Ali al-Khalifa, ignored Riyadh's reasoning and insisted that lower oil prices would, over time, benefit producers with large reserves.[34] Kuwait, furthermore, was the most successful OPEC producer in developing its international downstream operations (through its Q8 oil company) and its income from investments in the industrial countries accounted for a sizeable part of its total revenues.

Notwithstanding Saddam Hussayn's strong warning to 'quota-busters' in the Arab League's Baghdad summit at the end of May (see below), Kuwait and the UAE continued to exceed their quotas significantly. Subsequently, OPEC's oil price declined in June to about 14 dollars a barrel. Saudi Arabia's projected budget deficit of about 6 billion dollars for 1990 (to be financed through an additional bond issue),[35] could thus have been increased by an additional 4.5 billion. Such a development would have gravely undermined the kingdom's hopes for the economic recuperation essential to preserve the regime's stability. Saudi Arabia, therefore, joined Iraq and Iran in exerting massive pressure on Kuwait and the UAE to abandon their oil policy and to help raise oil prices by observing their respective quotas.

To appease the Gulf giants, Shaykh 'Ali Al Khalifa, responsible for the Emirate's oil policy for more than a decade, was replaced in a cabinet reshuffle on 23 June by a technocrat, Dr Rashid Salim Al-'Umayri. Shaykh'Ali, appointed minister of finance could, nevertheless, still influence his country's oil policy. Indeed, shortly after his appointment, Dr Al-'Umayri declared that there was no reason to change the Emirate's oil policy.[36] Yet, Sa'dun Hamadi, Iraq's deputy prime minister, who carried a strong letter of warning from Saddam Hussayn to both Kuwait and the UAE's rulers, declared after a meeting with Kuwait's Amir on 26 June that he was told by the latter that it was Kuwait's 'keen interest to abide by its OPEC quota (1.5 m.b.d.) in order to safeguard OPEC's interests'. Hamadi added that Iraq believes that '25 dollars per barrel is a fair price'.[37]

In view of the situation in the oil market and the approaching OPEC summit (26 July), Saudi Arabia invited the petroleum ministers of Kuwait, the UAE, Iraq and Qatar to attend an emergency conference in Jedda on 11–12 July. During two days of deliberations, chaired indirectly by King Fahd through Hisham Nazir, Kuwait and the UAE capitulated and agreed to support an OPEC production ceiling of 22.5 m.b.d. (compared with 24 million produced in June), strictly to observe their quotas, and to support a proposal to raise OPEC's reference price. Immediately after the meeting, both Kuwait and the UAE began to reduce their production, causing OPEC's oil price to increase to about 16.5 dollars a barrel.[38]

OPEC's Geneva summit on 26–7 July was among the shortest ever, because the framework for its decisions had been agreed upon at the Jedda meeting two weeks earlier. The 22.5 m.b.d. production ceiling was adopted unanimously and all OPEC members undertook strictly to observe their quotas. Furthermore, to please Iraq, which demanded a 25-dollars-a-barrel price, OPEC, led by Saudi Arabia and Kuwait, agreed to a 21-dollar reference price, instead of their proposed 20 dollars a barrel.[39] While successfully protecting what was considered a reasonable price at a time when the world economy was believed to be recuperating, Riyadh badly needed the additional revenue to cope with internal developments in the kingdom.

GOVERNMENT, ELITES AND INTERNAL SECURITY (1988–90)

The wide support for King Fahd's government among all classes of Saudis which emerged in the mid-1980s was still in evidence in 1989, despite the prolonged economic crisis. Even the leftist Arab press grudgingly conceded the universal support for King Fahd's regime, the cessation of the power struggle within the ruling family and that '. . . Saudi Arabia could be considered one of the most stable states in the region'.[40] Though the new elites', particularly its nationalist, anti-American part, and 'non-conformist' young ulama's criticism of the regime was increasing, it was offset by the religious establishment's traditional alliance with Al Saud and the latter's power. Iranian-directed subversion and threats related to the hajj 'quota' also helped consolidate popular support for King Fahd.[41] Yet, under the surface, the regime's stability was being challenged by both external and internal forces.

In the first months of 1989, Persian Gulf and inter-Arab politics and the traditional struggle between conservatives and modernists began again to undermine the ruling oligarchy's solidarity. Ayatollah Khomayni's death in June and Iraq's renewed involvement in regional politics caused the faction in the ruling class, led by Saud al-Faysal, to advocate again the improvement of relations with Iran. Another faction, led by Crown Prince Abdallah, wished to strengthen relations with the Arab world and Syria in particular. Both were unhappy with Fahd's close relations and co-operation with Washington. The Sudayris, no longer able to afford to buy their Arab neighbours' goodwill and uneasy about Saddam Hussayn's aspirations, continued to develop, through Prince Bandar, low-profile relations with the US (and covertly with the American Jewish community) and encouraged American 'over the horizon' presence in the region. They also increased efforts to cultivate Cairo's friendship and to have Saudi Arabia play the mediator role in the Arab camp. Overall, Fahd's prestige and the cohesiveness and power of the Sudayris were still sufficient to contain their rivals within the royal family and to maintain, at least outwardly, its unity.[42]

An urbane monarch who preferred Hijazi towns, with their 'soft cosmopolitan society', to Riyadh in the Najdi heartland, 'with its more direct abrasive society',[43] Fahd was well aware of the rising influence of militant, fundamentalist ulama and of the conservative character of the majority of Saudis. The appeal of the former increased in this period owing to the hardship suffered by lower-income Saudis in the major towns and in parts of the rural areas owing to the economic recession.[44] Hence, although surrounded by reform-advocating Western-trained technocrats and personally willing to grant the intelligentsia limited participation in policy-making, Fahd was careful not to antagonise the religious establishment and their conservative supporters. Among other things, the costly National Consultative Assembly building, whose construction had been completed in 1986, was used only for exhibitions and similar purposes. The establishment ulama and their Morality Police, moreover, seemed to gain more power as the ageing monarch continued to depend on them for legitimisation and to maintain the regime's stability.

The liberal intelligentsia, supported by young princes desiring a truly modernised Saudi Arabia, privately admitted their disillusionment with Fahd's costly 'modernisation' policy, which they considered a 'non-policy'. Nevertheless, they remained relatively weak. The majority of the expanding educated middle class, largely the product of domestic universities, is conservative by nature and does not want 'radical' changes in the 'Saudi way of life'. They agreed, however, with the liberals' criticism about the wasteful and costly achievements of the kingdom's modernisation which, many believed, benefited US and European economies more than Saudi Arabia's. The same applied, they asserted, to the Saudi armed forces, trained by a host of foreign experts, which remained weak and inconsequential, despite the enormous investment in it. This, they claimed, was the intention of the regime, which refused to establish a universal military service in the kingdom.[45]

Fahd's pro-American policy, vindicated during the Iran–Iraq war, was still unpopular in 1990. This was an outcome of the US' special relations with Israel and due to the fact that many educated and semi-educated Saudis believed that Western interests were not compatible with Arab-Muslim aspirations. Above all, to conservative Saudis, the US represents materialistic, Christian 'infidel' values and power, which challenge Islamic values and Muslim power. Hence, Saudi relations with Washington between 1988 and 1990 seemed occasionally strained, largely as the result of Riyadh's wish to demonstrate, to its nationalist intelligentsia and ulama, its independence of American policy or its displeasure with America's support of Israel.[46]

While Saudi Arabia's Sunni majority, with negligible exceptions, consolidated its ranks behind the regime until and after the end of the Iran–Iraq war (August 1988), the same could not be said about the kingdom's Shi'ites. The Mecca massacre (July 1987) and its aftermath, Fahd's decision to limit the number of the Iranian pilgrims, the struggle for power in Tehran and Shi'ite-sponsored terrorist activities in the kingdom, each exacerbated the tension between Saudi Arabia and Iran and affected the Saudi Shi'ite population. Security measures were bolstered in the kingdom's different provinces, particularly in the Eastern one. Suspected members of Shi'ite clandestine and leftist organisations were rounded up for interrogation and many were arrested. The latter included Saudi political exiles, who had returned to their country following a general amnesty declared by Riyadh at the beginning of 1988. Indeed, the growing number of political prisoners in the Eastern Province necessitated the construction of a new prison in Al-Hasa. The security services were also greatly expanded and their training improved with American help.[47]

Tension between Tehran and Riyadh over the hajj quota in 1988, a major cause for the eruption of acts of sabotage in major oil and other industrial installations in the Eastern Province, resulted as well in the extension of terrorist activities, largely by foreign Shi'ites, to Hijaz.[48] This wave of violence culminated in the killing of three policemen in Al-Qatif by a local Hizbollah (Party of God) cell which intended to attack oil installations and government offices.

Endorsing once again the historical alliance between 'state and church' in Saudi Arabia, the Council of the Assembly of Senior Ulama (*Majlis Hay'at Kibar al-'Ulama*), convened in Ta'if (Hijaz) between 20 and 24 August, produced a *fatwa* permitting the execution of terrorists who destroyed property and human lives and undermined the security of the state.[49] Following the issue of that *fatwa* four Saudi Shi'ites, responsible for the killing of the three policemen in Al-Qatif, who underwent training in Iran and later smuggled explosives into the kingdom, were publicly executed. Shortly afterwards, several members of the Lebanese Hizbollah responsible for bombing incidents in the Hijaz and Riyadh, which resulted in several deaths, were also executed.[50]

Notwithstanding continued attempts to improve relations with Tehran and Arab radical states, the Saudi regime was determined to suppress any militant opposition group, whether fundamentalist or leftist, Shi'ite or Sunni. Hence, a wide-scale hunt for members of such groups began at the end of 1988 and many were arrested. Indeed, even a verbal attack on a government official, or 'spreading rumours', became a criminal offence punishable by imprisonment.[51]

The death of Ayatollah Khomayni in June 1989, which exacerbated the struggle for power in Tehran, and the 1989 hajj season gave rise to a new wave of Shi'ite terrorist activities in Saudi Arabia and against Saudi targets and diplomats abroad. Two bombs exploded near the Grand Mosque in Mecca on 10 July, causing the death of several pilgrims. Subsequently, about 30 members of a Kuwaiti-dominated Shi'ite terrorist group called 'The Arab Fury Generation' were arrested. Of the 19 Kuwaitis who were found guilty of involvement in the Mecca incident, 16 were publicly executed in September and three were given prison sentences. During the trial, it became evident that the newly re-established Iranian embassy in Kuwait had co-ordinated the activities of this group and supplied it with explosives and weapons. The beheading of the Kuwaiti Shi'ites caused general consternation in their country. Although the Kuwaiti government did not publicly criticise Riyadh, relations between the two countries further deteriorated.[52]

Offshoots of the Lebanese Hizbollah and other extremist Shi'ite groups took revenge for the execution of the Shi'ite terrorists by bombing Saudi targets and assassinating Saudi diplomats in the Middle East, South East Asia and Europe.[53] It also became evident that militant Sunni fundamentalist groups were directly, or indirectly, being supported by Tehran, or were co-operating with Arab Shi'ite fundamentalist organisations, supported by the Iranian *Da'wa*. The Egyptian authorities, for instance, arrested at the beginning of August a fundamentalist terrorist group which had been trained by Saudi Shi'ites based in Damascus. The group, composed of 52 Egyptians and 4 Saudis and Iranians included university professors, doctors and students, some of whom converted to Shi'ism.[54] Saudi Sunni, largely tribal, 'neo-fundamentalists', allegedly belonging to a group called 'The Martyr Juhayman ibn Saif al-'Utaybi', trained abroad and later incarcerated in Saudi Arabia, were said to have entered the kingdom via Yemen.[55] A group of Egyptian fundamentalists were also arrested by the Saudi authorities in the Hijaz and extradited to Egypt. Other Arab–Sunni fundamentalists, some Sudanese and some North Africans, who had found refuge in the Hijaz, were also expelled to their respective countries, but not before producing neo-Ikhwan and 'neo-fundamentalist' disciples in the kingdom.[56]

It seems that the Hijaz, which had been in the past a haven for Arab and other Muslim Brothers (Ikhwan), had become since the 1970s, particularly following the success of the Iranian Islamic revolution, a centre of activity of Arab militant fundamentalist groups.[57] Apprehensive about the growing influence of such groups among the kingdom's younger conservative population in the 1980s, the Saudi security services closely watched them and incarcerated their members, including ulama, teachers, businessmen, administrators and Saudi-Aramco employees.[58] Such steps, coupled with tighter security measures instituted by Riyadh during the conflict with Baghdad, and the Shi'ite clandestine groups' decision temporarily to stop their operations against the Saudi regime during the Iraq crisis, were probably responsible for the absence of serious anti-government and anti-American terrorist activities in the kingdom between August 1990 and April 1991.[59]

Generally speaking, the intelligentsia's discontent and subversion by Shi'ite fundamentalists or tiny leftist groups in the 1980s was relatively insignificant. Undoubtedly, the most serious challenge to the Saudi regime up to August 1990 emanated from the prolonged economic recession. Businessmen, entrepreneurs, unemployed graduates and, above all, the Saudi masses, who continued to suffer from the economic crisis despite Riyadh's optimistic promises, began to question Fahd's ability to deal with the situation and increasingly criticised the behaviour of members of Al Saud. Notwithstanding the monarch's reiterated declarations in 1989 that the economic crisis was over, the Saudi people did not sense the change. This was why Riyadh needed quickly to increase its oil revenue and why it reversed its oil pricing policy. Increased revenue, the regime believed, was also essential to its ability to manoeuvre in inter-Arab politics.

SAUDI ARABIA AND INTER-ARAB AFFAIRS

Riyadh's influence in the Arab world was an outcome of its oil wealth. Generous donations to Muslim, especially Arab, countries enhanced Saudi Arabia's position in this group and enabled it to play the role of arbitrator in Arab and Muslim politics. But, as its oil revenue and financial reserves rapidly declined in the 1980s, Riyadh's ability to grant aid to its poor co-religionists and neighbours, Iraq excluded, rapidly diminished. By the late 1980s, even its aid to the 'confrontation countries', i.e. Syria, Jordan, Iraq (the PLO excepted) and to Egypt, dwindled to a trickle. Naturally, this seriously reduced Saudi influence in Arab politics.

Saudi Arabia had played a major role in the GCC since its inception in 1981. As a result of its coaxing, the GCC became a mutual defence organisation which even Kuwait, despite previous reservations, joined in 1986. Even earlier, Saudi Arabia and Kuwait had closely co-ordinated their policies concerning the Iran–Iraq war. Yet it was Kuwait, rather than Riyadh, that overcame its apprehension of pan-Arab nationalist and Shi'ite reactions and facilitated the massive American naval build-up in the Gulf in 1987.

As discussed above, Saudi relations with Kuwait gradually deteriorated in the last months of 1988 partly because of the Emirate's oil policy. With its 30 per cent Shi'ite population Kuwait rapidly improved its relations with Iran after the latter agreed to an armistice with Iraq and the two countries reopened their embassies in each other's capital. Kuwait city thereafter became a base for anti-Saudi terrorist operations. The conservative Saudi regime also viewed with displeasure Kuwait's renewed experimentation with 'democracy' and its competition with it for the role of a 'peace broker' in the Arab camp.[60] The Emirate, no longer endorsing Riyadh's support for a strong US naval presence in the Gulf, insisted on the removal of an American floating base from its territorial water and deflagged several of its American-registered tankers. To add insult to injury, Kuwait, which hosted a Gulf football tournament in 1989, tactlessly chose as the emblem for these games the image of two horses, symbolising its victory over a Saudi invading force in 1920;[61] this caused Riyadh to boycott the games. Lastly, the execution of the Kuwaiti Shi'ites responsible for bombings in Mecca in July 1989 further strained relations between the two countries.

To offset their weakness both Kuwait and Saudi Arabia competed for the role of a mediator in the Arab camp, especially with regard to the civil war in Lebanon. Most annoying to the Saudis was the fact that, from mid-1989, when Saudi Arabia desperately needed additional income, Kuwait (and the UAE) caused oil prices to decline through overproduction. Hence, the Saudis allied themselves on this matter with Iraq (and Iran), and, even earlier, disregarding the GCC mutual defence pact, signed two non-belligerence pacts with Baghdad in March 1989. Indeed, Riyadh's lukewarm co-operation with Baghdad before August 1990 may have been a contributing factor to Iraq's invasion of Kuwait.

IRAQ'S REGIONAL ASPIRATIONS RE-EMERGING

Saddam Hussayn emerged from the war with Iran with enormous prestige and self-confidence and a powerful and seasoned army. Still devoted to the Ba'th party's pan-Arab ideology, the Iraqi president aspired to establish Iraq's hegemony in the Gulf, if not in the Arab world as a whole. Hence, he strove to rehabilitate his country's economy quickly and was determined to strengthen further his military power and political clout through the rapid expansion of Iraq's conventional and unconventional weapons industry and arsenal.

The war with Iran had practically driven Iraq to bankruptcy. It owed 35-40 billion dollars to its Gulf benefactors and more than that to its Soviet, French and other arms suppliers, to foreign trade partners, contractors and banks.[62] In so far as its rich Gulf neighbours now refused to help finance Saddam Hussayn's plans, Baghdad was practically unable to obtain credit abroad. With OPEC's oil price around 15 dollars a barrel in 1988, Iraq's petroleum industry was generating a revenue of about 12 billion dollars annually, hardly sufficient for a nation of 17 million people with ambitious economic development and military programmes and an enormous foreign debt. Thus, the Iraqi leader opted to maximise his country's revenue by expanding its oil production and export capacity and by increasing oil prices.

Aware that Iraq's demands in the peace negotiations with Iran were unrealistic, Riyadh, although it tried privately to mitigate them, publicly sided with Baghdad. It also continued to grant Iraq some financial assistance from the sale of the neutral zone's oil; and when Saddam Hussayn attended the Ta'if Islamic conference in 1988, he was received with the highest honours. In addition Riyadh was instrumental in the Reagan and especially in the Bush administrations' decisions greatly to increase, from 1988, the Office of Agriculture's Commodities Credit Corporations guarantees to Iraq to help rehabilitate its economy. Yet, Saudi support for Iraq was born of sheer political necessity. The Sauds well remembered that before Iran's 'Islamic revolution' Baghdad was considered the regional predator and its Ba'thist regime was anathema to the Wahhabi ulama.

By 1989 Saddam Hussayn fully realised that the bi-polar world order, which previously he had shrewdly exploited, was rapidly changing. His old ally the Soviet Union, no longer a superpower, had different priorities; he could not count on its help to achieve his ambitions. Yet

Saddam was determined to continue to build up his military industry and power despite his financial difficulties. Thus, he even diverted funds from the US credit guarantees to his weapons development programme and paid with American wheat for arms obtained from Soviet-bloc countries. This was revealed in the ongoing US Congress' investigation of the Banca Nazionale del Lavoro (BNL) Atlanta branch, whose manager enabled Iraq to use American guaranteed agriculture credit to the tune of about 5 billion dollars for different purposes.

Exasperated by Kuwait's and Saudi Arabia's refusal to continue their financial support to Iraq and their objection to its joining the GCC, Saddam Hussayn was the driving force behind the formation in Baghdad, on 16 February 1989, of the Arab Co-operation Council (ACC) together with the rulers of Egypt, Jordan and North Yemen. Although ostensibly an economic co-operation organisation, the ACC was a strange collection of unequals, with different types of regime. As a political body, it was meant to counterbalance the Saudi-led GCC. The only factor common to all the ACC members was their need for financial aid, which the GCC countries were no longer willing, or able, to grant.[63]

Not wishing to antagonise the Saudis, the ACC partners, particularly Egypt, exerted themselves to convince Riyadh that the organisation was purely an economic one, not aimed against the kingdom. Hence Taha Yassin Ramadan, the Iraqi president's deputy, arrived in Riyadh on 25 February to explain the nature and aims of the new organisation. Notwithstanding, Riyadh's and its allies' suspicions of the ACC were exacerbated when Iraq's leaders reverted to traditional Ba'thist slogans, increased their pressure on Kuwait concerning territorial and financial claims and intensified their involvement in the Lebanese and Arab–Israeli conflicts.[64]

The Saudi rulers' uneasiness following the emergence of the ACC was to be expected. They resented King Hussayn's role in initiating this alliance, were angry at the inclusion in it of Yemen, which they considered to be in their own back yard, and were displeased by Cairo's participation in this body. Above all, they were apprehensive of Baghdad's aspirations in the region. Following President Mubarak's visit to Riyadh at the end of February to explain the ACC's aims, King Fahd announced his intention to visit Cairo at the end of March. Yet, following deliberations in the royal family, Fahd flew first to Baghdad on 25 March to meet with Saddam Hussayn and, the next day, signed with the Iraqi ruler two non-aggression pacts. Considering all the help that Riyadh had rendered to Iraq during its war against Iran, it seems strange that the two 'fraternal' countries needed such pacts. Yet, remembering Iraq's subversive activities in the Arabian Peninsula in the 1970s and aware of Saddam's renewed pan-Arab ambitions, Riyadh now needed reassurance concerning Baghdad's future intentions.[65]

In the coming year Riyadh endeavoured to drive a wedge between Egypt and Iraq, responded positively to Syria's efforts to overcome its isolation and supported Damascus against Iraqi attempts to undermine its position in Lebanon. Indeed Saddam's efforts to eject Syria from Lebanon at the Arab League's summit meeting in Casablanca in May failed, largely owing to Riyadh's behind-the-scenes intervention. Further, a Saudi-initiated conference of Lebanese leaders convened in Ta'if in August, led to the 24 October Ta'if pact to end the Lebanese civil war and essentially recognised Syria's hegemony in Lebanon. Lastly, after Ayatollah Khomayni's death in June 1989, Riyadh, following its GCC allies, renewed its efforts to improve relations with Tehran thus hoping, *inter alia*, to offset Iraq's power in the region.[66]

Saudi suspicions concerning the ACC in general, and of Saddam Hussayn's aspirations in particular, were exacerbated following an ACC summit in San'a in September 1989. There, the Iraqi delegation, using traditional Ba'thist terminology, endorsed the forthcoming unification of the two Yemens – anathema to Riyadh. Hence, by the end of 1989, as Saddam Hussayn's pan-Arab ambitions became more evident, Prince Bandar, the Sudayris' ambassador in Washington, declared that he expected the US to protect his country if attacked. He described Iraq 'as the most immediate potential threat' to Saudi Arabia 'because of its ideology' and because of historical border problems between the two countries. Iraq, he added, considered itself the local superpower and the vanguard of pan-Arab ideology.[67]

The ACC meetings and summits in the year following its inception provided Saddam Hussayn with a platform to further his pan-Arab ambitions and efforts to establish Iraq as the leading Middle East power. The ACC's Amman summit in the last week of February 1990, which focused on the 'threat' to the Arab countries from the immigration of Soviet Jews to Israel, was a crucial one. It not only enabled Saddam to appear as the champion of the pan-Arab and Palestinian causes, but also openly to attack an 'American–Zionist conspiracy' aimed at undermining Iraq's efforts to acquire 'technology' and to develop a sophisticated weapons industry. The Iraqi president bluntly challenged the continued American naval presence in the Gulf and involvement in its affairs. He also called upon the Arab countries 'to withdraw their investments in the United States until it stopped its aggressive policy against the Arabs, its activities to prevent Iraq from acquiring technology and its support for Israel'. Indirectly, he criticised the Gulf rulers for co-operating with America and serving its interests.[68] Obviously, in addition to challenging the US, this was a challenge to both Kuwait and Saudi Arabia.

Determined to expedite the development of Iraq's conventional and unconventional military industry, Saddam Hussayn, using part of Iraq's oil revenue and credit obtained by devious means (largely from the US),[69] expanded in Europe and in America the network which acquired, by all possible means, factories, machinery, parts, chemicals and technology for that industry. All the above, however, necessitated resources beyond those available to Iraq. Thus, the refusal of both Kuwait and Riyadh to renew their massive financial aid to Iraq once Iran no longer posed a threat to it may have caused Saddam to contemplate Kuwait's (and possibly Saudi Arabia's) annexation as early as 1988.

Iraq's efforts to acquire advanced technology and components for its conventional and unconventional weapons industry did not escape the attention of some US government officials and agencies (for instance the CIA's detailed report from 4 September 1989, according to *NYT*, 2 August 1992) and of Israel. Thus, the purchase of 'insecticide factories' and chemicals in West Germany, and the acquisition of 'dual purpose' machinery, foundries and components of different types, claimed to be for Iraq's agriculture, oil and other industries, in America and Europe, but truly intended for Saddam's missile and unconventional weapons industry, began to unravel in 1989 and the beginning of 1990.[70] The BNL scandal (the extent of which and the Bush administration's appeasement policy towards Baghdad has partly emerged through the investigation of the US Congress' banking committee led by Representative Henry Gonzalez in 1992), followed by the assassination in Belgium of Dr Bull, the Canadian developer of the 'super gun', supposedly capable of firing chemical, bacteriological and nuclear shells at targets about a thousand miles away,[71] opened a pandora's box. Information concerning the procurement, in European countries, of different items for Iraq's poison gas and missile industries and, above all, for nuclear facilities came to light. In April 1990, British customs confiscated switching devices to be used as triggers for nuclear bombs, smuggled out of America and destined for Baghdad. This further vindicated claims that Iraq was rapidly developing its nuclear capability, a matter strongly refuted by Baghdad and conveniently ignored by UN agencies and many of Iraq's industrial trade partners until August 1990. Israel pointed out, moreover, that despite his financial difficulties Saddam had not demobilised his one-million-strong army following the 1988 cease-fire with Iran.

The efforts co-ordinated by the Americans thereafter to foil Iraqi military aspirations so enraged Saddam Hussayn that they triggered his accusations in the Amman conference about an 'American–Zionist conspiracy' aimed at halting Iraq's 'scientific advancement'.

Soviet Jewish immigration to Israel, which gained momentum at the end of 1989, awakened strong emotional opposition in the Arab world. Arab politicians and journalists claimed that the wave of Jewish immigrants would accelerate Jewish settlement in the occupied territories and help Israel's 'expansionism' in the Middle East. Yet, above all, this migration seemed to end long-standing Arab hopes that the Palestinians' high birth rate would eventually submerge the Jewish state. Coupled with hurt pride and anti-American sentiments prevalent among Arab nationalists and fundamentalists, this became a vehicle for Saddam's regional and pan-Arab aspirations.

Most Arabs approved of Saddam Hussayn's efforts to change the balance of power in the Middle East and to acquire 'a military option' against Israel. An Arab nuclear capability to offset Israel's alleged capability was (and still is) desired by several Arab leaders. But only Saddam was on the verge of achieving it when, in 1981, Israel destroyed his Tamuz nuclear reactor and complex, and again in 1991, as revealed by the findings of the UN inspection teams. Saddam Hussayn, previously, did not hesitate to make indiscriminate use of unconventional weapons against Iran and the Kurds. Thus, some Arab leaders who previously supported him, and the US from the second part of 1989, suspected that he was capable of exploiting his unconventional capability, including a nuclear one, as leverage to achieve his aspirations in the region and, possibly, in the world.

IRAQ, PAN-ARABISM AND THE GULF OIL

In interviews following the Amman summit (February 1990), Saddam reiterated his call to end the American naval presence in the Gulf. A presence, one source claimed, which 'prevents Kuwait from returning to the Arab fold'.[72] Thus, Riyadh became even more concerned about Saddam's intentions.

To allay Saudi anxiety, Saddam Hussayn prudently accepted Fahd's invitation to visit the kingdom and explain his position. An Iraqi summary of this visit (17-18 March) claimed that besides condemning the danger of the immigration of Soviet Jews to Israel, the purpose of the Iraqi president's visit was to refute, 'in the most frank and friendly manner, allegations which had reached King Fahd and the Saudi government' (about his aspirations?). The talks also touched 'on bilateral relations . . ., the advancement of security in the region (the American naval presence?) and the prevention of any attempt to undermine' it.[73]

A more vitriolic attack by Saddam Hussayn on America, the West and Israel on 2 April followed the execution of *The Observer*'s correspondent, Farzad Bazoft, who attempted to investigate an explosion in an Iraqi nuclear installation and was accused of spying for Israel. Saddam asserted that there was an 'American-British-Zionist' plot to prevent Baghdad from obtaining advanced military technology and that the 'Powers' were 'falsely accusing Iraq of developing nuclear bombs'. Admitting that Baghdad possessed chemical weapons, he threatened 'to burn half of Israel, if the latter attacked Iraq or the Arabs'. Deriding America's capability as a superpower, he pointed out the US vulnerability to the 'oil weapon'. Lastly, he underscored another 'conspiracy' to undermine Iraq's economy by reducing the price of oil and threatened those who were helping it.[71]

The escalation of Saddam's bellicose rhetoric and references to the Gulf countries' oil policy and their US ties caused grave concern in Riyadh and Cairo. President Mubarak, who did not relish playing second fiddle in the Arab leadership and did not wish for an Arab–US confrontation nor another round of war with Israel, flew to Baghdad shortly after Saddam's 2 April speech. He tried to restrain his Iraq ally and to postpone the Arab League's summit on Soviet Jewish immigration, which Saddam planned to convene in Baghdad. Mubarak had Riyadh's blessing for both goals; like him, Fahd was convinced that Saddam Hussayn on his home field, manipulating the Arab masses' minds, would control the summit and exploit it for his own aims and for self-aggrandisement.[75]

It did not take Mubarak long to realise that the Iraqi president was determined to hold the summit in Baghdad. He became convinced as well that Saddam Hussayn, carried away by his own rhetoric, was ready to lead the Arabs to a confrontation with the United States over its Middle East policy and its 'embargo' on the transfer of military technology to Baghdad. Mubarak, therefore, arranged in the middle of April for visiting US senators, led by Robert Dole, to meet Saddam in Baghdad and listen to his grievances against the US, which many Arabs shared. On this occasion the Senate's republican minority leader who was close to President Bush apologised to Saddam Hussayn for a Voice of America attack on him for human rights violations and the gassing of thousands of his Kurdish citizens.

Even before the May Arab League summit in Baghdad, which again established Saddam's claim to pan-Arab leadership, the Iraqi leader's defiance of the US had made him a hero of the Arab masses who had craved such a leader ever since Nasser's death. The fact that Saddam was a cruel tyrant was irrelevant, for he rekindled in the Arabs' hearts a sense of pride and a feeling of power. In a speech on 18 April, the Iraqi president again emphasised Iraq's 'duty' to protect all the Arabs against any aggressor. He also claimed for Iraq the role of a champion of non-aligned states against the superpowers and the leadership of the Arabs in their long-standing conflicts with the 'Persians and the Jews'.[76]

Many Arabs welcomed Saddam's defiance of the world and his attempts to counteract 'the shameful and prevailing image of Arab weakness'. The Arab press, even in Egypt, repeatedly praised the Iraqi leader's stand against Israel and the West and fully supported Saddam in the face of what was portrayed as a Western-inspired campaign against him.[77] Although the Saudi and other moderate Arab rulers feared the outcome of

Saddam's fiery rhetoric, they were incapable of challenging him because, like Nasser, he inspired popular Arab support.

The extraordinary Arab League summit convened in Baghdad on 28 May 1990 was meant to discuss the Soviet Jews' immigration to Israel. This summit marked the climax of Saddam's endeavours to attain recognition as a pan-Arab leader. He managed to overshadow his rivals, Mubarak and Assad (who did not attend the summit) and his bellicose stance regarding America and Israel, which won popular Arab support, was adopted by the summit. Mubarak's moderate approach, arguing that improving relations with Washington would cause America to coerce Israel to attend a peace conference and relinquish the occupied territories, was ignored even by the moderate Arab leaders who covertly supported it.[78]

As the conference's host, Saddam delivered the keynote speech, whose introduction dwelt on the unification of the two Yemens which took place on 22 May (a slap in Riyadh's face). Much of the speech was devoted to the importance of Arab solidarity and of pan-Arabism. In the name of the Arab masses Saddam called upon the Arab rulers to unite in common action and policy and indirectly demanded that the pro-Western oil regimes reverse their policy and support 'those capable of leading the Arabs'. A united Arab nation, he asserted, would persuade America to stop its support of Israel and accept Arab demands.

Saddam also had his own axe to grind. He stressed the need to confront 'American imperialism', warning that weakness in the general Arab stance *vis-à-vis* foreign powers 'could manifest itself in granting facilities to them'. The Arabs, he said, should withhold their resources (oil) and wealth (investment) from those who are fighting us or 'opposing our scientific and technological progress'. His attack on Israel and its American benefactor was entwined with strong criticism of the GCC members' unwillingness to support Baghdad while co-operating with the US.[79]

Undoubtedly, Saddam Hussayn moved, at the Baghdad summit, one step closer to a regional role. Yet, his rivals, Mubarak and Hafiz al-Assad, who in the meantime overcame their differences, could also count on the support of the conservative Arab rulers led by King Fahd. Obliged to attend a summit they did not wish to take place, Fahd and Mubarak were now even more concerned about Saddam's ambitions and apprehensive about his confrontational attitude towards America and Israel. In the summit's closed sessions they challenged Saddam over his policy, which could push the region into war and chaos. On his part the Iraqi president took to task the 'quota-busters' and their low oil price policy, claiming that '. . . this is in fact a kind of war against Iraq'.[80]

The GCC summit, which met in Ta'if in the first week of June did not reflect the Gulf rulers' anxiety over Saddam's accusations a few days earlier. Rather, in the opening speeches, tribute was paid to the Baghdad summit and the Kuwaiti delegation congratulated the two Yemens on their unification.[81] None the less, Riyadh was disturbed by Saddam's latest accusations and greatly concerned as well about developments in Yemen. Unified Yemen had a population of 12-13 million citizens, compared with Saudi Arabia's six million and its militant republican regime was unfriendly to the 'reactionary' Saudi monarchy which had opposed the Yemens' unification. Nearly two million Yemenis, moreover, were employed in the kingdom, mainly low-paid manual labourers. The Saudis were also worried about Baghdad's expanding relations with San'a and the fact that Iraqi officers were training the Yemeni army. Above all, large sections of the border regions between Saudi Arabia and the new Yemen, containing sizeable oil resources, remained undefined, a matter that in the past had caused many clashes between Saudi Arabia and both Yemeni republics.[82]

Commemorating the 22nd anniversary of the Iraqi Ba'th's revolution, Saddam Hussayn delivered a speech on 17 July which constituted the opening shot of the Iraqi conquest of Kuwait. Most of the speech was an expansion on his 28 May attack on Israel, underscoring Iraq's present military–scientific capabilities, and the alleged 'Zionist–American–British conspiracy' to deprive Iraq of modern technology. Yet, towards the end of his speech, Saddam referred to an additional 'imperialist–Zionist conspiracy' aimed against Iraq's economy and scientific advancement through the reduction of oil prices. Saddam claimed that 'a decline of every dollar a barrel in oil price resulted in a drop of one billion dollars in Iraq's annual revenue'. As OPEC's oil price 'fell in recent years from 27 dollars or 28 dollars a barrel to the current level' Iraq has been losing 14 billion dollars annually.

'Certain Arab oil regimes', Saddam added, 'were co-operating with America, who wishes to control Arab oil and buy it as cheaply as possible and thus undermine Arab capability and power. The US, which will need to import increasing quantities of Arab oil, is striving to ensure its flow to it . . . and to increase its strategic oil reserve. That would guarantee its position as a superpower able to control the instigation of wars . . . and when and how to impose stability . . .'.

'The convergence of interests between (the) US . . . and the policy of certain Arabs who trade in oil and politics – some of whom are oil ministers and some of whom are at a higher level – constitutes the most important feature of this subversive policy.' ' . . . The United States and Israel would then be out to start wars . . . without worrying about a potential halt to the flow of oil to American and other world markets [referring to the 'oil weapon' strategy]' '. . . Hence, the policies pursued by certain Arab rulers are American-inspired and detrimental to the interests of the Arab nation . . . they . . . have thrust their poisoned dagger into our back.' Finally, Saddam threatened to punish the traitors and the 'quota-busters'.[83]

In a letter to the Arab League's Secretary General on 16 July, which was immediately released to the Iraqi media, Tariq Aziz, Iraq's foreign minister, mentioning Kuwait and the UAE, but not Saudi Arabia, by name, asserted that they had deliberately undermined Iraq's economy by exceeding their OPEC quotas and thereby depressing oil prices. He also claimed that Kuwait had encroached on Iraq's territory and its Rumayla oil field and 'stolen' from it 2.4 billion dollars' worth of oil, and that Kuwait refused to write off the sums it had lent to Baghdad during the war. 'We register', continued Tariq Aziz, 'Iraq's right to get back the stolen amounts . . . Things have developed to a level which we can no longer ignore.'[84]

Responding to the Iraqi letter, Kuwait on 19 July not only rejected the Iraqi claims but accused Baghdad of repeatedly violating its territory. The Kuwaiti government called for Arab League mediation between it and Iraq. Subsequently, Shazli Klaybi, the League's Secretary General, visited both Kuwait and Baghdad.

King Fahd and President Mubarak telephoned the Iraqi and Kuwaiti rulers on 20 July, urging them to settle their differences amicably. Yet, on the same day the Iraqi government-controlled press viciously attacked Kuwait's rulers for supporting 'American and Zionist conspiracies' against Iraq.[85]

Iraq, immediately after its independence, had invaded Kuwait in 1961 and 1973 and had never renounced its claims to Kuwait's territory. Even during the war with Iran, when Kuwait's and Saudi Arabia's financial and logistical support saved Iraq, Saddam occasionally revived some of Iraq's territorial claims against Kuwait. Such claims focused on the strategic Bubyan and Warba Islands, which block most of Iraq's narrow Persian Gulf coast.

The peace negotiations between Iraq and Iran were stalled by the beginning of 1989 because of Baghdad's insistence on full control of the Shatt-al-Arab and other territorial concessions by Tehran. Temporarily despairing of opening its ports along the Shatt-al-Arab, Iraq undertook in mid-1989 a major project of rehabilitating and expanding its oil terminals along its Persian Gulf coast. In October 1989, Iraq announced the beginning of the construction of a major port at Umm Qasr at the head of Khor Abdallah, which it shares with Kuwait. This announcement coincided with the termination of the construction of the IPSA2 pipeline from Iraq's Rumayla fields through Saudi Arabia to a terminal south of Yanbu on the Red Sea. With an initial capacity of 800,000 barrels daily, the pipeline was projected eventually to carry 1.5 m.b.d. of Iraqi oil to the world's markets.[86]

Iraq revived its territorial claims against Kuwait, particularly concerning Bubyan and Warba, at the beginning of 1989 and even more forcefully in the second part of the year and also requested a 10-billion-dollar loan. Kuwait, on its part, decided to build a town on Bubyan and connect it to Kuwait proper by a causeway in order to establish its sovereignty over the island.

In the face of mounting Iraqi hostility, Shaykh Sa'd Al Abdallah al-Sabah, Kuwait's crown prince and prime minister, visited Baghdad in February 1989, attempting to solve Kuwait's border problems with Iraq. His visit was followed in May by a visit from Kuwait's defence minister, Nawwaf Al Ahmad al-Sabbah, whose efforts also failed. The tension between the two countries seemed to abate after the visit to Baghdad in September of Kuwait's Amir, Shaykh Jabir, when, it was claimed, Iraq did not press its territorial demands, nor its request for a 10-billion-dollar loan.[87] An incursion of Iraqi forces into Kuwaiti territory at the end of 1989, however, suspiciously coincided with Baghdad's disclosure of its intention to deepen and widen Khor Abdallah. Subsequently, in the first months of 1990, Iraq frequently reiterated its demands for the control of Bubyan and Warba.[88]

Critical of Kuwait's oil policy, Baghdad began in mid-1989 to exert pressure on the former to stop exceeding its OPEC quota. Kuwait did not hide the fact that its over-production, an outcome of its long-range policy aimed at blocking any rise in oil price, had resulted from growth in demand. Hence, the Emirate (and the UAE) again exceeded its production in the first months of 1990, causing prices to decline sharply. Iraq's conquest of Kuwait was thus prompted by the latter's manipulation of oil prices, its refusal to lend Baghdad 10 billion dollars which it badly needed,[89] and rejection of Iraq's territorial demands concerning Bubyan and Warba. More fundamentally, Baghdad had always considered Kuwait part of 'historical Iraq' and coveted its wealth.

While Arab leaders were attempting to defuse the tension between the two countries, Baghdad began, in the third week of July, to move military forces to Kuwait's border. Simultaneously, the Iraqi press published vicious anti-Kuwaiti editorials, *inter alia*, accusing Kuwait's foreign minister (the amir's brother) of involving the UN in an 'Arab conflict' and of being an 'agent' of US policy in the Gulf.[90]

Saddam Hussayn's speech in the Baghdad summit, it seems, caused Saudi Arabia and Egypt to co-ordinate their policies more closely. This was reflected in exchanges of messages between the two leaders and a visit of President Mubarak to Fahd in Jedda on 11 July. The talks were described as having to do with 'Arab national security and the advancement of the peace process'. Mubarak, moreover, did not send a representative to the Arab foreign ministers' meeting in Tunisia, a follow-up of the Baghdad summit. For this he was accused by Tariq Aziz (and Yassir Arafat) in Tunis of being too friendly with the United States.[91]

The Saudi and Egyptian rulers' mediation brought Tariq Aziz to Alexandria on 22 July for a meeting with President Mubarak. King Hussayn joined the talks on the following day. Immediately afterwards, Mubarak flew to Baghdad and Kuwait, where he held talks with both Saddam Hussayn and the Kuwaiti Amir. On 25 July, King Fahd and President Mubarak announced that Iraq and Kuwait had agreed to discuss their differences in Jedda at the end of the month. Saddam, moreover, promised both Mubarak and King Fahd that he had no intention of invading Kuwait.[92]

Riyadh was greatly disturbed by Saddam's tactless accusations that the US was building up its oil stockpile with the help of Arab rulers to undermine Iraq's economy and 'Arab' achievements and that 'the policies of some Arab rulers are American'. King Fahd and other moderate Arab rulers had become convinced that Saddam Hussayn was not concerned just with the price of oil, but with much broader financial and political aims that had to do with his pan-Arab aspirations.[93] Indeed, both Kuwait and the UAE had totally capitulated in the Jedda meeting, several days before Saddam's 17 July speech. Yet, this did not deter Saddam Hussayn from his vicious attacks on their rulers. Even Kuwait's and the UAE's support at the Geneva summit on 26-7 July, for all the points agreed upon in Jedda two weeks earlier, did not alter Iraq's bellicose stance.

Talks between Iraqi representatives led by Izzat Ibrahim, Saddam's deputy, and the Kuwaiti delegation, led by Crown Prince Sa'd Al Abdallah, opened on 31 July in Jedda. In the first working session on 1 August it became clear that the Iraqis were not interested in a peaceful solution. In addition to exorbitant financial demands from Kuwait as 'compensation', and writing off the Iraqi debt, Baghdad insisted on the acceptance of all its territorial demands. The Kuwaitis were willing to pay a fraction of the sum demanded by Baghdad in addition to writing off the Iraqi debt. They were also ready, they later claimed, to lease Warba Island to Iraq, but not Bubyan. Rather than continue the negotiations, the Iraqi delegation immediately left for Baghdad and Saddam's army invaded Kuwait on the following day.[94]

171

10

SAUDI ARABIA AND THE WAR
WITH IRAQ

THE IRAQ-KUWAIT CRISIS AND SAUDI ARABIA

Saddam Hussayn's Baghdad summit speech left Riyadh with no illusions about the direction which Iraqi policy was taking.[1] Yet, Saudi Arabia's traditional timid and indecisive foreign policy, as well as disagreement within the ruling elite on how to cope with the Iraqi leader's increasing militancy, caused Riyadh to opt for inertia. Indeed, Washington still believed that the Iraqi president's belligerence was a ploy to gain him concessions and leadership in the Arab camp and it continued to cultivate his friendship and grant him economic aid. Thus, Riyadh maintained its co-operation with Baghdad on OPEC's price and production policy, even though it was directed against its GCC allies. It also supported Saddam Hussayn's campaign to stop the immigration of Soviet Jews to Israel and paid lip service to his condemnation of Western efforts to prevent Iraq from obtaining sophisticated military technology.

After Saddam Hussayn's 17 July speech, the Saudi regime, if not most Saudis, became apprehensive about Iraq's next step. A Saudi delegate to OPEC's 26-7 July summit, 'familiar with Saudi official thinking', claimed that 'many Saudis had concluded that Iraq has become a much more serious threat to the Arab world than Israel'.[2] At this critical time, the royal house was split into several camps concerning the policy to be adopted *vis-à-vis* Baghdad. While some senior princes advocated the continuation of Iraq's appeasement, others recommended the creation of a Saudi-Syrian-Egyptian axis instead of, or in addition to, the feeble GCC. For their part, the Sudayris, through Prince Bandar, frequently discussed the situation in the region with Washington but were unwilling to involve the latter in it.

Previously, Washington had largely ignored warnings about Saddam's efforts to build up an unconventional weapons arsenal and industry that could change the Middle East balance of power and endanger the region's stability. Even after the Iraqi president's plans and endeavours to acquire sophisticated military technology and develop a nuclear capability became known, the Bush administration continued to provide Iraq with agricultural products and military intelligence and helped it obtain credit in the US, practically until 2 August. It not only ignored CIA reports on Baghdad's unconventional weapons development and use of poison gas, but shielded Iraq as well from sanctions which the Congress was contemplating following Saddam Hussayn's use of chemical weapons against the Kurds and his threat on 1 April 'to burn half of Israel'.[3]

Yet, reacting to Saddam's 17 July speech, US Defense Secretary, Richard Cheney declared (20 July) that America's commitments to Kuwait had not changed and added that the US took very seriously any threat that would put at risk US interests or friends in the Gulf. As Iraq began to move troops to Kuwait's border several days later, the US warned Iraq (24 July) not to use force in its conflict with Kuwait and began to deploy naval and air force units in the Gulf.[4] Subsequently, April Glaspie, the American ambassador in Baghdad, was summoned to meet Saddam. Instead of inhibiting Iraqi plans to invade Kuwait, it seems that Ms Glaspie's lukewarm warning and earlier talks held between Secretary James Baker and Foreign Minister Tariq Aziz left Saddam with the impression that Washington's reaction to Kuwait's conquest would be limited to condemnation of Iraq in the Security Council or, at most, a demand for some sort of sanctions against it. (For an excellent evaluation of Ambassador Glaspie's capability and her being a scapegoat of the Bush administration's Iraq policy, see: Robert D. Kaplan, 'Tales from the bazaar', *The Atlantic Monthly*, August 1992.) Washington began a serious re-evaluation of its relations with Iraq, but not till the last week of July.[5]

Iraq's invasion of Kuwait on 2 August took Riyadh completely by surprise, particularly as Saddam's delegates had just begun to negotiate with the Kuwaitis in Jedda a day earlier. Saddam Hussayn had given his word to King Fahd, President Mubarak, King Hussayn and to the US, that he had no intention of invading Kuwait. In the first two days after the invasion of Kuwait, Riyadh was totally paralysed by fear. Its media did not even report the event. Though it was in effect the GCC's leader, Saudi Arabia did not even denounce at first the conquest of Kuwait, a signatory of the organisation's mutual defence agreement. In this crucial period, the region's – even the world's – history could have been altered, if the Iraqi forces had continued their advance into Saudi Arabia.[6]

An Arab foreign ministers' meeting convened, at Kuwait's request, on 3 August, as well as Arab officials who gathered earlier in Cairo under the auspices of the ICO, seemed incapable of acting. Even Syria, Iraq's traditional foe, did not call for anything more meaningful than an extraordinary Arab summit. On the other hand, the Security Council, led by the US and with the USSR's full co-operation, acted swiftly. It promptly adopted (2 August) a resolution (660) condemning Baghdad's aggression and demanded 'an immediate and unconditional' Iraqi withdrawal from Kuwait's territory. It also threatened 'to use sanctions and military action, if compliance was not forthcoming'.[7] Indeed, the Soviet Union's rapid disintegration and co-operation with the US was a major factor in shaping the course of this crisis.

Although Saudi Arabia could well become Saddam's next victim, its royal leadership disagreed on whether to turn to the United States for help. The conservatives, led by Abdallah, supported 'an Arab solution' to the crisis and abhorred the very idea of having American 'infidel' troops on Saudi territory. Nationalists, such as Prince Talal, objected to the possibility of fighting 'fraternal' Iraq.[8] The Sudayri brothers, Na'if and Salman, it is claimed, were convinced of the inevitability of requesting US help and of acting resolutely against Iraq but Sultan expressed reservation. Fearing an Islamic and Arab nationalist backlash, Fahd hesitated. Only face-to-face talks with the US Secretary of Defense, sent by President Bush to Saudi Arabia (5 August), convinced Fahd that his kingdom was at risk. In the early hours of 7 August, he agreed to apply to the US for protection.[9] Having received Riyadh's request for aid, Washington immediately despatched air and additional naval forces to Saudi Arabia and to the Persian Gulf.

Despite denials of the fact, Riyadh began to move some reinforcements to Kuwait's border the day after the Iraqi invasion. But only on 4 August did it strongly condemn Iraq's aggression, declaring its full support for the exiled Kuwaiti government in Ta'if. Simultaneously, the Saudis endorsed in Cairo (on 4 and 5 August), Arab League and ICO resolutions denouncing Iraq's conquest of Kuwait.[10]

In the following days, Iraq greatly reinforced its army in Kuwait, part of which was now deployed along the Saudi border. Yet Riyadh, still afraid of Baghdad's reaction, denied reports that it had sent tank units to its Eastern Province. It also continued to permit the flow of Iraqi oil through IPSA2 to its Red Sea terminal until 14 August. Only the arrival of sizeable American forces in Saudi Arabia in the coming days calmed Riyadh's fears. Thereafter, its policy towards Baghdad became far more assertive. Indeed, on 9 August King Fahd made his first public speech since the invasion of Kuwait in which he strongly denounced Iraq's aggression. He also stated that the US military presence in Saudi Arabia was a necessary *temporary* measure and called upon Arab and other friendly forces to participate in Saudi Arabia's defence.[11]

Still apprehensive of Arab and Muslim reaction to its request for US help, which Iraqi propaganda claimed amounted to inviting 'infidel' forces 'to Islam's holy towns',[12] Riyadh badly needed the presence in the kingdom of Arab and 'international' forces to mitigate the American military presence. Such a fig-leaf was provided by President Mubarak, who successfully manipulated the Arab League's Cairo summit to condemn Iraq's aggression and to permit its member states to send troops to protect Saudi Arabia. Thus, Egyptian troops arrived in the kingdom on 11 August, followed by Syrian and Moroccan contingents.[13] Moreover, the Security Council's resolutions 661 and 662, again supported by the Soviets, imposed sweeping trade sanctions on Iraq (blocking its oil exports), and authorised the use of minimal force to implement them. Several European countries, led by the UK and France, also provided international 'cover' for the American operation.[14]

The Soviet Union's co-operation with the United States against its former ally, Iraq, was not achieved, despite the monumental change in the world order, without a price. Indeed, Saud al-Faysal flew to Moscow in mid-September and, following lengthy talks, relations between the two countries were restored and a substantial loan was promised to the USSR. On this occasion, both countries condemned Baghdad for its aggression.[15]

It was now clear that the vast military infrastructure built up by Riyadh over more than a decade, at a cost of tens of billions of dollars, was destined all along for a crisis such as the present one, not for the minuscule Saudi army. The rapidly increasing American land, air and naval forces found ready in Saudi Arabia and the Gulf superb military facilities and installations and stockpiles of munition and spare parts. Yet, the presence in Saudi Arabia of such a large number of American servicemen, including servicewomen, created grave problems for the conservative Wahhabi kingdom, whose ramifications still threaten Saudi Arabia's stability.

Although warned not to offend local sensitivities, it was to be expected that the foreign troops, their lifestyle, behaviour and very presence in the kingdom, would affect, if not offend, many Saudis. Furthermore, this American presence increased existing tensions within Saudi society. Enjoying, for a time, a relaxation of the ulama's tight control over their life, some freedom of expression and access to news sources, the Saudi new elites hoped that the arrival of the Americans heralded a new era in the kingdom. Thus, the liberal intelligentsia in the Eastern Province, now the centre of the American forces, in Riyadh, and particularly in Jedda, began to ignore some of the strict Saudi–Wahhabi prohibitions. They openly discussed politics, and enjoyed a somewhat freer press and access to the international media through the thousands of antenna dishes which mushroomed on rooftops in the kingdom's main cities.

The middle class was frustrated, nevertheless, by the double standard practised by the regime; this still enabled the ulama and their Morality Police strictly to control everyday life in the kingdom, while the royalty's ostentatious lifestyle and corruption were overlooked. They were enraged as well by the commission system and other practices which enriched the aristocracy while all other citizens were called upon to tighten their belts during the recession years. Above all, in this period the middle-class new elites again brought up demands for reform and for wider participation in decision-making.[16]

The dependence of Saudi Arabia on foreign help to protect it caused bitter queries, both among the conservatives and the liberal new elites. Why, despite the 200 billion dollars spent by the government on defence since about 1970, were the Saudi armed forces only about 58,000 strong and totally incapable of defending the kingdom? The establishment ulama were greatly disturbed, on their part, by the US military presence in Saudi Arabia and the liberties taken by the new elites. Indeed, some extremist 'neo-fundamentalist'[17] *fuqaha*' (theologians: singular *faqih*), who represented a new trend among the orthodox in the late 1980s, openly preached against the government policy and America, and called for an Islamic–Arab solution to the crisis, rather than allowing non-believers to protect the holy land of Islam and to fight Muslim Iraq in order to liberate Kuwait.

Questions were also raised, by both liberal and traditional intelligentsia, about the logic of the timid Saud policy in the past and the support given to Baghdad, which practically encouraged the Iraqi aggression, as well as about the regime's 'riyal politik', aimed at acquiring goodwill and influence in the Arab–Muslim world, which proved to be a mirage. Indeed, Saudi nationalism (*wataniyya*) now replaced vague pan-Arab tendencies among elements of the new elites who became sceptical concerning their 'fraternal' relations with other Arab countries.[18] The immediate victims of this new trend were the Palestinians, Jordanians and Yemenis whose governments openly identified with Saddam Hussayn's policy.

Violent anti-Saudi Iraqi propaganda was directed at two target audiences in the Arab camp. The first was Arab nationalists, whose admiration Saddam had won by defying the West and becoming the champion of the 'have-nots' and the Palestinians and by creating a linkage between the solution of the Kuwait crisis and Israel's 'occupied territories'. The second was Islamic conservatives and fundamentalists, to whom the presence of 'infidels' in Arabia was anathema. The latter were told that Fahd, who claims to be 'the protector of Islam's holy shrines', had enabled the Americans to garrison and defile Mecca and Madina.[19]

Riyadh could do little to combat Iraq's pan-Arab propaganda. Anyway, Saudis were not enthusiastic about sharing their oil wealth with the Arab multitudes and were now most unfriendly to the Palestinians. On the other hand, Saddam Hussayn, the head of the secular Ba'th, was never known for his Islamic devotion; but his allegations found an attentive ear among the new generation of militant Wahhabi fundamentalists. Fahd, therefore, endeavoured to disprove the Iraqi claims concerning his piety by further strengthening the Morality

Police's authority and by legitimising the invitation of Western forces to protect Saudi Arabia through a *fatwa* which he requested from the establishment ulama.

Saudi Arabia's foreign policy, guided by Saud al-Faysal, not only became more assertive in this period, but also abandoned pan-Arab motifs and the effort to please all the major players in the Arab camp. It strongly censured the PLO, Jordan, Yemen and, to some extent, Sudan, Algeria and Libya, for their support of Iraq or their sympathy for Saddam Hussayn's cause. This policy was clearly reflected in Saud al-Faysal's speech in the United Nations at the beginning of October, as well as in declarations of Saudi leaders, *inter alia*, rejecting any attempt to buy off Iraq with concessions. An interview in September with Prince Sultan, the defence minister, in which he strongly opposed the use of Saudi territory to attack Iraq, was attributed to misinterpretation. Henceforth the official Saudi policy, co-ordinated by Fahd, was much more in line with Washington's uncompromising position concerning Iraq, than with France's and the USSR's more moderate stance.[20]

Simultaneously, Riyadh became more receptive to Tehran's attempts to improve relations between the two countries despite the latter's declared neutralism concerning the Kuwait crisis, accompanied by strong denunciation of the American intervention. Furthermore, although Iran condemned Kuwait's conquest by Iraq, it seemed to be tilting towards Baghdad after the latter, in a sudden move aimed at securing its flank, accepted all Tehran's demands concerning the peace agreement between the two. Yet, it was also signalling to Riyadh and Washington its intention to remain neutral in the conflict. Iran's policy was undoubtedly influenced by President Rafsanjani's pragmatism; but it was also affected by the power struggle in Tehran and the influence of the radical, dogmatic, strongly anti-American opposition. The Saudi regime, in this critical moment, wished to entice Tehran, as far as it could, away from Baghdad.

Insensitive American journalists and television networks made Fahd's task more difficult by writing about, or displaying footage of, entertainers performing before American troops, and females dancing in front of US soldiers in Dhahran. These performances were taped by Baghdad and broadcast on Iraqi TV, and copies of the tapes gained wide circulation in the kingdom. So did a flood of cassette tapes of sermons by the few score of 'neo-fundamentalist' Saudi *faqihs* who capitalised on the American presence in Saudi Arabia and denounced the regime for inviting 'infidels' to Islam's heartland, and viciously attacked the US and its 'Zionist policy'.[21] The above notwithstanding, the great majority of the ulama, much as they disliked the American presence in their country, were even more apprehensive of the Iraqi threat to the Wahhabi kingdom's very survival and, therefore, fully supported the Saudi regime's policy.

Shortly after he requested US help to defend his country, a major departure from the traditional Saudi 'over the horizon' policy, Fahd convinced the establishment ulama that they must legitimise this act. Subsequently, Saudi Arabia's leading, arch-conservative *'alim*, Shaykh Abd al-Aziz bin Baz, issued a *fatwa* 'that even though the Americans are, in the conservative religious view, equivalent to non-believers as they are not Muslims, they deserve support because they are here to defend Islam'.[22]

In view of the ongoing debate among Muslim theologians on whether Muslims are allowed to use infidels' support in battle (*al-istia'nat al-muslimin bi'l-kufar fi'l-kital*), Fahd invited 350 Islamic leaders and scholars to Mecca to discuss 'the theological justification for calling in non-Muslim troops to defend their kingdom'. Riyadh made certain that its guests toured Mecca and Madina to see for themselves that no American, or other 'infidel' troops, were there.[23]

By September, following reports about Iraqi atrocities in Kuwait and its systematic looting, most Saudis, now aware of what they were being spared, fully supported the regime's decision to invite American forces to defend their country. Thus, Shaykh Sa'd bin Fa'iz al-Mudarah, rector of Prince Abd al-Aziz mosque in Dhahran declared that: 'as a principle, nobody liked the American troops coming here. But we are forced to accept it as a temporary measure.' Moreover, the regime emphasised the fact that once the Americans were no longer needed, they would immediately leave the kingdom.[24]

As the immediate danger to Saudi Arabia receded, the American presence in the kingdom increasingly became an embarrassment to King Fahd. Moreover, the extremist *'alims*, with followers among the Morality Police *muttawwa'in* (volunteers), claimed that the Westernised liberal intelligentsia had conspired with the Americans to annihilate the conservative religious elements in Saudi society. It was even rumoured in Najd that the conservative tribal National Guard (commanded by Crown Prince Abdallah), was being despatched to the border so that it would be destroyed by the Iraqis. Some 'neo-fundamentalist' *'alims* even advocated the extermination of the liberal intelligentsia.[25] Finally, as the size of the American forces in Saudi Arabia continued to grow, while the Iraqis did not make any move against the kingdom, many 'lower-class' semi-educated Saudis began to believe allegations that the American army had come to stay.

The threat to the 'Saudi way of life' was highlighted, as far as the conservatives were concerned, by growing demands for reform expressed by young princes and the intelligentsia. Photocopiers and fax machines were widely used in the controversy between the ulama and the liberal intelligentsia and for the distribution of a 'set of change-demands that circulated in Jedda but were never delivered to the king'. Leading members of Saudi Chambers of Commerce and the middle class as a whole, nevertheless, petitioned the monarch 'for more representation . . . and some women argued that they should be allowed access to more jobs and be permitted to drive cars'.[26]

The above notwithstanding, the majority of the Saudi religious hierarchy and conservative population identified with the leadership of the establishment ulama, who publicly supported the regime's policy. The latter were responsible, *inter alia*, for obtaining the condemnation of Iraq at the meeting of the World Muslim League in the last week of September, where Saddam Hussayn was described as a 'blasphemer'.[27] Yet they and the majority of the tribal population became apprehensive when King Fahd, under pressure from the intelligentsia to establish a universal military service, announced (but did not carry out) his intention to abolish the tribal quota system for recruitment to the armed forces. Even worse, succumbing to middle-class elite pressure, he declared that in certain circumstances he foresaw the possibility of women's deployment in the areas of human and medical services while fully preserving Islamic social values and behaviour.[28] Lastly, also under pressure from the new elites and, it is claimed, by his Western allies, Fahd again announced at the beginning of November his intention to reform the provincial government and the 'legal procedures' (a challenge to the ulama who controlled the *shari'a* system), and to establish an appointed National Consultative Assembly.[29]

The false dawn of 'liberalism' in the kingdom culminated in November with a 'demonstration' (forbidden by law) of 47 women, largely employed in the education system. In defiance of the custom forbidding women from driving themselves, they drove cars in a procession in the centre of Riyadh. This seemingly harmless event badly backfired as far as the liberal elites were concerned and played into the hands of the ulama and their conservative supporters.

Already agitated by the American presence in Saudi Arabia, its cultural impact and the liberals' growing audacity, the orthodoxy treated the women's 'demonstration' as a *casus belli*.[30] King Fahd may have sympathised with the women's cause, but was coerced to side with the establishment ulama and the conservatives, whose grudging support for his policy he badly needed. Thus, the prohibition on women's driving, a custom that has nothing to do with the *shari'a*, was now sanctified by an edict of Prince Na'if, the minister of the interior, in an attempt to appease the ulama.[31] The 'demonstrators' were immediately dismissed from their jobs, their passports were confiscated and they were called whores by the clergy and hounded by Najdi fanatics.

The women's 'demonstration', coming on top of a threat of 'sweeping' reforms, was too much for the conservatives and the establishment ulama to accept, not to mention the outrage of the extremists in the latter's ranks. The outcry was such that the regime, soon afterwards, renounced the planned reform of the 'procedures of the legal system', which the ulama denounced as 'secular'. Fahd's intended 'political reforms' were also strongly opposed. The religious establishment rejected, as it always did, any attempt at 'democratisation' because, as a leading *'alim* claimed, 'the people's will is fickle'.[32]

Within the royal family, the conservatives, led by Crown Prince Abdallah, were also displeased with the monarch's 'reform' tendency. Prince Abdallah, echoing the growing criticism from extremist ulama, still questioned the advisability of having invited an infidel army to protect the kingdom. It was claimed that 'only Prince Abdallah . . . has managed to dissociate himself effectively from the presence of the US troops in Saudi Arabia'.[33] Thus, with the final stage of the confrontation with Iraq rapidly approaching, Fahd gave in to the conservative majority's pressure and again abandoned his proposed reforms.

The ulama and their conservative supporters pressed their advantage to the limit. The more fanatic opened an all-out offensive against the 'Westernised' regime and the liberal intelligentsia. The latter they called 'apostates' and 'corrupters of the faith' and practically invited their assassination. Some, wishing to exploit the regime's presumed weakness, also demanded that non-*shari'a* commercial laws, courts and banks be abolished and replaced by 'Islamic' ones.[34] Yet, most ulama lobbied the Sauds for the expansion of their control over the kingdom. Coupled with an outburst of militant fundamentalism in this period, the relaxation of government control was undoubtedly responsible, among other things, in the coming year for a major change in the ulama–regime relationship.

THE ULAMA AND THE REGIME
(AUGUST 1990 – MAY 1991)

The Iraq-Kuwait conflict and its aftermath brought to the surface the cleavage between the older, powerful establishment ulama and younger, 'non-conformist' *'alims*, largely graduates of Islamic universities, and between both of these and a few score of popular, fanatic, largely Najdi, 'neo-fundamentalist' theologians. These 'political ulama', claimed Dr Ghazi al-Gosaybi, a leading Saudi scholar who carefully studied their 'Islamic cassettes' and pamphlets, wished to usurp the Saudi regime and replace the Wahhabi system based on the traditional alliance between Al Saud and the ulama with Khomayni-type 'Governance of the Jurist' (*vilayat faqih*).[35]

By the 1990s, the traditional alliance between 'state and church' in Saudi Arabia, conditional on the regime's preservation of Wahhabi Islam's hegemony and the 'Saudi way of life' in the kingdom, was no longer unchallenged as it had appeared to be after the·Ikhwan rebellion in the late 1920s and the abortive Mecca rebellion of 1979. Dissatisfaction with the regime, on one hand, and with the establishment ulama's leadership, which almost automatically legitimised every act of the Sauds and benefited from their largess, on the other hand, was rife among the junior, better-educated, ulama and professors of Islamic and other universities.

The rise of 'non-conformist', university-educated junior ulama and professors of Islamic studies within the ranks of orthodoxy is an outstanding phenomenon in Saudi Arabia. This development, an outgrowth of the late 1970s and 1980s, confronted the Sauds with a new and complicated challenge because these elements, although not militant, could not be bought off. Like their liberal-intelligentsia counterparts they, too, desired to reform the system and privately questioned the rulers' lifestyle, justice values and conduct of government. They also wished to expand participation in the decision-making process beyond the ranks of the oligarchy, although they were still willing to accept the primacy of Al Saud. Yet, their perception of reform and of the future character of the Saudi kingdom differs markedly from that of the liberal intelligentsia; their goal is to transform Saudi Arabia into a 'modern' Islamic–puritanic theocracy, governed strictly according to the *shari'a* under the supervision of appropriate independent ulama, through an Islamic *majlis al-shura.*

Even more outstanding is the emergence of 'neo-fundamentalism' led by about two or three score of militant popular, largely Najdi, theologians (not necessarily ulama). These made their criticism of the regime and its policy known even before 1990, in lectures in Islamic universities, theology faculties and other institutions and in Friday sermons at different mosques in Riyadh and in Najd's lesser towns and villages and, to some degree, in Asir. Yet their most effective weapons were pamphlets and 'Islamic cassettes'.[36] In contrast with the humility of the 'soft' middle-class and liberal intelligentsia and the timid, 'non-conformist' junior ulama, this group of theologians did not hesitate publicly to challenge the regime's policy and even its legitimacy[37] and dwelt as well on socio-political subjects that were considered taboo, as far as the ulama were concerned, after the 1920s.

This group of extremist *fuqaha'* probably emerged during the economically difficult period in the 1980s. They are far more politically knowledgeable than their forerunners, the uncouth fanatic *'alims* who joined the Ikhwan rebellion in the 1920s and others who opposed modernisation under Faysal and Khalid. They differ completely from the older-generation extremist, narrow-minded, establishment ulama. The neo-Ikhwan of the 1970s, largely bewildered, ex-bedouin, fundamentalist militants, who turned to jihadist messianism and rebelled in Mecca in 1979, were students of extremist establishment ulama (such as Abd al-Aziz bin Baz) in the 1970s. They soon turned their backs on them, however, when they became aware of their hypocrisy when dealing with the Al Saud regime and the benefits they reaped from their position.

Even more xenophobic and anti-Western (and anti-Shi'ite) and supportive of Islamic solidarity than the ultra-conservative establishment ulama, the new breed of 'neo-fundamentalist' *'alims* are far more sophisticated than the former. Indeed their criticism of the regime after August 1990 combined religious, socio-economic and political themes. Indirectly, and even directly, they took the Sauds to task for their deviation from the principles of Wahhabi Islam and a puritan state; above all they were uncompromising in rejecting the regime's decision to invite 'infidel' troops to protect the kingdom and fight Muslim Iraq and in their attacks on the US and its 'Zionist allies'.[38]

The relatively late eruption of 'neo-fundamentalism' in Saudi Arabia is related to the evolution of militant fundamentalism elsewhere in the Arab world, which was fanned by the success of the (Shi'ite) Islamic revolution in Iran. Prior to the 1960s, fundamentalist movements, such as the Muslim Brothers in Egypt or *salafi* movements elsewhere in the Arab world or in the Indian sub-continent, largely wished to reform Muslim societies and rulers and to establish the *shari'a* as the Muslim state's unchallenged code of behaviour and law. Such movements were by nature anti-colonialist and anti-Western but did not aspire to replace their respective regimes by force as long as they did not subvert the principles of Islam or conduct their government in a manner detrimental to their (Muslim) subjects' well-being. This was in essence the consideration which had theoretically guided the Saudi ulama ever since the Ikhwan movement was defeated by Ibn Saud.

Militant 'neo-fundamentalism', which has emerged in the Muslim–Arab world since the 1960s, is totally intolerant of 'despotic' Muslim secular regimes, or ruling classes which, it believes, have totally deviated from the path of true Islam and abetted social injustice. The government of the believers, the 'neo-fundamentalists' asserted, is to be entrusted only to the most qualified and pious among the *fuqaha'*, who will cleanse the Muslim *umma* from *jahili* (non-Islamic, literally 'pre-Islamic polytheist') influences and govern it according to the laws of true Islam. Determined to overthrow and replace such regimes, which they consider 'infidel', and forcibly, if necessary, reform their (Muslim) societies, the militant 'neo-fundamentalist' movements do not hesitate to resort to terrorist tactics (jihad) to achieve their goal.

By 1979 'Governance of the Jurist' (*vilayat faqih*) was established by Ayatollah Khomayni in Shi'ite Iran. However, attempts to establish 'Islamic' (Sunni) governments in Egypt and Syria were crushed with an iron fist. Nevertheless, such a fundamentalist government was forcibly set up in Sudan by 1989. Militant fundamentalist movements, exploiting the

(Western) democratic system which they condemn (supported by Iran), are also challenging the governments of Egypt, Algeria, Tunisia and Jordan. The neo-Ikhwan rebellion in Saudi Arabia in 1979 failed to attract popular support among the Wahhabi kingdom's masses who enjoyed a relatively high standard of living, although their heritage is still alive among marginal bedouin elements and students of Islamic institutions.

The traditional alliance between the ulama and the Sauds in the modern Wahhabi state, and the rising standard of living of all Saudis helped to ward off the challenge to the regime of 'neo-fundamentalism', as the Mecca rebellion demonstrated. But discontent with pseudo-fundamentalism and hypocrisy in the kingdom obviously survived that traumatic event. Extremist fundamentalism in Saudi Arabia, undoubtedly nurtured in the 1980s by prolonged economic recession and unemployment among high school and university graduates, continued to spread under the surface, particularly in Najd, in Asir and in the poorer sections of the kingdom's major cities. This process was further assisted by the fact that while the common people suffered increasing hardship, the Sauds, many of whom abused the principles of puritanic Wahhabism, continued to exploit their positions for their own enrichment.

The development of 'neo-fundamentalism' in Saudi Arabia was facilitated as well by the special relationship which the Wahhabi establishment ulama had developed in recent decades with militant fundamentalist movements elsewhere in the Muslim world and the aid and refuge Riyadh granted, whenever necessary, to their leaders. Such movements (Egyptian, Afghani, Syrian, Sudanese, Algerian and Tunisian) established a presence in the kingdom and its Islamic universities which had an impact on elements in Saudi society. Furthermore, as was the case with the Afghan Islamic Party, Saudi volunteers who underwent military and ideological training in their camps were made aware of the contempt felt by their activities for the Saud regime and its establishment Wahhabi ulama.[39]

The Gulf war and the presence in the kingdom of hundreds of thousands of 'infidel' soldiers as well as the temporary relaxation of the strict supervision of freedom of speech and censorship, undoubtedly increased 'neo-fundamentalist' tendencies in Saudi Arabia. Exploiting the pulpits of different mosques (largely in Najd), and through pamphlets and 'Islamic cassettes', the militant *'alims* not only challenged Fahd's decision to invite 'infidel' soldiers to protect the kingdom, but lashed out at America and its regional policies and accused the Saudi Western-trained technocrats of being the agents of an American conspiracy to corrupt the kingdom and of serving Western intelligence services.[40] Indirectly, they also challenged the credibility of the leaders of the establishment ulama for the *fatwas* they issued to legitimise Fahd's policy and the war against Iraq. Indeed, when some of the more extreme and popular Najdi *'alims* were reprimanded for exceeding the permissible by their interference in politics and attacks on the rulers and were denied the pulpits of mosques, anti-government demonstrations erupted in some Najdi towns known for their conservatism.[41]

'Islamic cassettes' with sermons of 'neo-fundamentalist' preachers, attacking the government for inviting 'infidel' troops to Saudi Arabia and concerning its policy regarding Iraq (and attacking Saudi Shi'ites), gained wide circulation in the kingdom, particularly in Riyadh and in Najd's smaller towns and villages, during the autumn months of 1990. The matter was considered sufficiently serious for the interior ministry to forbid the trade in such cassettes and to try to supervise the Friday sermons of the 'neo-fundamentalist' theologians by demanding that taped copies be deposited with the authorities beforehand.[42]

At the beginning of November, Washington obtained Riyadh's consent to increase the complement of the US forces in Saudi Arabia to about 500,000, in order to acquire an offensive capability. This was done in view of the vast and well-equipped army concentrated by Saddam Hussayn in and around Kuwait.[43] When economic sanctions failed to coerce Iraq to evacuate Kuwait unconditionally, military action became inevitable. The Soviet military and Moscow's foreign office 'Arabists' endeavoured to prevent the allied attack, but failed to convince Saddam Hussayn of the futility of his policy. To 'help' Moscow overcome its reluctance over the planned offensive against Iraq, Riyadh agreed to lend the Soviet Union 1.5 billion dollars. Yet, it was largely due to Washington's pressure that the five permanent members of the Security Council voted unanimously on 29 November to permit the allied forces to take the necessary steps to free Kuwait.[44] Subsequently, President Bush informed Saddam Hussayn that he must comply with the Security Council's resolutions not later than 15 January 1991 or else suffer the consequences.

As 15 January approached, an outcry arose from the Saudi fundamentalists and 'nationalists' against the use of the kingdom's territory for a Western–American attack on Muslim–Arab Iraq. Disagreement broke out in the royal family (Prince Abdallah, the conservative, joined forces with Prince Talal, the modernist–nationalist, and with Prince Turki, Fahd's full brother and the Sudayris' 'black sheep') and within the ulama's ranks, over King Fahd's policy. Cassette tapes with sermons of 'neo-fundamentalist' preachers attacking the regime and its stance again freely circulated in the kingdom, but particularly in the kingdom's main towns and Najd. Possibly the most popular anti-regime and anti-Western cassettes were the ones of Shaykh Salman al-Odah, a Najdi *'alim* whose words could be heard through mosque loudspeakers in many towns and villages of the central province. Indeed, 100,000 copies of

184

his violent anti-American book, published at the beginning of 1991, were sold within a month.[45]

Travellers coming from Saudi Arabia at the beginning of January 1991, reported that King Fahd and his regime were being openly attacked in sermons in different mosques in the kingdom, the Hijaz included. The 'neo-fundamentalist' theologians denounced the intention to fight for the disliked Kuwaitis and advocated that negotiations be opened with Iraq. They chastised Fahd for becoming an American tool and the Egyptian and Syrian troops for supporting him.[46]

Opposition among the other ulama to the American presence in the kingdom (but not to the government's policies) was also on the increase, as many Saudis believed that the US would not relinquish its bases in the kingdom after the war. Yet, the great majority of the establishment ulama continued to support the regime and its policy despite their concern about foreign influences on the Saudi society. Indeed, Shaykh Muhammad bin Salih, considered the second-ranking (establishment) 'alim in the kingdom, announced that the presence of the American soldiers in the kingdom 'was the lesser of two evils' and, thus, was a sufficient justification for the invitation extended by the government to the American troops.[47]

Shaykh Abd al-Aziz bin Baz was again called to the rescue in January and he issued a controversial *fatwa* authorising a jihad against Saddam Hussayn. Furthermore, in a 'jihad convention' at the Imam Muhammad bin Saud Islamic University, ulama loyal to the ruling family justified the war against Iraq, asserting that Muslim law allows believers to call on non-believers for assistance in a jihad.[48]

Be that as it may, the majority of Saudis and most of the new and old elites supported the planned offensive against Saddam Hussayn's regime, fearing that inaction would lead to his eventual domination of Saudi Arabia. Inevitably, once Scud missiles began to fall upon Riyadh, even the extremist ulama temporarily fell silent and the Saudi royal house and people consolidated their ranks behind King Fahd and his policy.[49]

11

DEMANDS FOR SOCIO-POLITICAL CHANGE IN THE POST-WAR ERA

THE LIBERALS' 'OPEN LETTER' TO KING FAHD

The short 'mother of all battles' (to quote Saddam Hussayn), which ended so disastrously for Iraq, was not an occasion for rejoicing, nor for victory parades, in the kingdom, but rather a cause for soul-searching for many Saudis. The swift destruction of an Arab–Muslim army by the 'infidels' brought back the bitter memory of the Six Day War with Israel. Combined with the sight on the TV screens of an Iraqi soldier kissing the boots of an American marine, it was deeply humiliating and produced a religio-nationalist backlash against the Americans. Some Saudi nationalists even claimed that their country had been used by the West and that if anyone benefited from Iraq's defeat it was the 'Zionists and the Americans'.[1]

The above notwithstanding, King Fahd and his Sudayri brothers emerged from the war with strengthened prestige and with their pro-American policy again vindicated. They faced, nevertheless, challenges exacerbated by the war, whose ramifications had their impact upon both the liberal and middle-class intelligentsia minority and the great majority of the conservative fundamentalist population.

Demand for change and reform of the kingdom's political system rose to a pitch in the first months of 1991. It was enhanced before and during the war months by the partial relaxation of censorship and restrictions on freedom of speech and access to the world media.

> Saudis at all levels of sophistication and wealth are passionately debating their future. Almost everyone accepts the rule of the Saud family and the notion that the country should be strictly governed by the laws of Islam. But for the first time there are public, and growing, demands for increased participation in decision-making and for greater accountability . . . [and to] end the corruption . . .[2]

Some of the Western-trained technocrats went even further and demanded the right to organise politically and socially and '. . . the right to debate

186

publicly without fear of being ostracised or stigmatised by the dreaded appellation "kafir", nonbeliever'.[3]

The middle-class businessmen who suffered from the long recession were angered, as well, by the monopolisation of a declining pool of business by members of Al Saud. Dissatisfaction also spread among the 'non-conformist' 'alims who were no longer willing to accept their mentors' hypocrisy concerning the regime, the excesses of members of the royal house and injustice in the kingdom. Thus, although in total disagreement about the character of the reforms which they envisaged, both orthodox and liberal new elites found themselves united in demanding change in the Saudi system.[4] Yet, they were still a minority compared with the establishment ulama and the conservatives who wished for an immediate restoration of the traditional 'Saudi way of life'.

Once the war was over and most of the foreign troops were prudently and rapidly withdrawn from the kingdom, the monarch and his royal counsellors, faced with growing tension in the kingdom, again opted for the traditional alliance with the conservative majority of Saudis, rather than for the new Saudi Arabia envisaged by the relatively small group of the liberal intelligentsia, or even the larger moderate middle class. Subsequently, the regime clamped down on the liberties assumed by the new elites during the previous months and media coverage returned to the controlled 'Islamic' format. The Morality Police, hundreds of whom were transferred from the Eastern Province to Hijaz after August 1990 in order to avoid friction with the foreign troops, extended their activity to Jedda and even raided houses of influential technocrats and merchants, previously believed to be immune to such treatment. With the departure of the foreign troops, the muttawwa'in 'have again gone to work with a vengeance', even in the Eastern Province's oil towns, where previously their activity was restricted because of the presence there of large Western communities. Indeed, occasionally they even harassed the companions of royal princes.[5]

In a speech on 5 March to Muslim religious leaders, King Fahd reiterated Saudi Arabia's commitment to the shari'a, suggesting that 'some Saudis' expectations of liberalisation in domestic policies may be premature'.[6] Yet, at the same time, the monarch appointed a moderate 'alim, Shaykh Abd al-Rahman al-Sa'id, to head the Morality Police, with a budget of 18 million dollars for the training of the 3,000 semi-educated, largely of bedouin origin, muttawwa'in, as well as for recruiting a better-educated manpower for his organisation.[7]

The craving for change, which manifested itself all over the kingdom, particularly in the capital and the main towns of the Hijaz, Asir and the Eastern Province, now incorporated both liberal and orthodox new elites, commoners and aristocrats, rich and poor. Of course, there was a meaningful difference between the changes espoused by the liberals and those desired by the new generation of religious scholars. But the great majority of both new elites were critical of Al Saud double standards, corruption and nepotism and united in their wish for some degree of participation in political decision-making. Despite the reinstituted restriction on freedom of speech, representatives of the middle-class and liberal elites, on the one hand, and 'non-conformist' ulama and Islamic universities' professors, on the other, were ready to petition the king for political and other reforms, in line with what each believed appropriate.

After the flurry of intensive pro-change activity in the last months of 1990 and the beginning of 1991, however, the liberal intelligentsia, aware of the monarch's increased power following Iraq's approaching defeat, resigned itself to lobbying minimal reforms acceptable to the regime. The clamour of the Kuwaiti opposition for the democratisation of their government's system, supported by the Western media, they realised, did not help their cause because it alarmed the conservative Saudi oligarchy.[8] Nevertheless, 43 moderate liberal businessmen and intellectuals from Hijaz, Najd, Asir and the Eastern Province wrote King Fahd an open letter, distributed in the kingdom and published in a Cairo opposition newspaper and some Jordanian ones at the beginning of February.[9]

Addressed to the monarch with the utmost respect, pledging to uphold 'the existing ruling system' and the *shari'a* as Saudi Arabia's constitution, the petition called upon the monarch to establish national, provincial and municipal consultative councils, to promulgate a 'Basic Order of Government' and to curb the activities of the Morality Police and of the strict censorship on the press. The signatories seemed to take it for granted that, at most, King Fahd would only appoint a council of 'wise men', representing various spheres of opinion in the kingdom, to serve as a traditional Muslim *shura* (council) with limited consultative powers.[10]

According to a biased and distorted version, published by the Jordanian newspaper *Al-Liwa*, the petition expressed strong reservations about the war against Iraq and the hope that, once Kuwait was liberated, the foreign forces would leave the kingdom's soil and their 'imperialist fleets should not be allowed to establish permanent bases in the region and through them control its resources'. Such extremist demands do not appear in a more reliable version of the petition published by another Jordanian daily several weeks later.[11]

Ms J. Caesar, an American who had taught at a women's college of King Saud University in Riyadh, analysing the petition, observed that 'Perhaps more significantly it [the letter] . . . demands that all citizens will be equal before the law, regardless of race, tribe, social status or gender . . . within the Islamic context.' Clearly the signatories had in mind the women who drove in a convoy in Riyadh, whom pamphleteers accused 'of having renounced their religion'.[12]

Less obvious about the demand for equal rights, continues Ms Caesar, is that the open letter objects to a system of justice under which all members of the royal family and their associates are immune from prosecution. It carefully balances demands for basic human rights and avoids any appearance of questioning Islam. Yet, while accepting that the Qur'an is God's word, those who interpret it, the signatories hint, are fallible. Thus, the law should be interpreted by ulama independent of, and not appointed by, the government.[13]

A realistic executive of the Riyadh Chamber of Commerce and Industry remarked, in relation to the petition, that 'the consultative council is a symbol of participation and will help educate the public . . . We are not ready for free elections but it is a step forward.' Moreover, the ulama were apprehensive lest such a council, albeit without muscle, might serve as 'a forum for people to speak out against their [the ulama's] excesses'.[14]

In sum, the changes requested in the liberals' open letter to King Fahd were far less meaningful than those demanded by the liberal elites in the early 1980s. The petition does not dare mention a fundamental law (constitution) that will curb the authority of the ruler and the ulama or challenge the position of the *shari'a* as the kingdom's fundamental law. The opinions expressed in the letter were, in fact, a watered-down version of a set of demands, never presented to the monarch, which circulated among the Hijazi intellectuals in Jedda during the autumn of 1990. The outspoken authors of the previous document, circulated through fax machines only a few months earlier, now feared that they would be castigated like the 47 women 'demonstrators' in Riyadh, lose their jobs and privileges, and be harassed by the fundamentalists.[15] Undoubtedly, they and the rest of the intelligentsia were also intimidated by the regime's decision to clamp down on the liberties that they had taken to themselves before and during the war with Iraq.

The petition to the king probably influenced the monarch, among other things, to reiterate in April his promise from November 1990 and of many occasions before, to establish an appointed consultative assembly. Fahd may have become convinced that this was the appropriate step to take at the time and, possibly, may have wished to shield his regime from criticism in the West, similar to that which appeared in the world press regarding Kuwait's rulers.[16]

THE ULAMA PETITION – A CHALLENGE TO THE SAUDS' REGIME

The liberal intelligentsia's petition, followed by King Fahd's declaration of the planned reforms in April, precipitated another petition on 30 April (or in mid-May),[17] which was far more astounding because it was signed by more than 400 ulama and professors from the kingdom's Islamic and other universities. Among the signatories were over 50 (nearly 100, according to one source) leading establishment ulama.[18] The majority of the signatories, however, were younger, 'non-conformist' *'alims* and university professors and a score of the most popular 'neo-fundamentalists'. Indeed the delay in the ulama's reaction to the earlier petition was caused by the difficulty the 'non-conformist' initiators of the petition faced in bringing together the three streams of orthodoxy and working out a formula acceptable to all. Once such a formula was found and the petition signed, its content was immediately published in the Egyptian opposition press.[19]

On the surface the ulama's memorandum seemed an Islamic version of the petition of the liberal intelligentsia. *De facto* it was a delayed reaction of the Wahhabi theologians to the decline of their power in the kingdom, the regime's continuous attempts to erode their control of the legal system, and the kingdom's modernisation and 'Westernisation'. It reflected as well the wish of the militant *'alims* to re-establish the kind of relations between 'state and church' that existed before the conquest of the Hijaz and the decline of the Ikhwan's power or, as the 'neo-fundamentalists' wished, to control the government and its policies, if not to get rid of the Sauds' regime altogether.

The petition practically demanded the abolition of all non-*shari'a* legal codes, especially banking and commercial laws. In fact it demanded the re-examination of all the laws and regulations promulgated by the government since the days of Ibn Saud.

By demanding freedom of expression within the Islamic context, it meant to establish 'Islamic media' controlled by the ulama. It wished for the reform of the foreign service suitably to represent the Wahhabi state and the establishment of an 'Islamic army'. Most outstanding was the demand that the theologians control, through the *majlis al-shura*, the government's internal and external policies, including oil production, pricing and marketing. In short, the aim of the petitioners was totally to change the fundamentals of the relationship between 'state and church' and establish in Saudi Arabia an 'Islamic government' resembling, to some extent, Tehran's Shi'ite Islamic regime modelled upon Ayatollah Khomayni's principle of *vilayat faqih* (as pointed out in Ghazi al-Gosaybi's book, *Hatah la takun fitna!!*, published several months earlier).

The ulama's opposition to the regime's encroachment on areas which traditionally they controlled had not abated even during the reign of King Faysal, who did not shrink, whenever necessary, from a confrontation with them. Under the more conciliatory Fahd, who bypassed the *shari'a* and the ulama in matters concerning modernisation, finance, oil and external policy, the religious establishment bitterly criticised Saudi co-operation with the US. They particularly condemned the 'Westernisation' of the Wahhabi kingdom and its legal (Islamic) system which the regime gradually developed alongside the *shari'a*, for which they accused the American-trained technocrats. Overt attacks on the regime, its legitimacy and its policy, including oil and foreign relations, by popular 'neo-fundamentalist' theologians, including *aadis, khatibs* (preachers), imams and professors in Islamic universities gradually gathered momentum during the 1980s. This process was probably enhanced by the lengthy recession, when many graduates of Saudi universities, particularly the Islamic ones – a hotbed of anti-regime fermentation – could not find employment suitable for their qualifications and training.[20]

Steps taken by the regime to prevent the militant *'alims* from exploiting their pulpits in the mosques and the universities to spread 'sedition', caused the 'neo-fundamentalist' *fuqaha'* (theologians), following the Iranian example, to reach the public through 'Islamic cassettes'; this was already occurring in the late 1980s, and even more so after August 1990. The relatively 'gentle' reaction of the authorities, interpreted as a symptom of the regime's weakness and the economic crisis, encouraged the younger generation of religious scholars, particularly after the Iran–Iraq war ended, to increase their scathing attacks on the process of 'Westernisation' of the kingdom. For that they largely accused the American-trained technocrats, whom they often accused of being agents of, and serving, American intelligence, in undermining Saudi Arabia's Islamic–Wahhabi character.[21]

By 1989–90, ferment among the ulama seemed to have reached a boiling point. The activity of the Morality Police's *muttawwa'in* was stepped up and even members of the entourage of royal princes were not immune to harassment.[22] In the Islamic universities, 'non-conformist' or 'neo-fundamentalist' professors, some of them non-Saudi Arab *salafis*, constantly brainwashed their students. Even within the 'secular' universities, many Saudi and foreign Arab professors belonging to the ultra-religious camp endeavoured to 'Islamicise' these institutions and their students.[23]

On the surface it seemed that King Fahd had opted to follow the time-honoured Saudi practice of doing nothing. Relating to both liberal and ulama petitions, he stated that the Saudi rulers 'had always consulted with a range of qualified religious and liberal men'.[24] Yet, the '400 ulama's petition' seriously shook the monarch and most Sauds because it signified the emergence of a broad-based coalition between the different streams in the ranks of the ulama. It also represented a departure from the traditional alliance between 'state and church' within the framework established by Ibn Saud after 1930 and, therefore, a threat to the regime's authority and legitimacy. It reflected as well the growing militancy among the Wahhabi theologians in Najd and to a lesser extent in Hijaz and Asir, which was winning increasing support among the students of Islamic institutions and the rank and file of the armed forces and the National Guard.[25] Hence, the monarch, probably after consulting the most senior members of Al Saud, took unprecedented steps against the signatories of the petition. Their passports were confiscated and many were interrogated, harassed and humiliated by the police. Some were barred from using the pulpits of their mosques or from lecturing in the universities. The most militant were practically hounded by the *mabahith* and a few popular extremist preachers, previously opposed to the infidel troops' presence in Saudi Arabia and the war against Iraq, were even incarcerated. Yet, they were soon released, their arrest having sparked demonstrations in Najd and Asir.[26]

The fact that well over 50 leading establishment ulama signed the petition and that it was immediately leaked to Egyptian opposition press and widely distributed in the kingdom, caused the monarch to convene on 3 June the government's Higher Legal Council, established within the framework of the Ministry of Justice. The council not only authorised the steps against the rebellious ulama proposed by the government but published a declaration forbidding any attempt to exert pressure on the regime by the publication of petitions and memoranda intended for the rulers. Simultaneously, gauging the anger of the regime, the Council of the Assembly of Senior Ulama strongly denounced the petition of the 400 *'alims*, and especially its being made public. It emphasised the fact that although a Muslim has a right to counsel his leader in private, such advice must not be made public nor used to incite others.

As members of the latter council (including the kingdom's two leading arch-reactionary ulama, Bin Baz and Muhammad ibn 'Uthaymin) were signatories of the above petition, its denunciation was considered an apology of a sort to the regime and reflected the renewed cleavage between the establishment ulama and the younger generation of 'non-conformist' and 'neo-fundamentalist' *'alims*. The declaration of the Council of the Assembly of Senior Ulama could also be seen as an attempt by most of the senior ulama to isolate the more militant signatories of the petition who, it was indirectly hinted, were responsible for purposely leaking the substance of the document to the public and the foreign press and for exploiting the political *naïveté* of the upper-crust of the religious leadership.[27]

While adopting strong measures against the militant signatories of the petition, King Fahd rescinded some minor taxes and annulled several monopolies related to the registration, transfer and annual inspection of motor vehicles held by members of his family, mentioned in the petition. The senior editors of three leading Saudi newspapers, *Al-Sharq al-Awsat*, *Al-Majalla* and *Sayyidati*, accused by the orthodox of an anti-Islamic stance, were moreover dismissed from their positions[28] and the liberal middle class and young princes were told to restrain their demands for more rapid changes in the kingdom. Indeed, in a cabinet reshuffle, announced on 31 July, the only changes made were the appointment of three new ministers who were old retainers of, or related to, the Sudayris. Yet, simultaneously, steps to rehabilitate the women who took part in the 'driving demonstration' were taken. Their passports were returned in order to enable them to travel abroad and they were granted some financial compensation for being suspended from their jobs in the previous year.[29]

The regime also hoped that rising revenue from oil, which contributed to its ability to increase the expenditure budget, would help renew the kingdom's prosperity and mitigate the population's dissatisfaction. In the meantime the government increased the grants and loans available to citizens for home building and for business development, in addition to the many billions already spent for this purpose. Furthermore, on the occasion of 'Id al-Adha (the sacrifice holiday) the government proclaimed a general amnesty to most political prisoners serving sentences of up to 25 years (largely Shi'ites) and the Ministry of Information reviewed the prohibition on the sale of opposition papers published abroad 'as long as they did not include attacks on members of the royal family and the regime'.[30]

Aware of the unfavourable reaction of the majority of his colleagues to the 'petition of the 400' and the anger it had aroused among the senior members of Al Saud, Abd al-Aziz bin Baz invited some of his co-signatories to prepare an explanatory memorandum addressed to him which could be made public without contravening the new prohibition on the publication of petitions to the monarch.

Through a watered-down explanation of each of its twelve main sections, this memorandum attempted to undo some of the damage caused by the confrontational tone of the petition. The most important point, underscored on several occasions in the memorandum, was the claim that the original petition was meant only to advise the ruler on necessary reforms and not to demand their execution or to criticise the regime. The writers apologised for the fact that the content of the original document was leaked to the press by explaining that when the draft was circulated among more than 400 signatories, the danger that someone would make its contents known was unavoidable. Moreover, they did not dismiss the possibility that the leak was done deliberately by 'hypocrites who wish this country and society ill and who seek to undermine its unity by spreading rumours, sedition and apprehension'.[31]

Notwithstanding their apologetic tone, the writers again recommended the establishment of a majlis al-shura for both internal and foreign affairs, free of outside pressure ('an Islamic principle'), the members of which should combine Islamic learning, integrity and experience. Denouncing the Iraqi 'despot', they pointed out, none the less, the friendly relationship that Saudi Arabia maintains with other despotic regimes (Syria, Egypt?) and rulers who practically 'fight Islam and tyrannize the faithful' (the US and USSR?). In addition, they advocated the protection of national resources (oil) against waste and exploitation.

The writers stressed the need to cleanse the kingdom's judicial system from non-*shari'a* temporal legal codes which contain 'blatant violations of Islamic law'. They again recommended the principle of equality before the law and censured 'favouritism, nepotism and corruption'. They condemned the poverty of sections of the Saudi population in places such as the Tihama and in the big cities while some Sauds use their position to amass great wealth. They suggested a purge of public and private banking which they accused of usury, and of the media for its un-Islamic stance and influence, for which they accused the liberal intelligentsia which dominate it.

Lastly, the memorandum complained about the persecution by the authorities of the 400 ulama, *qadis*, imams and university professors who signed the petition to the king and their humiliation and harassment by the police for 'no legitimate reason'.[32]

MILITANT FUNDAMENTALISM, REGIME AND REFORM (JUNE 1991 – MARCH 1992)

After the establishment ulama, Bin Baz included, had practically apologised to the rulers for signing the petition to the king, they also unreservedly restated their support of the alliance between 'state and church' and legitimised the regime's policy. Hence, the cleavage between the older generation and the militant younger ulama again surfaced.

Simultaneously, the monarch increased his endeavours to strengthen the regime's relations with the rural population (partly to erode Crown Prince Abdallah's power base). Members of the Sudayri group, King Fahd included, frequently visited the peripheral, less developed, provinces and met with their tribal shaykhs, ulama and *a'yan* in order to study the needs of each region. They also held *majalis* in many villages and small towns and dealt with the population's requests and grievances. Similar tours were undertaken by the 'young' aristocratic provincial governors, many of whom were Fahd's appointees. On all such occasions the royal visitors (*hukuma*) announced major development projects and the establishment in the provinces of different institutions or branches of the Saudi universities.[33]

Despite Washington's pressure, the Saudi regime repeatedly rejected US proposals for a Gulf defence pact (see below); tension concerning this matter was occasionally reported within the royal family and in the relations between Riyadh and Washington.[34] Prince Sultan, considered the more conservative among the Sudayris, who in September 1990 openly rejected a joint US–Saudi operation against Iraq, now strongly opposed any co-operation with the US concerning the Gulf's defence that might necessitate an increased American presence in the kingdom. Indeed, his son, Major General Khalid, who commanded the Arab forces during operation 'Desert Storm', claimed that such co-operation and the presence of US soldiers in the holy land of Islam would be condemned by most Saudis and other Muslims and could undermine the regime's stability. Prince Khalid, according to an Egyptian opposition newspaper, also rejected the US plans on the ground that they might lead to more meaningful ties between his country's defence and that of Israel.[35] Yet King Fahd, supported by Sultan's second son, Prince Bandar, was far more co-operative with Washington in regard to its regional policy and underscored Saudi friendship with the United States and President Bush's traditional support for the Saudi kingdom.[36]

Indeed, once it had overcome its initial apprehension concerning its promises to Washington to help in organising a Middle East peace conference, Riyadh persuaded the GCC foreign ministers to agree to send an 'observer' to the planned peace talks. On 20 July Saudi Arabia even declared its support for an Egyptian proposal to end the Arab boycott of Israel if it agreed to stop the establishment of new settlements in the 'occupied territories'.[37] Subsequently, Riyadh's co-operation with the United States' Middle East policy and OPEC became a major target of anti-regime sermons and 'Islamic cassettes' of militant ulama in the following months.

Baghdad's audacity in its treatment of the UN inspectors, and Saddam's efforts to circumvent the Security Council's resolutions caused the US and UK to call for a renewed military action against Iraq in September. Washington's plans were shelved, however, because Riyadh, whose bases were essential for such an operation, refused to allow America to use them, fearing internal and general Arab anger. Prince Sultan, it seems, again led the opposition to the US request; but his son, Major General Khalid, proved to be even more adamant on the matter. In this he was supported by Crown Prince Abdallah, who objected to any Saudi involvement in the American plans.[38] As King Fahd was not pleased with General Khalid's attitude and his pressure to be appointed chief-of-staff of the Saudi armed forces, a position traditionally held by a commoner, Khalid, promoted to lieutenant general, 'decided', or was told, to resign from the armed forces. The above notwithstanding, King Fahd again took great pains to deny the existence of tension in the relations between his country and the US.[39] Indeed, when the American-initiated Arab–Israeli peace conference opened in Madrid at the end of October, Prince Bandar, as Fahd's representative, was instrumental in Damascus' decision to attend the conference and played a role far beyond that of a mere observer.[40]

Riyadh's involvement in the Arab–Israeli peace talks was a marked example of changes in King Fahd's policies, which became increasingly assertive after mid-1991, especially concerning relations with the ulama. Not only was the monarch now determined to crush any militant opposition to his regime, he was also resolved to carry out the reforms which he had been planning for more than a decade. He was even more resolved to accelerate the kingdom's development and to revive the prosperity of its population. For that purpose Riyadh, among other things, negotiated with a consortium of foreign banks additional loans of about 10 billion dollars at a preferential rate of interest, much to the disgust of the ulama. Moreover, to overcome the reluctance of domestic and foreign banks to lend money to Saudi businessmen and entrepreneurs, and to bypass the *shari'a* courts, a special office was established in every chamber of commerce in the kingdom to deal with non-payment of loans or IOUs.[41]

In a speech to the nation, broadcast on Saudi television and radio network on 15 November, King Fahd again announced his intention to carry out soon a series of reforms in the government of Saudi Arabia, including the formation of a Consultative Council, the reorganisation of the government of the provinces (*nizam al-muqata'at*) and the introduction of a 'Basic Order of Government'. In contrast with similar vague announcements in previous years, the monarch, this time, presented his plans to the Saudi people in detail.

On the same occasion the monarch frankly informed the Saudis that their government was forced to borrow abroad 10 billion dollars, in addition to 7 or 8 billions which it intended to raise in 1992 through another domestic bond issue. Fahd assured his subjects, none the less, that their standard of living, subsidies and the other privileges would be protected and that they could expect an improvement in the kingdom's economy on account of the government's substantially increased expenditure budget for 1992 and higher revenue from oil.[42]

King Fahd's use of the term 'Basic Order of Government' was meant to underscore the fact that it was not intended in any way to be a substitute to the *shari'a* 'as the kingdom's constitution'. Yet, it left room for the establishment of a parallel 'secular' legal system to deal, *inter alia*, with finance, banking, transportation and other matters.

To satisfy popular demand, Fahd also pledged to increase the strength of the Saudi armed forces to about 200,000 and to provide it with the best and most sophisticated armaments.[43] Yet, the monarch did not tell the Saudis about the 60 billion dollars which the kingdom had pledged to its allies to defray Gulf war expenses, nor did he mention the fact that Saudi liquid financial reserves had diminished to about 10 billion dollars.[44]

Fahd's determination to carry out his reforms was emphasised at the end of December, when Ali Sha'ir, the minister of information, declared in the king's name that the creation of a Consultative Council and other legislative and political changes would be announced at the end of

February. The setting of an exact time signalled to all Saudis that, this time, the monarch fully intended to carry out his reforms.[45]

Notwithstanding the ruler's intentions to curb the excesses of the Morality Police, the activities of the *muttawwa'in*, encouraged by the militant ulama, intensified in the second half of 1991, to the disgust of the younger Sauds, the intelligentsia and Westerners living in Saudi Arabia. Finally, by the year's end the monarch, with the co-operation of the new directors of the *muttawwa'in*, ordered the Morality Police to restrict their activities to what was permissible.[46]

Despite the condemnation of the militant younger *'alims* by the establishment ulama for extremism and intervention in matters traditionally considered the domain of the rulers, and their being harassed by the authorities, support for them did not diminish, particularly in Najd's heartland.[47] Defying tighter police supervision, the militants became, after mid-1991, more audacious in their attacks on the regime, on America and on their older mentors, sensing that a confrontation with the Sauds was now inevitable. In so far as their sermons and cassettes became far more intently focused on Saudi regional and international policies, a Saudi source claimed that 'they make it their business to know about oil policy and they watch things like our relations with the US and how this ties in with the Palestinians and Israel'.[48]

After they succeeded in creating a rift between the establishment ulama and the militant *'alims*, the authorities took a much harsher line in dealing with the latter. Some were detained without trial, others were being harassed by the police, and still others were deprived of pulpits or appointments in the universities. The distribution of 'Islamic cassettes' was again strictly prohibited (to no avail) and in the last months of 1991 many imams and preachers of different mosques were arrested for challenging the Saudi support for the Arab–Israeli peace talks. Simultaneously, foreign Arab fundamentalists (largely Egyptians, Sudanese or Syrians) who taught in Saudi universities or had found refuge in the kingdom were deported to their respective countries.[49]

The dissension between the establishment ulama and the militants became increasingly evident in the second part of the year when many 'non-conformist' young *'alims* joined the extremists in criticising the regime for its policies and their mentors for condoning them. For their part, the establishment ulama coalesced with the regime and took the militants to task for 'deviation' from the true faith and interfering in matters for which they were not trained and which are a recognised prerogative of the rulers. While Islamic cassettes enjoyed wide circulation, particularly among the 'hundreds of thousands' of unemployed graduates, the majority of the conservative Saudis still followed the establishment ulama and remained loyal to the Sauds.[50]

The attacks on the regime by the 'neo-fundamentalists' escalated in the last months of 1991. This became especially noticeable after King Fahd informed the nation on 14 November of his intention to announce soon his political and judicial reform plans. By the end of December it was quite evident that a confrontation between the bellicose ulama and the regime was imminent. Encouraged by the growth of their camp and the success of militant fundamentalism elsewhere in the Middle East, the extremist *'alims* no longer attempted to mitigate their attacks on the Sauds, their older peers and the Western-trained technocrats, whom they frequently accused of being agents of American intelligence and of spreading anti-Islamic cultural influence.

Since the autumn of 1991 Saudi militants, wishing to avoid government intervention, had co-ordinated their activities through religious societies (for instance *Al-Nahda al-Islamiyya* – the Islamic resurgence) and 'adopted a strategy of attacking government policies in public speeches in the mosques and in lectures at some of their religious universities'. Cassettes, in hundreds of thousands, containing their sermons assaulted government policies and personalities, ministers, columnists and senior religious leaders. Indeed, they focused on virtually every aspect of domestic and foreign policy including oil prices, banking and financial laws, government borrowing abroad, co-operation with the US during and after the Gulf crisis, and Riyadh's involvement in the peace talks with Israel. In December they crossed the red line by attacking the female education system and accusing leading women educators of being whores. The same type of slander was used against the Saudi Women's Renaissance Association, whose membership included several princesses and other prominent Saudi women.

These slanderous attacks enraged the religious establishment, allied to the Sauds, which controlled the female education system. It was also an open insult to members of the ruling family. Thus, ironically, both Shaykh Bin Baz, the arch-reactionary and Prince Turki, the London University graduate son of the late King Faysal and the head of the Saudi intelligence services (*Istikhbarat al-'Amma*), found themselves on the same side of the fence. In an article published in *Al-Sharq al-Awsat* (associated with the Saudi intelligentsia) and in other Saudi papers (29–30 December 1991), Bin Baz denounced 'the recording of poisonous allegations on cassettes and their distribution to the people' and described the extremists' assertions as 'lies and conspiracies against Islam and Muslims'. The behaviour of the authors of such cassettes, he added, 'is against the will of God'. Highly respected by most of the conservatives for his independent (yet reactionary) views, Bin Baz found his condemnation of the militants well received by the masses, who rejected the unbridled extremism of the 'neo-fundamentalists'.

Prince Turki, in a rare speech in a mosque, made public in the Saudi press, warned the militants that they had gone too far and accused them of slandering some of his relatives and acquaintances. He challenged the extremist ulama either to prove their charges or be held accountable for them. This represented the beginning of an open confrontation between senior members of the royal house and the 'neo-fundamentalist' *'alims*.[51] It also indicated the new alliance between the third-generation Sauds, led by Al Faysal, Al Saud (King Saud's offspring) and Al Fahd.

Soon afterwards the Saudi security authorities launched a wide-scale operation against the militants, arresting about a dozen of the most extremist ulama for attacking the regime's policy concerning the peace talks with Israel, Riyadh's willingness to attend the multilateral peace talks in Moscow and criticism of Prince Bandar (Prince Turki al-Faysal is his brother-in-law) for meeting American Jewish leaders. The militants also accused the regime of deviation from the *shari'a* and adoption of a pro-Western policy. Above all, the 'neo-fundamentalists' attacked Saudi support of a decision taken at the Dakar Islamic summit (December 1991) not to use the term 'jihad' in relation to the struggle against Israel, as proposed by Yassir Arafat.

The regime no longer handled the militant ulama with kid-gloves, nor did it adjust its policy, as it did in the past, in order to mitigate the ulama's criticism.[52] Indeed, a group of Jewish American leaders was officially invited to Riyadh in the second part of January 1992. There they met with Saud al-Faysal, the foreign minister, and with Prince Salman (a Sudayri), the powerful governor of Riyadh and its province, and other Saudi officials. The meeting followed an earlier relaxation of Saudi policy concerning the granting of visas to non-Israeli Jews or to anyone with an Israeli visa stamped in his passport. During these talks the Saudi leaders stated that 'the Arab–Israeli conflict is not a religious but a political one and, therefore, it is possible to solve it by peaceful means'. They also stressed, however, that the termination of the conflict depended on a just solution of the Palestinian problem and the return of the 'occupied territories'.[53]

Furthermore, when the multilateral Middle East conference opened in Moscow on 28 January, the Saudi kingdom was represented by Saud al-Faysal who, following a low-key and relatively moderate speech, stated: 'we cannot make or attain specific progress if Arab land continues to be occupied and the Palestinian people continue to be deprived of their right of self-determination'.[54]

The confrontation between the regime and the militant ulama came to a climax in the last week of January when the fundamentalists and their supporters, under the umbrella of the movement called *Al-Nahda al-Islamiyya* (the Islamic resurgence), began to organise a public demonstration against the regime, an action which was strictly prohibited. The demonstration was, however, called off after the organisers had received a stern warning that the security forces would arrest everyone involved in it.

Referring to the above and to the recent 'outrageous behaviour' of the religious militants, King Fahd told his cabinet on 27 January: 'I am following things with wisdom and patience, trying to resolve issues in amicable ways. But . . . if things transgress all limits, there shall be another way.' The monarch's remarks were widely publicised by the Saudi media which indicated that the regime, supported by most Sauds and the senior religious establishment, was ready to suppress by force the activities of the militant groups.[55]

By this time the 'neo-fundamentalists' had succeeded in consolidating their power in the many Islamic universities and institutions that thrived throughout Saudi Arabia. In addition 'the movement has fed off the frustrations of hundreds of thousands of university graduates, who have been unable to find jobs'. The militants, both ulama and students, were tolerated as long as they remained under the control of the establishment. After the middle of 1991, however, their mentors could no longer restrain them. The 'neo-fundamentalists' became increasingly concerned about Fahd's plans to institute reforms by the end of February which, among other things, would enable citizens 'to obtain rulings from civil judges', a matter which would undermine the role of the *shari'a* in the Wahhabi kingdom.[56]

At the end of 1991 the militant ulama focused on the Saudi participation in the peace talks with Israel and the regime's refusal to endorse a call for a jihad at the Dakar Islamic summit. Some 'neo-fundamentalists' also attacked other Arab countries, including Syria, Egypt, Jordan and the PLO, for participating in the Arab–Israeli peace talks.

When gentle coercion failed to stop the extremists' attacks, the regime decided at the end of 1991 to take a firmer stand against the rebellious *'alims*, as was done during the reign of Faysal. Thus, even a well-known veteran preacher of a Riyadh mosque, who repeatedly incited his audience against the regime, was arrested.[57] Furthermore, in an interview to *Al-Sharq al-Awsat* (30 January 1992), General Abdallah bin 'Abd al-Rahman Al al-Shaykh, the director of Saudi internal security, declared that the Gulf crisis caused the emergence of groups of 'sick-minded people'. He added that the security authorities would severely punish anyone encroaching 'on society's rights'.

King Fahd also became more assertive because 'there is a general public antipathy towards these extremists even among the conservatives in Saudi society, which form the majority'.[58] The fact that the country's economy was again thriving and that government expenditure in the 1992 budget was projected to be nearly 50 billion dollars (excluding special allocations for weapons procurement) undoubtedly increased the confidence of many Saudis in the future prosperity of their country and their support for the regime.[59] Ironically, this new prosperity was reflected, as in the case of Kuwait in the mid-1980s, in a feverish activity in the newly established stock exchange, where new share issues were snapped up by the public which realised immediate profits on its investment. The fundamentalists, who strongly condemned such 'un-Islamic' practices, did not endear themselves, of course, to the middle class and other elements of the Saudi public who now participated in the stock exchange. The new confidence of the private sector in the future of the kingdom's economy was also reflected in the return to the country of capital which had sought shelter abroad at the beginning of the Kuwait crisis.[60]

The budget for 1992, published at the end of December 1991, indicated a further rise in government expenditures and Riyadh's belief that a revenue of over 40 billion dollars would be generated by the sale of its oil. Yet, the budget also reflected the need for internal and external borrowing and the government's expectation that the private sector would take a more active role in the kingdom's development plans. Special attention was paid to the creation of employment opportunities for school and university graduates, particularly those of Islamic institutions and faculties of humanities and social sciences.

In the meantime, the Sudayris were not resting on their laurels. They managed to win the support of most of the liberals and middle class by their determination to promulgate reforms, their stand against the ulama and because of renewed prosperity in the kingdom. They consolidated their power in the cabinet and in the provincial government and continued to strengthen their contacts with their subjects in the rural areas and less developed provinces where paternal relations between rulers and ruled are still extremely important. Thus, at the end of January, just before launching the new campaign against the militant fundamentalists, King Fahd completed a lengthy tour of the provinces. Moreover, even the 31st session of the constituent council of the Islamic World League, meeting in Mecca in the last week of January, was used to strengthen the regime's position against the militant fundamentalists. Shortly afterwards, it is claimed, hundreds of *muttawwa'in* who were banned from entering a shopping mall in Riyadh and, therefore, demonstrated before Prince Salman's palace, were arrested.[61]

The frequently-promised reforms of the government system and the establishment of a Consultative Council were finally announced by King Fahd on 1 March. The new council was to consist of 60 appointed members and a chairman; their names would be announced by the monarch within six months. Their appointment was to be for four years and they were to be chosen for their ability, experience and integrity. The council would review foreign and domestic policies and bring its opinions to the government. If they were to agree with the government's policy their suggestions would be adopted without royal intervention. In case of disagreement, the monarch was to be the final authority on which policy to follow or which law to promulgate.

King Fahd would remain prime minister and commander-in-chief of the armed forces and would retain the power to choose and dismiss ministers and council members. In addition to a declaration that the government of the kingdom would remain in the hands of the Saudi royal family (Al Abd al-Aziz), an important innovation concerning the succession to the throne was the proposed creation of an electoral college of 500 princes, including representatives of the third-generation Sauds. Undoubtedly this was welcomed by the 'younger' generation of Sauds, who had no say in the succession process in the past.

The *nizam al-muqata'at* (provincial government) is also meant to decentralise the power of the government and give more authority to the provincial governors and the local assemblies that will be established in the kingdom's fourteen provinces. This was indeed in line with King Fahd's policy of limiting somewhat the power of the central government. Yet it also enabled the leadership of the provincial population to take a more active role in the running of their provinces and to be chosen eventually to sit on the national *majlis al-shura*.

Although the kingdom's constitution and source of legal system is the *shari'a*, 'The Basic System of Government', composed of 83 articles according to King Fahd, is intended to help continue the kingdom's modernisation. Among other things, 'The Basic System of Government' stresses the right to privacy and forbids government authorities from arresting, spying and violating basic human rights without cause. Article 37 states that 'private homes have their sanctity' and cannot be entered without the permission of their owners and cannot be searched unless there is a legal requirement to do so. (Nothing is said about the preservation of human rights in general, nor of freedom of expression.)[62]

Undoubtedly, these provisions are aimed at restricting the activity and power of the Morality Police. The *muttawwa'in*'s increased activities in the second part of 1991, even against people close to the rulers, enraged most younger Sauds, a large part of the middle class and Saudi Arabia's foreign community.

In line with the 'democratisation' of other GCC countries (Kuwait included), the appointed Saudi *majlis al-shura* is meant to enable selected sectors of the population to participate to some extent in the formulation of their kingdom's policy. It is also meant to serve as a steam valve and further consolidate the middle class's and other elements' support of the regime. The six months that Fahd had allotted for naming the members of the *majlis al-shura* were probably needed to compose carefully a balanced list that would represent the leading segments of the population, in suitable proportions.

The early reaction of the middle-class elites to King Fahd's announcement, despite the limited authority of the Consultative Council, was generally positive. The better-educated, third-generation Sauds, many of whom wish gradually to turn the kingdom into a modern constitutional monarchy and to curb the power of the ulama, generally welcomed Fahd's limited reform of the government system. Indeed, for the first time they are given a meaningful role not only in influencing policy-making but also in the succession process. Possibly they consider this as the first step towards broader reforms and the eventual transfer of power from their mentors to themselves.[63]

In order to win further popular support prices of gasoline, electricity, water and telephone fees were drastically cut and payments for exit visas were totally annulled. Simultaneously, to ensure the loyalty of the officer corps an additional 3,603 officers were promoted in the Saudi armed forces, which total 67,500 men. The growing revenue from oil enabled the regime, moreover, to divert additional funds to the development of agriculture and farmers were granted soft loans whenever needed.[64]

The establishment ulama were unhappy with Fahd's announced reforms and objected to some of them. Yet, as in the case of previous reforms, they continue to co-operate with the regime, hoping to gain some control of the *majlis al-shura* and the provincial consultative councils and curb meaningful changes in the *status quo*. The regime, moreover, increased its spending on the construction of mosques (nearly one billion dollars in recent years) and the Ministry of Pilgrimage and Endowments (*Awqaf*), already employing 54,000 'religious personnel' in the mosques, announced its intention to employ an additional 7,300 graduates of Islamic universities in 1992. As for the militant *'alims*, they totally reject the proposed reforms as being anti-Islamic because they are meant, they claim, to replace the *shari'a* with a civil code of law, to further erode the ulama's power and change the Wahhabi kingdom's character. Furthermore, it was claimed, the regime did not grant the non-royal elites true participation in decision-making while further cementing the absolute power of the monarchy.[65]

12

OIL AND GULF SECURITY

OIL AND POLITICS

The Security Council's sanctions against Iraq from August 1990, leading to the cessation of Iraq's and Kuwait's oil exports, created a shortfall of about 4.2 m.b.d. in OPEC's supply to the market. The expansion of Saudi and other OPEC members' production, to offset the shortfall, was not achieved overnight. Yet, by the beginning of 1991 Saudi Arabia's oil production had increased to 8.5 m.b.d. from 5.7 m.b.d. in August 1990. Consequently, oil prices, which had risen by October to nearly 40 dollars a barrel, declined by the beginning of 1991 to just over 20 dollars a barrel and to 16.5 dollars (OPEC) by mid-year. Thus, Riyadh fulfilled its obligation to the US, its protector, to keep the Gulf oil flowing to the world market at a 'reasonable price'.

Saudi Arabia's windfall profits, both from the rise of oil prices and from its increased production, were reported to be only 16 or 17 billion dollars.[1] That was in addition to about 22 billion dollar revenue from oil originally projected in the 1990 budget. Riyadh's income from oil in 1991 is estimated at over 40 billion dollars, resulting from an average export of nearly 8 m.b.d. at about 16 dollars a barrel. On the other hand, Saudi war expenses were estimated at 60–70 billion dollars. These include grants to countries which sent forces to protect the kingdom (25 billion dollars to the US), the cost of maintaining those forces in Saudi Arabia, and grants to friendly countries, such as Turkey and Egypt, which suffered losses owing to the UN sanctions against Iraq. The higher figure includes about 5 billion dollars, the cost of expanding Saudi oil production to 8.5 m.b.d.[2]

For internal political reasons, mainly because it did not wish to inform its citizens of the immense cost of the war and payments to the US, Riyadh did not produce a budget for 1991. Yet its budgetary deficit for 1990, originally projected to be between 6 and 7 billion dollars, rose to 15 billion dollars and to an estimated 25 billion in 1991. Thus, in addition to the annual bond issues of between 6 and 8 billion dollars and drawing again on its limited liquid reserves, Saudi Arabia was coerced to borrow heavily abroad for the first time in the kingdom's history.[3]

The above notwithstanding, Riyadh increased its expenditure budget (besides the war-related one) from 37.5 billion in 1989 to nearly 45 billion in 1991. Its projected expenditure budget for 1992 is approaching 50 billion dollars, not including special allocations for arms procurement paid for with oil. This, and the billions spent annually on expanding the Saudi oil production capacity, are bound directly to help Saudi Arabia's economic growth and prosperity. Furthermore, the presence in the kingdom of about half a million Western soldiers for eight months must have channelled substantial sums of money to the Saudi merchant class.[4] War-related contracts, worth billions of dollars, moreover, were won by Saudi companies and entrepreneurs. Indeed there are many signs that after years of recession, the Saudi economy and population are again thriving. Nevertheless, Riyadh is still hard pressed for cash to accelerate its economic development, to pay its war debts, to create jobs for unemployed school and university graduates, and to expand and upgrade its armed forces.

Fahd's recently announced *majlis al-shura* may give the ulama and middle class a limited advisory role in policy-making. Yet paramount in the regime's apprehension is a possible fusion between the economic problems and the rise of militant 'neo-fundamentalism' in the kingdom. Indeed for the first time since the suppression of the Ikhwan rebellion in the 1920s, the Saudi regime adopted harsh measures against ulama who challenged its legitimacy. As we have seen, it also resorted to the age-old tactic of buying the population's goodwill by improving their standard of living through a meaningful increase in government spending (including the expansion of the administration), salary increases and increased subsidies to electricity, water, gasoline, telephone services and the like. Such measures necessitate substantial funds. Unpopular internal bond issues and borrowing abroad – an anathema to all the ulama and their conservative followers – cannot solve the problem for long. Thus Riyadh faces a serious dilemma.

At 8–8.5 m.b.d., Saudi Arabia is producing in the third quarter of 1992 at near capacity. Hence the only option open to it is to increase its revenue by raising OPEC's oil price. While Riyadh badly needs higher oil prices, it cannot agree to demands by OPEC's price hawks, led by Iran and Algeria and supported by most other members, to contribute further to production cuts in order to again push oil price to OPEC's 21-dollars-a-barrel ceiling. Such a price hike would not only contradict Fahd's philosophy concerning the kingdom's long-range oil policy and interests, but could undermine the recovery of the world's, and particularly of the US, economy at a period when President Bush, considered a true friend of the Saudi regime and the Arabs in general (King Hassan of

Morocco to MBC TV, 25 May 1992), is standing for re-election. Moreover, Riyadh and Washington are also apprehensive about Iran's determination and efforts to develop quickly its military power and influence in the Muslim world, which higher oil revenue would assist.

Riyadh's elasticity concerning oil price is limited. While determined to keep its 35 per cent share of OPEC's market (particularly when Russian oil production is declining) it cannot afford to allow OPEC's oil price to decline beneath 17–18 dollars a barrel. Even such a price is hardly sufficient to support its efforts quickly to revive the kingdom's prosperity and stability and increase its military power.[5]

None the less, Saudi Arabia, it is evident, has decided to assume again its long-range oil policy, which supports a relatively low price, and is clearly co-ordinating this policy with Washington, whose balance of payments would be adversely affected by a significant rise in oil price.[6] Both are also concerned about the impact of higher oil prices on the hoped-for recovery of the world's economy.

Contributing over a third of OPEC's total oil production, Saudi Arabia dominated the organisation's summit in Geneva in November 1991. Although it agreed to a symbolic cut in production, such a cut was insufficient to raise OPEC prices from about 16.5–18 dollars a barrel to its 21-dollars-a-barrel reference price. In OPEC's February 1992 summit, Riyadh undertook to reduce its production to eight m.b.d. in the second quarter of the year, when demand for oil declines seasonally, in the context of the organisation's decision to cut its total production by 1.2–1.3 m.b.d. It adamantly refused, on Fahd's direct order, to reduce its and OPEC's production by an additional 300,000–400,000 b.d., as demanded by Iran, because this was bound to push OPEC's oil price to about 21 dollars a barrel. Yet in OPEC's May summit the Saudis supported only a small increase in the production ceiling for the third quarter when demand begins to rise. Thus, they caused OPEC's prices to rise up to 19 dollars a barrel, signalling its displeasure with the EC's unilateral decision to tax oil by three dollars a barrel (rising to ten dollars by the year 2000), conditional on US and Japanese approval. The US immediately announced its opposition to the EC proposal. Riyadh also expects Washington to continue to oppose any relaxation of the Security Council's conditions concerning the export of Iraqi oil.

The seasonal rise in demand in the fourth quarter of 1992 and the first quarter of 1993 and a possible revival of the world's economy may offset Kuwait's rising production (expected to reach 1.5 m.b.d. by the end of 1992) and increased output of other OPEC members. Riyadh, moreover, will essentially have paid its war debts by the end of 1992.[7] Thus, its cash-flow problems seem likely to be short-lived. It can, therefore, afford to help Washington and the other industrial countries to overcome the present economic recession by maintaining relatively low oil prices if the

EC oil taxation proposal is shelved. Indeed its revenues from oil, which more than doubled compared with 1989, will continue to rise as its production gradually rises and if the present relative stability in the oil market is maintained. An improvement in the world economy may even enable Riyadh eventually to support OPEC's 21-dollars-a-barrel ceiling price, and its revenue from oil will substantially increase and again enable it to build up the size of its liquid reserves and investments in downstream operations.

In the meantime, Riyadh is proceeding with its special five-year plan (1989–94) to expand its production capacity to about 10–10.5 m.b.d. It is also determined to retain its increased share of OPEC's market. Thus, in co-operation with the US, Riyadh will be able to preserve its hegemony in OPEC and essentially control the world's oil market and prices in the coming years. Such ability will not diminish even if Iraq is permitted, eventually, to utilise its full export capacity. All this depends on whether the US and its Western allies will continue to prevent Iraq from re-establishing itself as a local military superpower and the leader of militant pan-Arabism and to terrorise its weaker and more conservative neighbours. It will also depend on developments in Iran, which is rapidly building its military power and which, despite its assumed pragmatism, still hopes to control the region by exporting militant fundamentalism to the Arab–Muslim world. That, of course, is related to the success, or failure, and continuity, of the US efforts to maintain the stability in the region which is so important to the world economy and to restrain Baghdad's and Tehran's military–political aspirations.

'GULF SECURITY' AND IRAN

The rout of the Iraqi army, followed by the Shi'ite rebellion, which engulfed southern and south-central Iraq and the short-lived success of the renewed Kurdish rebellion in the north, caused grave concern in Riyadh. The possible emergence of a Shi'ite Islamic republic in southern Iraq, or possibly even in Baghdad, was a nightmare to the Saudis and their Arab allies. So was the possible disintegration of Sunni-Arab-dominated Iraq, a pillar of the Arab world. King Fahd and President Mubarak, therefore, endeavoured to convince Washington of the inexpediency of such a development. But, Washington itself believed that Iraq's collapse might adversely affect the whole region's stability and undermine Western interests there. Thus although Saddam Hussayn's overthrow remained a priority, the preservation of Iraq's territorial integrity even under a Ba'th regime, was preferred by Washington, Riyadh and Cairo. That led to the controversial cease-fire with Baghdad, which saved a good part of Saddam Hussayn's military machine.[8]

Once the US and Saudi Arabia reconciled themselves to the survival of

Saddam Hussayn's, or a Ba'th, regime, a strong Gulf defence pact seemed more essential than ever before.

The Gulf war demolished the taboos concerning overt co-operation and defence relations between the GCC countries and America. Yet, as far as Riyadh was concerned, the first premise of any defence arrangement was to reduce to a minimum the presence of US troops on the kingdom's territory.[9] In fact, during the last stages of the war against Iraq, it was agreed between Egypt, Syria and the GCC countries (the Damascus declaration of 6 March 1991) that, in addition to maintaining stronger Saudi armed forces, the main responsibility for protecting the kingdom was to be entrusted to a joint Egyptian–Syrian 'Arab army'.

Yet, by April it had become apparent that both Saudi Arabia and Kuwait were unwilling to undertake the financial commitments demanded by Egypt and Syria and 'viewed even the Egyptians as potentially destabilising if they became a semipermanent feature of these unchanging Gulf societies'.[10] Both Saudis and Kuwaitis preferred to rely on US 'intervention' forces which would have the use of several air and naval bases and facilities in Oman, the UAE and Qatar and the expanded base in Bahrayn. At this time, moreover, the US had just begun to evacuate its huge army stationed in Saudi Arabia and Kuwait.

Humiliated by the 'ungrateful' Gulf countries, President Mubarak declared in May that he was withdrawing the Egyptian troops from Saudi Arabia and Kuwait. Syria had already begun to do so even earlier. A compromise solution to the problem agreed upon during the Arab foreign ministers' meeting in Cairo in May 1991 proved to be mere lip-service to 'Arab consensus' and ended in failure. Tension between Cairo and Riyadh actually increased, following media reports about mistreatment of Egyptian workers in the kingdom and elsewhere in the Gulf and complaints by returning Egyptian soldiers about racist remarks made by Saudi and Kuwaiti troops.[11]

As the stationing of a large number of US troops in Saudi Arabia was not feasible, the US defence department believed that the second-best alternative for protecting the GCC countries and their oil was to stockpile, largely in Saudi Arabia, armour, artillery and heavy equipment and munitions sufficient for a corps of 150,000 soldiers. This plan, however, was scaled down drastically owing to the State Department's strong objections to turning Saudi Arabia practically into an American base, a matter that would enrage both Saudis and other Muslims. Riyadh even refused to consider a scaled-down plan to position on its territory US armour and support equipment for one division, which would necessitate servicing and guarding by American personnel. Such a presence of US troops in the holy land of Islam, the Saudis claimed, would be anathema to most Saudis, but particularly to their militant fundamentalists. This matter was the main reason for the tension in US–Saudi relations reported in June 1991.[12]

Determined to conclude a Gulf defence agreement, Washington tried to negotiate a long-term bilateral security alliance with the GCC. By the end of July an agreement framework was 'finalised', providing for joint military exercises, the sale of American arms to GCC countries, and the use by the US of several Gulf emirates' air and naval bases. Yet, the most politically sensitive issue, that of stockpiling American military equipment on Saudi soil, remained unsolved.[13]

Attempts to reach a final agreement with the GCC also failed in the coming months because each country insisted on different conditions. Some shaykhdoms wished US or UK troops to be physically stationed on their territory (unacceptable to the US and UK). Others insisted that the US sell them vast quantities of sophisticated arms and still others wished Iran to become party to this agreement. Saudi Arabia, the linchpin of the US plan, continued to resist Washington's request to position armour and heavy weapons in King Khalid military city near Hafr al-Batin (northern Saudi Arabia). The Saudis insisted that they buy the weapons and fully control them. Riyadh, it was claimed, overestimating its capabilities and achievements in the Gulf war, wished to transform its defensive-oriented army into a highly sophisticated mobile offensive force of 150,000 soldiers modelled upon the American force which had operated against Iraq earlier in the year. The US, according to this plan, was to supply the Saudis with the appropriate weapons and equipment and to train their new armed forces. Aware of the limitations of the Saudi capabilities and apprehensive of the ramifications of creating such a force in the kingdom, Washington rejected the Saudi proposal.[14]

Iraqi incursions into Kuwaiti territory since July, the most outrageous of which was a raid on Bubyan,[15] and Saddam's renewed belligerence, caused great anxiety in Kuwait. As talks between America and the GCC about a regional defence alliance were stalled, Kuwait, followed by Bahrayn, opted for a bilateral arrangement with Washington and, on 4 September 1991, signed an agreement with the United States for a ten-year security pact. Although Washington rejected Kuwait's request to station US troops permanently on its territory, this agreement provides for the positioning of American weapons and equipment in Kuwait, periodic joint exercises, and training of the Kuwaiti forces by the US. This development signalled the breakdown of efforts to forge a defence agreement with the GCC and the beginning of an attempt to replace it by bilateral agreements with each GCC country. It also indicated US determination to maintain Gulf security and the extent of Washington's pragmatism concerning this delicate matter.

Similar agreements are being negotiated with Qatar and the UAE and a 1980 agreement between the US and Oman was recently renewed. Yet, the problems which prevented Saudi Arabia from reaching an agreement with the US have not been overcome (second half of 1992). Nevertheless, the ongoing military co-operation between the two countries is based on a 1977 strategic co-operation pact. Thus, Mr Cheney, the US defence secretary, authorised in April the allocation of ground support equipment for 400 airplanes to be positioned in 'southwest Asia'. Pentagon directives for 1992 also refer to 200 battle tanks and 200 APCs that would be stored in the above region.[16]

Undoubtedly, the Saudi position concerning a military alliance with the US which would necessitate a meaningful American presence on its territory was influenced by the strong objections to it by some senior Al Saud princes, the establishment ulama and nationalist-oriented elements of the intelligentsia. The Saudi view was also influenced by the escalating clash between the militant *'alims* and the regime and, to some extent, by Riyadh's apprehension concerning the reaction of some Arab countries and of Iran to a large American military presence on Saudi soil.

Notwithstanding, as Saddam Hussayn succeeded in reconsolidating his power while he continuously defied the Security Council's resolutions, and as the scope of his military endeavours became known, the Gulf countries re-evaluated their defence problem. Although Riyadh remained opposed to a formal military agreement with the US, it closed its eyes at the end of 1991 to continued US control of the Dhahran base and its relatively large military presence in the kingdom.[17] The Saudis, more realistic now, aim to increase their armed forces to 90,000 and not 150,000.[18]

Furthermore, in spite of its efforts to improve its relations with Tehran and Rafsanjani's government's pragmatism, Saudi Arabia became increasingly suspicious about Iran's endeavours to build up rapidly a substantial military power and develop its conventional and unconventional weapons industry. Iran's much heralded pragmatism, moreover, stood in stark contradiction to its covert efforts to spread militant Islamic fundamentalism in the Arab countries and the Muslim world as a whole.

Following Saddam Hussayn's defeat and the Tehran-supported abortive Shi'ite uprising in southern Iraq, Iran accelerated its efforts to improve its relations with Riyadh. Diplomatic relations between the two countries were re-established in March 1991 following Iraq's defeat. This was followed by a visit to Jedda in April by Iran's foreign minister Ali Akbar Velayati. The latter's visit was reciprocated when Prince Saud al-Faysal arrived in Tehran in June to discuss, among other things, the problem of Iran's pilgrims quota. Velayati again visited Jedda at the end of June to finalise an agreement to raise the Iranian pilgrim quota from 45,000 to 115,000.

In so far as the Iranians were allowed in the 1991 pilgrimage season to demonstrate against America and Israel, such demonstrations were orderly and no anti-Saudi slogans were chanted by the participants. Hence, in an interview at the beginning of October, following a GCC foreign ministers' meeting with Velayati in Kuwait, Saud al-Faysal commended Iran's positive policy since President Rafsanjani's election, which had contributed to Gulf stability. The GCC ministers agreed to hold another meeting with their Iranian counterpart in early 1992 to 'establish a framework for the strengthening of their relations'. The Iranian–Saudi *rapprochement* culminated with Rafsanjani's visit to Riyadh in December.[19]

Well aware of the 'new world order' and the importance attached to the security of Persian Gulf oil by America (and the West), demonstrated by its war against Iraq, Iran reconciled itself, at least temporarily, to the US presence and hegemony in the region. Tehran's intensified endeavours to re-establish its membership in the community of nations were probably aimed, *inter alia*, at insuring recognition of its interests in the Gulf region and its defence.[20]

Iran opposed plans for an Arab Gulf security pact which disregarded its interests in the region and advocated a defence arrangement in which it could play a role of regional importance. It even exploited its close relations with some GCC countries to undermine American-sponsored Gulf defence plans which excluded Iran. The fact that they could not ignore Iran's growing regional importance caused the GCC foreign ministers who met in Kuwait at the end of 1991 to discuss Gulf security arrangements and to invite Velayati to the meeting for an exchange of views. Yet, Tehran's increasing military might, on the one hand, and its export of militant fundamentalism to the Arab–Muslim world, on the other, emphasised the need for an understanding with the US over Gulf defence.

Iran's revenue from oil had risen significantly since the end of 1990 after it expanded its production from 3.4 to nearly 4 m.b.d. in 1991, which generated a revenue of about 14 billion dollars. Yet, in spite of its pressing socio-economic problems, Tehran increased its allocation for defence in 1991 to about 4 billion dollars (compared with 12 billion dollars for the whole war period 1980–8) and more than that in 1992.[21] To bypass the American-initiated weapons embargo, Tehran obtained arms and military technology wherever it could. Thus, from 1990 on, focusing on missile and nuclear development, it carefully nurtured its ties with China and North Korea.[22] It also obtained large quantities of conventional sophisticated weapons, such as Mig-29 fighters, Sukhoy-23 fighter bombers and T-72 tanks from the disintegrating former Soviet Union.[23]

Obviously, Iran is determined to build up both its conventional and non-conventional military capability to the point where it could in the

211

future dominate the Gulf, or at least not be taken lightly, even by the United States.

Simultaneously, Tehran has been active in establishing its influence in the ex-Soviet Muslim republics of Central Asia (and Azerbaijan), although the majority of their population is Sunni. The low-profile development of these relations during the Gorbachev era has been replaced since mid-1991 by a major drive to establish Iranian influence in the Muslim republics. In addition to promises of financial aid, oil and membership in the Muslim Common Market, Iran is trying to exploit Muslim solidarity and ties with some fundamentalist ulama (especially in Tajikistan) to help advance its cause.

Iran finds itself in Central Asia in competition with (Sunni) Turkey. The latter has revived its early twentieth-century pan-Turanian aspirations based on common origin, language and culture with the four Central Asian republics. Turkey's secularism, relative modernism and special relations with the West are much more appealing than the extremist fundamentalism of war-ravished and relatively backward Iran. Saudi Arabia has also become increasingly concerned about Iranian activities in Central Asia and elsewhere in the Muslim world. It is using its wealth, the pan-Islamic organisations which it controls, and its status as guardian of Islam's holy places, sometimes in co-operation with Turkey, to counter the Iranian offensive in the ex-Soviet republics.[24]

Far more worrying to Riyadh is the fact that despite the image of moderation which Tehran has presented since the end of 1989, an image which helped to some extent to improve its standing in the world community, and despite the release of Western hostages in Lebanon, Iran is secretly promoting militant fundamentalism in the Arab–Islamic countries on a larger scale than in Khomayni's days. For some time, Tehran has been channelling funds to the Egyptian, Tunisian, Algerian and Moroccan militant fundamentalist movements and is training their cadres. The growth of the power of these movements came to a climax in the Algerian elections in February 1992; and consequently Iranian diplomats, involved with the local Islamic movement, were declared *persona non grata*.[25]

Even earlier Iran was deeply involved in the consolidation of the power of Sudanese General Beshir, who overthrew the government in Khartoum in 1989 and who shares power with Dr Hassan al-Turabi, the leader of the Islamic Front Organisation (previously Muslim Brothers). Cadres of Turabi's (Sunni) organisation were trained in Iran and Beshir's regime received funds and weapons from Tehran. That the relations between Iran and Sudan have the blessing of Iran's government was demonstrated by the visit to Khartoum in December 1991 of President Rafsanjani, followed by the arrival in Sudan of a larger number of Revolutionary

Guards from Iran and from Hizbollah camps in the Lebanese Bika' in 1992.

Sudan has become, in the last year or so, the base for Islamic militants' activities in Africa and the Arab world. Training camps, other facilities and weapons are provided to members of Egyptian, Libyan, Tunisian, Moroccan and Syrian fundamentalist and terrorist organisations. This has so worried President Mubarak's regime that the Egyptian government warned Khartoum to stop its support for Egyptian fundamentalist groups and intervention in Egyptian affairs, or suffer the consequences.[26] Ironically, even Libya's Mu'ammar Gadhafi, who previously supported Sudanese Islamic revolutionaries, is worried by the anti-Gadhafi activities promoted by Khartoum.

It could be that Tehran's ambivalent policy is an outcome of the struggle for power in Tehran between President Rafsanjani's pragmatic faction and the more dogmatic radical opposition, still quite powerful in Iran. That Iranian officials are involved in clandestine terrorist operations, that Rafsanjani's government overtly supports Islamic movements in the Maghreb, and especially the extremist Sudanese regime, and that Iran is endeavouring to build up its unconventional military power could be an indication that Tehran's seemingly dichotomous policy is, in fact, a shrewd strategy to 'have one's cake and eat it too'.

In the last months of 1991, when Fahd's government decided to adopt a more assertive policy concerning its radical ulama and began more openly to co-operate with the US it also became evident that Riyadh had begun to reassess its stance concerning Iraq. By then, it was obvious that Saddam Hussayn's regime was not likely to collapse because of economic sanctions and that the Iraqi leader, who was openly defying the UN inspectors, was determined to rehabilitate his military power. Thus Riyadh began to press Washington to take more determined steps against the Iraqi dictator. Although in September 1991 it refused to allow the US to use its bases to attack Iraq, by the year's end Riyadh had practically implored Washington to help bring down the Ba'th regime, whatever the consequences to the Sunni–Arab hegemony in Iraq.[27]

Riyadh also gave its blessing to a congress of Iraqi opposition movements, including Shi'ites, Kurds and inconsequential leftist and other organisations, which met in Damascus in January 1992. The Saudi regime hosted the leaders of this coalition in Riyadh at the end of February. Crown Prince Abdallah, Syria's ally, who now supports closer relations with Iran to counter Iraq's power and US hegemony in the region, even received in audience the head of the Tehran-based Iraqi Shi'ite opposition, Ayatollah Muhammad Bakr al-Hakim and other Iraqi Shi'ite leaders. Riyadh undertook, moreover, to supply the Kurds and the other opposition factions with weapons, including anti-air and anti-tank missiles, and funds in order to rekindle the revolt against Saddam

213

Hussayn. The Saudis promised that if they were to rise again, they would be given air cover against attacks by Iraqi helicopters and airplanes.[28] (In September 1992 the US declared Iraq south of the 32 parallel a 'no fly zone'.)

American and British pressure, through the UN, on Iraq increased again in March 1992. Unlike Cairo and Damascus, who both objected in principle to a planned American operation to enforce Baghdad to co-operate with the UN inspection teams, Riyadh favoured it. Following a Security Council meeting in mid-March, Iraqi foreign minister Tariq Aziz was told that unless Iraq co-operated with the UN inspectors and carried out the council's resolutions, it would suffer grave consequences. Despite Aziz's attempt to obtain some concessions from the UN concerning terms for the sale of Iraq's oil, none were given. Simultaneously, American and British naval and air units moved into the Gulf and to other bases and positions, including Saudi Arabia, within striking distance of Iraq.[29] The boycott on Baghdad was to be more strictly enforced by closing the Jordanian loophole (Jordan failed to abide by its promises to Washington). Subsequently, Iraq temporarily became again more co-operative with the UN inspection teams (until the next crisis in July 1992).

Now that it has crossed the Rubicon and no longer allows its militant ulama to inhibit its policy, Riyadh's relations and co-operation with Washington are stronger than ever. Furthermore, not only does the Saudi regime feel threatened by a revival of Saddam Hussayn's power and Iraqi anti-Saudi propaganda, but now it is increasingly apprehensive concerning Iran's growing military capabilities and ambitions in the region and in the Muslim world in general. Riyadh realises that, even if it were to build up the power of its armed forces and obtain the most sophisticated armament, it could not aspire to match the far superior military power of its larger neighbours.

Saudi Arabia's dependence on the US protective umbrella and its need to co-operate with Washington (oil pricing included) is now obvious not only to Fahd's regime and its Western-trained technocrats, but also to the larger part of the younger-generation Sauds and, much as they may dislike it, to the majority of the middle class and intelligentsia. Even if Riyadh is still reluctant, for obvious reasons, to formalise the presence of 'infidel' troops on its territory, the need to stockpile heavy weapons and equipment in Saudi Arabia cannot be ignored, even if the Saudis were to buy warplanes and other weapons from European countries. For the time being, however, the presence of the American navy in the Gulf region, the facilities that the US armed forces enjoy in Saudi Arabia (informal) and the GCC countries, and bilateral agreements such as that between America and Kuwait may suffice to ensure the region's stability. This stability is essential to the world's economy as well as to the survival of the Saudi and other GCC regimes. But such protection against outside aggression cannot ensure Riyadh against internal upheavals.

13

CONCLUSION

Despite the rapid modernisation of Saudi Arabia its rulers managed to avoid the socio-political dislocations that often accompanied development in the Arab–Muslim and Third World countries. This was due to the relative cohesiveness of the wide-based ruling house, the policies of the monarchs, and to the inability of the new social forces unleashed by modernisation to mount serious challenges to the Saudi regime. In addition, the modernisation of the kingdom and its government undermined the power of the non-royal traditional elites (tribal *umara*' and ulama) and, to a lesser degree, that of the royal family's partners, i.e. the Jiluwis, the Thunayans and Al al-Shaykh. Thus, today, it is the senior princes of Al 'Abd al-Rahman, and especially of Al 'Abd al-Aziz, who dominate the kingdom's informal consultative and policy-making organs.

Far from being an absolute monarchy, or a desert democracy, the Saudi regime is an oligarchy, whose cornerstone is the principle of consultation and consensus. Its collective leadership, which became more prominent after Faysal's demise (1975) and the 1982/3 royal family crisis, has been strengthened by the Gulf crises.

The policies of the Saudi rulers were guided by several 'golden rules' instituted by King Ibn Saud. For instance, whenever possible, the regime preferred to 'buy off' the opposition rather than fight it. Above all, it endeavoured to safeguard the alliance between 'state and church' which practically legitimised the regime (and usually its policy). On the other hand, it crushed with an iron fist the militant opposition which challenged its authority or attempted to overthrow the Sauds' government.

Unlike Iran under the Shah, where only a tiny ruling family and a small, self-indulgent upper middle class monopolised the country's oil wealth, the wide-based Saudi regime prudently channelled the kingdom's growing oil revenue, however unevenly, to all classes of Saudis. The ensuing modernisation and the rapid urbanisation of the rural population in the 1960s, 1970s and early 1980s helped transform the majority of

Saudis into a multi-layered, relatively prosperous bourgeoisie, mostly conservative and supportive of the Al Saud regime. Oil wealth also facilitated the process of national integration and the gradual emergence of a Saudi identity. Cohesion occurred despite the survival of traditional differences, such as those between *hadr* and *badu*, Najdi and Hijazi, Sunni and Shi'ite. The decline of oil prices and the resulting economic recession in the 1980s could have reversed this process, had it not been for the Iran–Iraq war and the Kuwait crisis.

Again following the example of Ibn Saud, his successors Faysal, Khalid and Fahd adopted policies aimed at pre-empting the consolidation in the kingdom of alternative power centres. Hence, they strove to incorporate the rapidly expanding middle-class elites into the Sauds' power base. For its part the middle-class intelligentsia opted on the whole for collaboration with the rulers, gaining in the process prestige, influence and wealth. Yet, despite this collaboration and the greater authority delegated to technocrats since the mid-1970s, the new elites, after some 25 years of faithfully serving the regime, failed to penetrate the ruling class and, until 1992, were excluded even from participation in policy-making.

The Mecca rebellion in 1979 seemed to demonstrate that, in contrast to other Arab and Muslim countries, 'neo-fundamentalism' in Saudi Arabia appeals only to peripheral elements. Most Saudis were quite happy with the apparent synthesis of formal puritanism, modernism and material prosperity, provided by the regime and legitimised by the establishment ulama. That consensus, however, began to change from the late 1980s.

Aware of the deeply-rooted conservative outlook of the Saudi masses and apprehensive about the kingdom's accelerated development, the rulers repeatedly granted the ulama's demands for stricter observance of Wahhabi doctrines and for the protection of the 'Saudi way of life'. As long as the ulama did not interfere with the kingdom's politics and modernisation programmes, King Khalid, and later even King Fahd, preferred to risk the alienation of Western-educated and other middle-class elites rather than lose the ulama's support. But in recent years better-educated, younger *'alims* became increasingly critical of the Sauds' government and of their peers, the establishment ulama, who nearly always legitimise the regime's character and policy and close their eyes to its (claimed) injustices and to the ostentatious lifestyle of many Sauds.

Following the 1979 and 1980 Shi'ite riots in the Eastern Province, Fahd not only accelerated the development of this region but, ignoring Najdi ulama objections, initiated a far more tolerant policy towards his Shi'ite subjects. Shi'ites are still discriminated against despite the regime's policy. Yet, they are now benefiting from the kingdom's development and prosperity and their status has been considerably improved. All that, the termination of the Iran–Iraq war and the *rapprochement* between

Tehran and Riyadh after Khomayni's demise, caused most Saudi Shi'ites to become much more supportive of Fahd's regime.

The replacement of older provincial amirs since 1980 with younger, modern-educated and capable ones, and the proliferation of royal technocrats in the central government, was partly meant to strengthen support for the Sudayris among the conservative rural population, Crown Prince Abdallah's traditional power base, and to reduce discontent among the younger Sauds. But it was meant, above all, to accelerate the development of the rural areas, to improve the inhabitants' standard of living (including that of the newly urbanised population) and to strengthen their allegiance to the Sauds' *hukuma*.

The new social forces that emerged with the kingdom's modernisation failed to undermine the bases of the regime. Only a small fraction of the middle class and the oil industry's workforce endorsed radical Arab nationalist and fundamentalist ideologies. Power and wealth, together with conservative nationalism, served the new elites as a surrogate for the pan-Arab and revolutionary ideologies which they had espoused in the 1950s and 1960s. The Iraqi invasion of Kuwait and Saddam Hussayn's demands that Arab 'haves' share their wealth with the 'have-nots', eroded any significant support in the kingdom for pan-Arabism.

The activity of the small Saudi militant opposition in the 1980s, occasionally evident in Asir and Hijaz, was limited largely to the Eastern Province. There, the Shi'ite 'proletariat', the fundamentalists and elements of the nationalist intelligentsia would probably be among the first to join a popular anti-Saud uprising if it were to erupt. Yet a Shi'ite uprising in Al-Hasa would be likely to backfire. In such an event, the Sunnis would rally behind Al Saud because of their almost universal aversion to Shi'ites and their concern lest they lose the Eastern Province's oil revenues.

Saudi Arabia's rural population, a major source of support for Al Saud, has rapidly declined in size in the last three decades but it still comprises about a third of the kingdom's population. The newly urbanised masses have also retained their relations with, if not their allegiance to, their traditional socio-political institutions and to the Sauds' *hukuma*. Such support depends, however, on Al Saud's ability to continue to improve the population's standard of living and to preserve the façade of a mildly fundamentalist state and the 'Saudi way of life'. Should the regime fail to do so, a fusion between socio-economic problems and religious fermentation may seriously threaten its stability. Cognisant of the above, King Fahd, helped by the establishment ulama and by the renewed rise in the kingdom's oil revenues, exerts himself to prevent such a development.

The unemployed intelligentsia in Saudi Arabia has become a most serious problem. As the increase of university graduates coincided with the decline of the Saudi economy in the 1980s, the competition for government positions among graduates of foreign, domestic secular and religious universities was exacerbated. In the second half of the 1980s the economic recession peaked and unemployment among Islamic school and university graduates and their 'secular' counterparts rose sharply, thus further aggravating the three-sided competition for government appointments. The regime's ability to deal swiftly with this situation depended on the continued growth of its oil income.

The country's enormous oil reserves and financial resources endowed Saudi Arabia with power and influence in the Arab and Muslim camps and in the international arena out of proportion to the size of its population and level of development. Saudi Arabia demonstrated its solidarity with its Arab and Muslim sister countries by supporting them financially and politically. They, in turn, helped consolidate the regime's prestige and stability. Yet, as its oil revenues dwindled in the 1980s, and correspondingly its grants to Arab and Third World countries, the kingdom's influence in the Arab camp and in the world gradually waned and relations with poorer 'fraternal' Arab states became soured. The foundation of the ACC in 1989 was an outcome of these developments.

As far as Saudi Arabia's socio-political and economic development is concerned, the conflict with Iraq was a watershed. The conflict brought into the open, or precipitated, processes that have their roots in the 1970s and 1980s.

Most assuredly, Saudi Arabia's 'seven lean years' are over. Even if the average (OPEC) oil price for 1992 remains about 18 dollars a barrel, Riyadh's average oil export, at less than 8 m.b.d., will generate more than 40 billion dollars annually, twice the 1989 figure. Furthermore, Riyadh's future output will continue to rise as its production capacity, and the demand for OPEC's oil, grows in future years. It can be expected, therefore, that Saudi Arabia's rising oil revenues will provide its citizens with higher *per capita* income, a higher standard of living and even better welfare and other services. Even the problem of the unemployed graduates is likely to be gradually solved by accelerated development spurred by increased government spending and intensified private-sector activity. All this will help the regime maintain itself in power and continue its evolutionary rather than revolutionary reforms.

Notwithstanding the kingdom's gradually renewed prosperity, the middle-class intelligentsia remains impatient with the Sauds' involvement in business, their special privileges and their 'high' lifestyle. By the beginning of the 1990s, the new elites were far more numerous and powerful and their expectations now go beyond the satisfaction of material needs. Their wish for a role in decision-making, debated during the war with Iraq and made public in watered-down form in the 'open letter' to the king, is unlikely to be satisfied by minor participation in decision-making in an appointed *majlis al-shura*. Yet, for the time being, in the face of 'neo-fundamentalist' reaction, they will probably opt, as they have done since the reign of Faysal, to co-operate with the Saudi regime.

The war with Iraq has amply demonstrated Saudi Arabia's vulnerability. Thus, Riyadh's defence programme envisages the 'substantial' strengthening of its armed forces advocated by both new elites and ulama in view of the kingdom's recent dependence on foreign troops. The institution of universal military service, repeatedly promised by the Sudayris, has not been carried out. With a citizen population of about six million, of whom about 60 per cent are women and Shi'ites, only a relatively small proportion of Saudis are eligible, or willing, to serve in the armed forces. That percentage declines further if 'undesirable' elements are excluded and if a prosperous economy offers young educated Saudis more tempting incentives than a military career. This, and American objections, may have caused Riyadh to scale down the planned size of its armed forces to about 90,000 servicemen.

With a territory of about a million square kilometres, and meagre manpower to defend it, Riyadh justly focuses on the development of its air power and air defence and the acquisition of costly state-of-the-art weapons for an army with an offensive capability and not just a defensive one.[1] The pool of young princes, encouraged by the regime to join the armed forces, who dominate the air force and sensitive command positions in the army and special services, is not unlimited. Additional educated manpower is more available in the relatively densely populated and sophisticated Hijaz and in some urban centres in other provinces. Simultaneously, the semi-educated para-military bedouin National Guard is declining in importance and the reservoir of volunteers for the army from loyal 'noble' bedouin tribes is rapidly shrinking, because of urbanisation and mass education. A new elites' upheaval in the future, spearheaded by 'Young Turks' from among the cadres of young officers, will be thus more conceivable than in the past if plans for a substantial expansion of the armed forces were to be carried out.

The Kuwait–Iraq crisis, which removed the taboo concerning Riyadh's (and GCC's) military co-operation with the West, has also undermined pan-Arab sentiments in the kingdom. No longer inhibited by fear of Arab reaction to their overt co-operation with Washington, the Sudayris, none the less, are well aware that an 'infidel' military presence on Saudi territory is anathema not only to the establishment ulama and their conservative supporters but also to a majority of the domestically trained intelligentsia. Yet, even an 'expanded' Saudi army will not be a match for Iraq's and Iran's rapidly growing military might. Having repeatedly rejected the 'Arab' defence agreement, and being incapable of accepting the American Gulf defence plans, Riyadh faces a dilemma. Hence its support of the US position concerning Iraq's disarming and its attempts to block Iran's expanding influence in the Arab–Muslim world and acquisition of conventional and unconventional weapons. On the other hand Crown Prince Abdallah is not alone in advocating an alliance with Tehran to counterbalance Baghdad's potential power, rather than be so dependent on an American presence in the region.

The Carter Doctrine of 1980 was a milestone in the US commitment to the preservation of stability in the Persian Gulf and, especially, the well-being of Saudi Arabia. But American commitment to the protection of Saudi Arabia and its oil goes back at least to the 1950s, and particularly to the 1960s, when demand for oil gradually overtook supply, and to 1970, when the US became a net oil importer.

By the early 1980s, new sources of oil, conservation and alternative sources of energy seemed about to bring the 'oil era' to an end. None the less, since the late 1980s, OPEC has been rapidly regaining its lost market share as demand for oil increases while other oil sources dry up. Indeed, by 1992, the United States, the world's largest consumer of oil, whose own production continues to diminish, is already importing about half its oil requirement. Oil prices, however, are now lower, in real terms, than they were in 1974, thanks to the policy of Saudi Arabia and its smaller Gulf allies. Controlling about 50 per cent of the world's proven reserves, the GCC countries co-operate with the US to ensure the flow of Gulf oil to the market at 'reasonable prices'. Hence, *inter alia*, America's determination to protect the Saudi regime (and its GCC allies) – considered by Washington the US's most important strategic asset in the region.

The major operation which America undertook to defend Saudi Arabia, dislodge the Iraqi army from Kuwait and break Saddam Hussayn's power, is ample proof of Washington's sensitivity concerning the Persian Gulf's stability.

Saddam Hussayn is well aware of Washington's unwillingness and inability to mount again a full-scale military operation against Iraq. He also believes that the West's resolution to maintain the sanctions against his country and destroy its military capability will erode with time. But he misjudged President Bush's determination and commitment, supported by the UK, to maintain the stability of the Gulf regimes and ensure the undisturbed flow of relatively cheap Persian Gulf oil to the world market.

For the time being it seems that the West's determination has overwhelmed the Iraqi dictator. Yet much will depend in the future on the continued resolve of Washington and its allies not to permit Saddam Hussayn's attrition tactics to succeed. The US policy, moreover, hinges on Saudi Arabia and its allies' co-operation concerning Gulf defence, particularly in the face of Tehran's endeavours once again to become the regional 'superpower'.

Riyadh's co-operation with the US is inhibited by internal factors. Although the Saudi new elites' ranks are constantly being expanded by new generations of university graduates, the intelligentsia and its middle-class allies are still a minority. The conservative majority strongly identifies with the establishment ulama (and with the Al Saud *hukuma*) and wishes to preserve the 'Saudi way of life', which helps them adjust to modernisation and to a rapidly changing social structure and environ-ment. Some who could not, or did not wish to, adjust are the ones who have turned, or are turning, to 'neo-fundamentalism'.

The emergence of a large group of relatively young 'non-conformist' *'alims* and professors in Islamic universities, within the ranks of the ulama, signalled an important change in the traditional relationship between 'state and church' in the kingdom. Though not as militant as their 'neo-fundamentalist' counterparts, and still acknowledging the primacy of Al Saud, they are unhappy with their mentors' almost automatic legitimisation of the regime's policy and hypocrisy concerning the Sauds' personal behaviour. Above all, they advocate a revision in the relationship between the regime and the ulama which would enable the latter to control practically all aspects of government activity.

A more serious challenge to the Sauds emanates from the overtly militant and popular 'neo-fundamentalist' theologians and preachers who emerged in the 1980s. These publicly challenge the policy and behaviour of Al Saud and the regime's very legitimacy. Like their Ikhwan predecessors in the first decades of the century and the 'neo-Ikhwan' in the 1970s, they are fanatically xenophobic, extremely anti-American and strongly supportive of Islamic solidarity. Also, they are more sophisticated, and their attacks on the regime combine religious, social and political themes.

The wide circulation, during and after the war with Iraq, of vitriolic 'Islamic cassettes' that were directed against the regime, against the US and against Western-trained technocrats undoubtedly influenced Riyadh's repeated rejections of the US Gulf defence plans. Ironically, it also influenced King Fahd to go ahead with his plans for evolutionary reform and liberalism. The continued militant–fundamentalist fermen-tation is evidence that the rise of 'neo-fundamentalism' in Saudi Arabia is not a passing phenomenon. Rather, it is a major undercurrent in Saudi society, greatly enhanced by the rapid modernisation which the Saudi kingdom underwent in the 1970s, which was accelerated by the economic hardships of the 1980s.

The fact that Saudi Arabia is now again entering a period of prosperity may mitigate the impact of the militant fundamentalists' message. Indeed, their stance concerning the war against 'Muslim Iraq' and extremism was, and is, rejected by most ulama and Saudi conservatives, not to mention the middle-class elites. Nevertheless, their continued belligerence, despite their harassment by the regime, and their influence on part of the Saudi population, and indirectly on the government's policy, should not be underrated.

In his article, 'The end of pan-Arabism',[2] Fouad Ajami analyses the rise and decline of pan-Arabism, calling it a myth that held back the Arab countries' adjustment to the realities of the modern world. Ajami's brilliant analysis has been challenged by several supporters of Arab nationalism who assert that even if pan-Arabism temporarily suffered a setback after Nasser's demise, Arab solidarity, which existed before Nasser, is very much alive.[3] Yet, the Iran–Iraq war proved that even Arab solidarity is dependent on personalities and self-interest.

By the end of the 1980s, the disintegration of the 'Arab system' reached such a degree that economic factors, self-interest and regionalism, rather than ideology, were the main driving forces behind the Arab countries' re-grouping. Leaving the Maghreb Co-operation Council (MCC) aside, the ACC was clearly an alliance of 'have-nots' with a grudge against the GCC, which was no longer able or willing to support them. The oil-rich GCC, supposedly also an economic co-operation body, focused above all on its member states' defence and the security of their regimes.

The Kuwait–Iraq crisis reflected the deep antagonism of the poor, culturally more developed and densely-populated Arab countries towards their past benefactors, the sparsely-populated, backward and archaic, oil-rich regimes. Paradoxically, Baghdad, which fomented the reaction against the haughty behaviour of the latter, was temporarily impoverished through the poor judgment of its ruler, and was previously unwilling to share Iraq's oil wealth with its needy 'Arab sisters'. It was, ironically, the promise of wealth-sharing that Saddam Hussayn exploited to gain widespread Arab support for his annexation of Kuwait. The Palestinian cause, also exploited by him, was one of the only issues to produce Arab solidarity, because of the Arabs' (and fundamentalist Muslims') total rejection of Jewish Israel, 'the outpost of Western culture and imperialism'.

The myth of Arab unity (to quote Ajami), and what remained of the credibility of Arab solidarity, suffered badly from the Gulf war. The deep dislike and suspicion between 'haves' and 'have-nots' which existed before the Kuwait crisis was greatly enhanced by Iraq's brutal aggression against Kuwait and Arab nationalists' sympathy for Baghdad. Iraq's performance in 'the mother of all battles', moreover, dealt Arab pride an additional severe blow. All that, undoubtedly, encourages each Arab country to seek its own salvation and pursue its own national interests.

Betrayed by those whom they had previously supported financially, the Saudi-led GCC countries' fear and suspicion of their 'fraternal sisters' was greatly enhanced. No longer worried about antagonising inimical

Arab militant nationalists, they now openly turn to their Western patrons for protection.

The 'new world order', resulting from the USSR's disintegration, deprived the Arab radicals of their former ability to exploit the Powers' rivalry. This, and the war with Iraq, enabled America to establish its hegemony in the Gulf and in the Middle East as a whole. The wealth and influence of the Gulf oil countries is now protected by the umbrella of a higher-profile American presence in the region. The militant Arab states are no longer able (at least for the time being) to intimidate the moderate pro-Western oil countries. Nevertheless, the rift between rich and poor in the Arab world, which will continue to widen in the future, coupled with the Gulf regimes' weakness, archaic character and rising militant fundamentalism, are all bound to undermine the region's stability. That is, unless the GCC countries – whose wealth will continue to increase in the coming years – are going to be willing to share their fortune with their poorer brethren and/or reform their regimes.

The war with Iraq demonstrated how the Arab–Israeli conflict could easily be manipulated to destabilise the entire region. The decline of the radicals in the fragmented Arab camp, together with the emergence of the 'new world order', enhanced the chances of a settlement of the long-standing conflict. Adjusting to the 'new world order', even Syria's Hafiz al-Assad moderated his antipathy for America and his total rejection of Israel and agreed, after gentle coercion by the Saudis and the Egyptians, to participate in the American-initiated Middle East peace talks.

Yet American hopes, during the Gulf war, that the Saudi-led GCC countries would take a leading role in the planned Arab–Israeli peace negotiations, proved, at first, overly optimistic. Aware of the strong detestation felt by most Saudis for Israel, Riyadh informed Secretary Baker on 22 April (1991) that the kingdom had no intention of participating in the planned Arab–Israeli peace talks. Soon afterwards, however, under pressure from Washington (and Prince Bandar), and once he began to follow a more assertive policy, King Fahd became committed to the US endeavours to end the Arab–Israeli conflict (a position he had supported as early as 1981). This, however, further inflamed the militant fundamentalists' incitement against the Saudi regime.

Some members of the middle-class elites hoped for an alliance with the discontented third-generation educated Sauds that might lead to more rapid political reform. Indeed, many younger princes, including royal officers and technocrats, frustrated by their mentors' policies, impatiently awaited their chance to reform the kingdom's political structure, but they prudently avoided such overtures. Fahd's new 'Basic Order of Government', however, will involve some of the third-generation Sauds, for the first time, in the succession process. That, and their participation in the central and provincial government and administration, the king hopes, may win their support for his evolutionary reforms.

Despite disagreement on major policy matters, largely between the Sudayris and the conservative senior princes led by Abdallah, the ruling family still maintains its outward unity and consensus and commands considerable support among the population. In the expectation of a challenge to their hegemony or over the next round of succession, the Sudayris, moreover, have strongly fortified their position in the government, provincial administration and the security and armed forces. It is widely believed that Prince Sultan still nourishes hopes of replacing Crown Prince Abdallah as heir apparent. This could partly explain his resistance to closer co-operation with the US concerning Gulf defence. Yet, even if Abdallah were to succeed Fahd, he will have to delegate substantial authority to Sultan, the next in line of succession, and will be surrounded by Sudayris, or Sudayris' appointees, in all key positions. Furthermore, Abdallah's anti-American stance and his having become the main protagonist of a pro-Iranian policy (detestable to the ulama) aimed at counterbalancing Iraq's potential threat and US Gulf defence plans, does not endear him to Washington. Nor is he the favourite choice of the younger Sauds, the middle-class intelligentsia or the technocrats. It is possible to envisage, therefore, a situation in which, to please everyone concerned, the relatively liberal, likeable and capable youngest Sudayri, Prince Salman, may emerge as a compromise candidate. In view of the new circumstances, it is also not totally inconceivable that the next Saudi monarch could be one of the more outstanding third-generation Sauds.

Often accused of weakness and indecisiveness, King Fahd, nevertheless, managed successfully to navigate the Saudi regime through the difficult social, economic and political challenges of the 1980s and the Iraq crisis of 1990-1. In the early 1990s he was also required to deal with the new elites' growing demand for liberalisation and political reform and converse demands by the ulama and their 'neo-fundamentalist' offshoot that practically amounted to a challenge to the Sauds' authority and the very existence of their regime. In his relations with the ulama Fahd resorted, as long as he could, to consultation and consensus to avoid a confrontation, but once they exceeded the permissible, he did not hesitate to coerce them to accept again the Sauds' primacy and simultaneously dealt harshly with the militants who continued to challenge the regime and its policy.

Always the advocate of modernisation and evolutionary reforms King Fahd sympathised with the new elites' wish to participate to some extent in policy-making. When he overcame his reluctance to confront the orthodox and his conservative peers, the monarch declared the creation of an appointed (albeit with limited authority) *majlis al-shura*. Once established, this body may become, nevertheless, a platform for vocal criticism of the government's performance and policy, as was the case with the Kuwaiti parliament dissolved in 1986. Moreover, the middle-class elites and the younger Sauds, on whose support Fahd (and possibly his American allies) is counting, are likely to press later on for additional concessions. On the other hand, the still powerful *ahl al-hal wa'l-'aqd* and the establishment ulama are most likely to slow down such a process.

For the time being, the Saudi regime's stability seems secure. The new Consultative Assembly will serve as a steam valve for the new elites' frustration, and the fundamentalist threat to the Sauds has already peaked and is less serious than it may seem.

NOTES

INTRODUCTION

1 On urban population: Kingdom of Saudi Arabia, Ministry of Planning: *Fourth Development Plan 1405-1410 AH - 1985-1990 AD*; Kingdom of Saudi Arabia, Ministry of Finance and National Economy, Central Department of Statistics, *The Statistical Indicator*, Eleventh Issue, 1406 AH - 1986 AD; *The Economist Intelligence Unit (EIU)*, Saudi Arabia - Country Profile 1990-1, pp. 7-8. Jedda and Riyadh each have a population of over a million. Mecca is the third largest town. Dammam, Al-khobar, Dhahran and Hufuf in Al-Hasa follow it. See also, M. Abir, *Saudi Arabia in the Oil Era. Regime and Elites; Conflict and Collaboration* (London, 1988), Introduction.

1. THE CONSOLIDATION OF THE RULING CLASS

1 Al, equivalent to *Ahl*, meaning family, clan or tribe.
2 Amir can denote in Saudi Arabia: prince, provincial or district governor, tribal shaykh or village headman.
3 The majority novice ulama, some of tribal origin.
4 J. S. Habib, *Ibn Sa'ud's Warriors of Islam* (Leiden, 1978), p. 222; C. Moss Helms, *The Cohesion of Saudi Arabia* (London, 1981), pp. 137-8; also, H. St John Philby, *Sa'udi Arabia* (Beirut, 1968), p. 265.
5 On the Ikhwan rebellion see below.
6 O. Y. Al-Rawaf, 'The concept of the five crises in political development: relevance to the kingdom of Saudi Arabia', unpublished PhD thesis, Duke University, 1981, p. 329.
7 *Majlis*, lit. 'council' or 'audience' (reception room) – a forum for discussion and for petitions, held by every Saudi of consequence. Royal *majalis* are theoretically open to every Saudi.
8 On this phenomenon, see Abir, *Saudi Arabia*, chapter 2. In 1991 King Fahd appointed a second Al-Shaykh technocrat to his cabinet: *New York Times (NYT)*, 6 August 1991.
9 F. A. Shaker, 'Modernization of the developing nations. The case of Saudi Arabia', unpublished PhD thesis, Purdue University, 1972, p. 169 and D. Van Der Meulen, *The Wells of Ibn Sa'ud* (London, 1957), p. 255: 'desert democracy'. M. Wenner, 'Saudi Arabia: survival of traditional elites' in F. Tachau (ed.), *Political Elites and Political Development in the Middle East* (New York, 1975), p. 180; 'modernizing autocracy'. A. H. Alyami, 'The impact

of modernization on the stability of the Saudi monarchy', unpublished PhD thesis, Claremont Graduate School, 1977, p. 175: 'almost absolute autocracy'.

10 Called also *Al-Lajnah al-'Ulyah* – the Supreme Committee.

11 The document sanctioning King Saud's deposition and Faysal's enthronement (1964) was signed by 68 princes, of whom 38 were Ibn Saud's sons, and 12 distinguished ulama, four of whom were Al-Shaykhs: Al-Rawaf, 'Five crises', pp. 320, 326; W. Ochsenwald, 'Saudi Arabia and the Islamic revival', *International Journal of Middle East Studies (IJMES)*, Vol. 13 (1981), p. 274. Also, A. I. Dawisha, 'Internal values and external threats', *Orbis* (spring 1979), p. 130.

12 See Abir, *Saudi Arabia*, chapter 1, note 20.

13 Leading tribal amirs were consulted in the 1979 crisis and they are again courted by King Fahd: J. Kraft, 'Letter from Saudi Arabia', *The New Yorker*, 4 July 1983, p. 51; Chung In Moon, 'Korean contractors in Saudi Arabia: their rise and fall', *The Middle East Journal (MEJ)*, Vol. 40, No. 4 (autumn 1986), p. 628.

14 Abir, *Saudi Arabia*, chapter 1, notes 22, 23.

15 N. H. Hisham, 'Saudi Arabia and the role of the Imarates in regional development', unpublished PhD thesis, Claremont Graduate School, 1982, p. 9.

16 D. Ottaway, *The Washington Post (WP)*, 27 November 1984.

17 Al-Rawaf, 'Five crises', pp. 326-7; A. Bligh, 'The Saudi religious elite (ulama) as participant in the political system of the kingdom', *IJMES*, Vol. 17, No. 1 (February 1985), pp. 10-15.

18 Bligh, 'Religious elite', p. 38; A. Layish, 'Ulama and politics in Saudi Arabia', in M. Heper and R. Israeli (eds), *Islam and Politics in the Modern Middle East* (New York, 1984); Ochsenwald, 'Islamic revival'.

19 The ulama leadership, largely Al al-Shaykh, participated in the final deliberations leading to Saud's dethronement. Saud's removal from office, an extreme step, was in line with tribal custom and Muslim concepts.

20 See below chapter 11.

21 The conservatives claimed that TV has become a channel for Western influence. See Abir, *Saudi Arabia*, p. 105, note 68.

22 A. H. Said, 'Saudi Arabia: the transition from a tribal society to a nation', unpublished PhD thesis, University of Missouri, 1979, p. 111; Al-Rawaf, 'Five crises', pp. 187-8; S. S. Huyette, *Political Adaptation in Sa'udi Arabia* (Boulder, 1985), p. 117.

23 R. Schulze, 'The Saudi Arabian 'ulama and their reaction to Muslim fundamentalism'. A paper prepared for a colloquium on Religious Radicalism and Politics in the Middle East, the Hebrew University (Jerusalem, May 1985), pp. 9-10, 20, 23; Al-Rawaf, 'Five crises', pp. 359-60; Ochsenwald, 'Islamic revival', pp. 283, 277; Layish, 'Ulama', pp. 46-57; Shaker, 'Modernization', p. 138.

24 On claim of a growing rift between the senior and younger radical *'alims*: A. Bligh, *From Prince to King. Royal Succession in the House of Saud in the Twentieth Century* (New York, 1984), p. 100. Of ulama who publicly challenged the authorities and were quietly deprived of a public platform: M. Field, 'Why the Saudi royal family is more stable than the Shah', *Euromoney* (October 1981); *Financial Times* (London. Henceforth *FT*), 21 April 1986, supplement, p. VIII. Also, chapters 10, 11 below.

25 See Abir, *Saudi Arabia*, pp. 148-52.

26 J. Shaw and D. E. Long, The Washington Papers: *Saudi Arabian*

Modernization: The Impact of Change on Stability, No. 89 (1982), p. 44; D. Holden and R. Johns, *The House of Saud* (London, 1982), pp. 402, 519; T. Sisley, *The Times* (London), 22 May 1980; *FT*, 24 April 1984, supplement, p. II.
27 See below chapter 5. Also, Abir, *Saudi Arabia*, pp. 151-2, 159.
28 Schulze, 'Saudi Arabian 'ulama', pp. 22-3; J. A. Kechichian, 'The role of the ulama in the politics of an Islamic state: the case of Saudi Arabia', *IJMES*, Vol. 12, No. 1 (February 1986), pp. 59-60.
29 Ochsenwald, 'Islamic revival', p. 277. See below pp. 169-70.
30 P. Mansfield, *FT*, 21 April 1986; Huyette, *Adaptation*, p. 93.
31 Al-Rawaf, 'Five crises', p. 527; also, M. Field, *FT*, 21 April 1986, supplement, p. VIII; Huyette, *Adaptation*, p. 117; Layish, 'Ulama', pp. 54-7.
32 See chapters 10, 11 below.

2. MODERN EDUCATION AND THE RISE OF NEW ELITES

* For a detailed discussion of this subject see Abir, *Saudi Arabia*, chapter 3.
1 H. Lackner, *A House Built on Sand* (London, 1978), p. 74; Al-Rawaf, 'Five crises', p. 244.
2 *Aramco Handbook* (Netherlands, 1960), p. 161; A. L. Mosley, *Power Play. The Tumultuous World of Middle East Oil 1890-1973* (Birkenhead, 1973), p. 327.
3 R. F. Nyrop (ed.), Area Handbook Series: Saudi Arabia: A Country Study (Washington, DC, 1982), pp. 102-3, 105; M. E. Faheem, 'Higher education and nation building, a case study of King Abdul Aziz University', unpublished PhD thesis, University of Illinois at Urbana-Champaign, 1982, p. 77; D. P. Cole, *Nomads of the Nomads. The Al Murrah Bedouins of the Empty Quarter* (Chicago, 1975), pp. 141-2, 153; M. Katakura, *Bedouin Village. A Study of a Saudi Arabian People in Transition* (University of Tokyo Press, 1977), pp. 64, 115, 118, 157-9.
4 M. M. Kinsawi, 'Attitude of students and fathers towards vocational education in economic development in Saudi Arabia', unpublished PhD thesis, University of Colorado at Boulder, 1981, pp. 9-10, 90-1, 104; Said, 'Saudi Arabia' pp. 94-5; *FT*, 5 May 1981, supplement.
5 For instance 22.8 billion dollars in the second development plan (1975-80). On vocational schools in 1980s: *Saudi Gazette* (Saudi Arabia), 17 September 1986, p. 3.
6 Handbook (1982), pp. 100-1, 112; F. A. S. Al-Farsy, *Saudi Arabia: A Case Study in Development* (London, 1982), pp. 164-5.
7 *Saudi Arabia: Education and Human Resources*, the Royal Embassy of Saudi Arabia, Information Office (Washington, DC, 1989); Kingdom of Saudi Arabia, Ministry of Planning, *Fifth Development Plan 1410-1415 AH - 1990-1995 AD* (Human Resources Development); Kingdom of Saudi Arabia, Ministry of Finance and National Economy, Department of Statistics: *The Statistical Indicator*, Eleventh Issue 1406 AH - 1986 AD.
8 On provinces' schools: *The Middle East* (London), November 1984, p. 69.
9 On Shi'ites see below pp. 33-4 and 48.
10 Handbook (1982), p. 105. See A. A. Al-Ibrahim, 'Regional and urban development in Saudi Arabia', unpublished PhD thesis, University of Colorado at Boulder, 1982, for instance, pp. 151, 153-5, 211; E. B. Gallagher, 'Medical education in Saudi Arabia: A sociological perspective on modernization and

language', *Journal of Asian and African Studies*, Vol. XX, Nos. 1–2 (1985), pp. 7–10; *WP*, 15 February 1987, p. A28.

11 The term 'lower class' (classes), used in this book for the sake of convenience, refers to most of the rural, and the lower-income urbanised (lower-middle-class), population.

12 Kingdom of Saudi Arabia, Centre for Statistical Data and Educational Documentation: *Development of Education in the Ministry of Education During 25 Years 1954–78* (Riyadh, 1978), pp. 13–15; A. L. Tibawi, *Islamic Education: Its Tradition and Modernization Into the Arab National Systems* (London, 1972), p. 182; W. Rugh, 'Emergence of a new middle class in Saudi Arabia', MEJ (winter 1973), p. 11.

13 N. A. Jan, 'Between Islamic and Western education: a case study of Umm Al-Qura University, Makkah, Saudi Arabia', unpublished PhD thesis, Michigan State University, 1983, pp. 58–9; Tibawi, *Islamic Education*, pp. 182–3; Said, 'Saudi Arabia', p. 111; Faheem, 'Higher education', p. 77.

14 On higher education institutions in Saudi Arabia: Abir, *Saudi Arabia*, pp. 41–8.

15 Faheem, 'Higher education', p. 159

16 *Middle East Economic Digest (MEED)*, 12 October 1984, p. 47; Gallagher, 'Medical', pp. 2–5, 7–10; *WP*, 15 February 1987. In 1986/7, 70 per cent of KSU students were in humanities and social sciences: *International Herald Tribune (IHT)*, 20 February 1987, p. 2.

17 Foreign Broadcasting Information Service (FBIS), 26 September 1985, Riyadh in Arabic, 22 September 1985. On diminishing employment opportunities for women: *MEED*, Special Report, July 1984, p. 2.

18 *Fifth Development Plan 1410–1415 AH – 1990–1995 AD*; *Saudi Arabia: Education and Human Resources* (Embassy of Saudi Arabia, Washington, DC, 1989).

19 Abir, *Saudi Arabia*, p. 58, note 33.

20 *WP*, 27 November 1984. On students' unemployment: *Al-Yamama* (weekly, Saudi Arabia), 20 June, 4 July 1986; also, *Saudi Gazette*, 1 August 1986; *IHT*, 20 February 1987, p. 2.

21 Faheem, 'Higher education', pp. 111–12, 117–18; M. M. Marks, 'The American influence on the development of the universities in the kingdom of Saudi Arabia', unpublished PhD thesis, University of Oregon, 1980.

22 On ulama's increasing power and criticism by extremists of Western-trained technocrats, see below chapter 10. Also, Ghazi b. Abd al-Rahman Al-Kosaybi (Gosaybi), *Hatah la takun fitna!!* (n.p., 1991), pp. 167–8, 175.

23 *The Statistical Indicator*, 1406 AH – 1986 AD. The 1985/6 education budget was reduced by a third compared with previous years. See below p. 140 on royal family's intervention to annul reduction of subsidies by government in view of population anger.

24 A. Thomas, *FT*, 22 April 1985, supplement, p. II.

25 Ochsenwald, 'Islamic revival', pp. 278–9.

26 See below pp. 170–2, 178–81, 193 and *IHT*, 31 December 1991 – 1 January 1992.

3. THE REIGN OF SAUD (1953-64): STRUGGLE FOR POWER AND NATIONALISM

1 *Al-Hayat* (Beirut), 25 November 1953; *NYT*, 6 December 1953; *Mideast Mirror* (Beirut), 2 January 1954; *Hamizrah Hakhadash* (Israel), Vol. 6, No. 1 (1955), p. 67.
2 J. Buchan, 'Secular and religious opposition in Saudi Arabia' in T. Niblock (ed.), *State, Society and Economy in Saudi Arabia* (London, 1982), p. 119. On the Shi'ites see below pp. 84-8.
3 Van Der Meulen, *Ibn Sa'ud*, pp. 200, 250-1; *Al-Dustur* (Weekly, London), 4 February 1979, p. 8.
4 The petition was attributed to Palestinian and communist agitators: *The Times*, 19, 20 October 1953; *Al-Dustur*, 4 February 1979, p. 8.
5 Lackner, *House*, p. 96; M. Cheney, *Big Oil Man From Arabia* (New York, 1958), pp. 227-36; *The Times*, 19, 20 October 1953; *Al-Hayat*, 25 November 1953; Alyami, 'Modernization', p. 182; *Al-Dustur*, 4 February 1979, p. 8.
6 Labour and Workers Regulation Act of 10 October 1947: G. M. Baroody, 'The practice of law in Saudi Arabia' in W. A. Beling (ed.), *King Faisal and the Modernisation of Saudi Arabia* (London, 1980), pp. 121-2; Cheney, *Oil Man*, p. 221.
7 A high proportion were educated Hijazis. The less prestigious armed forces did not attract Najdis, except to top command positions.
8 Consultative Assembly, Council of Deputies. F. Hamzah, *Al Bilad al-'Arabiyah al-Sa'udiyya* (Mecca, 1937), pp. 90-1, 98-100; H. Wahba, *Arabian Days* (London, 1946), p. 73; C. W. Harrington, 'The Saudi Arabian council of ministers', *MEJ*, Vol. 12, No. 1 (1958), pp. 3, 12.
9 Of Hijazi separatism in late 1970s: Gh. Salameh, 'Political power and the Saudi state', *Merip Reports*, No. 91 (October 1980), p. 21. In 1969: Holden and Johns, *House of Saud*, pp. 280-1.
10 *Qadaya Sa'udiyya*, pp. 3-5; *Al-Dustur*, 4 February 1979, pp. 8-9. Educated Shi'ites are heavily represented in the small militant Saudi socialist and Marxist organisations.
11 On Saudi opposition in the 1950s and 1960s: Abir, *Saudi Arabia*, pp. 74-8.
12 J. Arnold, *Golden Swords and Pots and Pans* (New York, 1963), p. 205; *Haaretz* (Israel), 27 June 1956; *Qadaya Sa'udiyya*, p. 5; *Al-Hawadith* (Beirut), 23 November 1962, interview with Nassir Sa'id. The nationalisation of the Suez Canal by Nasser intensified demands in the Hijaz and Al-Hasa to nationalise Aramco and annul the Dhahran air base agreement: *Al-Dustur*, 4 February 1979, p. 9.
13 See Abir, *Saudi Arabia*, p. 79.
14 On Shi'ites' dissatisfaction: *Al-Bilad* (Saudi Arabia), 13 September 1960; *Al-Hayat*, 17 November 1960. On opposition: *Qadaya Sa'udiyya*, pp. 5-7.
15 *Al-Dustur*, 4 February 1979, p. 9.
16 Schulze, 'Saudi Arabian 'ulama', pp. 10-14; N. O. Madani, 'The Islamic content of the foreign policy of Saudi Arabia. King Faisal's call for Islamic solidarity 1965-1975', unpublished PhD thesis, The American University, Washington, DC, 1977.
17 Huyette, *Adaptation*, p. 75.
18 T. Niblock, 'Social structure and the development of the Saudi Arabian political system', in T. Niblock (ed.), *State, Society and Economy in Saudi Arabia* (London, 1982), pp. 99-100; Buchan, 'Religious opposition', p. 113; *Al-Jarida* (Beirut), 30 December 1960; *Al-Hayat*, 12 November 1963.

19 See Abir, *Saudi Arabia*, pp. 85-6.

20 *Al-Haqa'iq* (Egypt), 16 March, 16 November 1961; *Al-Hawadith*, 5 May 1961; Holden and Johns, *House of Saud*, p. 214; Bligh, *Succession*, p. 70; *Al-Hayat*, 14 March, 10 June 1961, 22 February 1961; Lackner, *House*, p. 98; Salameh, 'Political power', p. 20; *Afrique Action* (Tunis), 27 February 1961.

21 *NYT*, 17 March 1961. In line with his appeasement policy, Faysal supported demands to rescind the Dhahran agreement: *Al-Hayat*, 18 March 1961.

22 Schulze, 'Saudi Arabian 'ulama', pp. 11-12, 18; Ochsenwald, 'Islamic revival', p. 278; Madani, 'Foreign policy', pp. 78-9; also Holden and Johns, *House of Saud*, p. 215; *Al-Hayat*, 7 May 1961; *Akhir Sa'ah* (Egypt), 3 May 1961.

23 See Abir, *Saudi Arabia*, p. 89. Faysal's fundamentalist nephew was killed by the police in a demonstration against the establishment of a TV station in Riyadh in 1965. His brother assassinated Faysal in 1975.

24 This was the beginning of the rise of the 'Sudayri Seven', sons of Abd al-Aziz by Hassa bint Ahmad al-Sudayri, led by Fahd, the eldest. They form the most cohesive and powerful group within the senior sons of Ibn Saud: Sultan the defence minister and now second in line of succession; Na'if the interior minister (1975); Salman the governor of Riyadh (1962), considered the most capable, far-sighted and likable. Turki, until the 1970s Sultan's deputy, a 'progressive', was dismissed because of a marital scandal. Ahmad became in 1975 Na'if's deputy and Abd al-Rahman, who represents the family's business interests.

25 Huyette, *Adaptation*, p. 72.

26 *Mideast Mirror*, 27 February 1954. See Abir, *Saudi Arabia*, p. 53, Table 3.3.

27 Kingdom of Saudi Arabia, Ministry of Information, *Faisal Speaks* (1 December 1963); G. De Gaury, *Faisal King of Saudi Arabia* (New York, 1966), appendix 1, according to Saudi radio, 7 November 1962.

28 Bligh, 'Religious elite', p. 42; Layish, 'Ulama', p. 34. Both institutions were reorganised and became state-supervised and state-funded in the early 1970s. See above pp. 9-10.

29 Abir, *Saudi Arabia*, pp. 94-6.

30 '. . . his (Faysal's) progressive policy in 1962 gave new hope to the people': Shaker, 'Modernization', p. 312.

31 Ibid., p. 227, note 104; L. Blandford, *Oil Sheikhs* (London, 1976), pp. 123-4; *FT*, 22 April 1985, supplement, p. VI; Huyette, *Adaptation*, p. 77; Holden and Johns, *House of Saud*, p. 280.

32 Shaker, 'Modernization', pp. 306-8, 311; *Faisal Speaks* (1963), p. 12; *Al-Hayat*, 7 November 1964.

33 Holden and Johns, *House of Saud*, pp. 252, 280-1; Alyami, 'Modernization', pp. 182, 201. Alyami was an eyewitness to the 1967 rioting in Al-Hasa. Also, B. Williams, *FT*, 5 May 1981.

34 *Qadaya Sa'udiyya*, pp. 6-7; Lackner, *House*, p. 188; *Al-Nahar* (London-Beirut), 2 April 1964. Shaker ('Modernization', pp. 306-7) relates the intensification of anti-government activities to Faysal's failure to carry out the promised constitutional reforms.

4. THE REIGN OF FAYSAL (1964-75): NEW ELITES, OIL AND RAPID DEVELOPMENT

1 Dr Ghazi al-Gosaybi, a leading intellectual, who held several ministerial positions until 1984, Hasan al-Mash'ari (minister of agriculture under

Faysal), Dr Abd al-Rahman al-Zamil (deputy minister of commerce): Abir, *Saudi Arabia*, chapter 5, note 3.

2 Schulze, 'Saudi Arabian 'ulama', pp. 20–1; Holden and Johns, *House of Saud*, p. 249; N. Safran, *Saudi Arabia: The Ceaseless Quest for Security* (Cambridge, Mass., 1985), pp. 121–2.

3 Holden and Johns, *House of Saud*, pp. 250, 278–80; *Qadaya Sa'udiyya*, p. 7; Buchan, 'Religious opposition', pp. 114–15; Lackner, *House*, p. 101; Safran, *Saudi Arabia*, p. 121; *Sawt al-Tali'a* (Baghdad), No. 6, June 1974. See also, Abir, *Saudi Arabia*, p. 98.

4 M. Abir, 'The manpower problem in Saudi Arabian economic and security policy', colloquium paper, Woodrow Wilson International Center for Scholars (Washington, DC, April 1983), appendix A.

5 Abir, 'Manpower', pp. 44, 79 (note 73); Holden and Johns, *House of Saud*, pp. 244–5.

6 Abir, 'Manpower', appendix A; also, M. Abir, *Oil Power and Politics: Conflict in Arabia, the Persian Gulf and the Red Sea* (London, 1974), pp. 102–3.

7 Alyami, 'Modernization', p. 168; *Al-Akhbar* (Lebanon), 13 July 1969. On Nassir Sa'id: *Al-Hadaf* (PFLP, Beirut), 7 March 1981, p. 27; Bligh, *Succession*, p. 86; Salameh, 'Political power', p. 23 and note 20.

8 Hisham Nazir joined Tariki's Directorate of Petroleum in 1958. In 1962, he became Zaki Yamani's deputy: Huyette, *Adaptation*, p. 75.

9 Lackner, *House*, p. 190. For text and curriculum of the 1969 labour law: *Qadaya Sa'udiyya*, p. 7 onward; also, Baroody, 'Practice of law', p. 122; Holden and Johns, *House of Saud*, p. 271.

10 Abir, 'Manpower', p. 22.

11 F. A. Hafiz, 'Changes in Saudi foreign policy behaviour 1964–75. A study of the underlying factors and determinates', unpublished PhD thesis, University of Nebraska–Lincoln, 1980, p. 63; Madani, 'Foreign policy', p. 129.

12 Safran, *Saudi Arabia*, p. 129.

13 On the 1969–70 attempted coups and widespread arrests: Abir, *Saudi Arabia*, pp. 114–17 and relevant notes.

14 Remnants of the NLF and some of the released prisoners formed the Saudi Communist Party in the mid-1970s: *Handbook* (1984), p. 301. Fahd was displeased with Faysal's indiscriminate arrests: M. Field, *FT*, 22 April 1985, supplement, p. VI; R. Lacey, *The Kingdom* (London, 1981), p. 441.

15 Holden and Johns, *House of Saud*, pp. 278–9.

16 Shaker, 'Modernization', pp. 311–15.

17 Blandford, *Oil Sheikhs*, pp. 124–5; *Al-Hurriyya* (PFLP, weekly, Beirut), 18 May 1970; *Al-Ahrar* (Lebanon), 19 June 1970.

18 *Al-Ahrar*, 28 November 1969; also, Abir, 'Manpower', pp. 33–6.

19 Abir, 'Manpower', p. 41; Gh. Salameh, *Al-Siyassa al-Kharijiyya al-Sa'udiyya mundhu 1945* (Beirut, 1980), pp. 525, 532, 577.

20 Huyette, *Adaptation*, pp. 75, 78, 80; Lackner, *House*, p. 73. Until 1975 only Faysal could authorise visas 'to Jews and journalists': Holden and Johns, *House of Saud*, pp. 379, 459.

21 Shaker, 'Modernization', p. 308.

22 Huyette, *Adaptation*, p. 96. On Fahd's derogatory words on ranking officials with PhD: Holden and Johns, *House of Saud*, p. 460.

23 Until its modernisation in the late 1960s the administration was composed of 70 per cent offspring of traditional civil servants, merchants and other *hadr*. Of the total in 1970 over 60 per cent were still Najdis and less than 30 per cent Hijazis: I. M. Al-Awaji (deputy minister of the interior), 'Bureaucracy and

society in Saudi Arabia', unpublished PhD thesis, University of Virginia, 1971, p. 179. Najdis also dominated the religious institutions: F. M. Al-Nassar, 'Saudi Arabian educational mission to the US', unpublished PhD thesis, University of Oklahoma (Norman), 1982, pp. 47–8, 50; also, Huyette, *Adaptation*, pp. 75, 95–6. The above proportion gradually changed from the late 1960s in favour of the Hijazi technocrats: Al-Awaji, 'Bureaucracy', pp. 176, 179–80; Said, 'Saudi Arabia', pp. 17, 76, 185. On nepotism: Al-Nassar, 'Mission', p. 58; Al-Awaji, 'Bureaucracy', pp. 232, 236.

24 Muhammad Aba'l-Khayl was appointed minister of finance in 1975, Sulayman Solaym became deputy minister of commerce in 1974 and minister in 1975. Ghazi al-Gosaybi (Najdi from the Eastern Province), appointed minister of industry and electricity in 1975, was previously dean of faculty of commerce in Riyadh university and Faysal's adviser. Since 1984, ambassador in Bahrayn.

25 Al-Awaji, 'Bureaucracy', pp. 179–80; Huyette, *Adaptation*, pp. 95–6.

26 On Najdi 'mafia' controlling administration in late 1970s: J. Robenson, *Yamani. The Inside Story* (London, 1988).

27 Mashaal Abdullah Turki Al Saud, 'Permanence and change: an analysis of the Islamic political culture of Saudi Arabia with a special reference to the royal family', unpublished PhD thesis, Claremont Graduate School, 1982, p. 116. A conservative, the writer is clearly jealous of the power and success of the technocratic upper-crust. Also, Shaker, 'Modernization', p. 317.

28 Al-Rawaf, 'Five crises', pp. 341, 369. On erosion of *umara*'s authority by rise of central government: Said, 'Saudi Arabia', pp. 104–5; A. M. Al-Selfan, 'The essence of tribal leaders' participation, responsibilities, and decisions in some local government activities in Saudi Arabia: a case study of the Ghamid and Zahran tribes', unpublished PhD thesis, Claremont Graduate School, 1981, p. 151.

29 Al-Rawaf, 'Five crises', pp. 366–7.

30 See above chapter 2.

31 See Abir, *Saudi Arabia*, chapter 7, pp. 171–4.

32 Shaker, 'Modernization', p. 315. Cited as written. Also, Lackner, *House*, p. 88.

33 V. Sheean, *Faisal – The King and His Kingdom* (Tavistock, 1975), p. 119. Cited as written.

34 F. Halliday, *Arabia without Sultans* (Manchester, 1975), p. 69; Salameh, 'Political power', p. 23; M. Field, 'Why the Saudi royal family is more stable than the Shah', *Euromoney* (October 1981); *Al-Mawqif al-Arabi*, 20 April 1981.

35 See Abir, *Saudi Arabia*, p. 127.

5. POWER STRUGGLE, MODERNISATION AND REACTION (1975–80)

1 On the 'Sudayri Seven': Abir, *Saudi Arabia*, p. 105, note 76. The powerful Sudayri bedouin clan of northern Najd has intermarried with all the main branches of Al Saud. When the term 'Sudayris' is used in this book by itself it refers to the 'Sudayri Seven' and their descendants, also called the Al Fahd. Within the 'Sudayri Seven' Sultan and Na'if, known for their conservatism, are occasionally critical of Fahd's policy. Salman is considered a liberal and the closest to Fahd. See also, G. S. Samore, 'Royal family politics in Saudi

Arabia (1953-1982)', unpublished PhD thesis, Harvard University, 1984, pp. 347-55.

2 *Al-Hawadith*, 4 April 1975 (interview with Fahd); *Al-Usbu' al-'Arabi* (Lebanon), 12 May 1975; Salameh, 'Political power', p. 20.

3 Lackner, *House*, p. 88; *Qadaya Sa'udiyya*, pp. 5-6; Blandford, *Oil Sheikhs*, p. 123; H. Shaked and T. Yagnes, 'The Saudi Arabian kingdom', in C. Legum (ed.), *Middle East Contemporary Survey*, Vol. 1 (New York, 1978), p. 570.

4 Buchan, *FT*, 5 May 1981, supplement. On special security forces and US assistance to the above: Holden and Johns, *House of Saud*, pp. 518, 522. On US: Lackner, *House*, p. 173. The amirs in the rural areas and the *'umda* – the neighbourhood head in the towns and the village shaykh – became part of the interior ministry's security apparatus: *Al-Yamama*, 4 January 1984.

5 The GCC covertly co-ordinated its members' security activities. With the outbreak of the Iran–Iraq war (1980) it also became a mutual defence organisation. After Iraq's conquest of Kuwait (1990) it was used to help the US operations in the Gulf.

6 Huyette, *Adaptation*, p. 12, also, pp. 78-80, 126; Lackner, *House*, p. 73; Holden and Johns, *House of Saud*, p. 459.

7 Of alleged Najdi mafia run by Aba'l-Khayl in the administration: Robenson, *Yamani*.

8 *FT*, 14 June 1982. On involvement of US Corps of Engineers: Salameh, *Al-Siyassa*, pp. 320-3.

9 Farmers and semi-nomads made up about 20 to 25 per cent in 1981: Kingdom of Saudi Arabia, Ministry of Planning, *Employment by Sector* (Riyadh, 1982). In 1970 the rural population made up 75 per cent of the total: Shaker, 'Modernization', p. 186. Also, S. Al-Turki and D. Cole, *Arabian Oasis City* (University of Texas Press, 1989).

10 Moon, 'Korean contractors', pp. 625-9; S. E. Ibrahim, *The New Arab Social Order. A Study of the Social Impact of Oil Wealth* (Westview Press, 1982), pp. 8-13. King Khalid benefited from defence contracts and Fahd's son Muhammad earned hundreds of millions of dollars in commissions. Al-Rawaf, 'Five crises', pp. 332, 350, 487.

11 Lackner, *House*, p. 72; Salameh, 'Political power', p. 13.

12 Al Saud, 'Permanence', p. 146 (note 20), p. 166 (note 24); J. Nevo, 'The Saudi royal family: the third generation', *The Jerusalem Quarterly (JQ)*, No. 31 (spring 1984).

13 See below pp. 112-13.

14 Shaked and Yagnes, 'Saudi', p. 570.

15 J. Keegan, *World Armies* (New York, 1979), pp. 617, 620; A. I. Dawisha, 'Saudi Arabia's search for security', *Adelphi Papers*, No. 158 (winter 1979-80), p. 7; Shaked and Yagnes, 'Saudi', p. 567.

16 A. McDermott, *FT*, 20 March 1978.

17 *Al-Dustur*, 4 February 1979; *Handbook* (1984), p. 51; Buchan, *The Middle East* (September 1980); Salameh, 'Political power', p. 21; F. Halliday, 'The shifting sands beneath the House of Saud', *The Progressive* (March 1980), p. 39.

18 The IRO was founded in 1974/5 and began its operations in 1979: *Merip Reports*, February 1985. The IRO maintains relations with Middle Eastern Marxist organisations: *8 Days* (weekly, London), 23 May 1981; *Al-Mawqif al-'Arabi*, 20 April 1981.

19 M. Collins, 'Riyadh: the Saud balance', *The Washington Quarterly* (winter 1981), p. 207; Bligh, *Succession*, p. 93. Criticism of Fahd's oil and pro-US

policies, impact of the Camp David agreement and the fall of the Shah: *Al-Watan al-'Arabi* (Beirut–Paris), 28 March 1980; Salameh, *Al-Siyassa*, pp. 603–11, 670–4.

20 See below pp. 94–6.

21 Holden and Johns, *House of Saud*, pp. 464, 519; Lacey, *The Kingdom*, p. 436.

22 Al-Farsy, *Saudi Arabia*, p. 172; Al Saud, 'Permanence', p. 152; Ibrahim, *Social Order*, p. 7; Collins, 'Riyadh', p. 202; Field, 'Royal family'.

23 Al-Rawaf, 'Five crises', p. 361; ibid., pp. 359–60; *Al-Da'wa* (Riyadh), 5.3.98 (AH), p. 45; *Time* (magazine), April 1978. On renewed attacks on Al-Gosaybi on this matter: Al-Gosaybi, *Hatah*, p. 103.

24 Holden and Johns, *House of Saud*, p. 517. Also, *Handbook* (1984), p. 113; *Al-Safir* (pro-Libyan, Lebanon), 9 January 1980, an interview with Crown Prince Fahd.

25 Al-Rawaf, 'Five crises', p. 356; *Al-Mawqif al-'Arabi*, 20 April 1981.

26 Holden and Johns, *House of Saud*, pp. 515, 518; *Al-Safir*, 9 January 1980, an interview with Crown Prince Fahd; Kechichian, 'Ulama', p. 59; Buchan, 'Religious opposition', pp. 120–3. For full text of pamphlets: Abu Dhurr (pseud.), *Thawra fi Rihab Makka* (Dar Sawt at-Tali'a, Kuwait, 1980), pp. 265–73.

27 See Abir, *Saudi Arabia*, p. 163, note 41. On alleged support for rebels in Islamic universities: *Al-Thawra al-Islamiyya*, June–July 1990.

28 Hufuf, the Al-Hasa oasis capital had a population (largely Shi'ite) of about 200,000. On politically-motivated absence of statistics relating to Shi'ites: P. T. Kilborn, *NYT*, 9 February 1987.

29 B. Williams, *FT*, 5 May 1981; J. S. Rossant, *NYT*, 3 January 1980; Al-Ibrahim, 'Urban development', p. 150.

30 *NYT*, 3 January 1980, p. A2; also, M. Field, *The Merchants. The Big Business Families of Arabia* (London, 1984), p. 82; *Handbook* (1984), pp. 113–14; T. R. McHale, 'A prospect of Saudi Arabia', *International Affairs* (autumn 1981), p. 635. Of National Guard in Hufuf: Cole, *Nomads*, p. 111.

31 See above and *Handbook* (1984), p. 51. On recent political developments among the Shi'ites and claims that they make 20–25 per cent of total Saudi population: *Al-Jazira al-'Arabiyya* (Saudi Arabia–London), July 1991, pp. 22–4.

32 M. Field, 'Society, the royal family and the military in Saudi Arabia', *Vierteljahresberichte*, No. 88 (June 1982), pp. 217–18; *NYT*, 6 December 1979; Salameh, 'Political power', p. 21; *Handbook* (1984), p. 51.

33 On Shi'ite riots: Abir, *Saudi Arabia*, p. 164, notes 53–5.

34 B. Williams, *FT*, 5 May 1981; M. Field, *FT*, 17 September 1982; Field, 'Royal family'; Buchan, *The Middle East* (September 1980).

35 *FT*, 27 September 1980; *Al-Hadaf* (PFLP), 18 April 1981, pp. 30–1, according to *Al-Masira* (publication of Saudi Workers Socialist Party).

36 M. Field, *FT*, 17 September 1982; B. Williams, *FT*, 5 May 1981; *Al-Mawqif al-'Arabi*, 20 April 1981.

37 See below pp. 112–13, 150–1. Also, *Al-Jazira al-'Arabiyya*, July 1991, pp. 22–4. In recent years the IRO was overshadowed by the Hizbollah (The Party of God).

38 About 2,000 people were arrested in the Najd and in the Hijaz in temporary detention camps. They were largely from the town of Sajar, inhabited by 'Utaybi tribesmen: *Al-Thawra al-Islamiyya*, June–July 1990, p. 21.

39 Huyette, *Adaptation*, p. 117.

6. THE ZENITH OF THE NEW ELITES' POWER: A FALSE DAWN (1979–83)

1 Abir, *Saudi Arabia*, pp. 51-5, Tables 3.1-3.5. Also, *Al-Watan al-'Arabi*, 28 March 1980; *The Middle East and North Africa 1980/1* (Europa Publication, London 1980), p. 661.

2 Al Saud, 'Permanence', p. 115; also, Al-Rawaf, 'Five crises', pp. 364, 366-7, 370-1.

3 Kraft, 'Letter', p. 50.

4 Of regional cleavages about 1980: N. N. M. Ayubi, 'Vulnerability of the rich: the political economy of defense and development in Saudi Arabia and the Gulf', a paper prepared for The Gulf Project, Center for Strategic and International Studies, Georgetown University, Washington, DC (Los Angeles, May 1982), pp. 13-14.

5 *Al-Watan al-'Arabi*, 28 March 1980; *Al-Riyadh* (Saudi Arabia), 10, 13 January 1980; *Al-Siyassa* (Kuwait), 10 January 1980. See below pp. 104-5, 186-7.

6 *Ukaz*, 22 March 1980; *Al-Riyadh*, 10, 13 January 1980.

7 *Al-Jazira* (Saudi Arabia), 8 September 1980, 19 March 1982; *WP*, 22 July 1980.

8 Gallagher, 'Medical', p. 12; also Lackner, *House*, p. 72; *The Economist* (weekly, London), 13 February 1982; Shaked and Yagnes, 'Saudi', pp. 566-7; Abir, *Saudi Arabia*, pp. 45-6, 47-8, 49-50.

9 Al Saud, 'Permanence', p. 173. A special pay scale existed for ministers and equivalent ranks. On Hisham Nazir's business interests: Moon, 'Korean contractors', p. 624, also pp. 625-7. On kickbacks: ibid., pp. 620-1.

10 On revived influence of traditional rural elites: Moon, 'Korean contractors', p. 628; Kraft, 'Letter', p. 51. On present standard of living of bedouin: J. Craig (UK ambassador to Saudi Arabia until 1984), confidential report No. 5184 to the Secretary of State for Foreign and Commonwealth Affairs, *Glasgow Herald*, 9 October 1986.

11 See Abir, *Saudi Arabia*, p. 176, note 20.

12 Ibid., note 21.

13 R. Kavoussi and A. R. Sheikholeslami, 'Political economy of Saudi Arabia' (University of Washington, January 1983), pp. 32-5, 54-5; Lackner, *House*, p. 211. On failure of the 1969 coups because of relationship between masses and *hukuma*: Halliday, *Arabia*, p. 69. Also, Gallagher, 'Medical', p. 11.

14 On this policy in the early 1990s see below pp. 186-7, 240, note 33.

7. THE REIGN OF KING FAHD: ECONOMIC CRISIS AND OPPOSITION (1982–7)

1 Kraft, 'Letter', p. 53; *Al-Tayar* (Iraqi opposition, London), 27 June 1984, p. 1. Fahd's eight-point plan was abandoned in the face of Syrian opposition.

2 On widescale bankruptcies: *FT*, 21 April 1986, supplement, p. II; *IHT*, 4 June 1986. Also, *Ma'riv* (Israel), 8 March 1987; *EIU*, No. 3 (1986), Country Report – Saudi Arabia, p. 4; R. Knauerhase, 'Saudi Arabia faces the future', *Current History*, February 1986, p. 75.

3 *WP*, 27 November 1984, 15 February 1987; *NYT*, 28 January 1986; *Al-Shahid* (Tehran), 23 October 1985.

4 Abir, *Saudi Arabia*, p. 206, note 5.

5 *IHT*, 27 November 1985; *Saudi Gazette*, 17 September 1986.

6 Abir, *Saudi Arabia*, p. 206, note 8.

7 *Wall Street Journal* (*WSJ*), 19 July 1985; *NYT*, 28 January 1986.

8 *Ukaz*, 19 March 1985; *Al-Riyadh*, 26 March 1985. On enormous capital flight: Field, *FT*, 21 April 1986, supplement, p. I.

9 By August 1986 Saudi financial reserves, over 150 billion dollars in 1982, declined to less than 40 billion.

10 *Al-Riyadh*, 11 March 1986.

11 *IHT*, 7 January 1987, p. 7.

12 *Al-Siyassa*, 22 March 1983. Also on this crisis: *Al-Masa'* (Egypt), 13 June 1983; Kraft, 'Letter', p. 53.

13 On above and development of National Guard: Abir, *Saudi Arabia*, p. 206, note 15.

14 Al Saud, 'Permanence', p. 157.

15 *Al-Siyassa*, 22 March 1983; also, *Al-Jarida*, 23 March 1983; *WP*, 27 March 1983; *Al-Thawra al-Islamiyya* (London), October 1984, p. 56; *FT*, 24 April 1984.

16 Abir, *Saudi Arabia*, p. 207, note 19.

17 Ibid., note 20. On new armed forces' fourth command: *EIU*, No. 3 (1986), Saudi Arabia, p. 7.

18 On Special Security Forces and new force to protect economic installations: *Al-Safir*, 9 January 1980, pp. 8–10; Buchan, *FT*, 5 May 1981, supplement; *Al-Yawm* (Saudi Arabia), 21 January 1984; *Al-Thawra al-Islamiyya*, July 1984; also, Samore, 'Royal family', pp. 457–8. On new highway policy: *Al-Riyadh*, 3 January 1991.

19 *Al-Sharq al-Awsat* (London–Saudi Arabia), 29 March 1984; *Ukaz*, 4 May 1984; Field, *FT*, 22 April 1985 (supplement, pp. VI–VII), 15 February 1985.

20 Bandar's crucial importance in Saudi foreign relations was demonstrated during the Gulf crises, and in the negotiations leading to the Arab–Israeli peace talks (see below).

21 *Al-Thawra al-Islamiyya*, according to *Haaretz*, 19 February 1987.

22 Al-Ibrahim, 'Urban development'. On accelerated development of the southern provinces: *Al-Hawadith*, 5 July 1991.

23 W. Lancaster, *The Rwala Bedouin Today* (Cambridge, Mass., 1981), p. 18; Al-Ibrahim, 'Urban development', pp. 113, 200, 210–11, 215, 285, 317; Al-Awaji, 'Bureaucracy', pp. 236, 238; A. M. Al-Selfan, 'Essence of tribal leaders' participation', p. 128; *Merip Reports*, February 1985. The south's population's poverty was emphasised in the ulama's petition to Fahd in 1991 (see below).

24 Abir, *Saudi Arabia*, p. 208, note 29. On Fahd's policy concerning rural population and Prince Ahmad's (deputy minister of interior) visit to the southern provinces, one of frequent meetings with rural population concerning their needs: *Al-Hawadith*, 5 July 1991.

25 *MEED*, Special Report, July 1984.

26 Ibid., pp. 65–7, 78; *Al-Yawm*, 18 October 1984; *Al-Madina* (Saudi Arabia), 29 December 1984; *Al-Jazira*, 18 November, 3 December 1984, 2 February, 2 March, 22 April, 16 July, 10 October 1985; *Al-Riyadh*, 1 March 1985; *MEED*, 21 July 1985; *Saudi Gazette*, 23 July 1986.

27 *Ukaz*, 25 March 1984; Field, *FT*, 21 April 1986, supplement, p. VIII; *Saudi Gazette*, 29 September 1986.

28 *Al-Thawra al-Islamiyya*, April 1985, p. 8.

29 Abir, *Saudi Arabia*, p. 208, note 36; *Handbook* (1984), pp. 112, 300; *The Times*, 23 May 1980; Ochsenwald, 'Islamic revival'; *WP*, 20 December 1982; *MEED*, 1 March 1985; *FT*, 22 April 1985, p. VI; Field, *FT*, 21 April 1986, supplement, p. VIII; also, *WSJ*, 19 July 1985; *FT*, 20 May 1986; *The Times*, 15 July, 3 November 1986.

30 *Al-Madina*, 29 July 1984, interview with Shaykh Abd al-Aziz Al al-Shaykh; also, *FT*, 21 April 1986, supplement. On reorganisation of *muttawwa'in* and of 'Islamic propagation' in rural areas: *Al-Madina*, 30 November 1983; *Ukaz*, 9 February, 8 July 1984; 5 May 1985; *Al-Riyadh*, 17 July 1984, 28 October 1985; Ottaway, *WP*, 27 November 1984; *NYT*, 23 May 1985.

31 The term 'neo-fundamentalist(s)' is used hereafter to denote the new wave of militant fundamentalist theologians and preachers (not necessarily ulama) in Saudi Arabia, who challenge the Al Saud's legitimacy and, like their counterparts in other Muslim countries, call for the establishment, by force if necessary, of a truly Islamic state. *FT*, 23 May 1984; Ottaway, *WP*, 27 November 1984; *Ma'riv*, 29 October 1986; *Handbook* (1984), p. 112; Knauerhase, 'Future', p. 78. On curbing of militant fundamentalist ulama and extremism: *Ukaz*, 4 May 1984; Field, *FT*, 21 April 1986, supplement; *Al-Thawra al-Islamiyya*, June–July 1990, pp. 24–5. See also below chapter 10.

32 *IHT*, 17 May 1985.

33 *WP*, 20 December 1982. Interview (1984) with Saudi Socialist Labour Party representative: *Merip Reports*, February 1985.

34 *Al-Siyassa*, 22 March 1983; *Al-Hurriyya*, 3 April 1983; *Al-Nashra* (Arab left; Cyprus–Nicosia), 14 November 1983 (quoting *Al-Thaqafa al-Mu'asara*, organ of the Saudi Nationalist Writers Union), 14 July 1986, p. 7; *Daily Telegraph* (London), 25 February 1983, p. 32; Kraft, 'Letter', p. 46; *Economist Foreign Report*, 19 May 1983; *Al-Yasar al-Arabi* (leftist; Egypt), March 1984, quoting Saudi leftist periodical *Tariq al-Qadahin*. Also Committee for Defence of Political Prisoners in Saudi Arabia: Abir, *Saudi Arabia*, p. 209, note 45. On plot in Najran, allegedly leading to the dismissal and arrest of former information minister, Muhammad Abdu Yamani: *Sunday Times*, 11 January 1984; also, *Ma'riv*, 11 January 1984, quoting *Nidal al-Shabab*, publication of Saudi Union of the Democratic Youth. The above are tiny Marxist front groups.

35 *Merip Reports*, February 1985; *Al-Thawra al-Islamiyya*, October 1984. On co-operation between the leftist faction of the PLO and Hizbollah in smuggling arms into Saudi Arabia: *Ma'riv*, 29 January 1985. Also, *Al-Shahid*, 23 October 1985.

36 Pamphlets of Committee for Defence of Political Prisoners in Saudi Arabia, London, August–September 1986 and advertisements in *The Guardian* (London), 5 August 1986; *NYT*, 20 August 1986. On latest activity of such committees: FBIS, 5 April 1991, according to AFP Paris in English, 29 March 1991.

37 For sources and details: Abir, *Saudi Arabia*, p. 209, note 46. Of tension between Sunni nationalist organisations and the IRO: *Al-Thawra al-Islamiyya*, October 1984 (p. 56), March 1985. On continued co-operation: *Al-Hadaf*, 18 March 1991; *Al-Jazira al-Arabiyya*, August 1991.

38 *Al-Thawra al-Islamiyya*, October 1984, p. 56; *Haaretz*, 19 May 1985; *FT*, 20 May 1985; *October* (Cairo), 3 August 1985. Also, *Al-Yawm*, 21 January 1984; *Al-Thawra al-Islamiyya*, July 1984, November 1984 (p. 4), July 1985; *Al-Dustur*, 30 March 1986; *Saudi Gazette*, 1 August 1986.

39 *Merip Reports*, February 1985; Field, *FT*, 21 April 1986, supplement, p. VIII; A. Dawisha, *IHT*, 25 November 1986.

40 See Abir, *Saudi Arabia*, pp. 170–1, 176, note 17.

41 Ottaway, *WP*, 27 November 1984; *MEED*, Special Report, July 1984, p. 67; *The Middle East*, February 1987, p. 29.

42 Ottaway, *WP*, 27 November 1984; *Al-Nashra*, 8 September 1986, pp. 23–4.

43 *Al-Nashra*, 8 September 1986, pp. 23-4; Faheem, 'Higher education', p. 124. On similar demands in the 1991 liberals' 'open letter' to Fahd: *Akhir Khabar* (Amman), 25 March 1991, p. 6.
44 Field, *FT*, 9 September 1982, p. 12; *WP*, 20 December 1982.
45 *Sunday Times*, 2 December 1984; *FT*, 3 January 1985; also, *MEED*, Special Report, July 1984, p. 4; *MEED*, 28 September 1984, p. 32; Field, *FT*, 23 May 1984.
46 Field, *FT*, 22 April 1985, supplement, p. I; Ottaway, *WP*, 31 May 1986.
47 *FT*, 4, 8 July, 18 December 1986; *The Times*, 5, 15 July 1986.
48 On liquid assets: *FT*, August–September 1986; *WP*, 15 February 1987.
49 Ottaway, *WP*, 27 November 1984; *WSJ*, 31 July 1984.
50 Ibrahim al-'Anqari, Ali Sha'ir and Muhammad Ali al-Fayiz: Huyette, *Adaptation*, p. 95; also, Samore, 'Royal family', pp. 270-7, 347-82, 539.
51 *Sunday Times*, 2 December 1984. On 1991 'open letter' see below pp. 348-50.
52 *FT*, 25 April 1984; Ottaway, *WP*, 27 November 1984. On Al-Gosaybi's attack on the neo-fundamentalists' assault on the regime, below, chapters 10, 11. Al-Gosaybi was appointed ambassador to the UK in April 1992: *MEED*, Vol. 36, No. 19, 15 May 1992.
53 *The Middle East* (September 1984), p. 48; *WSJ*, 31 July 1984.
54 Abir, *Saudi Arabia*, p. 210, note 64.
55 *IHT*, 8 May 1985; *NYT*, 23 May 1985; *Saudi Gazette*, 13 July 1986.
56 *IHT*, 17 May 1985; also, *WSJ*, 19 July 1985.
57 Abir, 'Manpower' (pp. 40-57) and 'Saudi security and military endeavour', *The Jerusalem Quarterly*, No. 33 (autumn 1984); *FT*, 22 April 1985, supplement, p. VII. Although reduced slightly, Saudi defence expenditure constitutes 30 per cent of the kingdom's 1987 budget: *The Middle East*, February 1987, p. 19.
58 Abir, 'Saudi security', pp. 87-91 and 'Manpower'; Holden and Johns, *House of Saud*, p. 463; Salameh, 'Political power', p. 10; McHale, 'Political system', p. 203. See also Abir, *Saudi Arabia*, p. 207, note 20.
59 T. H. T. Al-Hamad, 'Political order in changing societies, Saudi Arabia: modernization in a traditional context', unpublished PhD thesis, University of Southern California, 1985, pp. 288-9.

8. SAUDI ARABIA AND THE IRAN–IRAQ WAR

1 Abir, *Oil Power*, Chapter 1.
2 See Chapter 6.
3 R. King, 'The Iran–Iraq war: the political implications', *Adelphi Papers*, No. 219 (spring 1987), p. 35. On Saudi armed forces, see: A. H. Cordesman, *The Changing Military Balance in the Gulf* (Washington, DC, 1990).
4 *FT*, 24 July 1987, supplement GCC; also, King, 'Iran–Iraq war', pp. 32-3. Differing attitudes of the GCC members towards Iran further reduced the organisation's questionable effectiveness.
5 To overcome this dangerous strategic–economic factor, Riyadh quickly constructed in 1985 an east–west Trans-Arabian pipeline with a capacity of about 3.5 million barrels daily (m.b.d.).
6 After the Arab League summit in 1983, Prince Saud al-Faysal visited Moscow with other Arab foreign ministers to explain the summit's resolution concerning the Arab–Israeli conflict.
7 King, 'The Iran–Iraq war', pp. 32-5.
8 A small GCC Rapid Deployment Force, established in 1984, was stationed in

Hafr al-Batin in Saudi Arabia not far from Iraq's border: King, 'The Iran–Iraq war', pp. 32–3, 36–7. Baghdad re-established its relations with Washington in 1984. On Saudi efforts to improve relations with Iran: J. Kostiner, 'Counter-productive mediation', *Middle East Review* (summer 1987), p. 42.

9 President Reagan's speech in London in June 1984. The US also turned down Riyadh's request for additional F–15s because they were to be based in Tabuk, near Israel, but helped bolster the kingdom's air defences: E. Karsh, 'The Iran–Iraq war: the military analysis', *Adelphi Papers*, No. 220 (spring 1987), pp. 30–1.

10 In 1981 Kuwait's foreign minister and his Soviet counterpart declared that the Gulf should be kept free of foreign bases: King, 'The Iran–Iraq war', p. 36.

11 Kostiner, 'Mediation', pp. 42–3. In previous *rapprochement* attempts Iran demanded that Riyadh and Kuwait stop their aid to Iraq.

12 *FT*, 17, 23 July 1984; *Al-Majalla* (London), 23 May 1985; *Al-Mustaqbal* (Paris), 1 December 1985; Kostiner, 'Mediation', pp. 42–3.

13 *Al-Majalla*, 29 May 1985; *Ittihad* (UAE), 26 October 1986; *Ma'riv*, 26 November (according to *NYT*), 27 November 1986 (according to *WP*); *IHT*, 1 December 1986; *NYT*, 19 December 1986; *Al-Sharq al-Awsat*, 7 August 1988.

14 *NYT*, 27 April 1988.

15 G. Nonneman, *Iraq, the Gulf States and the War. A Changing Relationship and Beyond* (London, 1986), p. 86.

16 The GCC's summit, which met in Riyadh in March 1986, strongly condemned the 'Iranian aggression'. Crown Prince Abdallah, the head of the Saudi conservatives and a friend of the Syrian leader, also criticised Iran for its uncompromising stance: FBIS, 28 March 1986.

17 *FT*, 26 May 1986; *Saudi Gazette*, 12 August 1986.

18 Prince Bandar masterminded the Chinese deal behind America's back. F. W. Axelgard, *A New Iraq? The Gulf War and Implications for US Policy* (Washington, DC, 1988), p. 75; *Al-Ahram*, 14 August 1986; *FT*, 27 November, 1 December 1986; *IHT*, 1 December 1986. 19 *FT*, 31 December 1987, 4 January 1988; *WSJ*, 21 January 1989.

20 See above. The number of Saudi students going abroad sharply declined after 1986: *FT*, 13 April 1988, supplement, p. II.

21 *FT*, 27 August 1987; *NYT*, 18 October 1987. For indications that Saudi Arabia facilitated Iraqi air strikes on Iran's terminals in the lower Gulf: Axelgard, *A New Iraq?*, p. 75.

22 Nonneman, *Iraq*, pp. 90–1; *NYT*, business section, 18 October 1987.

23 Sharam Chubin (*NYT*, 4 May 1988) estimated that Saudi–Kuwaiti financial aid to Iraq by 1988 amounted to about 60 (?) billion dollars, not to mention payments from the sale of 300,000 barrels daily from the neutral zone. This is obviously a greatly exaggerated figure.

24 *FT*, 28 August 1987.

25 *IHT*, 25–6 November 1988.

26 R. O. Freedman, 'Continuity and change in Soviet policy towards the Middle East under Gorbachev'. A paper presented at a conference of the Centre for Soviet Studies, The Hebrew University of Jerusalem, January 1989, p. 33.

27 *FT*, 23 July 1987.

28 *FT*, 27 August 1987.

29 *FT*, 4 August 1988. The Iranian version was partly vindicated by Saudi declarations following the settlement of the hajj quota dispute in 1991 (see below).

30 *FT*, 17 August 1987; *NYT*, 18 August 1987.

31 *FT*, 15 August 1987.
32 *FT*, 15, 27, 28, 31 August 1987; *NYT*, 25 August, 18 October (business section) 1987; *Globe and Mail* (Toronto), 29 August, 7 September 1987.
33 *Los Angeles Times*, 29 October 1987; *Globe and Mail*, 29 April 1988, Fahd's interview to a Kuwaiti newspaper.
34 *FT*, 4 August 1987; *NYT*, 1 September 1987. Mostly non-Saudi Shi'ites and a Hizbollah branch in the Hijaz were involved in several terror incidents in the kingdom in 1988 and in 1989, see below.
35 See below. Also, *NYT*, 3 September 1987; *Ukaz*, 21 January 1988; *The Middle East*, September 1989.
36 *FT*, 13 April 1988; also, *Al-Muharir* (Marxist PFLP, Paris edition), 9 July 1988.
37 *FT*, 24, 28 August 1987.
38 *NYT*, 18 October 1987; *FT*, 27 January 1988; *The Middle East*, November 1987, March 1988.
39 *The Middle East*, March 1988; *FT*, 27 January 1988. Soviet foreign ministry officials visited Riyadh in March/April and Qatar established diplomatic relations with Moscow in August.
40 A. Gowers, *FT*, 13 April 1988, supplement; also, *NYT*, 24 February 1988, interview with Bahrayni minister.
41 *NYT*, 2 April 1988; *FT*, 5, 8 April 1988; *WP*, 6 June 1988; *MECS*, Vol. II (1988), pp. 697-9.
42 *FT*, 13 (supplement), 27, 29 April 1988; *NYT*, 27, 29 April 1988. Also, *Arab Times* (Kuwait), 11 January 1988, interview with Prince Abdallah.
43 *FT*, 7 October 1988; *IHT*, 18 October 1988, 8-9 July 1989; *FT*, 21 October 1988; *Haaretz*, 5 December 1988; *MECS*, Vol. 11 (1988), pp. 691-2. See below chapter 9.
44 See also below pp. 150-1. *IHT*, 8-9 July, 22 September 1989; *The Observer* (London), 30 July 1989; *The Middle East*, September 1989, p. 5; *FT*, 23 September 1989.
45 Including the assassination of Iran's last prime minister under the Shah, Shahpur Bakhtyari, in Paris in August 1991.
46 On opposition claims about covert dissatisfaction among new elites concerning the regime's character and pro-Western policy: *Al-Ra'i al-Akhir* (London), February 1989.
47 See below chapter 9.
48 Ibid.
49 *Haaretz*, 28 October 1988; Radio Israel, 21 March, 4 April 1989; *IHT*, 3 April 1989; *The Observer*, 30 July 1989.

9. PRELUDE TO THE IRAQ-KUWAIT CRISIS

1 *FT*, 31 December 1987, 4 January 1988; *NYT*, 11 January 1988; *WSJ*, 21 January 1988; *The Middle East*, July 1988.
2 *FT*, 23 October, 12 November, 31 December 1987.
3 *Ukaz*, 21 January 1988; *WSJ*, 21 January 1988; *Al-Siyassa* (Kuwait), 28 April 1988.
4 *Saudi Gazette*, 9 April 1988; *IHT*, 18 April 1989.
5 *IHT*, 18 April 1989.
6 *FT*, 12 May 1988.
7 *Al-Thawra al-Islamiyya*, August 1989. On graduates' unemployment: *The Middle East*, December 1989, p. 24.

8 FBIS, 24 October 1988 (Radio Riyadh, 20 October 1988), 22 November 1988 (Radio Riyadh, 20 November 1988); *The Middle East,* December 1989, p. 24; *Al-Thawra al-Islamiyya,* November 1988.

9 *FT,* 13 April 1988, supplement, pp. I, VIII.

10 See above p. 146–7.

11 *Los Angeles Times,* 14 November 1988; *Al-Thawra al-Islamiyya,* August 1989; *The Middle East,* December 1989, p. 21; J. Miller, 'The struggle within', *The New York Times Magazine,* 10 March 1991.

12 *Al-Thawra al-Islamiyya,* August 1989; *Los Angeles Times,* 14 November 1989; *The Middle East,* December 1989, p. 24.

13 *Saudi Gazette,* 8 April 1988; FBIS, 27 July 1988, Radio Riyadh, 26 July 1988; *FT,* 21 January 1990; *Ma'riv,* 28 February 1990; *NYT,* 13 January 1991.

14 FBIS, 1 November 1988, Radio Riyadh, 31 October 1988.

15 In 1981 its share was 42 per cent but it declined by 1985 to about 20 per cent: *FT,* 22 January 1990.

16 King Fahd's speeches: FBIS, 27 July 1988 (Radio Riyadh, 26 July 1988), 10 October 1988 (Radio Riyadh, 3 October 1988), 24 October 1988 (Radio Riyadh, 20 October 1988).

17 Estimated to suffice for 150 years at its 1988 rate of production.

18 *FT,* 29 July 1987, 26 May, 22 September 1988.

19 *Haaretz,* 22 October 1988; *FT,* 6 December 1988.

20 *Saudi Gazette,* 9 April 1988; *Al-Siyassa* (Kuwait), 28–9 April, 28–9 May 1988; FBIS, 27 July 1988 (Radio Riyadh, 26 July 1988), 15 October 1988 (Radio Riyadh, 3 October 1988), 24 October 1988 (Radio Riyadh, 20 October 1988); *FT,* 6 December 1988.

21 *FT,* 22, 26, 28 September 1989; *NYT,* 10 October 1989.

22 *Haaretz,* 26 November 1989; *Al-Siyassa* (Kuwait), 27 November 1989; *FT,* 29 November 1989.

23 Interview with Shaykh 'Ali Al Khalifa al-Adabi: *Middle East Economic Survey (MEES),* January 1990, according to Israel Petroleum Institute's newsletter (henceforth, *IPI,* in Hebrew), 15 February 1990; *FT,* 22 February 1990.

24 *MEES,* 1 March 1990; *IHT,* 5 March 1990.

25 *FT,* 2 May 1990; *Al-Thawra* (Baghdad), 3 May 1990; *Haaretz,* 5 May 1990. On oil price: FBIS, 16 April 1990, Radio Riyadh, 15 April 1990; *FT,* 18–19 April 1990.

26 FBIS, 3 April 1990, Radio Baghdad, 2 April 1990.

27 *Al-Dustur* (30 July 1990) reported that Iraq suggested that if such a price were achieved, the Arab oil countries should donate one dollar per barrel to fund projects in the Arab world.

28 *The Middle East,* July 1988, October 1989, p. 26; *IHT,* 13 December 1988, 3 January 1989; *FT,* 4 January 1989, 2 January 1990; *Al-Siyassa* (Kuwait), 6 January 1990.

29 King Fahd's speeches: FBIS, 27 July 1988 (Radio Riyadh, 26 July 1988), 24 October 1988 (Radio Riyadh, 20 October 1988); *IHT,* 20 December 1989, supplement Saudi Arabia.

30 *FT,* 13 October 1989, 22 January 1990. According to *NYT* (21 August 1990) 30–40 billion for 1989–93.

31 *FT,* 22 January 1990.

32 *IPI,* No. 172, July 1989.

33 *NYT,* 4 May 1989; also, *Al-Siyassa* (Kuwait), 3 May 1989.

34 *FT,* 13 March 1990, supplement Kuwait, p. 32.

35 *IHT,* 11 July 1990.

36 *FT*, 13 March, 8 April, 22 June 1990; FBIS, 27 June 1990, KUNA in English, 26 June 1990; *Al-Majalla*, 31 July 1990, pp. 20–1.

37 FBIS, 27 June 1990, KUNA in English, 26 June 1990; also, *FT*, 22 June 1990; *NYT*, 28 June 1990; *Al-Majalla*, 31 July 1990, pp. 20–1.

38 *IHT*, 11 July 1990; *Al-Qabas* (Kuwait), 16 July 1990; *FT*, 25 July 1990; FBIS, 30 July 1990, Radio Riyadh (quoting Hisham Nazir), 27 July 1990.

39 *NYT*, 28 July 1990; FBIS, 30 July 1990, Radio Riyadh, 27 July 1990, OPEC News Agency in English, 27 July 1990.

40 *Al-Muharir*, 9 July 1988.

41 *FT*, 13 April 1988, supplement, p. II.

42 *MECS* 1989 (draft), p. 25. On the ACC, see below. Also, M. Field, *FT*, 9 August 1990.

43 *FT*, 8 September 1990.

44 *Al-Thawra al-Islamiyya*, June–July 1990, pp. 20–5; *Al-Quds al-'Arabi* (Fundamentalist Palestinian, London), 1 August 1991, p. 4. Interview with Ali Salim, member of the political bureau of the Saudi Communist Party, on Saudi economic situation, 500,000 unemployed and many bankruptcies (1990): *Al-Hadaf*, 18 March 1991.

45 *Al-Ra'i al-Akhir*, February 1989, p. 5; *Al-Ta'ir al-Shimal* (Norway), March–April 1989, pp. 8–9; *FT*, 9 August, 12 December (supplement, Saudi Arabia, p. VII) 1990; *NYT*, 8 November 1990.

46 *NYT*, 2 April 1988: on recall of US ambassador. Also, *Haaretz*, 22 November 1989, according to G. Brooks, *WSJ*; M. Field, *FT*, 9 August 1990.

47 *Al-Nashra* (Communist, Athens), 14 December 1987; *Al-Thawra al-Islamiyya*, May–June 1988, June–July 1990, pp. 20–5. On the security officers' college established near Riyadh with US help: FBIS, 13 April 1988, Radio Riyadh in Arabic, 12 April 1988; *Al-Thawra al-Islamiyya*, June 1989. On religious persecution of Shi'ites, probably by local Sunni fundamentalists and ulama: *Al-Thawra al-Islamiyya*, June–July 1990, pp. 22, 24.

48 FBIS, 13 April 1988 (Radio Riyadh in Arabic, 9 April 1988, Radio Tehran, 12 April 1988), 27 April 1988 (Radio Kuwait, 27 April 1988); *NYT*, 28 April 1988.

49 FBIS, 30 August 1988, Radio Riyadh, 29 August 1988. See also denouncement of above by Saudi opposition organisations abroad: *Al-Hillal al-Dawli* (London), October 1988; *Al-Hurriyya* (Nicosia), 9 October 1988; *Al-Yasar al-'Arabi* (Paris), December 1988.

50 FBIS, 3 October 1988, Radio Riyadh, 30 September 1988; *FT*, 7 October 1988; FBIS, 24 October 1988, Radio Riyadh, 20 October 1988.

51 *Al-Nashra*, 8 May 1989.

52 *IHT*, 8–9 July 1989; *The Observer*, 30 July 1989; *The Middle East*, September 1989, p. 5 See also above pp. 146–7 and below pp. 152–3.

53 *The Middle East*, September 1989; *IHT*, 22 September, 2 November 1989; *FT*, 23 September 1989; *MECS* 1989 (draft), pp. 26–87; *Haaretz*, 7 October 1989, 2 February 1990.

54 *The Times*, 22 August 1989.

55 *Al-Thawra al-Islamiyya*, August 1989. Further on the tribal neo-Ikhwan group: ibid., June–July 1990, p. 20. On deportation of foreign fundamentalists: ibid., p. 24.

56 On deportation of Egyptian, Sudanese and other fundamentalists: FBIS, 28 December 1989, Radio Tehran, 24 December 1989.

57 See Abir, *Saudi Arabia*, pp. 24–5; *FT*, 11 January 1990.

58 *Al-Thawra al-Islamiyya*, June–July, 1990, pp. 20–1.

59 A PLO faction attacked a bus carrying American servicemen near Jedda:

NYT, 26 September 1990; also, *IHT*, 28 May 1991; *FT*, 30 January 1992, supplement, p. V.

60 *IHT*, 9 June 1989; *MECS* 1989 (draft), pp. 50-1; *IPI*, 15 February 1990, according to *MEES*; *FT*, 5, 13 March 1990.

61 *FT*, 21 February, 13 March 1990, supplement Kuwait, p. 31; *Surkiyya* (London), 5 March 1990, p. 10; *MECS* 1989 (draft), pp. 50-1.

62 Iraq's foreign debt was estimated at between 70 to 100 billion dollars: *NYT*, 28 July 1990.

63 The establishment of the Arab Maghreb Union (AMU) practically isolated Syria, which prudently began to improve relations with Egypt and to move closer to Riyadh.

64 FBIS, 27 July 1988, Radio Riyadh, 26 July 1988: *FT*, 15 November 1988, 17 February 1989; *Haaretz*, 16 February 1989, 17 February 1989; *Al-Siyassa* (Kuwait), 4 May 1989. *Ma'riv* (3 June 1991) quoting *October* (Egypt) claimed that the ACC was King Hussayn's brainchild.

65 FBIS, 28 March 1989, Radio Baghdad in Arabic, 27 March 1989; *FT*, 12 April 1989.

66 *FT*, 30 May 1989, 14 June 1989; *The Times*, 28 August 1989; *IHT*, 25 October 1989; *IHT*, 25 October 1989.

67 *Washington Times*, 21 December 1989.

68 *Al-Anba* (Kuwait), 25 February 1990; FBIS, 25 February 1990, Radio Baghdad, 24 February 1990; *FT*, 26 February 1990. An early book on the Kuwait crisis by A. Ehteshami and G. Nonneman (*War and Peace in the Gulf* (Reading, 1991)) is largely a collection of documents and tables and misconstrues the background to the conflict (pp. 57-90).

69 Banca Nazionale del Lavoro's Atlanta branch: *FT*, 21 November 1989; *WP*, 28 July 1990. See also below p. 245 note 3 on disclosures in 1991-2 about credit granted to Iraq by Washington from 1989 to August 1990. Also, Irangate, Special Report, *U.S. News & World Report*, 18 May 1992, pp. 42-51.

70 On the above see *NYT*, business section, 25 August 1991; *FT*, 21 November 1989. See also disclosures of US Congress banking committee on various occasions during 1992.

71 *FT*, 21 November 1989; *Ma'riv*, 15 May 1991.

72 *Surkiyya*, 5 March 1990, p. 10.

73 FBIS, 20 March 1990, Radio Baghdad in Arabic, 18 March 1990.

74 FBIS, 3 April 1990, Radio Baghdad in Arabic, 2 April 1990.

75 Shortly afterwards, Crown Prince Abdallah visited both Damascus and Baghdad for the same purpose: *The Middle East*, June 1990, pp. 13-14; also, *FT*, 19 April 1990.

76 *FT*, 19 April 1990.

77 Ibid.

78 *FT*, 1 June 1990.

79 FBIS, 29 May 1990, Radio Baghdad (live), 28 May 1990.

80 *FT*, 1 June 1990. On Saddam Hussayn's 17 July speech: *FT*, 25 July 1990.

81 FBIS, 6 June 1990; KUNA, 5 June 1960.

82 *FT*, 16 May 1990; *The Middle East*, July 1990, p. 5.

83 FBIS, 17 July 1990, Radio Baghdad, 17 July 1990.

84 *FT*, 19 July 1990; also, *WP*, 20 July 1990; *Al-Dustur*, 30 July 1990.

85 *FT*, 21-2 July 1990; also, ibid., 20 July 1990; *WP*, 20 July 1990.

86 *IPI*, 1 August 1989 (according to *MEES*), 10 July 1989; *Haaretz*, 17 October 1989; *The Middle East*, January 1990, p. 13.

87 *Jerusalem Post* (*JP*, Israel), 13 July 1989; *FT*, 18 August 1989; *MECS* 1990 (draft), Kuwait.
88 *MECS* 1989 (draft), p. 490; *FT*, 12 April 1989; *The Middle East*, July 1989, p. 10, January 1990, p. 26, March 1990, p. 26. For the Iraqi version see: *Al-Dustur*, 30 July 1990.
89 *MEED*, 20 July 1990.
90 *FT*, 24, 25 July 1990; *WP*, 24 July 1990.
91 *WP*, 20 July 1990; *FT*, 23 July 1990.
92 *FT*, 23, 26 July 1990; FBIS, 25 July 1990, KUNA, 24 July 1990; *JP*, 25 July 1990; *WP*, 26 July 1990; *Haaretz*, 26 July 1990.
93 *FT*, 25 July 1990. Riyadh negotiated with Washington in September 1989 the leasing of Saudi oil for the American strategic reserves.
94 *NYT*, 2 August 1990; *Al-Siyassi* (Cairo), 5 August 1990; *Al-Mussawar* (Egypt), 17 August 1990, an interview with Kuwait's foreign minister; *FT*, 18 August 1990; FBIS, 1 November 1990, KUNA, 31 October 1990.

10. SAUDI ARABIA AND THE WAR WITH IRAQ

1 King Fahd claimed that Saudi Arabia had been aware of Saddam's Gulf ambitions for some time: *IHT* (*NYT*), 7 March 1991.
2 *FT*, 6 August 1990.
3 *WP*, 26, 28 July 1990: *NYT*, 27, 28 July 1990; *Los Angeles Times*, 23 February 1992; S. Emerson, CNN special report, 26 February 1992; A. Lewis, *NYT*, 14 March 1992. Intelligence-sharing with Iraq continued practically until Kuwait's conquest: *WP*, 28 April 1992.
4 *WP*, 20 July 1990; *NYT*, 25 July 1990; *JP*, 25 July 1990; S. Emerson, CNN special report, 26 February 1992.
5 *WP*, 26 July 1990; *NYT*, 27 July 1990, 23 March 1991; *IHT*, 18 July 1991.
6 In a speech on 26 March Saddam Hussayn admitted that his greatest mistake was that he did not march into Saudi Arabia following Kuwait's conquest and even after the first US forces arrived there: Radio Baghdad and television, 26 March 1992. On the same subject: R. J. Lieber, 'Oil and power in the aftermath of the Gulf war', *International Security*, Vol. 17, No. 1 (summer 1992). Also, *IHT* (*WP*), 18 March 1991.
7 *FT*, 3 August 1990; *WP*, 3 August 1990; *NYT*, 3 August 1990.
8 On Mohammed al-Fassi, Prince Turki's (Fahd's full brother) brother-in-law, who went to Baghdad in October to express support for Iraq: *IHT*, 23 November 1991, 17 February 1992.
9 *FT*, 6, 9 August, 12 December (supplement, p. I) 1990; *WP*, 14 August, 20 September 1990; H. F. Eilts, 'The Persian Gulf crisis: perspectives and prospects', *MEJ*, Vol. 45, No. 1 (winter 1991), pp. 8–9; *Haaretz*, 3 March 1991. According to *EIU* (No. 4, 1991, 15 November 1991) Sultan was reluctant to ask for US help and opposed the offensive against Iraq.
10 *Al-Ahram*, 5 August 1990; *WP*, 5, 6 August 1990; *FT*, 6 August 1990.
11 *Al-Riyadh*, 10 August 1990; *WP*, 10 August 1990; also, *FT*, 7, 10 August, 12 December (supplement, p. I) 1990; *NYT*, 11 August 1990.
12 Iraq called for a jihad, to save Mecca and Madina: *WP*, 11 August 1990.
13 *WP*, 12 August 1990. Riyadh was reluctant to increase the symbolic Egyptian and Syrian units which reached Saudi Arabia, fearing future intervention in Saudi affairs and excessive financial demands: *WP*, 29 August 1990.
14 *NYT*, 9 August 1990.

15 *NYT*, 19 September 1990.

16 *IHT*, 13 March 1991; J. Miller, 'The struggle', p. 46.

17 The 'neo-fundamentalists' challenged the historical alliance between the (Wahhabi) ulama (previously) led by Al al-Shaykh and the political leadership of Al Saud. They practically called for the regime's overthrow and the establishment of a true Islamic state guided by qualified *fuqaha*'.

18 *WP*, 20 September 1990; *NYT*, 5 October, 8 November 1990, 13 January 1991; *FT*, 12 December 1990, supplement, pp. I, VII: *Al-Bilad* (Beirut), 15 June 1991, p. 33.

19 On the impact of such propaganda on Egyptian Islamists: *Al-Sha'b* (Egypt), 14 August 1990; also, *FT*, 13 August 1990; *WP*, 13 August 1990; *Al-Thawra*, 12–15 August 1990; A. M. Lesch, 'Contrasting reactions to Persian Gulf crisis: Egypt, Syria, Jordan and the Palestinians', *MEJ*, Vol. 45, No. 1 (winter 1991).

20 *NYT*, 3 March 1990; *MEED*, Vol. 34, No. 41, 19 October 1990, p. 4; *IHT*, 24, 27 October 1990; *FT*, 24 October, 6 November 1990; *Haaretz*, 13 December 1990: On Saudi rejection of an Algerian mediation offer.

21 *FT*, 20 September 1990; *WP*, 10 October 1990; *Al-Jazira al-'Arabiyya*, July 1991, pp. 22–8. On sermons and cassettes by popular 'neo-fundamentalist' *'alims*, attacking the regime and its policy, graduates of American universities and the kingdom's Shi'ites: Al-Gosaybi, *Hatah*, pp. 106–10, 117, 120, 152–3, 173–4. Al-Gosaybi calls them 'political *fuqaha*'' and questions the Islamic scholarship of some of the most popular. Also, *Al-Thawra al-Islamiyya*, May–June 1990.

22 *NYT*, 8 November 1990; Eilts, 'Persian Gulf', p. 8.

23 *WP*, 20 September 1990. On Muslim World League conference in Jedda on 12 September justifying Fahd's invitation to non-Muslims to help defend Saudi Arabia: *Al-Riyadh*, 13 September 1990; *WP*, 14 September 1990.

24 *WP*, 10 August, 20 September 1990; also, *FT*, 20 September 1990.

25 Al-Gosaybi, *Hatah*, pp. 106–10, 117, 120, 152–3, 173–4; also, *WP*, 2 September, 10 October 1990; *NYT*, 16 September 1990; *FT*, 20 September, 24 October, 12 December (supplement, p. VII), 1990; *Al-Jazira al-'Arabiyya*, July 1991, pp. 22–8.

26 *FT*, 24 October 1990; *NYT*, 8 November 1990; *IHT* (*WP*), 7 April 1991; *Time* (magazine), 17 June 1991, p. 39.

27 *NYT*, 29 September 1990; also, *FT*, 20 September 1990.

28 *NYT*, 5 September 1990; also, *Middle East Report*, July–August 1991.

29 *FT*, 10 November 1990. According to *FT* (12 December 1990, supplement, p. VII), Fahd discussed the matter in September. Also, *Misr al-Fatat* (Cairo), 1 April 1991, p. 3.

30 *FT*, 16 August, 20 September, 24 October 1990; *NYT*, 26 August, 8 November 1990; *WP*, 20 September, 10 October 1990, 13 March 1991; *IHT*, 14 December 1990; J. Miller, 'The struggle', pp. 28, 30–1, 39.

31 FBIS, 16 November 1990, Radio Riyadh, 15 November 1990; W. Ross, *Middle East International* (*MEI*), No. 390, December 1990. On extremist ulama all-out attack on this matter: Al-Gosaybi, *Hatah*, pp. 97–9. On claim that Prince Salman practically authorised the women's demonstration and was coerced by the ulama to swear on the Koran that this was not true: *Al-Bilad* (Beirut), 15 June 1991.

32 *WSJ*, 2 May 1991; also, *IHT*, 14 December 1990; *Misr al-Fatat*, 1 April 1991, p. 3. See below ulama petition, pp. 381–6.

33 *FT*, 24 October 1990.

34 Al-Gosaybi, *Hatah*, pp. 96-7. Islamic commercial laws and courts: ibid., p. 153.
35 On the new phenomenon of 'political ulama', substantiated by many quotes from their cassettes: Al-Gosaybi, *Hatah*, pp. 142-3, 151-4, 157-8.
36 *Al-Jazira al-'Arabiyya*, June-August 1991; Al-Gosaybi, *Hatah*, pp. 117-18; J. Miller, 'The struggle', p. 46; *WSJ*, 2 May 1991; *Time* (magazine), 17 June 1991, p. 40. On 118 cassettes of A'its al-Qarny's sermons ('who had not published one book'): Al-Gosaybi, *Hatah*, p. 118. On dismissal of many imams, confiscation of cassettes and publications of sermons of nine ulama and arrest of about ten other *'alims* (names listed) by order of Salman, the governor of Riyadh, before Kuwait's conquest: *Al-Thawra al-Islamiyya*, June-July 1990.
37 Half a dozen hold a doctor's degree, several were lecturers, or MA students in Islamic universities: Al-Gosaybi, *Hatah*, pp. 97-177. Also *Al-Jazira al-'Arabiyya*, June-August 1991; *EIU*, No. 3, 1991, pp. 7-8.
38 On cassettes by Dr Safar al-Hawali, Salman al-Odah and other militants, practically calling for the regime's overthrow for having invited the Americans to Saudi Arabia: Al-Gosaybi, *Hatah*, pp. 152-3.
39 *Al-Jazira al-'Arabiyya*, August 1991, pp. 3-5; also, ibid., July 1991; *Al-Quds al-'Arabi*, 1 August 1991; Al-Gosaybi, *Hatah*, pp. 143-54, 155-8.
40 Al-Gosaybi, *Hatah*, pp. 106, 117-18, 174-5.
41 *Al-Thawra*, 10 October 1990; also, *EIU*, No. 3, 1991, p. 3; Al-Gosaybi, *Hatah*, pp. 152, 155, 158. Extracts from unsigned pamphlets inciting against the regime, the Americans and the 'secular' intelligentsia: ibid., pp. 173-5.
42 *Al-Thawra*, 10 October 1990. Also, *Al-Jazira al-'Arabiyya*, August 1991; *FT*, 24 October 1990; J. Miller, 'The struggle', p. 46. On fundamentalists' complaint of being deprived of access to 'government media': Al-Gosaybi, *Hatah*, p. 154.
43 Eilts, 'Persian Gulf', p. 9.
44 *Ma'riv*, 29 March 1991, special supplement, p. 23; *WP*, 3 April 1991.
45 *WSJ*, 2 May 1991. On demonstrations in Burayda (Najd), following rumours that Salman al-Odah had been arrested: *Time* (magazine), 17 June 1991, p. 40. Of Shaykh (Dr) Safar al-Hawali, a leading theologian 'who had circulated tapes criticising the Gulf war': *IHT* (*NYT*), 6 July 1991. On the above and on (Dr) Shaykh Nassir al-Omar, Shaykh A'its al-Qarny and other extremist *'alims*, whom Al-Gosaybi calls 'political ulama': Al-Gosaybi, *Hatah*, pp. 134-77; *Al-Jazira al-'Arabiyya*, June-August 1991.
46 *Haaretz*, 14 January 1991; Al-Gosaybi, *Hatah*, pp. 120, 152, 155, 165, 173-4.
47 *NYT*, 13 January 1991.
48 J. Miller, 'The struggle', p. 46; *FT*, 18 February 1991. To counter quotes used by 'neo-fundamentalists' that 'dependence on non-Muslim aid caused the fall of Muslim states': Al-Gosaybi, *Hatah*, p. 152.
49 *NYT*, 13 January 1991; also, *WP*, 20 September 1990; *Haaretz*, 3 March 1991; S. Coll (*WP*), *IHT*, 13 March 1991.

11. DEMANDS FOR SOCIO-POLITICAL CHANGE IN THE POST-WAR ERA

1 S. Coll (*WP*), *IHT*, 13 March 1991; *WSJ*, 5 May 1991.
2 J. Miller, 'The struggle', pp. 30-1; also, *IHT* (*WP*), 13 March 1991.
3 J. Miller, 'The struggle', p. 28.
4 Ibid., p. 31. Also, *Al-Jazira al-'Arabiyya*, July 1991; *Akhir Khabar* (*Amman*), 25 March 1991, p. 6.

5 J. Miller, 'The struggle', p. 46; *IHT*, 13 March, 17 April 1991; *WSJ*, 2 May 1991.

6 *Al-Riyadh*, 6 March 1991; *IHT* (*NYT*), 7 March 1991.

7 *WSJ*, 2 May 1991; *IHT*, 9 May 1991; *Time* (magazine), 17 June 1991, p. 40; *EIU*, No. 4, 1991, 15 November 1991, p. 8.

8 *Haaretz*, 16 May 1991.

9 *Al-Liwa* (Amman), 6 February 1991, pp. 3, 20; *Akhir Khabar*, 25 March 1991; *IHT*, 17 April (*WP*), 6 July (*NYT*) 1991; *EIU*, No. 2, 1991, Saudi Arabia Country Report, p. 10. Among the signatories were former information minister Abdu Yamani, an Asiri, and Ahmad Jamjum, the former minister of industry, a Hijazi.

10 *IHT* (*WP*), 17 April 1991.

11 *Al-Liwa*, 6 February 1991; *Akhir Khabar*, 25 March 1991; *Al-Bilad* (Beirut), 15 June 1991, p. 31.

12 J. Caesar, *IHT* (*NYT*), 6 July 1991. According to other sources, the memorandum alluded to sectarian discrimination – largely the treatmen of the kingdom's Shi'ites.

13 Ibid.; also, *IHT* (*WP*), 17 April 1991; *Al-Bilad* (Beirut), 15 June 1991, p. 31.

14 *Time* (magazine), 17 June 1991, p. 40.

15 *IHT* (*WP*), 17 April 1991.

16 *IHT*, 9 May 1991; *Time* (magazine), 17 June 1991, p. 39.

17 *Al-Jazira al-'Arabiyya*, August 1991. Other sources, including *Al-Quds al-'Arabi* (1 August 1991), claim that the petition was submitted in mid-May.

18 *Al-Jazira al-'Arabiyya*, August 1991, pp. 10–11 (over 50); *EIU*, No. 3, 1991, 16 August 1991, p. 7 (up to 100).

19 On the 400 ulama's petition: *IHT*, 27 May, 6 July 1991; *Al-Jazira al-'Arabiyya*, June, August 1991, pp. 10–14; *MEI*, 14 June 1991; *EIU*, No. 3, 1991, 16 August 1991, p. 7.

20 *Al-Thawra al-Islamiyya*, June–July 1990.

21 Ibid., p. 20; Al-Gosaybi, *Hatah*, pp. 106, 174.

22 'Letter from Riyadh', *MEI*, No. 390, December 1990.

23 *Al-Bilad* (Beirut), 15 June 1991, p. 32.

24 *NYT*, 6 August 1991.

25 *MEI*, 14 June 1991; *Al-Jazira al-'Arabiyya*, June–July 1990, August 1991; *EIU*, No. 3, 1991, 16 August 1991.

26 Explanatory letter to Abd al-Aziz bin Baz, July 1991, according to *Al-Quds al-'Arabi*, 1 August 1991, p. 4; *MEI*, 14 June 1991; *EIU*, No. 3, 1991, 16 August 1991; *Al-Jazira al-'Arabiyya*, August 1991, pp. 10–14.

27 *EIU*, No. 3, 1991, 16 August 1991.

28 *Al-Ahali* (Egypt), 19 June 1991; *EIU*, No. 4, 1991, 15 November 1991, p. 8.

29 *EIU*, No. 3, 1991, 16 August 1991, p. 7; ibid., No. 4, 1991, 15 November 1991, pp. 8–9.

30 *Al-Hawadith*, 21 June 1991, p. 15; *Al-Quds al-'Arabi*, 25 June 1991, p. 1; *Al-Bayadir al-Siyassi* (East Jerusalem), 7 September 1991, p. 8.

31 *Al-Quds al-'Arabi*, 1 August 1991, p. 4.

32 Ibid.; also, *EIU*, No. 4, 1991, 15 November 1991. On persecution of leading popular 'neo-fundamentalists': *Al-Jazira al-'Arabiyya*, August 1991, pp. 10–14.

33 *Al-Hawadith* (London), 5 July 1991, p. 28. On Prince Salman's (Riyadh's governor) analysis of 'direct democracy', interview with Prince Faysal, King Saud's grandson: *Al-Dawliyya* (Paris), No. 27, 17 November 1991, p. 19. On major dam built in Bisha province (south): *Ukaz*, 2 May 1991. The intensive

contacts with the poorer 'tribal' population were partly aimed at eroding Crown Prince Abdallah's power base.

34 *The Observer*, 2 June 1991.

35 *Misr al-Fatat*, 7 October 1991, pp. 1, 10; *EIU*, No. 4, 1991, 15 November 1991, p. 12.

36 *Al-Hawadith* (London), 21 June 1991, p. 16, interview with King Fahd.

37 *WP*, 21 July 1991; *NYT*, 21 July 1991; *EIU*, No. 3, 1991, 16 August 1991, p. 11. An editorial in *Al-Madina* from 22 August reflected the unhappiness with Fahd's policy concerning Israel of some influential Saudis.

38 *The Guardian*, 16 October 1991; *NYT*, 16 October 1991; *EIU*, No. 4, 1991, 15 November 1991, p. 12; *Misr al-Fatat*, 7 October 1991, pp. 1, 10.

39 FBIS, 1 October 1991, Radio Riyadh, 30 September 1991, FBIS, 22 October 1991, Radio Riyadh, 16 October 1991; FBIS, 29 October 1991, Saudi Arabian television network, 24 October 1991; *Misr al-Fatat*, 7 October 1991, pp. 1, 10; *EIU*, No. 4, 1991, 15 November 1991, p. 12; *MEED*, Vol. 35, No. 44, 8 November 1991, p. III.

40 *Haaretz*, 20 (according to the Saudi daily *Al-Bilad*), 31 October, 4, 14 November 1991; *Ma'riv*, 4 November 1991; FBIS, 19 November 1991, MBC television in Arabic, 14 November 1991, interview with King Fahd on the peace process.

41 *EIU*, No. 4, 1991, 15 November 1991, p. 17.

42 Never published, 1991 Saudi expenditure budget (other than payments to allies) rose to about 45 billion dollars (est.), compared with 37 billion in 1989. Saudi estimated oil revenue in 1991 rose to over 40 billion dollars, compared with just over 20 billion in 1989.

43 *MEED*, Vol. 35, No. 44, 8 November 1991, p. VI; FBIS, 19 November 1991, MBC television in Arabic, 14 November 1991; *FT*, 30 January 1992, supplement, p. II.

44 *FT*, 30 January 1992, supplement, pp. I, II.

45 *Al-Sharq al-Awsat*, 31 December 1991; *Al-Riyadh*, 31 December 1991; also, *FT*, 30 January 1991, supplement, p. V.

46 *FT*, 30 January 1992, supplement, p. V; also, *EIU*, No. 4, 1991, 15 November 1991, p. 8.

47 *WSJ*, 20 September 1991.

48 *FT*, 30 January 1992, supplement, p. V.

49 *WSJ*, 20 September 1991; *IHT* (*NYT*), 7 January 1992; *Al-Quds al-'Arabi*, 13 January 1992; *Haaretz*, 14 January 1992 (on escalation of the militants' activities at the end of 1991); *FT*, 30 January 1992, supplement, p. V.

50 *IHT*, 31 December 1991; *NYT*, 30 January 1992. On wide circulation of cassettes and attacks on the regime and the Sauds in general: *Ma'riv*, 26 February 1992, according to N. McParker, AP, Saudi Arabia.

51 *Al-Riyadh*, 29–30 December 1991; *IHT*, 31 December 1991.

52 *Al-Quds al-'Arabi*, 13, 28 January 1992. Salman al-Odah, the most famous popular 'neo-fundamentalist', an MA student according to Gosaybi and a lecturer in Riyadh's Islamic university according to another source, was prevented from travelling to America at the invitation of the association of Muslim students in the US.

53 *NYT*, 22 January 1992; *Haaretz*, 23 January 1992.

54 *NYT*, 29 January 1992.

55 *Al-Riyadh*, 28 January 1992; *Al-Bilad* (Saudi Arabia), 28 January 1992.

56 *NYT*, 31 January 1992; *Jordan Times*, 13 February 1992; FBIS, 18 February 1992, Radio Riyadh, 13 February 1992.

57 *Al-Quds al-'Arabi*, 28 January 1992; *Al-Hayat*, 29 January 1992.
58 *NYT*, 30 January 1992; *Jordan Times*, 12 February 1992.
59 *FT*, 30 January 1992.
60 *Haaretz*, 31 January 1992, according to *WSJ*. On capital return: *FT*, 30 January 1992, supplement, p. II.
61 *NYT*, 30 January 1992; FBIS, 4 February 1992, Saudi television network, 25 January 1992. On *muttawwa'in* arrest: *Jordan Times*, 12 February 1992.
62 *Al-Riyadh*, 2 March 1992; *FT*, 2 March 1992; *IHT*, 2 March 1992; *Al-Majalla*, 4-10 March 1992, pp. 15-23.
63 According to *Al-Bilad* (Beirut), 15 June 1991, America, 'which greatly influenced Fahd's policy', encouraged him to involve the third-generation Sauds in the government in order to consolidate the regime's future stability.
64 Jerusalem.
65 Jerusalem.

12. OIL AND GULF SECURITY

1 *WP*, 20 December 1990; *FT*, 2 January 1991; *Haaretz*, 3 January 1991.
2 *WP*, 3 April 1991; *FT*, 30 January 1992, supplement, p. II.
3 *IHT*, 6 March 1991; *WP*, 3 April, 24 September 1991; *Time* (magazine), 17 June 1991, p. 39. Riyadh borrowed nearly five billion dollars at the beginning of 1991 and ten billion at the end of the year. Saudi liquid reserves fell by the beginning of 1991 to less than ten billion dollars: *FT*, 30 January 1992, supplement, p. I.
4 *NYT*, 11 February 1991; *FT*, 30 January 1992, pp. I, II.
5 On the immense cost of sophisticated weapons orders by Riyadh: *FT*, 30 January 1992, supplement, p. IV.
6 *FT*, 14 March 1991; also, *IHT*, 6 March 1991.
7 *FT*, 30 January 1992, supplement, p. II.
8 J. Hoagland, *IHT*, 30-1 March 1991; L. Mylroie, *WSJ*, according to *Haaretz*, 16 April 1991.
9 *IHT*, 3, 30 April, 10 May 1991.
10 J. Fitchett, *IHT*, 18 April, 22 April (*WP*) 1991.
11 *IHT*, 17 May 1991; *Haaretz*, 4 June 1991; *JP*, 10 June 1991.
12 *The Guardian*, 14 October 1991; *EIU*, No. 4, 1991, pp. 11-12; also, *IHT*, 30 April (quoting General Prince Khalid ibn Sultan), 10, 18 May 1991; *NYT*, 27 September 1991.
13 *Time* (magazine), 17 June 1991; *FT*, 31 July 1991; *NYT*, 1 August 1991.
14 *EIU*, No. 4, 1991, 15 November 1991, p. 11; also, *NYT*, 27 September 1991.
15 *WP*, 29, 30 August 1991; *NYT*, 30 August 1991; J. Hoagland, *WP*, 12 September 1991.
16 *FT*, 5, 20 September 1991; *WP*, 6 September 1991, 31 May 1992.
17 There were 20,000 US troops still on Saudi soil and about 17,000 on board ships docked in Saudi ports in November 1991: *EIU*, No. 4, 1991, 15 November 1991, p. 11. Answering allegations that Saudi Arabia had transferred the Patriot missile technology to China, Secretary Cheney revealed at the end of March that all Patriot batteries in Saudi Arabia were being operated by US servicemen: Israeli radio and television, 31 March 1992.
18 *Jane's Defence Weekly*, Vol. 16, No. 24, 1991, p. 1175. On GCC Kuwait summit dealing with Gulf security and on facilities provided to the US and the UK: *Haaretz*, 23 December 1991. Also, note 14 above.
19 FBIS, 26 June 1991, Radio Riyadh, 25 June 1991; *EIU*, No. 3, 1991, 16 August

1991, pp. 8–9; *IHT*, 4 October 1991; *MEED*, Vol. 35, No. 44, 8 November 1991, p. III; *FT*, 30 January 1992, supplement, p. V.

20 *FT*, 14 March, 31 July 1991; *Haaretz*, 19 March 1991.

21 *FT*, 6 February 1992; *WSJ*, 18 March 1992. Tehran hopes to earn 19.8 billion dollars from the sale of oil and gas in 1992. Iran plans to raise its production to five m.b.d. by 1993: *NYT*, 16 September 1991; *FT*, 28 January 1992; also, P. Tyler, *NYT*, 13 September 1991; *Haaretz*, 11 November 1991.

22 *FT*, 27 October 1991; *IHT*, 31 October, 1 November 1991; *Haaretz*, 22 November 1991; *WSJ*, 18 March 1992.

23 *Ma'riv*, 14 November 1991; *Los Angeles Times*, 7 January 1992; *IHT*, 14 March 1992; *WSJ*, 18 March 1992. On delivery of North Korean Scud-B missiles in Iran (for Syria): *IHT*, 9 March 1992; *FT*, 9 March 1992.

24 *Ma'riv*, 31 December 1991; *FT*, 6 February 1992; *Tehran Times*, 9 February 1992; *Haaretz*, 27 February 1992. On Iranian mediation between Armenia and Azerbaijan over Nagorno Karabakh: Israel television, 15 March 1992.

25 Iranian influence in the main stream of Algerian Islamic Front competed with the Saudi-influenced, more moderate, stream: *Haaretz*, 5 January 1991, according to *The European*.

26 *Yedioth Aharonot* (Israel), 3 January 1992; *Ma'riv*, 6 January 1992; *Haaretz*, 14 January, 15 March 1992; *NYT*, 29 January 1992. On alleged Iranian–Iraqi supported plot to overthrow Mubarak's regime: *Ma'riv*, 10 March 1992. On additional Revolutionary Guard units: *Haaretz*, 3 April 1992.

27 Riyadh refused to permit the US to use its bases to attack Iraq after Baghdad detained a UN nuclear inspection team: *NYT*, 27 September 1991. On Riyadh's apprehension of Baghdad's military and nuclear endeavours and call for action against it: *Ukaz*, 17–18 January 1992. In September 1992 Saudi bases were used by the US to protect Iraq's Shi'ites from the Iraqi airforce.

28 *NYT*, 19 January 1992; *Haaretz*, 24 February 1992; *IHT*, 25 February, 12 March (according to *WP*) 1992; *FT*, 28 February 1992. Of Egypt's displeasure with the Saudis concerning the Gulf's defence: *Al-Quds al-'Arabi*, 23 April 1992.

29 King Fahd fully supports the operation, unlike Syria and Egypt who oppose it: *NYT*, 19 March 1992.

13. CONCLUSION

1 Riyadh threatens to acquire European-made warplanes if the US further delays permission to purchase 75 advanced F-15s with attack capabilities: *Haaretz*, 26 March 1992. President Bush intends to sell the 75F-15E to Saudi Arabia: *NYT*, 13 August 1992; *WP*, 2–3 September 1992.

2 *Foreign Affairs*, Vol. 57, No. 2, Winter 1978/9.

3 Hassan Nafaa, in Tawfic E. Farah, *Pan-Arabism and Arab Nationalism. The Continuing Debate* (Westview, 1987).

BIBLIOGRAPHY

UNPUBLISHED PhD THESES

Al-Awaji, I. M., 'Bureaucracy and society in Saudi Arabia', unpublished PhD thesis, University of Virginia, 1971.

Al-Hamad, T. H. T., 'Political order in changing societies, Saudi Arabia: modernization in a traditional context', unpublished PhD thesis, University of Southern California, 1985.

Al-Ibrahim, A. A., 'Regional and urban development in Saudi Arabia', unpublished PhD thesis, University of Colorado at Boulder, 1982.

Al-Nassar, F. M., 'Saudi Arabian educational mission to the US', unpublished PhD thesis, University of Oklahoma (Norman), 1982.

Al-Rawaf, O. Y., 'The concept of the five crises in political development: relevance to the kingdom of Saudi Arabia', unpublished PhD thesis, Duke University, 1981.

Al Saud, Mashaal Abdullah Turki, 'Permanence and change: an analysis of the Islamic political culture of Saudi Arabia with a special reference to the royal family', unpublished PhD thesis, Claremont Graduate School, 1982.

Al-Selfan, A. M., 'The essence of tribal leaders' participation, responsibilities, and decisions in some local government activities in Saudi Arabia: a case study of the Ghamid and Zahran tribes', unpublished PhD thesis, Claremont Graduate School, 1981.

Alyami, A. H., 'The impact of modernization on the stability of the Saudi monarchy', unpublished PhD thesis, Claremont Graduate School, 1977.

Faheem M. E., 'Higher education and nation building. A case study of King Abdul Aziz University', unpublished PhD thesis, University of Illinois at Urbana-Champaign, 1982.

Hafiz, F. A., 'Changes in Saudi foreign policy behaviour 1964-75. A study of the underlying factors and determinates', unpublished PhD thesis, University of Nebraska-Lincoln, 1980.

Hisham, N. H., 'Saudi Arabia and the role of the Imarates in regional development', unpublished PhD thesis, Claremont Graduate School, 1982.

Jan, N. A., 'Between Islamic and Western education: a case study of Umm Al-Qura University, Makkah, Saudi Arabia', unpublished PhD thesis, Michigan State University, 1983.

Kinsawi, M. M., 'Attitude of students and fathers towards vocational education in economic development in Saudi Arabia', unpublished PhD thesis, University of Colorado at Boulder, 1981.

Madani, N. O., 'The Islamic content of the foreign policy of Saudi Arabia. King

Faisal's call for Islamic solidarity 1965–1975', unpublished PhD thesis, The American University, Washington, DC, 1977.

Marks, M. M., 'The American influence on the development of the universities in the kingdom of Saudi Arabia', unpublished PhD thesis, University of Oregon, 1980.

Said, A. H., 'Saudi Arabia: the transition from a tribal society to a nation', unpublished PhD thesis, University of Missouri, 1979.

Samore, G. S., 'Royal family politics in Saudi Arabia (1953–1982)', unpublished PhD thesis, Harvard University, 1984.

Shaker, F. A., 'Modernization of the developing nations. The case of Saudi Arabia', unpublished PhD thesis, Purdue University, 1972.

UNPUBLISHED REFERENCE MATERIAL

Abir, M., 'The manpower problem in Saudi Arabian economic and security policy', colloquium paper, Woodrow Wilson International Center for Scholars (Washington, DC, April 1983).

Ayubi, N. N. M., 'Vulnerability of the rich: the political economy of defense and development in Saudi Arabia and the Gulf', a paper prepared for The Gulf Project, Center for Strategic and International Studies, Georgetown University, Washington, DC (Los Angeles, May 1982).

Freedman, R. O., 'Continuity and change in Soviet policy towards the Middle East under Gorbachev', a paper presented at a conference of the Centre for Soviet Studies, The Hebrew University of Jerusalem (Jerusalem, January 1989).

Kavoussi, R. and Sheikholeslami, A. R., 'Political economy of Saudi Arabia' (University of Washington, January 1983).

Schulze, R., 'The Saudi Arabian 'ulama and their reaction to Muslim fundamentalism', a paper prepared for a colloquium on Religious Radicalism and Politics in the Middle East, The Hebrew University of Jerusalem (Jerusalem, May 1985).

OFFICIAL DOCUMENTATION

Craig, J. (UK ambassador to Saudi Arabia until 1984), confidential report No. 5184 to the Secretary of State for Foreign and Commonwealth Affairs: *Glasgow Herald*, 9 October 1986.

Kingdom of Saudi Arabia, Centre for Statistical Data and Educational Documentation: *Development of Education in the Ministry of Education During 25 Years 1954–78* (Riyadh, 1978).

Kingdom of Saudi Arabia, Ministry of Finance and National Economy, Department of Statistics, *The Statistical Indicator*, Eleventh Issue, 1406 AH – 1986 AD.

Kingdom of Saudi Arabia, Ministry of Information, *Faisal Speaks*.

Kingdom of Saudi Arabia, Ministry of Planning, *Employment by Sector* (Riyadh, 1982).

——*Third Development Plan 1400–1405 AH – 1980–1985 AD.*

——*Fourth Development Plan 1405–1410 AH – 1985–1990 AD* (Education).

——*Fifth Development Plan 1410–1415 AH – 1990–1995 AD* (Human Resources Development).

Saudi Arabia: Education and Human Resources, The Royal Embassy of Saudi Arabia, Information Office (Washington, DC, 1989).

Saudi Budget Estimates, The Royal Embassy of Saudi Arabia, Commercial Office (Washington, DC, 6 August 1991).

BOOKS

Abir, M., *Oil Power and Politics: Conflict in Arabia, the Persian Gulf and the Red Sea* (London, 1974).
——*Saudi Arabia in the Oil Era. Regime and Elites; Conflict and Collaboration* (London, 1988).
Abu Dhurr (pseud.), *Thawra fi Rihab Makka* (Dar Sawt at-Tali'a, Kuwait, 1980).
Al-Farsy, F. A. S., *Saudi Arabia: A Case Study in Development* (London, 1982).
Al-Kosaybi (Gosaybi), Ghazi b. Abd al-Rahman, *Hatah la takun fitna!!* (n.p., 1991).
Al-Turki, S. and Cole, D., *Arabian Oasis City* (University of Texas Press, 1989).
Aramco Handbook (Netherlands, 1960).
Arnold, J., *Golden Swords and Pots and Pans* (New York, 1963).
Axelgard, F. W., *A New Iraq? The Gulf War and Implications for US Policy* (Washington, DC, 1988).
Baroody, G. M., 'The practice of law in Saudi Arabia' in W. A. Beling (ed.), *King Faisal and the Modernisation of Saudi Arabia* (London, 1980).
Blandford, L., *Oil Sheikhs* (London, 1976).
Bligh, A., *From Prince to King. Royal Succession in the House of Saud in the Twentieth Century* (New York, 1984).
Buchan, J., 'Secular and religious opposition in Saudi Arabia' in T. Niblock (ed.), *State, Society and Economy in Saudi Arabia* (London, 1982).
Cheney, M., *Big Oil Man From Arabia* (New York, 1958).
Cole, D. P., *Nomads of the Nomads. The Al Murrah Bedouins of the Empty Quarter* (Chicago, 1975).
Cordesman, A. H., *The Changing Military Balance in the Gulf* (Washington, DC, 1990).
De Gaury, G., *Faisal King of Saudi Arabia* (New York, 1966).
Ehteshami, A. and Nonneman, G., *War and Peace in the Gulf* (Reading, 1991).
Field, M., *The Merchants. The Big Business Families of Arabia* (London, 1984).
Habib, J. S., *Ibn Sa'ud's Warriors of Islam* (Leiden, 1978).
Halliday, F., *Arabia Without Sultans* (Manchester, 1975).
Hamzah, F., *Al Bilad al-'Arabiyah al-Sa'udiyya* (Mecca, 1937).
Holden, D. and Johns, R., *The House of Saud* (London, 1982).
Huyette, S. S., *Political Adaptation in Sa'udi Arabia* (Boulder, 1985).
Ibrahim, S. E., *The New Arab Social Order. A Study of the Social Impact of Oil Wealth* (Westview Press, 1982).
Katakura, M., *Bedouin Village. A Study of a Saudi Arabian People in Transition* (University of Tokyo Press, 1977).
Keegan, J., *World Armies* (New York, 1979).
Lacey, R., *The Kingdom* (London, 1981).
Lackner, H., *A House Built on Sand* (London, 1978).
Lancaster, W., *The Rwala Bedouin Today* (Cambridge, Mass., 1981).
Layish, A., 'Ulama and politics in Saudi Arabia', in M. Heper and R. Israeli (eds), *Islam and Politics in the Modern Middle East* (New York, 1984).
Middle East Contemporary Survey (MECS).
Mosley, L., *Power Play. The Tumultuous World of Middle East Oil 1890–1973* (Birkenhead, 1973).
Moss Helms, C., *The Cohesion of Saudi Arabia* (London, 1981).

BIBLIOGRAPHY

Niblock, T., 'Social structure and the development of the Saudi Arabian political system', in T. Niblock (ed.), *State, Society and Economy in Saudi Arabia* (London, 1982).

Nonneman, G., *Iraq, the Gulf States and the War. A Changing Relationship and Beyond* (London, 1986).

Nyrop, R. F. (ed.), Area Handbook Series: *Saudi Arabia: A Country Study* (Washington, DC, 1982), (Washington, DC, 1984).

Philby, H. St John, *Sa'udi Arabia* (Beirut, 1968).

Robenson, J., *Yamani. The Inside Story* (London, 1988).

Safran, N., *Saudi Arabia: The Ceaseless Quest for Security* (Cambridge, Mass., 1985).

Salemeh, Gh., *Al-Siyassa al-Kharijiyya al-Sa'udiyya mundhu 1945* (Beirut, 1980).

Shaked, H. and Yagnes, T., 'The Saudi Arabian kingdom', in C. Legum (ed.), *Middle East Contemporary Survey*, Vol. 1 (New York, 1978).

Shaw, J. and Long, D. E., The Washington Papers: *Saudi Arabian Modernization: The Impact of Change on Stability*, No. 89 (1982).

Sheean, V., *Faisal - The King and His Kingdom* (Tavistock, 1975).

The Middle East and North Africa 1980/1 (Europa Publication, London 1980).

Tibawi, A. L., *Islamic Education: Its Tradition and Modernization into the Arab National Systems* (London, 1972).

Van Der Meulen, D., *The Wells of Ibn Sa'ud* (London, 1957).

Wahba, H., *Arabian Days* (London, 1964).

Wenner, M., 'Saudi Arabia: survival of traditional elites' in F. Tachau (ed.), *Political Elites and Political Development in the Middle East* (New York, 1975).

ARTICLES

Abir, M., 'Saudi security and military endeavour', *The Jerusalem Quarterly*, No. 33 (autumn 1984).

Bligh, A., 'The Saudi religious elite (ulama) as participant in the political system of the kingdom', *IJMES*, Vol. 17, No. 1 (February 1985).

Collins, M., 'Riyadh: the Saud balance', *The Washington Quarterly* (winter 1981).

Dawisha, A. I., 'Internal values and external threats', *Orbis* (spring 1979).

——'Saudi Arabia's search for security', *Adelphi Papers*, No. 158 (winter 1979–80).

Eilts, H. F., 'The Persian Gulf crisis: perspectives and prospects', *MEJ*, Vol. 45, No. 1 (winter 1991).

Field, M., 'Why the Saudi royal family is more stable than the Shah', *Euromoney* (October 1981).

——'Society, the royal family and the military in Saudi Arabia', *Vierteljahresberichte*, No. 88 (June 1982).

Gallagher, E. B., 'Medical education in Saudi Arabia: a sociological perspective on modernization and language', *Journal of Asian and African Studies*, Vol. XX, Nos. 1–2 (1985).

Halliday, F., 'The shifting sands beneath the House of Saud', *The Progressive* (March 1980).

Harrington, C. W., 'The Saudi Arabian council of ministers', *MEJ*, Vol. 12, No. 1 (1958).

Hottinger, A., 'Saudi Arabia: entering a new era', *Swiss Review of World Affairs*, Vol. 26, No. 5 (August 1986).

Karsh, E., 'The Iran-Iraq war: the military analysis', *Adelphi Papers*, No. 220 (spring 1987).

Kechichian, J. A., 'The role of the ulama in the politics of an Islamic state: the case of Saudi Arabia', *IJMES*, Vol. 12, No. 1 (February 1986).

King, R., 'The Iran-Iraq war: the political implications', *Adelphi Papers*, No. 219 (spring 1987).

Knauerhase, R., 'Saudi Arabia faces the future', *Current History* (February 1986).

Kostiner, J., 'Counterproductive mediation', *Middle East Review* (summer 1987).

Kraft, J., 'Letter from Saudi Arabia', *The New Yorker*, 4 July 1983.

Lesch, A. M., 'Contrasting reactions to Persian Gulf crisis: Egypt, Syria, Jordan and the Palestinians', *MEJ*, Vol. 45, No. 1 (winter 1991).

Lieber, R. J., 'Oil and power in the aftermath of the Gulf war', *International Security*, Vol. 17, No. 1 (summer 1992).

McHale, T. R., 'A prospect of Saudi Arabia', *International Affairs* (autumn 1981).

Moon, Chung In, 'Korean contractors in Saudi Arabia: their rise and fall', *MEJ*, Vol. 40, No. 4 (autumn 1986).

Nevo, J., 'The Saudi royal family: the third generation', *The Jerusalem Quarterly* (*JQ*), No. 31 (spring 1984).

Ochsenwald, W., 'Saudi Arabia and the Islamic revival', *International Journal of Middle East Studies*, Vol. 13 (1981).

Rugh, W., 'Emergence of a new middle class in Saudi Arabia', *The Middle East Journal* (winter 1973).

Salameh, Gh., 'Political power and the Saudi State', *Merip Reports*, No. 91 (October 1980).

JOURNALS AND PERIODICALS

Adelphi Papers
Al-Jazira al-'Arabiyya (London – Saudi opposition)
Al-Thawra al-Islamiyya (London – Saudi-Shi'ite opposition)
Current History
Economist Foreign Report
Euromoney
Hamizrah Hakhadash (Israel)
International Affairs
International Journal of Middle East Studies (*IJMES*)
Israel Petroleum Institute's newsletter (*IPI*, in Hebrew)
Journal of Asian and African Studies
Merip Reports
Middle East Economic Digest (*MEED*)
Middle East Economic Survey (*MEES*)
Middle East International (*MEI*, Arab–Palestinian)
Middle East Report
Middle East Review
Orbis
Qadaya Sa'udiyya (Saudi opposition, n.p.)
Sawt al-Tali'a (Baghdad)
Swiss Review of World Affairs
The Economist Intelligence Unit (*EIU*)
The Jerusalem Quarterly (*JQ*)
The Middle East (London)
The Middle East Journal (*MEJ*)

The Progressive
The Washington Quarterly
Vierteljahresberichte (Forschungsinstitut der Friedrich-Ebert-Stiftung, Bonn)

NEWSPAPERS AND WEEKLIES

Afrique Action (Tunis)
Akhir Khabar (Amman)
Akhir Sa'ah (Egypt)
Al-Ahali (Egypt – opposition)
Al-Ahrar (Lebanon)
Al-Akhbar (Lebanon)
Al-Anba (Kuwait)
Al-Bayadir al-Siyassi (East Jerusalem)
Al-Bilad (Beirut)
Al-Bilad (Saudi Arabia)
Al-Da'wa (Riyadh)
Al-Dawliyya (Paris)
Al-Dustur (pro-Iraqi; weekly, London)
Al-Hadaf (PFLP, Beirut; in Damascus since 1983)
Al-Haqa'iq (Egypt)
Al-Hawadith (Beirut–London)
Al-Hayat (Beirut)
Al-Hillal al-Dawli (London)
Al-Hurriyya (Nicosia)
Al-Hurriyya (PFLP; weekly, Beirut)
Al-Jarida (Beirut)
Al-Jazira (Saudi Arabia)
Al-Liwa (Amman)
Al-Madina (Saudi Arabia)
Al-Majalla (London)
Al-Masa' (Egypt)
Al-Mawqif al-'Arabi (Beirut)
Al-Muharir (Marxist PFLP; Paris edition)
Al-Mussawar (Egypt)
Al-Mustaqbal (Paris)
Al-Nahar (London–Beirut)
Al-Nashra (Communist, Athens)
Al-Nashra (Communist, Cyprus–Nicosia)
Al-Qabas (Kuwait)
Al-Quds al-'Arabi (Fundamentalist Palestinian, London)
Al-Ra'i al-Akhir (London)
Al-Riyadh (Saudi Arabia)
Al-Safir (Pro-Libyan, Beirut)
Al-Sha'b (Egypt opposition)
Al-Shahid (Tehran)
Al-Sharq al-Awsat (London–Saudi Arabia)
Al-Siyasi (Cairo)
Al-Siyassa (Beirut)
Al-Siyassa (Kuwait)
Al-Ta'ir al-Shimal (Norway)
Al-Tayar (Iraq opposition, London)

BIBLIOGRAPHY

Al-Thawra (Baghdad)
Al-Usbu' al-'Arabi (Lebanon)
Al-Watan al-'Arabi (Beirut–Paris)
Al-Yamama (weekly, Saudi Arabia)
Al-Yasar al-'Arabi (leftist, Egypt–Paris)
Al-Yawm (Saudi Arabia)
Arab Times (Kuwait)
Daily Telegraph (London)
Financial Times (London)
Foreign Broadcasting Information Service (FBIS) – Middle East
Globe and Mail (Toronto)
Haaretz (Israel)
International Herald Tribune
Ittihad (UAE)
Jane's Defence Weekly (England)
Jerusalem Post (Israel)
Jordan Times (Amman)
Los Angeles Times
Ma'riv (Israel)
Mideast Mirror (Beirut)
Misr al-Fatat (Cairo, opposition)
New York Times
October (Cairo)
Saudi Gazette (Saudi Arabia)
Sunday Times (London)
Surkiyya (London)
Tehran Times
Time (magazine)
The Economist (weekly, London)
The Guardian (London)
The New Yorker
The Observer (London)
The Sunday Star (Toronto)
The Times (London)
Ukaz (Saudi Arabia)
US News & World Report
Wall Street Journal
Washington Post
Washington Times
Yedioth Ahronoth (Israel)
8 Days (weekly, London)

GLOSSARY

ahl al-hal wa'l-'aqd	lit. 'those who loosen and bind. The Muslim communities' leadership made up of the most distinguished personalities, largely religious scholars. In the Saudi context, the most senior members of the oligarchy
'alim (pl. *ulama*)	(recognised) religious scholar
'ashura	day of mourning sacred to Sh'ites
a'yan	notables
badu	nomadic people
bid'ah	heretical innovation
dawla	lit. government. In the Saudi context modern central government
fatwa	religious/legal opinion
faqih (pl. *fuqaha*)	theologian
hadr	settled people
hukuma	lit. government. Traditional government, headed by the Sauds
hujar	military-agricultural villages
ijma'	consensus
Ikhwan	lit. brotherhood. Extremist Wahhabi tribal paramilitary organisation. Established c. 1912
Jahili	pagan, pre-Islamic, or deviating Muslim
khatib	preacher
mabahith	security police
majlis (pl. *majalis*)	council. Audience held by personalities of different importance, including the king
majlis al-shura	consultative council
mudarris	teacher in a higher institution of learning
da'wa	organisation for religious propagation, used also for subversion and terrorist activities by Shi'ite empires/ kingdoms. a *da'wa* office was established in Iran in 1989. A *Da'wa* (clandestine) party was established in Iraq (and Kuwait) and was closely connected to the Iranian *da'wa* office but it was mercilessly suppressed by Saddam Hussayn
mujtahid	religious scholar who formulates decisions on religious-legal matters among Shi'ites
mushrikun	polytheists

259

GLOSSARY

muttawwa'in	lit. volunteers. In Saudi context ulama who instructed bedouins on principles of Wahhabi Islam during Ibn Saud's reign. In modern times – Morality Police
muwahhidun	those who profess the unity of God. The correct name for the followers of the teaching of Muhammad b. Abd al-Wahhab (Wahhabis)
nizam al-muqata'at	provincial government codex, or provincial government system
salafi	fundamentalist
shari'a	the canonical law of Islam
shura	consultation
umara' (sing. *amir*)	tribal shaykhs or governors of different ranks in Saudi Arabia
umara' al-manatiq	provincial governors
'umda	village shaykhs or neighbourhood heads in towns
umma	the Islamic community or nation
velayat faqih	governance of the jusrist. This is a corruption of the Iranian Shi'ite term *velayet-e-faqih*
waqf (pl. *awqaf*)	religious endowment

INDEX

Abd al-Aziz b. Abd al Rahman Al
  Saud *see* Ibn Saud
Abdallah ibn Abd al-Aziz 48, 60, 67,
  71, 74-5, 77, 97-8, 103-5, 127, 138,
  153, 169-70, 180, 184, 194-5,
  204n16, 244n75
ACC 144, 162-3, 213, 217, 220, 224,
  243n42, 244n64, 248n33
Administration of Scientific Study,
  [Religious] Legal Opinions,
  Islamic Propagation and Guidance
  89, 110
ahl al-hal wa'l-'aqd 7-10, 28, 45, 64,
  68, 91-2, 103, 121, 225
Ahmad ibn Abd al-Aziz 69, 85, 87,
  106, 231n22, 237n24
Al al-Shaykh 3, 6, 9, 22, 43, 104-6,
  215, 227n11 and n19, 245n17;
  officials and officers 16, 43, 105,
  110, 200, 225n8, 226n8, 237n30; *see
  also* ulama
Al Fahd *see* Sudayri (Seven)
'alim(s) *see* ulama
Al-Hasa (Al-Ahsa) *see* Eastern
  Province
Al-Majlis al-A 'la li'l-Qada see The
  Higher Council of Qadis
Al Saud *see* royal family (house)
Al-Sharqiyya *see* Eastern Province
Al-Shaykhs *see* Al al-Shaykh
America *see* United States
Arab Nationalists (*Qawmiyyin al-
  'Arab*) 35-6, 38, 52-3, 56, 59, 67, 84,
  112; *see also* opposition
  organisations
Aramco 2, 15, 28-9, 31-5, 45, 50, 54-5,
  83-4; Aramco (oil) towns 32-3, 44,
  53, 83, 85, 110, 187; Shi'ites and
  subversion and 17, 28, 32-5, 50-3,

56, 59, 65, 75, 82-8, 113; labour
  laws and unrest 33, 35-6, 52, 55, 76,
  84-5, 88, 101, 230n6, 232n9
armed forces 86, 88, 202, 208;
  America(ns) and expatriates and 31,
  112-13, 157, 210, 219; air force
  (Royal Saudi) 36, 53, 60, 69, 111,
  139, 172; history, expansion,
  upgrading benefits, military towns
  and manpower 28, 31, 34, 36, 40,
  44, 48, 76, 105, 108, 111, 120, 125,
  128, 131, 143, 148-9, 175, 203, 205,
  209, 219, 230-7, 235n17; officers,
  'Young Turks', 'Free Officers' *see*
  new elites; opposition to regime
  and attempted coups and 11, 34, 36,
  40-1, 44, 56-8, 60, 75-6, 113, 120,
  219; 'royal' officers 6, 74, 105-6,
  111, 131, 195, 219, 223-4
Asir xv, 4, 33-4, 36, 44, 49, 53, 56-7,
  76, 96, 107, 112, 181, 217

Baghdad *see* Iraq
Bandar Ibn Sultan (Prince) 106, 131,
  134, 140, 156, 163, 172, 195, 199,
  223, 237n20, 240n18
Ba'th: Saudi 35-6, 52, 56, 59, 65, 84,
  87, 112; Syrian and Iraqi 30, 36, 43,
  49, 54-5, 57, 60, 66, 125, 129-30,
  161-3, 168, 176
Baz, Abd al-Aziz bin 80-2, 110, 178,
  181-2, 185, 192-4, 198, 207-8, 213,
  248n26
bourgeois *see* new elites – middle
  class
bureaucrats *see* new elites – middle
  class

Committee(s) for Encouraging Virtue

261